THE EVANSTON REPORT

The Evanston Report

The Second Assembly of the World Council of Churches 1954

H B

Harper & Brothers Publishers

New York

Preface

In the Official Report the attempt has been made to present as full a record of the Second Assembly of the World Council of Churches as possible. In addition to the reports and other actions of the Assembly, a narrative account of each day's events has been prepared. The addresses are very briefly summarized in the narrative, but the reports of departments are only alluded to, inasmuch as they appeared in full in the Assembly volume, *The First Six Years*.

Appreciation is expressed to Dr. Robert S. Bilheimer and the Rev. John Garrett for their work during and after the Assembly in helping to prepare this Report.

W. A. Visser 't Hooft,
Editor

Contents

A Message from the Second Assembly of the World Council of Churches

To all our fellow Christians, and to our fellowmen everywhere, we send greetings in the name of Jesus Christ. We affirm our faith in Jesus Christ as the hope of the world, and desire to share that faith with all men. May God forgive us that by our sin we have often hidden this hope from the world.

In the ferment of our time there are both hopes and fears. It is indeed good to hope for freedom, justice and peace, and it is God's will that we should have these things. But He has made us for a higher end. He has made us for Himself, that we might know and love Him, worship and serve Him. Nothing other than God can ever satisfy the heart of man. Forgetting this, man becomes his own enemy. He seeks justice but creates oppression. He wants peace, but drifts towards war. His very mastery of nature threatens him with ruin. Whether he acknowledges it or not, he stands under the judgment of God and in the shadow of death.

Here where we stand, Jesus Christ stood with us. He came to us, true God and true Man, to seek and to save. Though we were the enemies of God, Christ died for us. We crucified Him, but God raised Him from the dead. He is risen. He has overcome the powers of sin and death. A new life has begun. And in His risen and ascended power, He has sent forth into the world a new community, bound together by His Spirit, sharing His divine life, and commissioned to make Him known throughout the world. He will come again as Judge and King to bring all things to their consummation. Then we shall see Him as He is and know as we are known. Together with the whole creation we wait for this with eager hope, knowing that God is faithful and that even now He holds all things in His hand.

This is the hope of God's people in every age, and we commend it afresh today to all who will listen. To accept it is to turn from our ways to God's way. It is to live as forgiven sinners, as children growing in His love. It is to have our citizenship in that Kingdom which all man's sin is impotent to destroy, that realm of love and joy and peace which lies about all men, though unseen. It is to enter with Christ into the suffering and despair of men, sharing with them the great secret of that Kingdom which they do not expect. It is to know that whatever men may do, Jesus reigns and shall reign.

With this assurance we can face the powers of evil and the threat of death with a good courage. Delivered from fear we are made free to love. For beyond the judgment of men and the judgment of history lies the judgment of the King who died for all men, and who will judge us according to what we have done to the least of His brethren. Thus our Christian hope directs us towards our neighbour. It constrains us to pray daily, "Thy will be done on earth as it is in heaven," and to act as we pray in every area of life. It begets a life of believing prayer and expectant action, looking to Jesus and pressing forward to the day of His return in glory.

Now we would speak through our member churches directly to each congregation. Six years ago our churches entered into a covenant to form this Council, and affirmed their intention to stay together. We thank God for His blessing on our work and fellowship during these six years. We enter now upon a second stage. To stay together is not enough. We must go forward. As we learn more of our unity in Christ, it becomes the more intolerable that we should be divided. We therefore ask you: Is your church seriously considering its relation to other churches in the light of our Lord's prayer that we may be sanctified in the truth and that we may all be one? Is your congregation, in fellowship with sister congregations around you, doing all it can do to ensure that your neighbours shall hear the voice of the one Shepherd calling all men into the one flock?

The forces that separate men from one another are strong. At our meeting here we have missed the presence of Chinese churches which were with us at Amsterdam. There are other lands and churches unrepresented in our Council, and we long ardently for their fellowship. But we are thankful that, separated as we are by the deepest political divisions of our time, here at Evanston we are united in Christ. And we rejoice also that, in the bond of prayer and a common hope, we maintain communion with our Christian brethren everywhere.

It is from within this communion that we have to speak about the fear and distrust which at present divide our world. Only at the

Cross of Christ, where men know themselves as forgiven sinners, can they be made one. It is there that Christians must pray daily for their enemies. It is there that we must seek deliverance from self-righteousness, impatience and fear. And those who know that Christ is risen should have the courage to expect new power to break through every human barrier.

It is not enough that Christians should seek peace for themselves. They must seek justice for others. Great masses of people in many parts of the world are hungry for bread, and are compelled to live in conditions which mock their human worth. Does your church speak and act against such injustice? Millions of men and women are suffering segregation and discrimination on the ground of race. Is your church willing to declare, as this Assembly has declared, that this is contrary to the will of God and to act on that declaration? Do you pray regularly for those who suffer unjust discrimination on grounds of race, religion or political conviction?

The Church of Christ is today a world-wide fellowship, yet there are countless people to whom He is unknown. How much do you care about this? Does your congregation live for itself, or for the world around it and beyond it? Does its common life, and does the daily work of its members in the world, affirm the Lordship of Christ or deny it?

God does not leave any of us to stand alone. In every place He has gathered us together to be His family, in which His gifts and His forgiveness are received. Do you forgive one another as Christ forgave you? Is your congregation a true family of God, where every man can find a home and know that God loves him without limit?

We are not sufficient for these things. But Christ is sufficient. We do not know what is coming to us. But we know Who is coming. It is He who meets us every day and who will meet us at the end—Jesus Christ our Lord.

Therefore we say to you: Rejoice in hope.

Introduction

The First Assembly of the World Council of Churches, held at Amsterdam in 1948, marked the beginning of a new phase in the life of the ecumenical movement. The churches themselves, by sending their officially elected representatives to the Assembly at Amsterdam, fully entered the scene.[1] Their purpose in doing so went beyond the holding of an impressive assembly; their principal business was the creation of the World Council of Churches, in order to have a permanent ecumenical structure within which the churches might continue to grow into unity and advance their common mission in the world.

Six years later, the Second Assembly was held at Northwestern University, Evanston, Illinois. Although, like the first, it was composed of the official representatives of the churches, its task was different, and it also in a sense marked a new stage in ecumenical development. At Amsterdam, the chief task had been to create the World Council of Churches. At Evanston, the Assembly had to examine the unity given to the churches in the past six years of life in the World Council, and to determine those areas in which disunity was most apparent, and in which unity was most effective. There were few tensions, whether arising out of the church situation or out of the world scene, which were not present at both Assemblies. Many of these tensions had become more clearly defined in 1954, as that between the political east and the political west; and some were faced more clearly, as that between social and ethnic groups. Theological differences which existed in 1948 were faced more directly in 1954. These variations, however, did not form the chief difference between the First and Second Assemblies. That lay in the distinctive function of each, the one to create a will and a structure for unity; the other to deepen and develop that which had been created earlier.

Fully aware of the importance and difficulty which were attached to the Second Assembly, the Central Committee began

[1] See *The History of the Ecumenical Movement*, Ruth Rouse and Stephen Neill, editors, 1954, SPCK and Westminster Press, pp. 697 ff.

preparations for it early. At Woudschoten, Netherlands, in 1948, first mention was made of the size of the Second Assembly, and of the place of meeting. It was clear to all concerned that it should be in the United States, and this initial conviction was made formal action upon the acceptance in 1949 at Chichester of an invitation from the member churches in the United States. The first consideration of a main theme for the Assembly was given at Toronto in 1950, and from 1951 until the Assembly convened both the Central Committee and the Executive Committee were occupied at every meeting with plans for the Assembly. The most comprehensive actions were taken at Lucknow (India) in 1952–53, when the Central Committee engaged in a thorough review of all plans, taking decisions on all major matters.

Under the supervision of the Central Committee, preparation proceeded in four stages. The first, and the most difficult, was the preparation for the main theme. The Toronto action called for a theme "along the lines of the affirmation that Jesus Christ is the hope of the world," and authorized the creation of a representative commission of lay and clerical theologians to study how this affirmation could be developed in meaningful terms for the modern world. Three meetings of the commission were held, each one a week or more in duration; two reports of their discussions were issued, the third report being the statement given to the Central Committee. This statement was presented to the Assembly by the Central Committee as the preparatory document on the main theme.

The selection of Christian hope, or as formalized for the Assembly "Christ—The Hope of the World," as the Assembly theme proved to be daring and provocative. It was daring because it touched a nerve centre of human need, both within the churches and outside. Too long neglected, in contrast for instance with Christian teaching about faith and love, the thought of Christians concerning their hope had become confused with purely secular hopes, as well as with aberrations in Christian doctrine. The trumpet of the Church sounded weakly on this note. People therefore looked with very great expectation to this ecumenical discussion. Moreover, the subject of hope raised more vividly than perhaps any other at this time the whole range of areas touched by Christian thought in general. The destiny of the individual and the human race, and the character of man and the effectiveness of his own efforts to control his destiny, were brought into sharp focus, at a time when these matters were, because of world conditions, of immediate and personal concern to all. God's purpose and the meaning of His revelation in Christ, were fundamental starting- and finishing-points in the entire discussion, and these in turn raised questions concerning the nature of His Kingdom on earth and the place of the Church in relation to it. Many said that no more thorny issue of Christian theology could have been chosen.

The main theme debate, as it was carried on for four years, was also very fruitful. It is a matter of record that no single issue in ecumenical history had aroused such widespread and well-articulated comment. Letters, articles in the press, statements of groups, formal statements of churches came to the commission in unlooked-for numbers, and with very little organized promotion, other than the issuing of the successive reports. This general discussion of the verities of Christian faith was of undoubted value. Moreover, the discussion helped to clear the theological atmosphere by revealing that theological trends could not be so easily classified and labelled as popular assumption had supposed. Opposition between Anglo-Saxon and Continental theology was taken for granted, and it was initially supposed that of two parties, one, more Pelagian, humanistic and activist would confront the other, more Augustinian, other-worldly and quietistic. The four-year discussion revealed a more complicated scene. Augustinians and Pelagians showed their colours, but activist and quietist could not be identified with either. Americans and Continentals spoke with vigour, but there was no common theological pattern among them. Nor did the many traditions represented among the Younger Churches fall into neat categories. All variations of conviction were found everywhere, with the result that the theological situation was discovered to be less simple and compact, but much more fluid than had been assumed. Furthermore, it was clear that much vigorous debate had been aroused, not only by the intrinsic merit of the subject, but by the growing consensus in the Advisory Commission—a unity of theological thought perhaps as remarkable as any in recent church history.

The account of the main theme discussion at the Assembly in the following chapters will speak for itself. All Assembly partici-pants received the Advisory Commission's report well in advance of the meeting. At the Assembly fifteen groups of about fifty each discussed the report for ten hours. A statement was drawn up and received by the Assembly (see page 70).

The second area of preparation included the topics of the six sections at the Assembly. Here again, first decisions were made at Toronto in 1950, and refined in subsequent meetings of the Central Committee, the management of the process being delegated to the Study Department Committee. The tangible objective of the preparatory plans was the production of an Ecumenical Survey and a working paper for each of the six areas.[1] The Survey was in each case a public document, designed alike to stimulate wide discussion and to provide Assembly participants with relevant material for their discussion. The working paper was not a public document, and was submitted to the members of the appropriate section at the Assembly as a starting-place for the development of the Section Report. For Faith and Order, the Working Committee of the Faith and Order Commission undertook preparation for the Assembly, building substantially upon the work of the Third World Conference on Faith and Order, at Lund in 1952. For International Affairs, the Commission of the Churches on International Affairs (C.C.I.A.) undertook preparations, and for the other four subjects (evangelism, social questions, intergroup relations and the laity) special international commissions were formed. All preparatory groups met in the summer of 1953, the meeting having been preceded by intensive correspondence and visitation, and drafts of the appropriate documents having been prepared in advance. A second meeting took place immediately prior to the Assembly, in order especially to refine the working papers.

It should be noted that the six section topics included two which entered ecumenical discussion in a new way. At Amsterdam, one of four "concerns of the Churches" dealt with work, vocation and the laity. In the intervening six years, interest in this subject had substantially increased so that full discussion of it as a subject on a par with others was indicated. On the other hand, race relations had not had any direct treatment in ecumenical conferences since 1937, although allusions to the matter were frequent and vigorous in all the ecumenical meetings since then. A full-scale treatment of

[1] Published as six separate booklets by the SCM Press, London, and in one volume *The Christian Hope and the Task of the Church* by Harpers and Brothers, New York.

the subject was felt to be required, and the Central Committee accordingly included it as one of the six Assembly topics.

The third area of the preparation concerned the structure and functioning of the World Council of Churches itself. At Amsterdam much attention had been given to these matters, but largely on the presupposition that existing departments, committees, and relationships between them would continue, save with the recommended addition of a very few others. As, however, the Central Committee took up its work in the years following 1948, it became convinced that the Second Assembly should consider the basic pattern of the World Council's structure, and the manner of its functioning. In part this conviction grew out of the need to re-think relationships between departments, commissions and committees which had been created at different times and in response to various needs. In part it arose from the need to complete in a final and satisfactory way the merger of Faith and Order and Life and Work into a World Council of Churches. In part also it was required by the growing closeness of association between the International Missionary Council and the World Council. Also it was needful because of certain additions to the World Council programme which were necessary and which would have to be put into proper relationship to other World Council structure. Finally there was a desire to give the whole a careful scrutiny in the light of the experience of the first six years.

Accordingly, the Central Committee at Rolle (Switzerland) in 1951 appointed a Committee on Structure and Functioning, charged with reviewing World Council organization and making such recommendations as might seem wise. An extremely careful and exhaustive survey resulted, with periodic reports to the Central Committee, culminating in the Report on Structure and Functioning presented by the Central Committee to the Assembly, and adopted with only a few amendments.

The transaction of World Council business at Evanston was cast, save for such strictly Assembly business as the hearing of the total Central Committee Report, the Credentials Committee Report, the Nominations Committee and the like, in the framework of the Report on Structure and Functioning. Two documents were prepared. The first contained reports of the departments, commissions, and committees under the title *The First Six Years*. The second, entitled *The Assembly Work Book*, contained the

Report of the Committee on Structure and Functioning, and a series of proposals for the future work of the Divisions and Departments envisaged by it. Seven committees of the Assembly were thus required, and the Assembly membership was divided among them. Reports of these committees were adopted by the Assembly, and became binding for the various parts of the World Council's organization.

The fourth area of preparation included the specific organization of the Assembly, and the local arrangements for it. This proceeded in the first instance under the direction of the Central Committee and Executive Committee, but arrangements in the United States were delegated to the United States Conference for the World Council of Churches. A chief task, at the outset and until the Assembly convened, called for such negotiations with the U.S. government as would ensure entry into the United States for all members of the Assembly. The long series of delicate and sometimes difficult negotiations came to the successful result that, with but very few exceptions, the delegates received their U.S. visas in time. This in turn meant that the Assembly met as a truly world-wide meeting, and the contribution of the American churches and their leaders at this point alone was of signal importance. In addition local arrangements called for extensive planning at Northwestern University and Evanston, where every facility of buildings and personnel, as well as of finance, was accorded in a co-operative and helpful spirit. The American churches also developed four projects related to the Assembly. A Chicago Summer Ecumenical Institute, sponsored by ten of the seminaries of Greater Chicago, attended by 1,785 ministers, and conducted by an international faculty, was held for the two weeks prior to the Assembly. A "Festival of Faith," a concert of sacred music and an exhibition of religious art, more fully described elsewhere in this volume, were also part of the total arrangements made by the American churches.

The public relations of the World Council of Churches and of the Assembly, especially in America, proved to be complex and of the highest importance. On the other hand, American Christians on the whole eagerly anticipated and welcomed the Assembly, especially since it was the first major ecumenical meeting to be held in the U.S.A. On the other hand, the very nature of the ecumenical situation and of the world political scene in the summer of 1954 presented sharp contrasts to American opinion, both within the churches and outside. In social, racial, political and theological realms, these contrasts could be felt in differing ways. It was therefore necessary to cast the public relations of the Assembly in such a way as to capitalize the widespread and deep interest in the Assembly, and at the same time with sufficient realism, so that expectations would not be raised too high nor hopes turned in the wrong direction.

The specially created Press and Broadcasting Committee proceeded with its task in three basic ways. First by creating a very modest organization and budget, thus refraining from over-promotion. Second, by using existing church channels of publicity, thus drawing the member churches fully into the common effort. Third, by giving to those elements of the Assembly which were contrary to American opinion publicity which was equal to—and in some cases greater than—that given to the parts of the Assembly congenial to American opinion. Of necessity, less intensive public relations were carried forward throughout the rest of the world. The use, however, of Assembly preparatory materials and of news about the Assembly was widely disseminated throughout the world, and in many cases, e.g. in Hungary, made the basis for intensive study.

The entire spread of preparations for the Second Assembly therefore covered a large territory, from the development of careful theological documents to the arrangement of a bus system in Evanston, from public relations flung far and wide to delicate and private negotiations with government officials, from precise organizational recommendations to statements of prophetic Christian principle. Those responsible would not pretend that the preparations were as thorough in concept or as efficient in administration as they should have been. Yet all concerned would agree that a meeting such as the Second Assembly without as extensive preparation as possible is folly, and that such preparation has value in itself as well as value for the meeting to which it leads.

The Structure of the Assembly

The organizational structure of the Assembly was relatively simple, in view of its size and the complexity of work required of it. Fundamentally, the Assembly consisted of three phases, in each of which the total Assembly participated, and for each of which there was a staffed organization. These were the consideration of the main theme, the work of the sections and the work of the committees. These were not the only parts of the Assembly structure and programme, but they formed the basis of it. For the main theme discussion, all participants except accredited visitors were divided into fifteen groups, each group having a chairman and secretary. These officers met together in the Main Theme Co-ordinating Group each day of group discussion, and it was through this Group that opinions concerning the Main Theme were registered and ultimately formulated into the Assembly's Statement on the Main Theme.

The sections likewise included all save the accredited visitors, and each had four officers: Chairman, Vice-Chairman, Secretary and Liaison Officer. These formed the nucleus of the drafting group for each section, others being added by the section from its own membership. The Liaison Officer functioned to keep in touch with related discussion in other sections. The Chairmen, Secretaries and Liaison Officers of the sections met daily during section meetings as the Sections' Co-ordinating Group for the purpose of general correlation and administration of the sections' work.

The committees were organized similarly. Again the membership of the Assembly, except accredited visitors, was divided among the seven committees, and each committee had its Chairman, Vice-Chairman, Secretary and Liaison Officer. The Committees' Co-ordinating Group served as the administrative and clearing agency for the total work of the committees. Most of the committees were forced to divide into sub-committees, usually to deal with departmental business as indicated in the Structure and Functioning Report.

The youth consultants participated fully in all parts of the Assembly. A pre-Assembly meeting at Lake Forest College provided opportunity to prepare finally for the Assembly, and during it the youth consultants attended the main theme, section and committee discussions as well as the plenary meetings. In addition some separate meetings were held to consider particular aspects of youth work.

The whole was supervised and co-ordinated by the Steering Committee, which in addition was responsible for the many issues of the policy of the Assembly. Main Theme, Sections' and Committees' Co-ordinating Groups reported to the Steering Committee, as did the Worship and the Press and Broadcasting Committees. Moreover, committees concerned with specific business of the Assembly—Credentials Committee, Nominations Committee, and Message Committee—were in the first instance responsible to the Steering Committee and carried on their work under its immediate supervision. Such diverse problems as difficulties in the public address system, or extra expenditure for the duplication of documents for the public, also came to the Steering Committee.

The work of the Worship Committee was done largely prior to the Assembly. Arrangements called for morning and evening worship services daily, an opening and a closing service of worship for the Assembly, a service of preparation for communion in the host church, and the communion services. The statement in the Official Handbook concerning the communion services reads :—

Communion Services. The recommendations of the Lund Conference regarding communion services at ecumenical gatherings were as follows :

(1) There should always be a united Service of Preparation for Holy Communion, with special emphasis on the note of penitence for our separation from each other.

(2) There should be opportunity for communion services at such times as will make it possible for every member of the conference to receive communion somewhere without violation of his own conscience or disloyalty to his church tradition. These should be held at different times.

(3) Though on the grounds already indicated there are some who object to open communion services, yet we believe there should be an opportunity of this kind for the many who

desire such services and are free to partake. Such services should where possible be held on the invitation of the local church or churches which sanction such services. (Usually a very large proportion of the members of a conference will partake. Notable examples of this were the communion service held in the Nieuwe Kerk of Amsterdam, in 1948, and in Lund Cathedral, in 1952, and many regard such memorable occasions as of historic importance. At the I.M.C. Conference at Tambaram in 1938 two open communion services were held, one of which was Anglican.) . . .

(5) It is important that those who cannot partake at a particular communion service should be invited to attend the service as worshippers, though they cannot receive communion. This has been found by many to be a means of real blessing, of spiritual communion, and of deeper understanding and fellowship. . . .

The authorities of the respective churches have desired that the following statements be printed in this Handbook concerning the Communion Services:

From the Methodist Church: The Council of Bishops of the Methodist Church in the U.S.A. has sent to the Executive Committee of the World Council of Churches an invitation for all in the Assembly free to do so to participate in the Service of Holy Communion, to be held on the morning of August 22 in the First Methodist Church at Evanston.

From the Protestant Episcopal Church: According to a statement of the House of Bishops of the Protestant Episcopal Church in the United States of America, baptized communicant members of the member churches of the World Council of Churches are invited to receive the Holy Communion.

From the Augustana Evangelical Lutheran Church: The Augustana Evangelical Lutheran Church is distinctly sensible of the honour of having you as our guest at this service of worship. In this holy morning hour may we be devoutly grateful for the universal fellowship of Christians which finds expression here. We share the common task of providing bewildered humanity with the consciousness of an eternal destiny and of inspiring the leaders of our respective nations with an earnest desire to achieve God's purposes. For that task we need constantly to acknowledge our own inadequacy and to seek daily forgiveness and restoration. In the most intimate spiritual association that Christians may experience, the Lord's Supper, we have specific assurance of "the remission of sins, life and salvation." In the name of the Lord Jesus Christ, our Redeemer, we invite to the Lord's Table this morning all who believe in His Actual Presence and that we receive His True Body and Blood in this Sacrament. May He "strengthen and preserve you in true faith unto everlasting life."

From the Greek Orthodox Archdiocese of North and South America: The Greek Orthodox Archdiocese of North and South America extends a cordial invitation to all the participants of the Second Assembly of the World Council of Churches to attend the Divine Liturgy of St. John Chrysostom which will be celebrated by the Orthodox Delegates.

From the Church of South India: The Service of Holy Communion, in accordance with the liturgy of the Church of South India, will be open to all Christians, and a general invitation is given to the whole Assembly to attend.

In addition, the Worship Committee issued a booklet of daily bible readings, based on I Peter, which Assembly participants were encouraged to use, and to which the daily services of morning worship were related.

The Press and Broadcasting Committee had an arduous task. More representatives of the press—both secular and religious— and of the field of broadcasting—both radio and television—were in attendance at this meeting than at any other church meeting: 646 were accredited, of whom 322 represented the secular press, 195 the religious press, 76 the foreign press, and 53 radio; many information agencies were represented by Assembly participants. Separate staffs to service the secular press, both daily newspapers and wire services, the religious press and the broadcasting facilities were organized. In addition a fourth staff was created to prepare digests of Assembly speeches and documents for the press. Two separate press rooms were organized, each completely equipped with teletype, typewriters, special telephones and the like. Daily press conferences and daily briefing conferences were held, and every facility was extended to assist in arranging smaller press interviews. Copies of every public document were made available to the press. On Saturday, August 17th, the Chairman of the Press and Broadcasting Committee gave a dinner for the press, attended by more than 300, which served as reception and briefing conference.

One of the most valuable and interesting aspects of the Assembly was the accredited visitors' programme. Unable, by the rules of the Assembly, to attend main theme groups, sections, and committees, the accredited visitors participated during the times when these groups were meeting, in a specially arranged programme of speeches and discussions. A wide variety of subjects of ecumenical interest was covered by a representative group of speakers drawn from the Assembly, and group discussion followed. The whole was supervised by the Accredited Visitors' Steering Committee.

The staff of the Assembly, which operated under the General Secretary and the Executive Secretary of the Assembly, numbered over 376 and fell into the following categories:—

> Main Theme Group staff
> Sections staff
> Committees staff
> Stewards and Aides
> Press and Broadcasting staff
> Information Office staff
> Interpreters and Translators
> Office staff
> Bookstore
> Accredited Visitors staff
> Liaison with Northwestern University
> and local committees.

Many were volunteers; a few were specially engaged; virtually all of the World Council regular staff were in attendance. This staff was co-ordinated administratively by the Executive Secretary of the Assembly, but functioned through the related committees or other structural elements.

Many special offices played an important role. The Information Office was a centre for varied and multitudinous services. The Photographic Display (see "Narrative") was visited by thousands. The Bookstore, arranged by the Publishers Associated Section of the National Council of Churches, displayed a large number of titles. The exhibit of missionary education materials, sponsored by the International Missionary Council, arranged by the Department of Missionary Education of the National Council of Churches, also attracted many, as did the Historical Exhibition in Deering Library arranged by Northwestern University.

Northwestern University, from the very first, was essential to the Assembly structure. Its ample and comfortable accommodations were of course basic. The services of its staff, especially that related to administration, public relations, dormitories and commons, buildings and grounds, were extensive. A contribution of $25,000 to the Assembly travel budget further demonstrated the interest of the University in the Assembly, and this, together with the very low daily rate charged, greatly aided Assembly finances. The Chaplain of the University co-ordinated all University functions and services with the Assembly administration.

In addition, other Evanston and Chicago agencies were a part of the Assembly structure. Garrett Bibilical Institute, Seabury-Western Theological Seminary and the First Methodist Church placed their full facilities at the disposal of the Assembly.

In Evanston, a Committee of 100 was organized months prior to the meeting, and carried on, at its own expense, work of public relations, the finding of rooms in Evanston homes for accredited visitors, the selling of 33,000 tickets to the public meetings and a host of other tasks. The Church Federation of Greater Chicago, together with the U.S. Conference for the World Council of Churches, organized the Chicago-Area–Midwest Assembly Arrangements Committee, for the dual purpose of organizing the Soldier Field "Festival of Faith" and carrying on a programme of public relations in the Greater Chicago area.

The Assembly programme, structure, officers and staff were described in the Official Handbook. All Assembly participants are listed in the *Who's Who*.

The Narrative Account

THE ASSEMBLY IN ACTION

"Christ is the Hope of the World." To bear witness to this truth about two thousand participants in the official life of the Assembly presented their credentials for registration in Patten Gymnasium on the spacious campus of Northwestern University, Evanston, Illinois, during Saturday, August 14th.

The day dawned wet and misty as old friends began to greet one another and make new friends in the cosmopolitan stream of people moving all day through the building. The expectancy of three years of careful preparation could be sensed. Members of the Assembly settled into their living quarters and halls of residence. They discovered where their meetings would be held during the next two weeks. "Evanston, 1954" began.

THE OPENING DAY

Sunday, August 15th, brought clear, sunny weather. Television cameramen and photographers took up vantage points outside the First Methodist Church in Evanston. The tree-lined streets filled with gay and sober garments—white surplices and saffron stoles, national costumes of Africa and India, bishops in great variety of vestments, laymen and women in summer dress.

The Opening Service, on which the thoughts of Christians all over the world were fixed, began at 11 a.m. As the organ played the Reformation Chorale *A Mighty Fortress is Our God* the procession of official delegates, consultants and staff moved through the doors, followed by the World Council's Presidium.

The building was filled with warm light cast by the concealed lamps especially installed to provide illumination for a nation-wide television programme. The eyes of the congregation turned with those of the unseen viewers to the figure of Christ the Shepherd, dominating the carved wooden reredos. The minister of the church and leaders of worship moved to their places in the sanctuary.

From this point forward the worship proceeded with dignity and precision, drawing upon traditions represented in the World Council's life. Dr. Harold A. Bosley, minister of the host church, called the people to worship. They answered him together, using first the words "Blessed be God." The Old Testament lesson was read in French by Dr. Marc Boegner of the French Reformed Church. The choral anthem "Let Thy Holy Presence come upon us" by Tschesnokov preceded the reading of the New Testament lesson (in Greek) by Archbishop Athenagoras of Greece (Philippians 2, 1–11). After choral response Bishop Eivind Berggrav of Norway (Lutheran) led the congregation in the Apostles' Creed (in German). The Bishop of Chichester then said the Lord's Prayer and the acts of Petition and Supplication. After the hymn "In Christ there is no East or West" Bishop G. Bromley Oxnam (Methodist), as American President of the World Council of Churches, preached the sermon.

The Bishop recalled the words of St. Paul in the closing verses of the eighth chapter of his Epistle to the Romans. He used them as a starting-point for his exposition of words used in the Message of the Amsterdam Assembly, when the World Council was constituted in 1948: "We intend to stay together." These words recurred in the sermon as a refrain. The preacher spoke of the remarkable fellowship within the World Council during the first years of its life. He described the unity given to the Assembly in Christ by virtue of the fact that He came to all as their Hope. He stressed the obligations placed upon clergy and laity in the Church and the world as they worked together for the liberties of men and against false theories and injustice. He said, "It must be made clear that we dare not identify the gospel of Jesus with any historically conditioned political, social or economic system. The gospel stands in judgment upon all of them." He said that "the Communion table should precede the conference table because conference with our fellows will be more productive when preceded by Communion with our Christ." Finally, the Bishop reminded the Assembly that Christians stood for peace and were resolved to work for law and order on the earth. "Nothing can separate us from the love of God," he concluded, "Let the redeemed of the Lord say so. Jesus Christ is to become the Ruler of the kings of the earth, King of kings and Lord of lords. In this faith we intend to stay together."

Isaac Watts's hymn, "Jesus shall reign," was sung. Bishop C. K. Jacob of the Church of South India led the General Confession and a prayer spoken in unison. The choir rendered the anthem "God be in my head." The note of hope sounded out clearly as the congregation sang Charles Wesley's hymn "Come Thou long expected Jesus." Then Archbishop Athenagoras pronounced the benediction.

THE OPENING PLENARY SESSION

McGaw Memorial Hall, a tremendous arched steel and concrete structure, had been especially prepared to receive the full sessions of the Assembly. As 2 p.m. approached, delegates took their places at their desks, facing the platform and a drape bearing the emblem of the World Council of Churches in deep blue and white. Behind the official group at the long table a structure had been built for the World Council's Presidium. Participants in the Assembly faced this living symbol of the unity among the confessional families, under the World Council's sign, throughout the meetings.

Accredited visitors, observers, consultants, fraternal delegates, youth, staff and non-accredited visitors were given their own places in the auditorium. Facing the platform at the far end were pilgrims from the United States and every part of the world. They lined the tiers of "bleachers," where followers of basket-ball on other days shout to spur on the teams of Northwestern University. Translation facilities were provided for all the delegates and official participants. As at Amsterdam in 1948, each person received a small portable receiving set with headphones which made possible the reception of speeches in the three official conference languages as the speakers' words were simultaneously rendered into English, French and German. Dr. Marc Boegner called the Assembly to order for prayer and the singing of the hymn "Jesus shall reign." He declared the Assembly open. He called upon Dr. Roscoe Miller, the President of Northwestern University, who conveyed a welcome to the Assembly and expressed the hope that the work of the Assembly would prosper. Dr. Boegner conveyed thanks for the hospitality of Northwestern University. Professor Edmund Schlink and Professor Robert L. Calhoun, the first from the University of Heidelberg in Germany, the second from Yale in the United States, delivered their addresses on the Assembly's main theme.

Professor Schlink said:

Whenever we ask about the future of the world, we come immediately and unavoidably in the New Testament to the announcement of the end of the world. Wherever the coming of Christ is spoken of as the Hope of the world, the end of the world is always spoken of, too.

There is an essential difference between the fears of modern men and the New Testament proclamation of the end of the world. Today we are afraid of men who may misuse the power entrusted to them and unleash horrible destruction upon the world. . . But in the New Testament the calamities of the last days are not merely human misdeeds nor are they the consequence of human frailty. They are rather the activity of God Himself. . . . If in our thinking about this subject, we place the emphasis on the preservation of this threatened world, then we shall miss the point of our Assembly theme completely. If we expect Christ to ensure this world so that men may continue undisturbed their pursuit of liberty, may carry on their business, and seek an improvement in their standard of living, then Christ is not the hope of the world, but rather the end of all the world's hopes. The name of Christ is taken in vain if it is used as a slogan in this world's struggle for its own preservation.

It is not essential for us to see what we call "results." The whole point of Christian hope is that we live and act in faith. Christian hope is based in Jesus Christ alone. . . . For that reason, Christian hope always looks for the best from God and is tireless in its struggle against the powers of darkness.

Dr. Calhoun, speaking of the Christian hope, said:

The fundamental reality is God, His Kingdom and His righteousness, ever-present and ever-coming to judge and to bless His creatures. He is our Hope, because in Jesus Christ He has come down in the midst of earthly history, taken our cross upon His shoulders and our wounds into His heart, met death and hell face to face for our sake, and filled the human scene with a vast new light in which we men are judged and blessed as never before. He is our Hope because in Jesus Christ, died and risen, He gives us promise of strength to endure the stress of earthly battle, and of life with Him beyond earthly bounds.

In America, theology has often been less concerned with

the structure of biblical and traditional doctrines and more with the redressing of injustice in society. The distortion of sound basic Christian doctrines is dangerous. We tend to confuse the will of God with our way of life, and to suppose that our version of the gospel of hope is the only one that is meaningful and true.

It is perilously easy for us to identify God's promises with the peculiarly American way of life: to suppose that the kingdom of God is, at least in principle, our republican form of government, the economic system we call free enterprise, the social and cultural heritage we cherish.

Comparing our days with those of the early Church Dr. Calhoun said:

> Once more death stands at our elbow, unforgettable, and goes with us wherever we go. The word of hope to such a world must still be the gospel on which the martyr bishop of Antioch staked his life: that the God of Hosts is with us, that in Jesus Christ He came down to share our lot and break the tyranny of sin and death, that therein "that which had been prepared by God received its beginning," and that the course of history and the end of all things are in His hand.

As the session closed Pastor Boegner drew attention to the presence of Dr. John R. Mott, the World Council's Honorary President. Dr. Mott rose gravely to acknowledge the ovation he received.

THE FESTIVAL OF FAITH

The Assembly travelled in the late afternoon to Chicago, where the Church Federation of Greater Chicago entertained delegates and other visitors at supper. While the supper was being held within the buildings surrounding Soldier Field, 125,000 Christians from distances as far away as 300 miles, but mostly from the State of Illinois and the Chicago area, poured into the stands completely encircling the field.

At eight o'clock the chorus selected for the Festival led the huge crowd in song. Dr. W. A. Visser 't Hooft, General Secretary of the World Council of Churches, spoke on the acts of God to which the Festival would render witness. "We are here," he said, "because God has taken the initiative, not because we have started a new movement. We are here because God has His plan for the world, not because we have a new blueprint for world order; we are here in order to respond to all that God has done and promised. It is therefore fitting that at the outset of this Assembly we should focus our attention on the mighty works of God." The Presidents of the World Council of Churches, in their robes, filed on to the field. They took up their places centrally on a silver dais with sloping sides which faced the main entrance. Darkness fell. The green field was flooded with light. The people sang together the stirring hymn "All Hail the Power of Jesus' Name" while the official procession of Assembly participants filed towards the presidents, then diagonally across the field, to take up their positions in the congregation.

From where they sat they could see the illuminated faces of the chorus grouped in a semi-circle under three towers draped with golden cloth. Upon these towers the leaders of the worship afterwards stood. The night was clear and dark, but the rapt faces of the crowd could be dimly seen as they entered into the praise of God.

Dr. Marc Boegner led the Interrogation saying,"Why have you come?" The whole congregation replied,"We have come to worship God." The Archbishop of Thyateira led in prayer and the Bishop of Chichester acted for the Archbishop of Canterbury in making a statement preparatory to the pageant in which he spoke of the work of God in creating the new fellowship of the ecumenical movement.

The Festival then began. The action chorus entered the field and grouped itself around the central dais as the narrator began the story of creation. Complete darkness fell over the field. Against a background of music and speech the dancers in their wide robes then acted the biblical story of creation, of redemption in Christ and of the consummation of all things. The culmination came as all lay prostrate in sacrifice before God and afterwards grouped once more in the centre with arms upraised. The Christian Hope rang out in the great New Testament invocation to the coming Christ: "Even so come Lord Jesus."

The Festival of Faith had been developed after long and elaborate preparation (see "Structure of the Assembly"). The fine script was from the pen of Miss Helen Kromer and production under the direction of John Becker. The whole Festival was recognized by the Assembly as a characteristically grand and generous expression of the joy the American churches had shown in the coming of the World Council of Churches to the United States.

THE SECOND DAY: MONDAY, AUGUST 16TH

Worship in the First Methodist Church was led by the Rev. Dr. Gerald R. Cragg of the United Church of Canada. The constituting actions of the Assembly in McGaw Hall followed. Bishop G. Bromley Oxnam took the chair and described arrangements for the Assembly's agenda. Presiding officers and special committees were swiftly approved. A drafting committee for the Message was appointed. Reports were received on two new applications for membership in the Council from the Dutch Reformed Church of the Cape Province in South Africa and the Bantu Presbyterian Church in the same country. These churches were received into membership by unanimous vote of the member churches. Bishop William C. Martin, President of the National Council of the Churches of Christ in the U.S.A., brought greetings in the name of the American churches and presented a special copy of the Revised Standard Version of the Bible bound in handsome red leather for the use of the World Council of Churches and as a "symbol of our increasing fellowship and unity in Him." Bishop Oxnam received the gift and expressed the gratitude of the Council. He proceeded to introduce Dr. G. K. A. Bell, Bishop of Chichester, as "the beloved Chairman of the Central Committee," shaking hands as Dr. Bell passed to the rostrum to deliver a report on the work of the Central Committee during its first six years.

In presenting the Report of the Central Committee, the Bishop of Chichester called attention to the volume *The First Six Years* which was the actual report of the Central Committee. From his experience as chairman he then gave his personal impression of the work and of the meetings of the Committee. He spoke of the changes in the world situation since the First Assembly had met at Amsterdam. During those years the Central Committee had been the one comprehensive body to which the member churches could look for the carrying on of the work of the World Council. He spoke of the harmonious relationship which had been built up between the responsible leaders of the churches represented on the committees and the staff.

Some of the most rewarding features of the work of the Central Committee, he said, had been the response of the committee and staff to the conditions of the times and needs of the churches in terms of "main themes." In 1949 the theme "Contemporary Issues of Religious Liberty" had been developed in reference to the conditions in certain countries in eastern Europe. After vigorous debate had come the clear statement, "The totalitarian doctrine is a false doctrine." The following year the discussion had centred on "Dominant Religions and Religious Liberty" and "The Nature and Theme of the Second Assembly." In 1950 when public interest had been focused on the Korea situation the discussion had centred on "The Role of the World Council in Times of Tension." In addition, another statement from the 1950 meeting, on "The Church, the Churches, and the World Council of Churches" occasioned wide comment in the member churches.

As the work continued, it had become clear that it was impossible to separate the ecumenical task from the mission of the Church—that the Church was not the Church if separated from its mission. A new theme had emerged: "The Calling of the Church to Mission and Unity."

In closing the Bishop stated: "What has engraved itself so clearly on my mind in the six years has been the steady growth of mutual trust, and deep understanding, as well as a greater sense of urgency. In subjects which ordinarily afford ample ground for controversy, whether political or theological, complete freedom, frankness and charity have prevailed. There has been no thought, even in the most difficult matters, of one bloc lining up against another bloc; but always the sense of being an instrument of a World Council of Churches, not of a Council of the West or of the East, or of the North or of the South, and of a common desire to know the mind of Christ and to follow its leading to the best of our ability in all our relationships." He concluded by saying,"It has been a very great privilege to be the Chairman of such a brotherhood of Christians."

The Bishop of Chichester was followed by the Council's General Secretary, Dr. W. A. Visser 't Hooft, who was introduced by Bishop Oxnam as "a man who was prepared providentially for this high task."

Dr. Visser 't Hooft said the real motivations of the ecumenical movement were "a sense of repentance that in the actual life of the churches the holiness, the apostolicity, the unity of the Church had been obscured, and a determination to manifest more clearly the true nature of the Church of Christ. It was discovered that in order to demonstrate these fundamental characteristics of the Church the churches needed each other. For how could they 'make all men see what is the fellowship of the mystery,' how could they convince men that 'the middle wall of partition' had been broken down if they continued to live in isolation from each other?"

The churches, he said, had been called "to go as far as conscience would permit them to go in showing that fundamentally there is one and only one Church of Christ."

Asking "What then is the World Council of Churches?" Dr. Visser 't Hooft said:

"The World Council of Churches is essentially an instrument at the service of the churches to assist them in their common task to manifest the true nature of the Church. It is an instrument and must therefore never be considered as an aim in itself. The important thing is not the World Council as an organization. What is important is that the churches should be the Church. It is therefore a sign of confused thinking to speak of the World Council itself as the World Church. And it is completely erroneous to suggest that the World Council is or has any ambition to become a Super Church, that is, a centre of administrative power. There is not a single church in the membership of the Council which desires this; there is not one which would tolerate this.

"But there is more to be said. When churches come together in the name of their common Lord they do not meet as self-contained organizational structures. They are gathered together by the Lord. The economy of the *charismata*, the spiritual gifts, begins to operate. They learn from each other. They see anew the full dimensions of the Church Universal. They feel compelled to render common witness. They undertake common tasks together. In other words there is born among and between them a *koinonia*, a fellowship of participation in the work of the Holy Spirit."

In the years since the Amsterdam Assembly, the General Secretary said, the churches had given clear indication that they stood behind the Council and did not think the Council had gone too far in its first years. Still remaining, however, was the task of reaching the lives of millions of church members with the challenge and encouragement of ecumenical fellowship.

He called attention to the fear expressed by some that making the World Council of Churches a body officially representing the churches might mean "freezing the ecumenical situation." In the first six years there had been no indication that such had happened and the Council continued to stand for "*manifest*" unity of the Church, but its own task in that realm was necessarily limited: "First to remind the churches again and again that co-operation or friendly relations are not enough, for unity means at least complete and unrestricted fellowship; second, to create the conditions in which the churches come to know each other, enter into searching conversation with one another and learn from each other so that the walls of partition become transparent and finally disappear altogether . . . The Council can and must work to create a situation in which there is so much in common between the churches, that there is no adequate reason for them to remain separate from each other."

He then spoke of the specific tasks of the Second Assembly: "We are here as men and women who are themselves bewildered, who have no ready-made solutions in our pockets, who disagree with each other over many things. We have no other distinction except that we are here in the name of a Lord who is constantly gathering His people together and who uses them to proclaim His word. And so we may confidently expect that in a real measure our divisions will be transcended and that beyond and above the loud voices of this world we shall hear together the eternal Word of God."

The Main Theme, he felt, would serve to bring the churches closer together because it lifts them from their self-centredness, calls them to give a convincing message to a world crying for hope, and shows them all how they have failed to render a sufficiently clear witness to the Christian hope.

He found cause for encouragement in the attendance at the Assembly. Speaking of those present and those absent he said, "With regard to the attendance at this second Assembly we have reason to be greatly encouraged. With very few exceptions the member churches have eagerly responded to the invitation and the vast majority have sent their full quota of delegates. It is especially remarkable that we have this time very much larger delegations from a number of countries in Asia. We can also note progress in the participation from Africa, though we must confess that the representation from this continent, as also that from Latin America, is not yet what it ought to be in view of the strength and growth of the churches concerned. . . .

"We are at one in our conviction that all churches should have full freedom to participate in ecumenical assemblies through their officially appointed delegates. We deplore therefore that certain churches do not enjoy that freedom. But while they may not be in direct contact with us, they remain more than ever part of the fellowship in Christ. From one of those churches we have received word that it remembered fellow Christians in other countries in its prayers and hoped that Christians elsewhere would remember this church in their prayers. We shall certainly want to respond to this desire and try to remember in all that we say and do that we have a very special responsibility for those who are absent against their will. . . .

"We express the hope that other Christian churches which share our faith in Christ as God and Saviour and as the Hope of the world, but which have had no contact with the World Council, will come to see that our one and only purpose is to be servants of the Kingdom of God and of Christ's Church on earth. We are ready at any time to enter into conversation with them so that they may come to know our true intentions and, if possible, join our fellowship.

"No unofficial observers from the Roman Catholic Church will be present among us. In view of the 1949 instruction of the Vatican and of the presence of such observers at the Faith and Order Conference in Lund (Sweden) in 1952 it had been expected that some observers would be allowed to attend this Assembly. Later on it was found that the necessary permission would not be given. The pastoral letter from the Archbishop of Chicago has stated the reasons for this refusal. It is surprising to find that this letter makes no reference to the Vatican instruction and shows a serious lack of understanding of our true purposes. On the other hand it is significant that a number of well-known Roman Catholic theologians in Western Europe have issued a substantial memorandum on the main theme of our Assembly which is a valuable contribution to our discussion. Introducing that document the review *Istina* expresses its sentiments of fraternal sympathy with the effort made in the ecumenical movement to render a common witness to Christ as the only Hope of the world. It is good to know that in spite of deep divergences there remains this precious link."

In conclusion, the General Secretary said, "If we can only hold to the one, overwhelming promise which God has given to His Church, if we can only have that acute sense of proportion which helps us to recognize the design of God in its greatness, and man-made designs in their smallness, if we can live in that glorious independence which comes from being rooted in faith, hope and love, we need not be fearful for the outcome of the Assembly."

A further Plenary Session in the afternoon proceeded immediately to receive the proposals of the Committee on the Structure and Functioning of the World Council of Churches. These were delivered on behalf of the Central Committee by Dr. Leslie Cooke (Congregational, United Kingdom). Informally introducing the text of his speech, Dr. Cooke remarked on the habit of using biblical texts in Assembly addresses and whimsically said that the text of his choice would be Ezekiel 37, 3 : "Can these dry bones live?" His address was the subject of immediate questions and comments, more particularly concerned with the future of the World Council's Presidium. Further discussion was then referred to a "hearing" on the report, to be held in another place.

Bishop J. E. L. Newbigin of the Church of South India briefly addressed the Assembly on the significance of the report of the Advisory Commission on its main theme and the work of the Main Theme Group. Dr. Franklin Clark Fry, the Vice-Chairman of the Central Committee, closed the session by presenting proposals concerning the best use to be made of this important document.

A special convocation of Northwestern University was summoned in McGaw Memorial Hall at 8 p.m. for the conferring of honorary degrees upon each of the Presidents of the World Council of Churches and the Chairman of the Central Committee.

The Assembly resumed in Plenary Session at 8.30 p.m. with Bishop C K. Jacob of South India in the chair. The Bishop introduced the Assembly's sub-theme of Evangelism. Dr. D. T.

Niles of Ceylon spoke briefly for the World Council's Evangelism Secretariat, indicating three main areas of work: the problem of communication between the Church and non-Christians, the question of the approach to industrial workers and intellectuals, and a clarification of the theology of evangelism.

Dr. Niles then delivered an address on evangelism, in which he said:

The modern scene is a midnight in the affairs of men. Yet even in the darkness lost travellers come knocking at the door of the Christian Church, and are often bitterly disappointed. The Church is often miserably unprepared for those who come. The Church's attempt to escape from its evangelistic responsibility to the world is again and again the result of seeking to dodge the issue of the Cross, and when that happens the Church ceases to understand the true dimension of the hope that is in Christ.

It is Jesus who is the evangelist, we but keep the door of the fold, we but keep the inn on the road; and where there is expectant love there are always callers, those whom Jesus brings. There are many causes for the Church's failure in evangelism, but the chief one is always a failure in expectant love. It is so easy to engage oneself in what are known as evangelistic activities, even to have a true theology of evangelism, and yet be and remain the kind of person into whose hands the Great Shepherd cannot entrust His sheep.

What about success? Surely we are faced with a basic contradiction between the command to succeed and the need to be faithful to the message with which we are entrusted. The truth is that many who are invited will not come, and that the Master will not send His invitation back to them in a more acceptable form.

In the face of this dilemma the churches are confused. Our present problem is that the churches are in large measure refusing to be led by the Spirit into the wilderness, there to be tempted by the devil. They seem to prefer to go to the Cross some other way.

Midnight is a difficult hour in which to be faithful or successful: but we shall find grace as we seek to minister to the real need of him who comes to us in the midnight.

Canon T. O. Wedel of the United States also spoke on evangelism:

The churches are under judgment when they fail to fulfil their task of evangelism. Every chiselled stone in our Gothic shrines, every carving on our pews, every cushioned parish house stands under God's judgment if it is not serving the apostolic calling of the Church—a Church on mission sent. Every human soul over the face of the globe has as much right to the gospel as we have.

Those who think of the Church as a family enjoying a rich inheritance on an ancestral estate, or islands of the saved in the midst of the lost, or an aristocracy among the future citizens of heaven, are wrong. The true Church is an evangelizing army on the march, and a haven of rest only between campaigns when it returns to home base to renew its strength and to receive fresh orders. We have no right to our Sabbath ease and our promised end until the gospel has been preached throughout the world.

The Church is faced with specific questions. Does it really want to carry the gospel out into the world? Does it have the power to evangelize? Does it as a group of people corporately bear witness to the redeeming power of God?

Unfortunately the Church is too often unable to give an affirmative answer to these questions. Carrying the gospel to the world does not mean merely welcoming those who find us attractive. It means moving out into the slums of our great cities, among the poor and down-trodden, the social and racial minorities, the sceptics and unbelievers and the unevangelized multitudes in distant lands.

Evening prayers were led in the First Methodist Church by Superintendent Albert Ricca of the Waldensian Church in Italy.

THE THIRD DAY: TUESDAY, AUGUST 17TH

When morning worship, led by Bishop Hanns Lilje of Germany, concluded, the Assembly divided for meetings of the fifteen groups on the Main Theme "Christ, the Hope of the world." Discussion centred on the difference of emphasis— clearly apparent in the addresses delivered on the first day by Professor Schlink and Professor Calhoun. A process of scrutiny and criticism began as the report of the Advisory Commission on the Main Theme was sifted and evaluated by the gathered representatives of the churches for whom it had been compiled. Among chairmen of the groups were Dr. Charles Malik of the Lebanon, Dr. Martin Niemöller, the Bishop of London (Dr. J. C. Wand), and Professor H. Alivisatos of Athens.

Between the hours of 4 and 6 p.m. delegates who were intimately concerned to voice their opinions on the Central Committee's Report on Structure and Functioning were given opportunity to do so at a special hearing held by members of the Structure and Functioning Committee. Some minor improvements in the report were willingly received. The Committee, however, stoutly defended the arrangement envisaged in the report for the election of new presidents. Under the plan set out it was intended that no retiring president of the World Council of Churches should be eligible for re-election at the Assembly following his term of office. The debate in the hearing was warm and at times even tense, but it was clear that the differences emerging could not be classified within geographical or denominational blocs.

The evening session in McGaw Hall introduced the Faith and Order sub-theme of the Assembly, "Our Oneness in Christ and our Disunity as Churches." Archbishop Yngve Brilioth of Sweden, one of the most notable and respected figures in the Faith and Order movement from its beginnings, presided.

The hymn "O Worship the King " was sung. The Archbishop alluded, in his introduction, to the importance of the Faith and Order movement as bringing "a noble heritage" into the life of the World Council. He said that the Constitution accepted at the Third World Conference on Faith and Order in 1952 had left the Commission with liberty to do its special work. He expressed his personal pleasure that "the Constitution provided that membership must not necessarily be confined to member churches but open to others which accept the Basis of the World Council."

Canon Oliver Tomkins of England, who had been an Associate General Secretary of the World Council of Churches until August, 1952, then took the rostrum in order to report on the new perspective given to Faith and Order studies by the decision of the Lund Conference to study the meaning of the presence

of Christ in the Church. In addition, the Commission continued
study of the traditions of worship, of intercommunion, and of
those social, political and cultural forces which so powerfully
affect the life and unity of the churches.

Bishop Anders Nygren of Sweden, Professor V. E. Devadutt
of India, and Professor Georges Florovsky of New York, in
three complementary speeches which followed, revealed the sharp
and seemingly irreducible differences still separating the member
bodies of the World Council.

Bishop Nygren pointed to the Lund Conference as an important turning point in the development of Faith and Order
discussions.

> The churches have come to realize that ecumenical labours
> must have a new focus. When we speak of the unity of the
> Church we speak of Christ and His Spirit. For that reason Lund
> set up its Commission on "Christ and the Church." This means
> that in their conversations the churches are moving from the
> periphery to the centre. Instead of registering our various con-
> ceptions—with eventual agreement or disagreement—we are
> led to the centre of Christian faith and required, not to present
> the peculiar conceptions of our denomination, but together to
> learn from the divine word. The Church of Christ *is* already
> a unity, and only because that is true does ecumenical work
> have promise. Just as there is only *one* Christ, so there is only
> *one* body of Christ, only *one* Church of Christ.

> Looking to the future, the distinctive element of our
> present situation is—as it appears—that to ecumenical study has
> been granted the privilege and responsibility of giving to
> Christianity this deeper insight into the essence of the Church.
> When the understanding of the Church as the body of Christ,
> which has now been discerned theoretically, becomes a mighty
> reality in the life of the Church, then the decisive step to the
> unity of the Church will have been taken.

Dr. Devadutt called unity an essential ingredient in the
Church's mission.

> The fellowship of believers suffers a reduction when there is
> no common ministry and no common Eucharist. Those who are
> ready to share the sacraments with all Christians freely, often

manifest an alarming lack of concern for the deep convictions of their fellow Christians.

There is a paradox in the life of the empirical churches. They affirm their unity in Christ, yet they are divided. This paradox is of serious import and if we realized the seriousness of its import, we would be challenged to set ourselves to resolve the tragic tension between our oneness and our divisions.

Church membership is not based on the pursuit of an ideal agreed to as desirable by its members. It is based on an historic and intractable fact—the life, death and resurrection of Jesus Christ. We are indeed one, for we are all delivered and saved by one objective fact.

If in all conscience some feel that the Christ whom they worship, and whose sacrifice for their redemption they commemorate with an exultant gratitude at the celebration of the Eucharist, bids them to exclude other believers in Christ from participation at the same celebration, then the Christ they worship and the Christ others worship is by positive implication not the same Christ.

Three misconceptions prevail in respect to church union: the identification of serious divisions with desirable diversity; the feeling that church union means the destruction of diversity and the achievement of dead uniformity; and the mistaken idea that in non-Roman Christendom church union could mean elaborate unified organizational structure with a central authority and an authoritarian government. Church union means primarily two things, "the unity of the ministry and the unity of the sacraments."

Father Georges Florovsky said he recognized that he was called to the defence of an unpopular cause, but that this defence must be undertaken.

Christians still meet each other as strangers. The ecumenical movement has done much to break down barriers of misunderstanding but it has been confined rather to an advanced minority.

The greatest achievement of the ecumenical movement is its courage in acknowledging that there is a major disagreement. This disagreement cannot be dismissed merely as the result of "non-theological" or social factors. The very sting of Christian tragedy lies in the fact that, in the concrete setting of history, many divisions have been imposed, as it were, precisely by loyalty to Christ and by a sincere zeal for the true faith.

Those who represent the "High" or "Catholic" view of the Church have to insist that in the process of Christian disintegration there have also been certain "structural losses." For them the separation goes so deep in Christian life that they cannot regard many of the existing denominations as "churches" in the full or true sense of the word, i.e. as living "parts" of the Church Universal. They would not impose their own convictions upon those who are unable to share them, but they are compelled, precisely by their love for the brethren and in an ultimate obedience to the will of God, to state their own convictions and to abstain accordingly from any action in which they cannot join without betraying their deepest loyalty.

This does not mean that the ecumenical movement has reached a dead end, but that it is this very tension which gives true "ecumenicity" to the ecumenical movement. The task might be easier if certain communions were dropped out of the picture, but it would no longer be an ecumenical endeavour.

While it is true to say that everything historical will be surpassed at the end of history, yet what is being done by men in history has its own status in the story of salvation. A new discovery of the historical church tradition is needed. Full knowledge and understanding are reserved for the Day of Judgment, but a knowledge of *direction* is available for the Church in her earthly pilgrimage. To recover this *sense of direction* is the first task of the ecumenical movement at the present.

The weariness and perplexity inevitably associated with the central and most difficult period of all ecumenical meetings could be felt unmistakably as delegates travelled in the buses sent to take them from the plenary session to evening worship; but the simple and moving words of Scripture, the familiar prayers, and the music of Bach assured them that a greater purpose was in and through all they were doing together. The evening prayers were led by the Rev. Lyall Dixon of Australia.

The Fourth Day: Wednesday, August 18th

The Rev. Elsie Chamberlain, of the Congregational Union of England and Wales, was leader and preacher at morning worship.

During the morning Dr. Franklin Clark Fry presided over the plenary session. A brisk discussion took place concerning the future of the Council's presidium. It was eventually decided to accept the advice of the Central Committee and to provide that no president should be eligible for immediate re-election (see page 178).

Group discussion on the main theme continued in the afternoon. In the evening the Assembly was brought to its feet by further outstanding addresses. Bishop Berggrav was in the chair as Dr. C. L. Patijn of the Netherlands presented the work of the Assembly Section on Social Questions.

Dr. Patijn gave a brief résumé of ecumenical thinking on social questions since the Stockholm Conference on Life and Work in 1925.

It is evident that we are still just beginning to elaborate a new social ethos, which will be truly Christian and truly relevant to modern society. Christian thinking crystallized at the Amsterdam Assembly of 1948 around the term "responsible society." This phrase indicated the Assembly's concern for the adequate protection in economic and political life of all those who need help in order to be freed from want and fear. At the same time the term "responsible society" sought to express the churches' concern for a social order which provides democratic ways of living for "little men in big societies," which does not regard man as a cog in a machine, but as a free and responsible person. However, the implications of the concept of a responsible society were stated in the Amsterdam report in broad outlines only, "more in terms of general attitudes than specific issues."

The Church must speak in language which drives home with regard to specific issues. It should speak in positive and not in negative terms. The Church should see the dangers and sins of society not as an object for mere criticism but as an object for responsible action. For example, freedom in a responsible society is not identical with freedom from all state-intervention but a God-given opportunity for responsible action. The Church should base its word with regard to society not on fear, but on hope. The real service it can render society is to understand society better than it understands itself. It is for the Church to deliver society from utopian illusions, from the fetters of political dogma, from the frustrations arising out of political forms of idolatry. It is for the Church to give power, motivation, and courage for Christian action in society by proclaiming that God reigns and that we are called to participate in His ministry of reconciliation.

The second speaker was Dr. Charles Malik, Ambassador of the Lebanon in the United States of America and a delegate of the Greek Orthodox Patriarchate of Antioch.

Dr. Malik began with a strong testimony to the truth and power of the revelation of God in Christ.

The challenge of Asia and Africa, so far as their present fundamental revolution is concerned, is for the Christian conscience, in all sympathy and love, to understand and be concerned about their political, economic, social and spiritual needs. Asia and Africa demand the necessary freedom to develop their own social and political forms and institutions. These will vary considerably from Western forms. The important thing is not uniformity of culture but the growth of an international and intercultural order wherein every people and every culture will freely develop its own genius as much as possible and as best it can, subject obviously to four conditions only: (a) that no culture or nation encroach on another, (b) that therefore they all voluntarily enter into some universal juridical order, (c) that there be free interchange of ideas and goods among them, and (d) that the enjoyment of a certain indispensable minimum of fundamental human rights be guaranteed within each of them.

The really significant question is what is happening to the mind and soul of Africa and Asia. The intellectual and spiritual problems are far more important than political social or economic questions. Christians have under-estimated the importance of liberal education for Asia and Africa. Thousands of students attend Western universities and return home proficient in certain techniques but with little knowledge of the deepest things in the West, and even less appreciation of the deepest values of their own culture. Asia and Africa demand a living message. And for the most part only spiritless secularism reaches the world from the West. At the present rate of spiritual impotence, with the protective covering of the hydrogen bomb, it is only a matter of time before the whole of Asia and Africa, and maybe even Europe, will be engulfed by communism. What is desperately needed, besides the highest political wisdom, is a ringing positive message, one of reality, of truth and of hope.

The Rev. Peter Dagadu, General Secretary of the Christian Council of the Gold Coast, was dressed in a rich blue national costume striped with irregular rows of inter-woven gold. No one who heard him could feel immune from the dynamic indignation and sense of the sacred he brought to the Assembly from his native continent.

Africa today is no more a continent of dark mystery, peopled by primitive folk little known and less understood. The agricultural, educational, political, economic, industrial, military and religious elements of western civilization have poured in as in a flood-tide upon Africans. Gratitude and appreciation for the gifts of science, of education and of Christianity are mixed with many questions in the minds of Africans as a result of this contact with the West. The woeful lack of understanding by the Western world of the life of the African, caused primarily by misinterpretation of Africa by representatives of the West engaged in commercial, political and missionary enterprises, constitutes no little bewilderment to the African.

The questions Africans are asking include the following: When will the West come to appreciate African abilities and gifts, in all types of labour and the professions and in the resources of faith and sacrificial service to be found in African personal, family and communal life? Are the admirable techniques and material inventions of the West for the good of mankind or for human destruction? Are Africans to have a full share in the management of their own affairs? How long are race and other discriminations to continue? The West condemns communism but exploits African land and labour. Which system of philosophy and religion and which government will help us to get a larger share of the benefits from our own land and labour? Will the Christian churches apply the gospel to their own work in Africa? To inter-church co-operation? To land acquisition and management? To training for political leadership? Alongside contemporary changes and questions there is a process of change belonging to God alone—the process of changing bad men and bad women into good men and good women. It is called the miracle of conversion, and the only institution in the world which has evidence of this miracle is the Church. The hope for Africa lies with men and women of the West and of Africa who are a living witness to this miracle.

Bishop Berggrav, who had chaired the meeting with his usual simplicity, drew the speakers in line behind him at the rostrum after the closing hymn, as the huge crowd in the hall joined in the words of the Lord's Prayer in many tongues.

The many visitors who had waited in the moist heat for the evening session left the hall in the knowledge that they had been present at a meeting that would be long remembered all over the world.

Evening prayers were led by Dr. Michael R. Zigler of the Church of the Brethren.

The Fifth Day: Thursday, August 19th

Pastor Pierre Maury, a well-loved ecumenical leader, began the Assembly's fifth day at worship.

Thursday of the first week was primarily set aside for work, though it was marked by two special events which provided some relief. Group discussion on the Main Theme in the morning gave place later in the day to the first meetings of the seven committees on the Business of the World Council. As the report of the Committee on Structure and Functioning had been adopted on the previous day it was now possible for the churches to bring their thoughts to bear on many tasks before the Council in its newly organized form. The committees on the new Divisions of Ecumenical Action and Studies were charged with particularly grave decisions; the Committee on General Policy with even weightier matters. While the committees were meeting, the President of the United States was travelling by air to Evanston at the invitation of the World Council to bring his message and greeting.

The Deering Meadow, an enclosed space of bright green, standing between Sheridan Road and the grey Gothic façade of the library of Northwestern University, had been furnished with seats for participants in the Assembly. A crowd of 23,000 people gathered there on a glorious afternoon of bright sunshine and shade. In a grove a platform had been erected. The people of Evanston knew that this was a moment of great significance for their city. A little after four o'clock perhaps the most splendid of all the Assembly processions descended the steps of the Library and made its leisurely way to the speaker's dais. County and city police stood in groups along the pathway. Black academic robes and sober hats were flecked with the bright relief of hoods. Silk gowns in many shades supported the gleaming chains and crosses of bishops and the decorations of members of national orders. As President Eisenhower appeared, the audience rose and applauded his progress. Bishop G. Bromley Oxnam led the prayers; the Archbishop of Canterbury voiced a welcome.

President Eisenhower then spoke. He asked that the Assembly "remind us again and again of the vision without which the people perish," and for "a practical demonstration of the Christian ethic." The President proposed that Christians lead the way to peace by "inviting every single person in every single country of the world who believes in the power of prayer to the Supreme Being to join in a mighty, simultaneous, intense act of faith."

Then followed the conferring of an honorary degree of the University upon the President.

The benediction was given by Bishop Berggrav of Norway.

The second event which provided relief in the full programme of the Assembly was an orchestral and choral concert in Ravinia Park, Chicago. The Chicago Symphony Orchestra presented, among other selections, the Stock arrangement of "Ein' Feste Burg," and the Symphony in G Minor by Mozart. Miss Carol Brice was the soloist, and few will forget her deeply moving interpretation of the spiritual, "Sweet Little Jesus Boy."

THE SIXTH DAY: FRIDAY, AUGUST 20TH

The Anglican Bishop of Durham, The Right Rev. Michael Ramsey, conducted prayers in the First Methodist Church.

The committees on World Council Business continued their

work in the morning and afternoon. They adjourned at four o'clock. At that hour meetings of the many confessions represented at Evanston were held, in most cases in the local churches bearing their names.

Mr. Dag Hammarskjöld, Secretary General of the United Nations, visited the Assembly for the evening session. His coming was especially welcome in view of his earlier relationship with Archbishop Nathan Söderblom of Upsala, one of the outstanding pioneers of the ecumenical movement. Mr. Hammarskjöld was accompanied by his executive assistant Mr. A. Cordier.

Mr. Hammarskjöld said:

The churches may be a decisive force for good in international affairs and in national political life, without assuming a political role or trying directly to influence political decisions, if they will speak out for justice, truth and trust in public affairs. Our time is characterized by two predominant trends. One towards social and economic equality within nations, the other towards equal rights and opportunities for all nations. But if there are no means provided for orderly development these trends may lead to cataclysms like those of the recent past. We must approach our task from two angles. First of all by practical action to help underdeveloped countries economically and to provide a framework for peaceful development of the independence and self-determination of nations. Secondly there is need for inspiration, for the creation of a spirit among the leaders of the peoples which helps them to use the forces which they have to master, for peace and not for war, for evolution and not for revolution.

The conflicts under the surface of international and national politics are conflicts whose battlefield always has been and always will be the hearts of men. The overwhelming task of the churches and of all men of good will is to fight in this war in the hearts of men for an ever wider recognition of their own ideals of justice and truth. And to show men the strength—so necessary today—that follows from the courage to meet others with trust. Further, the churches can help explain the failures and achievements of all work for peace, which is the responsibility of every one of us. The Cross, although it is the unique fact on which the Christian churches base their hope, should not separate those of the Christian faith from others, but should instead be that element in their lives which enables them to stretch out their hands to peoples of other creeds in the feeling of universal brotherhood which we hope one day to see reflected in a world of nations truly united.

Dr. O. Frederick Nolde, Director of the Commission of the Churches on International Affairs, then spoke. He reviewed the activities of the Commission and suggested ways in which the churches could contribute towards solving major international issues.

Christians recognize that the proclamation of the gospel and the growth of Christian fellowship are the main contributions of the churches towards peace. But more direct methods must also be tried. The Commission has sought to build an organization which will express an effective and timely Christian witness to the nations, and to offer such help for the solution of international problems as may be derived from the Christian faith and the experience of the churches. Utilizing a two-way line of communication, between church leaders and national church commissions, and with inter-governmental bodies the C.C.I.A. has: secured the incorporation of an acceptable standard of religious freedom in the Universal Declaration of Human Rights; initiated the idea of the U.N. Peace Observation Commission subsequently adopted by the United Nations; pressed for armaments reduction; supported the technical assistance programmes; secured favourable international actions on behalf of refugees; and sought to register Christian conviction on many occasions in recent years, at the time and place where international decisions have been made. Examples of the latter type of action were in Korea at the time of the conference on armistice arrangements, and at the Berlin Foreign Ministers' Conference, and the Geneva Asian Conference.

Dr. Nolde suggested that this co-operative witness of churches and national commissions of churches under the World Council and the International Missionary Council was becoming a new world peace movement, rooted in the life of the churches, seeking to express the meaning of the Christian faith for relations among nations. Looking ahead, the alternative to war could only be found in peaceful competition with a sincere commitment to growing co-operation. War is not inevitable. If competition could go forward peacefully, any system should be given opportunity to demonstrate its worth. While the World Council condemned all forms of totalitarianism, this ideological conflict could not be resolved by force. Christians and churches could support and urge their governments to support: development of a more balanced outlook among nations; purposeful negotiations of all crises; an end of imperialism; projects for achievement of human dignity, justice, freedom; reduction and regulation of armaments; development of the international family; and the building of a sound and healthy domestic society.

During the evening messages were read from the Director General of UNESCO, the President of the German Federal Republic, and the American Secretary of State, Mr. John Foster Dulles. The proceedings were symbolic of the new responsibilities assumed by the churches in the international arena since the establishment of the Commission of the Churches on International Affairs in 1946.

The Rev. Philip Potter of Jamaica led evening prayers.

The Seventh Day: Saturday, August 21st

Metropolitan Juhanon Mar Thoma, of South India, conducted worship on the Saturday morning at the end of the Assembly's first week.

Archbishop Athenagoras took the chair for the morning plenary session. Messages were read from the Isabella Thoburn College, Lucknow, India, where Sarah Chakko, the first woman president of the World Council of Churches, had been Principal until her death in February, 1954, from the Batak Church Council in Sumatra, and from the Reformed Evangelical Churches in Poland.

Bishop John Peter conveyed a message from the Hungarian delegation to the Assembly as a whole, in which he assured delegates that his delegation might come from "the other side of the world but not the other side of the Church."

At home, and here, too, we proclaim against all divisions and tensions the unbreakable oneness of the Church. It is in the conscience of our fellowship—yes, it was in joy and readiness to talk to you, that we came here. . . I wish to thank you in the name of our delegation for the profound signs of love we experience here whenever we meet gatherings of church delegates.

He appealed for a positive approach towards the evaluation of political positions and asked that Christians should not be negative in dealing with one another's social and political outlooks (see p. 120).

A final message came through the Bishop of Harrar, who brought greetings from the Emperor of Ethiopia.

The subject set down for consideration was the theme of the Fifth Assembly Section on Inter-group Relations. President Benjamin E. Mays and Dr. Ben Marais spoke in turn.

Dr. Mays said that research on the problem of race relations yielded no support for theories of racial superiority or inferiority which could lead to practices of segregation.

In the Old Testament the lines of separation are drawn only along religious and not along racial lines. In the New Testament it is equally clear that separateness was on the basis of religion and culture and not on the ground of racial or ethnic origin. Fourteen leading European theologians all agree that they cannot find any justification in the Bible for a segregated Church based on racial or ethnic origins. Examination of ancient and modern church history leads to the conclusion that nowhere in the early Church do we find distinctions drawn on the basis of country or race. In the mediaeval Church the basis of membership was faith not race, Christ not colour, credal acceptance and not nationality. The colour or racial bar in the Church is a modern development. It was when western imperialism began to explore and to exploit the coloured peoples of Africa, Asia and America that segregation and discrimination based on colour and race were initiated.

The questions naturally arise: How can segregation and discrimination in the Church be justified? What can the churches do to put themselves in line with the gospel, the practices of the ancient and mediaeval Church, and in line with the findings of modern science? If the churches cannot practise full Christian fellowship in worship and membership, how can they preach the prophetic word to secular organizations that discriminate on grounds of race, colour and caste? Another aspect of this subject is often overlooked: what discrimination does to the person who practises it. It sears not only the soul of the segregated but the soul of the segregator, as well. The churches must recognize the urgency of the present situation. We preach a universal gospel that demands that our deeds reflect our theory. The gospel on race has been preached for nineteen centuries, yet segregation remains the great scandal in the Church. Local churches permit secular bodies to initiate social change in the area of race, but both Negro and White follow slowly or not at all. If an atheistic communist can act on his belief and suffer for it, surely the followers of Christ can suffer for theirs. The Church must encourage its members to exemplify in their vocations and local churches this supra-racial unity in Christ. For the Church is God's creation and not man's and it belongs to God. And in God's domain all men are equal.

Dr. Ben Marais then spoke.

The great majority of churches find no justification for a policy of segregation within the Christian Church or even society. But within the universal Church there is a small body of opinion which bases a policy of racial segregation within the Church on Scripture. This group argues as follows: "It is clear that God willed the existence of separate nations and that He wills to perpetuate the division into races and nations. Restoration of the unity of mankind, we learn from Scripture, can be effected only through the conquest of sin. The concept of *apartheid*, or rather the maintenance of the racial identity of each nation, can for that reason not be regarded as a temporary measure but is a constant obligation of every nation out of respect for God's dispensation. Even in the Church of Christ, as it exists here in its instituted form, the gospel did not abolish differences. Any attempt to ignore this will be an attempt to build another Tower of Babel. The creation of separate churches is not only permissible but essential. Only when the Kingdom of God comes in perfection will these limitations pass away."

Dr. Marais stated clearly that this latter position was not his own, and went on to describe a third position more closely allied to his own views.

This third view agrees that exclusion as such is wrong but yet holds that Christian responsibility may lead us to acknowledge that while separate churches for different racial, ethnic, colour or language groups are not *the ultimate ideal*, it may *in certain situations* be at present the lesser of two evils.

The fact that segregated churches may still be necessary must lead us as believers to repentance. Dr. Marais quoted Professor Keet:

Judgment must begin at no other than the house of God. If the Church must, for practical reasons, take account of an existing situation, this accommodation must be seen clearly as a temporary measure, justified only on the ground that the ultimate goal may be missed if we proceed over-hastily to reach it. The goal itself may never be lost sight of.

Dr. Marais concluded:

In submitting this report with Dr. Mays I do it as one who believes that the Christian fundamentally knows only one *apartheid* (separation) and that is separation from sin, and is deeply disturbed by our failure in many respects, but as one on the other hand who is as deeply convinced of the extremely complicated situations some churches face. Let condemnation in these things be far from us and understanding, prayer and hope motivate and characterize our discussions and actions as men and as churches.

There was time at the end of the session for a further speech by Mr. Francis P. Miller of the United States, who introduced the Assembly Section on the Laity.

Human society furnishes the Christian with the raw material of life on which he can leave the imprint of his eternal citizenship. The Christian life is thus an effort to express the meaning of citizenship in God's Kingdom through our duties, responsibilities and opportunities as citizens of a particular society. God rules. God is at work accomplishing His purposes through men and through the society which man has created. But while God works so do "the principalities and the powers—the rulers of this present darkness" (Eph. 6, 12). A fateful struggle is engaged for the souls of men. The battle is fierce and long, but final victory will be won (and in one sense is already won) by

Jesus Christ. He is our Captain and He will assign to each of us our specific task and mission.

One of our greatest weaknesses as a world-wide Christian community is our failure to provide our laymen with the kind of religious education which makes them think of their work in secular society as being the place to which God has called them to serve Him. Some are called to a specific vocation. But every honourable job, no matter how mechanical or trivial, can become a vocation, the moment the man who holds the job understands the full meaning of being a Christian. Take politics as an example. Not many Protestants in my part of the world realize that to be a Christian means being a good citizen in a creative and constructive sense, one who acts responsibly on the basis of a Christian concept of society. Nor do the churches strive to send their ablest sons and daughters into public life, as they challenge them to go as missionaries to foreign lands. There are many churchmen in public life. But few realize that their Christian faith should have automatically converted their political activity into a Christian vocation. And the stark fact is that the survival of responsible freedom in the world depends upon Christians taking seriously their obligations and duties as citizens, and the Church sending her ablest members into public life.

As in politics so in any other job the layman does. It can, by the grace and love of God, become the Christian vocation to which he is called. His job can become that if the Church provides laymen with the instruction they need. It is our responsibility to see that it does.

The Archbishop of Canterbury, whose health had not been good enough to allow him to take part in the opening of the Assembly, was now on the platform. Many representatives of the churches noted the regular presence of John R. Mott, the Honorary President. True to his life-long tradition of punctuality and loyalty to the cause, Dr. Mott was often to be seen gazing out over the faces in the hall—faces of those who consciously or unconsciously owed so much to his genius and resourcefulness.

After a third meeting of committees on World Council Business during the afternoon, many in the evening attended the service of preparation for Holy Communion held in the First Methodist

Church. Dr. Ernest A. Payne of the United Kingdom preached the sermon. It was an occasion for reflection on the similar services held six years before at the First Assembly in the Nieuwe Kerk in Amsterdam. A deep unity sensed in worship and in the unspoken as well as the spoken penitence of Christians face to face with Christian disunity led fittingly into all the Communion services of the week that lay ahead.

THE EIGHTH DAY: SUNDAY, AUGUST 22ND

Holy Communion according to the rite of the Methodist Church in the U.S.A. was celebrated in the First Methodist Church on the morning of the second Sunday of the Assembly. In an impressive service the celebrants from among bishops of the Methodist Church were assisted by participants from other churches. Bishop Ivan Lee Holt, President of the World Methodist Council, presided. The invitation extended to all Christians was accepted by the majority of Assembly participants with profound gratitude for the unity thus given to them. Yet for them and for those unable to communicate there was also a sense of pain and contrition. Successive groups of communicants knelt at the rail to receive communion, knowing that the true unity in Christ had not yet been achieved, yet having that foretaste of it which inspires hope and faith in its full realization.

The great and widely attended Methodist service was the first of a series to be held during the Assembly's second week.

The afternoon gave the participants in the Assembly a breathing space. Women representatives, who were more numerous than they had been at Amsterdam, received a characteristically gracious welcome from the women of Evanston and Chicago. Nearly 5,000 women came to a long planned and well organized series of teas arranged in the various churches of the city, where they were received by the women members of the Assembly. Later they listened to an informative and thought-provoking address by Dr. Kathleen Bliss, in the First Methodist Church, filled to capacity. Other delegates took the opportunity to see the photographic display devised by Mr. John Taylor, a member of the World Council's staff. The display had been the subject of widespread appreciative comment throughout the Assembly, and had drawn the admiration of professional photographers and journalists seeking appropriate symbols to convey the meaning of the ecumenical movement and the World Council's work.

In McGaw Hall in the evening a large cast drawn in great part from membership of the churches of Evanston presented a "dramatic documentary" called *By the Waters of Babylon*. The platform in the hall had been converted for this occasion into a wide stage across which moved the figures of men and women dressed in grey, representing the procession of nameless and sometimes faceless refugees, vexing the conscience of the modern world. The script of the pageant had been written by Miss Janet Lacey of the Department of Refugee Service of the British Council of Churches. In the heat of the midsummer night, watching the glare of the spotlight on the actors and the three speakers who told of the World Council's work for refugees, the audience, drawn from all over the world, was vividly reminded of the continuing responsibility of the churches towards one another and the millions of hard-pressed and bewildered refugees in East and West. The three people who gave typical instances of what the World Council was doing were Bishop Dibelius of Berlin, the Rev. S. H. Myung of Korea, and Dr. Edgar Chandler, the Director of Service to Refugees for the World Council of Churches. Finally, Pastor Marc Boegner appealed to the huge audience to respond to the call that had been made.

THE NINTH DAY: MONDAY, AUGUST 23RD

The day began with the Anglican Service of Holy Communion, held in St. Mark's Protestant Episcopal Church at Evanston, with the Right Rev. Henry Knox Sherrill, Presiding Bishop of the Protestant Episcopal Church in the U.S.A., officiating. All baptized communicant members of the member churches of the World Council of Churches were invited to receive the Holy Communion.

During the morning the Assembly Sections met, and in the afternoon the committees on World Council Business met again.

At the evening plenary session Archbishop Athenagoras took the chair. The sweltering heat led even the most sober and formal members in the Assembly to remove their coats. Metropolitan Gennadios of Helioupolis read a message concerning the Assembly from the Oecumenical Patriarch, welcoming the atmosphere which was leading the churches into closer co-operation with one another. The message said the teachings of the Church Fathers indicated that there was always room within the Church for a diversity of rites and practices—provided there was unity of faith. Although by men's reckoning the time when full unity would be realized might seem far off, if Christians would confess that the will of their Lord was for such unity, that day would surely come. All must work towards that goal.

Dr. M. E. Aubrey of the Baptist Union of Great Britain and Ireland introduced the report of the Credentials Committee. The report was adopted unanimously (see p. 256).

The report of the Nominations Committee was presented by President Moreland, its chairman (see p. 259). Its proposal for the presidium was followed with marked interest. The advisability of appointing a layman to the presidium was to be discussed with great warmth in the Assembly during the next few days. The Bishop of Chichester received special applause when his name was put forward for election as an honorary president. Dr. John R. Mott received a similar spontaneous ovation.

Dr. Hendrik Kraemer delivered his report on the work of the Ecumenical Institute at the Château de Bossey. Speaking deliberately and modestly about what had been achieved at Bossey since 1947, he alluded to the pioneering work of its varied conferences, its sense of community, and to the links between the Institute and the World Council's concern with the task of the laity. He said that in his view the work of the Section on the Laity was the most important of all the Assembly's studies.

Dr. Henry P. Van Dusen, the Chairman of the Study Department Committee of the Council, after speaking briefly about the importance of proper study within the total pattern of ecumenical life, introduced Dr. Nils Ehrenström, the Study Department's Director. Dr. Van Dusen expressed appreciation of the long and distinguished service Dr. Ehrenström had rendered to ecumenical study since the Stockholm meeting on Life and Work in 1925. Before Dr. Ehrenström spoke, Dr. Van Dusen especially emphasized two other points—the danger that Anglo-Saxon thinking might dominate ecumenical study work as English assumed the status of a *lingua franca*, and the problems of communication with the member churches involved in the evolution of a rounded study programme.

Dr. Ehrenström followed Dr. Van Dusen by presenting the

report of the Study Department Committee, indicating that the key tasks are the selection of priorities in subject matter, cross-fertilization of varied convictions, integration of differing projects and studies, and the development of the partnership of a wide number and variety of agencies and persons in the advance of ecumenical thought.

Although the meeting had adhered fairly well to time, the large audience breathed a sigh of gratitude when Dr. Visser 't Hooft explained that Dr. Madeleine Barot, who was scheduled as the last speaker, had proposed that the Assembly should "no longer be exposed to the excessive heat of this night."

Bishop Mar Philoxenos, of the Orthodox Syrian Church of Malabar Catholicate, led evening prayers in the First Methodist Church.

THE TENTH DAY: TUESDAY, AUGUST 24TH

A third service of Holy Communion was sponsored by the Augustana Evangelical Lutheran Church and held at the Immanuel Evangelical Lutheran Church in Chicago. The celebrant was the Rev. Dr. O. V. Anderson, president-elect of the Illinois Conference of the Church. Many who journeyed to Chicago to worship in the service or to communicate spoke warmly of the way in which the quiet splendour of the Swedish rite had been made a living reality in the heart of American Middle West.

During the day the Assembly sections met twice more. When the plenary Assembly came together in the evening, Dr. Franklin Clark Fry assumed the chair as President Moreland brought forward a second statement from the Nominations Committee. He said that a courteous request, signed by more than sixty people, suggested that a layman be nominated for the presidium. A certain layman had been asked whether he was prepared to stand; he had declined. President Moreland therefore moved the adoption of that part of the report of the Nominations Committee that concerned the presidium as a whole. Pastor Martin Niemöller thereupon urged postponement of a decision so that other possible lay nominees could be approached. It was decided to postpone the election of the presidents to enable the Nominations Committee to study the position again.

Bishop Jacob took the chair as Dr. R. B. Manikam presented his report of his period of office as East Asia Secretary of the

World Council and the International Missionary Council. Dr. Manikam was introduced as an embodiment of the sense of working unity between the two world bodies. The speaker wore a golden turban to crown his national dress. He described his many journeys and the discharge of his trust, and spoke of the many new opportunities for missionary co-operation, responsible Christian action, and church union within the area he served.

To make the ecumenical movement more real to the Christian churches of Asia, an East Asia secretary had been jointly appointed in 1950 by the I.M.C. and W.C.C. Since 1951, in addition to Europe and North America, Dr. Manikam had visited churches in Malaya, Indonesia, India, Hong Kong, Japan, Korea, Formosa, Burma, Thailand, Indo-China, East and West Pakistan, Ceylon, Australia, New Zealand, the Fiji Islands and Hawaii. He attended regular conferences concerned with East Asian affairs and recently edited a book entitled *Christianity and the Asian Revolution*.

More than half of the world's population living in the area between Karachi and Tokyo, is today involved in a major political, economic and social revolution. Although only forty million Christians inhabit East Asia (out of 1,230 millions!), the Church has a glorious role to play in this fast-changing social setting. It must face the challenge of four great non-Christian cultures—Hindu, Buddhist, Islamic and Confucian—the handicap of preaching an apparently divided Protestant Christianity, and the counter-appeal of communism. But the Church in East Asia is moving forward. It is increasing its own missionary enterprise. It is strengthening its corporate life through national councils of churches. It is solidifying its relationships with the ecumenical movement.

Dr. Manikam cited the challenge set forth in the new book he had edited:

Two great convictions have grown in us. We Christians of East Asia should give far more to the Church than we are doing now. At least for the maintenance of the life and work of our churches we should make ourselves entirely responsible. Assistance received from abroad should be primarily utilized for forward movements in evangelism, newer experiments in Christian witness, production of evangelistic and apologetic literature, and maintenance of those institutions which are at present essential for the Christian enterprise.

The other conviction of ours is that the time has come when we of East Asia should regard the evangelization of this part of the world as our primary responsibility. Our sons and daughters should be challenged to go out as missionaries. We do not forget that we are part of the Church Universal. We are grateful for our God-given national heritage, and we shall strive together to hold to it so that it may never divide but enrich all nations.

Two speakers followed him in analysing the problems of "world-wide evangelization in this generation." They were Dr. Charles Ranson, the General Secretary of the International Missionary Council, and Canon Chandu Ray of the Bible Society in Pakistan.

Dr. Ranson stated that the one great task which has been given to the Church is to preach the gospel to the ends of the earth and to the end of time.

Although the situation which we face in the world today is very different from that confronting the Church in earlier centuries, there is only one answer to the question: what is the meaning of the present time? It is that this is the time given to the Church for the prosecution of its apostolic mission to the world. So long as time remains, the Church can never write "mission accomplished" against its great commission.

World-wide evangelism means that Christian World Mission can no longer be properly conceived in terms mainly of the outreach of the churches of the western world. It is the outgoing of a world-wide and supra-national fellowship. The magnitude of that task cannot be over-estimated. There are still vast areas of the world which have never heard the name of Christ, and where there is still no hindrance to the preaching of the gospel save the lack of a messenger. The hard core of ancient non-Christian tradition has not yet been deeply penetrated by Christian faith.

Today we must also recognize that the gospel is a gospel for man in this world and for the *whole* man including his environment. This is more than a matter of individual discipleship. It involves a tension in which the Church must live, choosing between living unto itself and living as a mission in the world. Concretely, this implies three things:

(1) the Church is summoned to encounter with the world:

(2) the Church is called not only to encounter with the world but to mobility in the world:

(3) we need, above all, a new initiative born of the Holy Spirit.

We cannot command the Spirit but we see some signs of His movement. There is particularly the deepening perception that world-wide evangelism cannot be divorced from the quest for Christian unity, and in view of this fact the traditional patterns of missionary oganization and action are being reviewed. The failure to express in visible form the unity given in Christ is a formidable obstacle to effective world evangelism.

The problem is that we already know more than we have the power to do. If we are tempted merely to look at the recumbent figure of the other disciple and ask "Lord, what shall this man do?" we may also hear the devastating word spoken to Peter: "What is that to thee? Follow thou me."

Canon Chandu Ray spoke as a convert from Hinduism and a missionary in his own country.

We of the younger churches are living as in apostolic times, with a very large percentage of non-Christians around us, whose attitude to Christianity is not always favourable. And yet we have tremendous encouragement in our work. This evening I want to bear witness to some recent experiments in evangelism, and share with you both the victories and the failures in our work.

Christianity has made great strides in some Asian countries through the joint efforts of foreign mission bodies, national mission groups, and evangelists. Housing, health, education, literacy, and the spiritual life of many Asians have greatly improved under the impact of the Bible and Christian evangelism. New techniques of spreading the gospel have been employed, including literacy instruction, progressive teaching, showing of lantern slides illustrating bible stories. And constantly there is the steady, effective way of "gossiping the gospel." Failures have been due to disunity of evangelistic efforts and comity of missions.

The world Church can aid the younger churches in their programmes of evangelism. It can encourage mission schools and colleges to bear a courageous and clear witness to Christ and to present His challenge. It can see that evangelists and new converts have sufficient food to eat and clothes to wear to allow them to carry on an effective ministry. It can make certain that the Bible is available in the local language or dialect. It can help provide special training for evangelists and special instruments for their trade, for example audio-visual equipment. It can work for greater unity throughout the Christian world and see that comity or divisions do not hinder the on-going, vital task of evangelization.

As the meeting closed, Dr. Franklin Clark Fry stepped forward to say that Dr. John R. Mott expected to leave the Assembly on the next day. All in the hall rose as Dr. Mott waved his hand in acknowledgment, at first almost dissuasively, and then in acceptance.

Pastor P. T. Poincenot of the Evangelical Lutheran Church of France led evening prayers.

THE ELEVENTH DAY: WEDNESDAY, AUGUST 25TH

At an early hour in the morning the Divine Liturgy of St. John Chrysostom was celebrated in St. Andrew's Greek Orthodox Church in Chicago. Archbishop Athenagoras of Thyateira was the celebrant, assisted by Bishop John Shahovskoy and priests from several Orthodox delegations.

The Assembly sections held a further meeting during the morning. A special plenary meeting took place in McGaw Hall at 2.30. The Archbishop of Canterbury was in the chair. Bishop Lilje presented an introductory statement from the group co-ordinating the discussions on the Main Theme. In this he described the use proposed for the report of the Advisory Commission on the Main Theme, and a "Statement on the Main Theme" compiled to reflect the state of discussion in the Main Theme groups. Considerable discussion on Bishop Lilje's introduction and the Statement on the Main Theme followed. It took some time for the Assembly to clarify the relationship between the Report of the Advisory Commission, the Statement now put forward, and the forthcoming "Message of the Assembly" (see p. 70).

At the opening of the evening plenary session the Archbishop of Canterbury introduced Mr. Melvin Nelson, the Chairman of the Evanston Committee of One Hundred. Mr. Nelson displayed to the Assembly a Bible bookmark consisting of three blue ribbons attached at one end to a bronze book-marker and at the other to a metal cross, anchor, and commemorative seal of the Assembly. He explained that this was the gift of his committee to official Assembly participants. The Archbishop of Canterbury received the gift and thanked the people of Evanston, especially Mr. Nelson and the members of his committee. Mr. Nelson warmly shook the hand of the Bishop of Chichester and Dr. W. A. Visser 't Hooft.

The Rev. David Say next came forward in place of President Moreland to convey the further advice of the Nominations Committee. He first moved the election of the Bishop of Chichester as an honorary president. The election was unanimous and immediate. The whole Assembly stood at this moment to applaud the Bishop. Mr. Say then repeated the six original names put forward for the presidium. After some discussion (see p. 262) the nominations were put to the Assembly and the new presidents were elected. They were: Principal John Baillie, Bishop Sante Uberto Barbieri, Bishop F. K. Otto Dibelius, Metropolitan Juhanon Mar Thoma, Archbishop Michael and Bishop Henry Knox Sherrill. The Archbishop of Canterbury congratulated the new presidium.

After a confessional and geographical analysis of the names brought forward for the Central Committee, the nominations were put and the Committee was elected with applause. It was agreed that the Chairman of the International Missionary Council should be asked to sit with all meetings of the Central Committee, and that Dr. John R. Mott should be asked to continue as an honorary president.

When the discussion on the Main Theme was resumed, Archbishop Michael read a statement for the Orthodox delegation in order that the position of the members of his own communion in relation to it should be quite clear (see Appendix 8, page 329).

Bishop Albert Bereczky of Hungary followed him by bringing forward a statement from the Hungarian delegation on the same subject, indicating their sense of solidarity with the ecumenical movement, the value which the Hungarian churches attached to the main theme and their hope for continued close association.

During the rest of the evening full consideration was given to a revised draft of the Statement on the Main Theme.

Evening prayers were led by the Rev. Michio Kozaki, Moderator of the Church of Christ in Japan.

THE TWELFTH DAY: THURSDAY, AUGUST 26TH

The final meeting of Assembly Sections took place after the morning service of worship, conducted by the Rev. J. H. Jackson, President of the National Baptist Convention U.S.A., Inc.

Speaking at the opening of the afternoon session at McGaw Hall, Bishop Oxnam announced with regret the sudden death on the previous evening of Mr. John Forrester-Paton, delegate of the United Free Church of Scotland. The Bishop said that due commemoration of Mr. Forrester-Paton, whose services to the ecumenical cause were distinguished, would be made in worship later in the Assembly.

He indicated that a new draft of the Main Theme Statement would be available at the end of the session so that final amendments could be submitted in writing before consideration of a final draft the next day.

A number of reports were then received—from the General Policy Committee (presented by Bishop Martin), from the Committee on the Information Department (presented by Dr. Payne), from the Committee on the Division of Studies (presented by Dr. Meyer)—and a further statement was made by Dr. Blake on behalf of the Finance Committee. Dr. Blake envisaged increased support for the World Council from many parts of the world, and asked for advice from any other churches considering an increase in their allocations. Final action was taken on the Report of the Committee on Structure and Functioning. Then Dr. Cooke explained small consequent changes in the Rules. All these were approved. Dr. Fry sponsored a resolution providing that the Central Committee should exercise its discretion in assessing priorities in expenditure in excess of the model budget. The Assembly agreed that this should be done.

Since the evening was officially left free, many took the opportunity to visit the exhibition of masterpieces of Religious Art displayed at the Chicago Art Institute on the occasion of the Assembly.

Commissioner W. G. Simpson, International Secretary of the Salvation Army, conducted the service of evening worship.

THE THIRTEENTH DAY: FRIDAY, AUGUST 27TH

Principal A. L. Haddon of the Churches of Christ in New Zealand presided at morning worship.

The Bishop of Chichester took the chair in the morning at the first of three plenary sessions held during the day. The Reports of Assembly sections were now coming to hand. The Assembly began to enter its final phase. The substance of its achievement became more clearly visible; at the same time the divisions and points of continuing debate were brought clearly into the open so that the chart for future work to be undertaken within the World Council's fellowship could be observed by all. The report of the Assembly Section on Evangelism was presented by Bishop Raines and received, subject to certain small changes being incorporated. Dr. Emmen brought forward the Report of the Working Committee on the Division of Inter-Church Aid and Service to Refugees. As this business was before the Assembly, a letter directed to the World Council by the United Nations High Commissioner for Refugees was read (see Report of the Committee on Interchurch Aid and Service to Refugees).

Section III put before the Assembly its document on "The Responsible Society in a World Perspective" during the afternoon. A feature of the debate immediately following, on the Statement on the Main Theme, was a sharp exchange of views on the advisability of including in it a reference to Christ as the hope of Israel. Eventually the Assembly did not speak on the issue raised, but received a statement on the subject from a minority (see Appendix 6, page 327) and asked the Central Committee to undertake further study of the question.

The evening session began agreeably when the Bishop of Chichester welcomed Dean Emeritus James of Northwestern University and made to the University a presentation of two large bronze plaques to be affixed to the walls of McGaw Hall in commemoration of the Assembly. Dean James responded, outlining the religious foundation of the University and its debt to the churches.

Three speakers proceeded to introduce one of the great themes chosen for special emphasis towards the Assembly's close. They were Bishop Eivind Berggrav of Norway, Mrs. Rena Karefa-Smart of West Africa, and Archbishop Michael of the Greek Orthodox Church in the United States. Their subject was "The Tensions of the World and Our Unity in Christ."

As the night was again humid, Bishop Berggrav abandoned formality and stood in his shirt sleeves, speaking in blunt and definite style. His incisive words were blended with piquant darts of humour, and these were naturally most welcome to his large audience at this stage in the Assembly's life. He said:

> The churches must confess their solidarity with the world because they not only share responsibility for creating tensions in the world, but they are in fact the source of the very greatest tensions and divisions. They produce these precisely on the basis of that which Christ offered them as His own life's heritage to make the bonds of unity strong among them. This paradoxical situation must make the churches very humble in speaking about the tensions of the world. Actually, tensions are included in the purpose of the Creator and are necessary to the growth of life. It is when sin in the form of fear and anger enters in that tensions become destructive. And we in the Church cannot convict the world for its destructive tensions as long as relations in the Church are also motivated by fear or anger. In the unity of Christ love is the constructive and overruling force.

> Today we can say that unity in Christ has become to some extent a force in the life of the Church. It serves as a constant reminder of, and gives us a bad conscience about, our destructive tensions; it creates a new willingness in us to listen to those with whom we are in disagreement; and it helps us to see that there is no "master church" but a "church family" in Christ. And when this spirit of unity in Christ comes to influence the life of the Church, then it may also influence the tensions between nations. For we must demonstrate love to man in political relationships also. This does not mean that we should overlook injustice and wickedness and "make a sweet soup of all the mess we are in." To be in unity in Christ means to be in unity with the full Christ, in unity with His love as well as in unity with His law.

When Bishop Berggrav finished speaking, his audience rose to clap for several minutes. Their appreciation was silenced only when he whimsically applauded them in return.

Mrs. Karefa-Smart took her stand at the reading desk wearing patterned and embroidered African national dress. She spoke with simplicity and vigour in these terms:

God has not left Himself without a witness in tropical Africa. Nevertheless the desperately strained condition of African society, resulting from tensions at the deepest levels of social relationships, intellectual development and spiritual life, presents to the Church a challenge to demonstrate clearly and convincingly that in the new life with Christ there is a way of power and hope for all persons and groups, and that this way triumphs here and now over the divisions, wants, fears and false hopes that beset men.

Three kinds of tension strain the fabric of African society: the struggles for independence and self-determination in political and economic life, the pressure of an increasing population upon an increasingly unproductive soil, and tensions produced by the present educational system which finds the Church reinforcing in effect an ecclesiastical *apartheid*. The churches are contributing to these tensions by remaining inactive and by continuing to be irrelevant to many of the situations more effectively ministered to by other religions. Most serious of all is the degree to which we Christians have professed to have answers to urgent needs without letting God use us in a demonstration of what those answers are. . . . The presence within church life of racial and ethnic groups living, worshipping and working separately and in more or less isolation from the world constitutes, I believe, one of the most acute problems for the Church in its witness in Africa.

Christianity has failed to meet tropical Africa at the only place where real rapport is possible—in its communal life and structure. Christians have failed in translating effectively the Gospel and its meaning into local mores and patterns. I believe that the churches must become *the Church* if the Kingdom of our Lord is to become a compelling reality for *all* men, and that two of the marks of that becoming will be the reorganization of church life along communal lines, and the achievement of unity between the divided and isolated sections of African Christendom.

The last of the three speakers, Archbishop Michael, said:

The greatest tension of the present time is that represented by the opposition of the two worlds divided by the Iron Curtain. Communism is permitted by God in order to teach us certain things. Of these, one which is fundamental is that the totalitarian claim of communism is the highest challenge to Christians, who are called to give complete devotion to Christ rather than to a political system or ideology. Another challenge is the comradeship among the communists, which in their own terms is like that which Christians should have for one another.

Faced with this tension, Christians should do certain things. First, it is imperative to avoid any proselytism among churches. Second, Christians, in the spirit of the Encyclical of 1920 of the Ecumenical Patriarch, should continue in love and earnest discussion with each other in order to promote unity. Third, Christians should together study the gospel of Christ in ever more penetrating ways, especially the Sermon on the Mount. Only conscientious Christianity and the pure life in Christ can cure the world of every evil vestige of totalitarianism.

The day ended in the knowledge that the session had covered what the Bishop of Chichester referred to as "a wide field from different angles."

Bishop L. G. Beecher of Mombasa conducted the evening service of worship, in which Mr. John Forrester-Paton was especially commemorated. Dr. Tracy Strong, until recently General Secretary of the World's Alliance of Y.M.C.A.s, spoke of Mr. Forrester-Paton's service to the Y.M.C.A. and the Church. Dr. Paul Limbert, the present General Secretary of the World's Alliance, read the Scripture. The blessing was given by Bishop Philipose of the Mar Thoma Syrian Church in South India.

THE FOURTEENTH DAY: SATURDAY, AUGUST 28TH

The Rev. R. Stuart Louden conducted the Assembly's worship.

Dr. Henry P. Van Dusen was in the chair as the Assembly resumed plenary session to continue its discussion of the Report of Section III on the Responsible Society. When the major discussion on the Report ended, Sir Kenneth Grubb introduced the Report of Section IV on International Affairs. Mr. Wikborg of Norway brought forward the recommendations from the Working Committee on the Commission of the Churches on International Affairs. As the session closed, a special welcome was extended to members of the General Council of the United Christian Youth Movement, who were seated in the Assembly as visitors.

Though the afternoon was set down as "free," a good deal of business in committees was furthered before the evening plenary meeting, when Bishop Oxnam was in the chair, and Dr. Madeleine Barot read the deferred report of the Department on the Life and Work of Women in the Church, reviewing the work of the Department, and indicating that in the future the Department, under the new name of The Department on the Co-operation of Men and Women in Church and Society, would work to promote study of issues concerning the relationship and common service of men and women in the churches and in society, and to promote an ecumenical consciousness in church women's organizations.

Dr. Fry then took the chair for discussion on the Main Theme Statement. He outlined the position up to that point, and explained that the situation was now largely clarified as the use of the document had been determined, and the discussion on the hope of Israel was referred to the Central Committee for future action. Bishop Oxnam resumed the chair as the Report of Section V on Racial and Ethnic Tensions came before the Assembly. At this stage the Rev. C. B. Brink, speaking for the Dutch Reformed representatives from South Africa, made an important statement (see Appendix 7, page 328) to the effect that the South African churches would not vote against the findings, as they wished to keep the door open to fuller conversation on the race question.

The evening service was read by Bishop John Shahovskoy of the Russian Orthodox Church in North America.

THE FIFTEENTH DAY: SUNDAY, AUGUST 29TH

Holy Communion in the First Methodist Church according to the rite of the Church of South India was attended by many participants in the Assembly. The invitation extended was broad enough to permit many who so desired to take communion, and interest in the blend of Catholic, Orthodox, native Indian, and Evangelical elements in the Liturgy drew other worshippers to attend and pray. The celebrant was the Right Rev. C. K. Jacob.

Worship and preaching followed in the local churches of
Evanston. In the late afternoon the second of the important
closing themes was presented to the full Assembly in McGaw Hall
by Bishop Dibelius of Berlin and Dr. Josef Hromadka of Czechoslovakia. A third paper on the same theme—"The Church's
Dependence on God and its Independence from Men"—was read
for Professor Reinhold Niebuhr, in his absence for reasons of
health, by Bishop Angus Dun of Washington.

Bishop Dibelius began by drawing attention to the Barmen
Declaration made by the Evangelical Churches in Germany
many years before.

In our time, the decisive test of the independence of the
Church from men is whether it will remain independent of the
state, from its propaganda, and from its political will. Christians
in Germany remember that twenty years ago in the Barmen
Declaration the Confessing Church clearly stated its dependence
upon God by refusing to put the Church at the disposal of
Adolf Hitler. And today Christians still stand behind the
Barmen Declaration. The Church has but one Master: Christ.
It acknowledges but one authority: the Word of God.

The most severe test of the freedom of the Church is in the
struggle with the totalitarian state. In this struggle the Church
and its members are called to make real sacrifices because the
state by its power puts them at great material disadvantage and
thus tries to force them to give up their independence. By
resisting the state with quiet martyrdom the Christian is a
living witness to the fact that there is another world, a world
over which the state possesses no power and which therefore
sets limits to the totalitarian demand. Thus the state is prevented
from becoming fully totalitarian when the Church fulfils its
duty. Practically, this means that the Church must help its
people to oppose those ideas and actions of the state which are
opposed to Christian teaching and doctrine. Decisions in some
cases will not be easy, as for example when the state asks the
Church to support its campaigns for peace. But the Church has
to remember the political thinking which motivates the state in
such campaigns and say to it: "Perform your task! As for us,
we will work for peace within the ambit of our own resources,
retaining our loyalty to the Word of Him who is our peace and

our hope, thus holding fast to our independence from you" (the state).

It is not given to any man to render much outward help to the Church engaged in this struggle for independence. Inner freedom must be fought for and won by a wrestle within. However, other Christians can do what Paul asked of the Christians in his time: "That ye strive together with me in your prayers."

Dr. Niebuhr had analysed the problem from a different point of view.

We must be prepared today to explain to a credulous world what we mean when we declare our faith in the God who has been revealed in Christ, who is both the lord of our life and the lord and sovereign of this strange drama of our human history. We must explain that our dependence upon God rather than men does not mean irresponsibility. Man must be responsible to the limits of the power with which God has endowed him. But the biblical message and particularly the drama of the Cross reveal that divine goodness was in conflict not chiefly with human evil but with human goodness. It was Roman justice, the best justice of its day, and Hebraic religion, the highest religion of its day, which were implicated in the Crucifixion. And it is in the light of this truth that the Church's duty is to point to God rather than any human virtue or power as our creator, judge and redeemer, and as the source of our peace.

That is why the Christian Church has the duty always to bear witness not to the righteousness of Christians but to the righteousness of God which judges all men, and to the grace of Christ which saves all who truly repent of their sins.

The ecumenical movement can be understood as a movement of God's grace in that it has helped us to see the reliability of God and the unreliability of men in maintaining the purity of the gospel. The movements which destroyed the unity of the Church for the sake of restoring the purity of the gospel succeeded in purging the gospel of Roman heresies but exposed it to the corruption of new nationalistic and parochial heresies. The ecumenical movement has provided a means which enables us all to perceive our particular heresies more clearly. Thus it is God's judgment and grace and not any virtue of our own which works mightily among us to heal the broken body of Christ and make us one.

In pronouncing our dependence on God we face two particular temptations. One is to renounce all traffic with the wisdom of the world because to do so might deflect us from the truth of the gospel. We must not bury our treasure in the ground. Ecumenical study and action have helped us to bring the gospel into a fruitful encounter with human experience and culture. The other temptation is to interpret the biblical insight that "all men are sinners" to mean that Christian faith transcends all political and social struggles. But we are men and not God and we must distinguish between the moral level of our decisions, where we are required to choose between possible alternatives, and the religious level on which indeed we acknowledge that both we and our most dangerous foes are equally sinners in God's sight and are equally in need of His forgiveness.

Professor Hromadka was introduced by Bishop Berggrav from the chair. "My heart is warm toward you with Christian brotherhood," Bishop Berggrav said. "I often disagree with you, you know that, Dr. Hromadka; but you are our Christian brother." Professor Hromadka delivered his address with his customary urgent insistence.

It is perhaps platitudinous to speak of the dependence of the Church on God and of its independence from men, for the biblical message and the creeds of the Church reiterate that the God of the prophets and the apostles is the God of sovereign, free grace, bound to no human ideas and institutions. He is beyond all human thought and speculation and beyond all human norms and moral judgments.

Nevertheless through our human ideologies we try to get hold of God and to subordinate Him to our human thoughts and systems; we try to use Him as our ally in ideological, political, and social struggles. It is the imperceptible temptation always confronting the Church that it also will use God for human ends, to convert the faith into safeguards of human earthly treasures and possessions. A godless world is much less dangerous than a Church thus made pagan. In striving to be true to its dependence upon God, the Church cannot desire an abstract independence from men. Jesus Christ made Himself a servant of men and He took upon Himself their burdens. He did not come into the world with any idea of independence but rather to do His Father's will. It is utterly wrong to express our independence from men in attitudes of superiority or religious self-satisfaction. We are independent in a truly biblical way when we, in self-denial, give ourselves in loving service to our neighbours. The Church of Christ finds her genuine freedom and independence in self-consecration unto her Lord and in self-dedication unto men in the spirit of love. The Church marches through our secular world avoiding and rejecting identification with any human absolute and rejecting also any efforts to look for an absolute evil in any secular institution or in any man. We must not apply human, civil, or political categories of freedom to the Church. Her freedom is the freedom of service. Her glory is glory in humility. Her majestic independence rests in her identification with poor, weak, destitute, despised, forsaken men.

Archbishop Brilioth of Sweden presented the Report of the Assembly's Section of Faith and Order in the evening. Dr. Henry P. Van Dusen was in the chair for the discussion. A statement on the Faith and Order Report was read for the Orthodox delegation by Archbishop Michael (see p. 92 in discussion of Faith and Order Report).

Bishop Lajos Vetö of the Lutheran Church in Hungary led evening prayers.

The Sixteenth Day: Monday, August 30th

Bishop S. U. Barbieri of the Argentine, and now one of the new presidents of the Council, conducted morning worship.

Pastor Marc Boegner was in the chair. The discussion on the Report of the Section on Faith and Order continued during the morning. Upon its conclusion, the resolutions from the Section on International Affairs were introduced and adopted. The Bishop of Chichester spoke during the session to commend an appeal to the nations concerning the peace of the world (see p. 146.)

The Bishop of Chichester was in the chair during the afternoon. Dr. Kathleen Bliss introduced the Report of the Section on the Laity. Before the ensuing discussion, Dr. Reinold von Thadden made a clear and forceful statement on the series of post-war Kirchentag meetings in Germany. He evoked memories of the recently-held 1954 Kirchentag at Leipzig, where the call to the Christians of the East and West zones had been "Rejoice in Hope." The resolutions from the Section on Inter-Group Relations were discussed and approved. The Report of the Finance Committee was introduced by Dr. Eugene Carson Blake. Final amendments from the Section on International Affairs were incorporated. Bishop Angus Dun reported for the Committee on the Division of Ecumenical Action. The last draft of the Section on Evangelism was approved. Minor additions and changes were made in the Report of the Section on Inter-Group Relations. In general the session gave opportunity for essential tidying up.

The Rev. Philip Potter delivered the Report of the Youth Department Committee to the evening session, calling attention to three aspects of the Youth Department's work: ecumenical conferences, notably the one at Travancore, the thirty ecumenical work camps conducted each summer, and the World Youth Projects. This is not an exhaustive list of Youth Department work, but illustrates the chief ways in which the Department functions.

Bishop Newbigin and the members of his Drafting Committee then came to the platform for the reading of the Message. The Assembly passed through its last high point of debate as it addressed itself to the heart of its own Main Theme. As the Drafting Committee wrestled on the platform with final problems which emerged, Dr. Fry presented a resolution on Religious Liberty. Dr. E. C. Blake of the Presbyterian Church, U.S.A., spoke for the Presbyterian World Alliance in supporting the resolution, which was adopted (see p. 149). Dr. Fry also announced that it was proposed to set up, through the Central Committee, machinery for the study of the issues of Proselytism and Religious Liberty, especially in the light of the fruitful work at the Assembly of an informal group under Bishop Sherrill. A final draft of the Message was promised for the last morning of the Assembly.

Evening worship was led by Dr. Heinrich Renkewitz of the Moravian Church in Germany.

The Seventeenth Day: Tuesday, August 31st

Bishop G. Bromley Oxnam took the chair as retiring American President at the last plenary session in McGaw Memorial Hall on the closing day. The hymn "O God our Help in Ages Past" seemed full of meaning. At its close the Assembly remained standing to repeat together in English the words of the 23rd Psalm. Dr. C. L. Patijn proposed one final change in the report of Section III. The Assembly accepted the final form of the Message and extended its unanimous thanks to those who had worked so long at drafting its central document. Bishop Lilje of Germany spoke briefly to commend *The Ecumenical Review*, the quarterly publication of the World Council of Churches. Dr. Kathleen Bliss gained approval for final changes in the text of the report of the Section on the Laity. Archbishop Brilioth brought forward final modifications in the text of the Faith and Order Report. Bishop Newbigin read the final form of the Message. The formal business of the Assembly itself gave way to a series of closing actions.

Invitations for the holding of the next Assembly came from Greece and Japan. Professor Alivisatos of Athens said that he spoke for the Greek Government with the Ecumenical Patriarchate in inviting the World Council of Churches to hold its third Assembly on the Island of Rhodes in 1960.

Dr. Michio Kozaki spoke as Chairman of the National Christian Council in Japan. He said that 1959 would mark the 100th anniversary of the inauguration of the Christian movement in his country. The third Assembly would be welcome. Bishop Oxnam expressed appreciation and said the invitations would be studied carefully.

Appreciation was expressed from the Chair to retiring staff members of the World Council—Dr. Nils Ehrenström, Mademoiselle Suzanne de Diétrich, Miss Jean Fraser, and Dr. H. H. Walz.

Pastor Marc Boegner voiced the thanks of the Assembly towards the American Churches, the people of Evanston, and the American committees that had worked to prepare the Assembly, and the Executive Secretary, Dr. Bilheimer. "God bless you, Mr. Chairman," he concluded, "God bless your churches, God bless your great nation." Bishop Oxnam said he was grateful for what had been said. He proceeded to lead the Assembly in giving instructions for the writing of a series of letters of thanks. He made special mention of some who were present in the session. As these filed by across the platform the Bishop spoke an appropriate cheerful word of gratitude for each, concluding with a special reference to the wisdom and organizing genius of Dr. Robert S. Bilheimer, who, as Bishop Oxnam said, had worked tirelessly for over two years, conceived all the special events, secured the co-operation of churches and civic bodies, and carried a position of great responsibility. "The World Council of Churches owes him a debt of inexpressible gratitude," the Bishop said. He also made mention of the work of Dr. Bilheimer's assistant, Mr. William DuVal. The Bishop presented a copy of *The History of the Ecumenical Movement*, inscribed by the Presidents of the World Council, to Chaplain Walter Wagoner of Northwestern University in recognition and gratitude for his services as the liaison officer between Northwestern University and the Assembly.

In a comment on the technical labours of many behind the scenes, Bishop Oxnam paid tribute to Mr. Melvin Nelson of the Committee of One Hundred and to Mr. Charles Parlin, the prominent Methodist layman who had acted as Chairman of the Press and Broadcasting Committee for the Assembly. The Evanston meeting had been one of the best reported conventions in the history of the nation. The office staff, under Miss Lucy Seidler, had consumed eight tons of mimeograph paper. The audience warmly applauded the aides and stewards under the leadership of Mr. George Booth. They were followed by the interpreters and translators led by Pastor Dominique Micheli. Miss Eleanor Kent Browne, who had been in charge of the Information Bureau, and the Rev. Howard Schomer, who had arranged the accredited visitors' programme, were last to take the platform, but the Bishop very warmly alluded to all those others whose work had meant so much to the Assembly's life.

In a previous ceremony the Bishop of Chichester had spoken with gratitude of the out-going presidents. He promised that each would receive a simple parchment scroll suitably inscribed. Bishop Berggrav responded for the presidium, drawing laughter by his undue modesty when he said, "We have been situated in this hall so that when we voted nobody took any notice of our votes. That is characteristic of our position in the World Council of Churches!"

Last of all the entire Assembly stood for several minutes to applaud the General Secretary, Dr. W. A. Visser 't Hooft, who rose to receive the gratitude due to him for his leadership in thought and action during the vital first six years of the World Council of Churches' life.

The plenary session ended with an act of worship as the six incoming Presidents were recognized together with the new Honorary President, the Bishop of Chichester. The hymn was "In Christ there is no East nor West." Bishop Oxnam commended the Presidents as members of "an endless line of splendour, those troops with heaven for home." He offered prayer, the Assembly sang the hymn "Love Divine, all Loves Excelling," and the proceedings in McGaw Hall were brought to an end with the Aaronic Blessing.

In the closing service the Assembly's work was offered to God, and the representatives of the churches again turned towards the world. The new Central Committee took its place in the front seats. There was no formal procession. The members of the Committee wore plain street dress and this was to some extent a symbol of their recognition that much hard work lay before them. The Bishop of Chichester who presided at the service entered with Bishop Eivind Berggrav, the preacher. The first wore surplice and stole, the second wore the traditional Norwegian ruffle. The new Presidents sat in the chancel. Dr. Visser 't Hooft read the lesson. In the prayers the Bishop of Chichester inserted an intercession for the World Council of Churches' member churches in China, which had not been forgotten during the Assembly. Bishop Berggrav spoke briefly and plainly. He based his sermon on the Epistle to the Ephesians, 4, 11–16, especially the words "until we all attain to the unity of the faith." "This word *until* is written also over the future of the ecumenical movement. . . Growth is always dependent upon God. *We* can't add one cubit to our stature (Mt. 6. 27). All growth is a process, more akin to creation than to fabrication. . . . Don't then be anxious about your life, World Council of Churches. If the leaven is of God, be sure that He Himself will guard and direct it *until* all of it is leavened!"

After the Bishop's address, the congregation rose to sing the Te Deum in unison. An action of dedication and silent prayer closed with the Benediction, setting a seal of completion and new resolve upon all that had been said and done. The Assembly was over.

The Statement on the Report of the Advisory Commission on the Main Theme

We are profoundly grateful for the work of the Advisory Commission. The Report exhibits a substantial ecumenical consensus. It indicates the direction in which we must all move: away from ourselves towards Christ, our only hope, away from human desires, doctrines and ideologies towards the Word of God which alone has eternal authority and power, away from the godless self-centredness of this world towards the kingdom of Christ.

As we discussed the Report at this Assembly, sharp differences in theological viewpoint were expressed among us. In view of the greatness of the theme, this fact should occasion no surprise. The nature of our disagreements and their reference to the contents of the Report are described in brief here and more fully in the précis of our discussions. But even our difficulties provided us with a common bond, as, confronted by this great theme, we saw our differences and disagreements become diverse insights into its richness.

Our major criticism of the Report relates not so much to its substance but to its mode of expression; not to what is said, but to what is not said. We find that the note of joyous affirmation and radiant expectancy which should mark a statement of the Christian hope does not sufficiently illuminate the Report. We find certain important *omissions*: the present work of the Holy Spirit in the Church and the world; specific reference to "signs of hope"; adequate treatment of the theme of creation and cosmic redemption.

We are not agreed on the relationship between the Christian's hope here and now, and his ultimate hope. As the précis of our discussion clearly reveals, we are not satisfied with the presentation in the Report of the so-called "rival hopes." Some held that a too sympathetic account has been given of these hopes, some ask for a more understanding treatment of them and many point out that the list is incomplete and should certainly include hopes which falsely bear the Christian name. We are not wholly satisfied with the treatment of the non-Christian religions and are not agreed on the correct definition of our hope as it applies to all who, while believers in God, do not know Him as revealed in Christ. There were many who felt that the Report should emphasize more strongly the solidarity between the people of the Western world and those of other continents. And some thought that too sharp a distinction was made between the Church and the world.

The Report has engaged the full attention of the Assembly. It moved us not only to agreement and disagreement, but to testimony. It is our desire that all who read it will be moved to give utterance to the Christian hope in their own words and with the additions which their thought and prayer discover. Our witness will thus become our united response to the Report, for by its aid, and with the guidance of the Holy Spirit, we shall then speak together of the living Christ, the hope of the world. The joyous word rings across the world and through all time: "Christ is risen." We cry: "Christ is risen indeed."

Because Jesus Christ died and rose again for the world and will come again to renew it and judge it in His glory and grace, this world is anchored to Him with unshakable hope. He rules over all history by the power of His cross and resurrection and nothing can pluck this world out of His hands. His eternal purpose of redemption will be brought to its complete consummation. Because Christ is the living Christ, He is able to meet us in every circumstance of life and every mood of our hearts.

The Holy Spirit is living and working within men. The steadfastness of Christian men and women in their daily work and their courage in times of trouble are tokens of our hope in Christ. The fruits of the Gospel when it is proclaimed in the world, the winning of the hearts and lives of men by Christ, are tokens of hope. A society which seeks to recognize human dignity, where there is an attempt to distribute justly the burden and benefit of labour, where there is effort to banish hunger, war and despair, is a token of hope.

All these witness to His coming: in our time where the Gospel is preached and the sacraments administered and the Holy Spirit descends and dwells in us; and to His coming in glory and triumph at the end of this age.

The Church witnesses to this hope when it seeks, in unity with its Lord, to be *His* Church; when it is in the world as He is in the world to seek all, to save all, to serve all; when it manifests growing unity in its fellowship; when in its sacramental life, the bread and cup are truly shared across all barriers of class and race, culture and wealth.

It is in this perspective that the Report of the Advisory Commission is presented to the churches. It cannot be represented as the only word of the Assembly on this subject. It is, however, a creative and provocative ecumenical statement of Christian hope for this day. And it is therefore forwarded to the churches, with the commendation of this Assembly, for their study, prayer, and encouragement.

Discussion of the Statement on the Report of the Advisory Commission on the Theme of the Assembly

First Discussion

The Archbishop of Canterbury was in the chair. Bishop Lilje presented two documents:

(1) an introductory statement from the Co-ordinating Group on discussion on the Main Theme,

(2) a draft supplementary statement on the report of the Advisory Commission.

The Archbishop of Canterbury said that the supplementary statement was not to be confused with the Message, but was open for discussion.

Dr. Fry, speaking for the Steering Committee of the Assembly, clarified the procedure for reception of the main theme documents, and proposed that the report of the Advisory Commission on the main theme be received for forwarding to the churches. This proposal was accepted and a debate proceeded concerning the text of the accompanying statement drawn up by the main theme co-ordinating group.

Professor Torrance drew attention to certain apparent contradictions and inappropriate phrases in the draft statement, more particularly in usages of the word "sign" and what he considered unscriptural use of the words "end of time." He moved an amendment arising from the need for a more succinct, joyful, and positive statement of belief in the actual return of Christ.

Bishop Lilje (for the main theme co-ordinating group) accepted the amendment in substance.

The Archbishop of Canterbury explained that the co-ordinating group would incorporate the sense of such amendments as were obviously acceptable to the Assembly, and declared the opinion of the Assembly preponderantly in favour of the amendment.

The Rev. Stuart Coles asked for specific inclusion among signs of hope in Christ of "the proclamation of God's Word in the Christian Scripture and preaching."

Bishop Lilje commented that this element was included under the phrase "the fruits of the Gospel."

The Archbishop of Canterbury, after a show of hands, declared support for the specific addition to be insufficient.

Archbishop Brilioth questioned the use of the word "obedience" in connection with commendation of the statement to the churches. He asked what the churches were to obey and said an unhappy impression could be created. He proposed to substitute the word "encouragement."

Bishop Lilje said that "obedience" implied that which every Christian owes to the Lord. He acknowledged the point made, however, and suggested "loyalty to their Lord" or some such expression.

The point was referred back to the co-ordinating group for attention.

Professor Kinder, speaking to the statement as a whole, criticized the disproportionate emphasis on the present reality of the Christian hope as against the ultimate hope, both in the statement and in the report of the Advisory Commission. He said his stand was not European but biblical in that what was ultimate gave vitality to the present hope. He asked for a far stronger emphasis on this ultimate New Testament hope as part of the supplement to the report of the Commission.

Professor O. H. von der Gablentz referred to the enumeration of "signs of hope" and said that the mention among these of "a society recognizing human dignity, where there is a just distribution of the burden and benefit of labour" suggested that there was such a society on earth. He recommended a change and drew attention to two other points: first, that the words "we are not agreed on the relationship between the Christian hope here and now, and the ultimate hope" suggested that the entire Assembly bluntly accepted such a disagreement, which was not the case; secondly the words "we cannot announce ourselves as wholly satisfied" indicated a similar disagreement, which was not as drastic as it seemed. Was not a further document, analysing the differences involved, required, in addition to the Commission's report and the present supplementary statement?

Professor Wingren drew attention to the subsuming of Christ's coming under the general category "signs of hope." In the New Testament a sign always means not the reality but a witness to it. But the coming of Christ is the reality. He could not find any biblical basis for using the word "sign" to describe such phenomena as the recognition of human dignity and the achievement of social justice. He proposed that the Report say that Christ was already coming, and then speak of the gospel, the community and other evidences of this main truth.

Dr. Van Dusen spoke as chairman of the Study Department Committee and a member of the Advisory Commission. No member of the Commission was "wholly satisfied" with the report's final text, but all felt it was a true representation of the consensus between them. Many of the criticisms made in the statement were identical with those of members of the Commission. Acceptance of the statement would not be received as a rebuke by the Commission. He was satisfied that the statement accurately represented the mind of the Assembly and seriously questioned whether major revision would be an improvement. Endorsement of the statement with authority for minor revision was all that was required.

Mrs. Karefa-Smart spoke for Africa. She expressed apprehension at the report and said that the use of the terms "they" and "we" made its tone too Western. She said that for Africans hope itself was sober and urgent rather than basically joyous, so that to this extent the restraint expressed was acceptable.

The Bishop in Jerusalem (Anglican) moved modification of references to Israel. He said that he lived where every statement about Israel was apt to become bitterly controversial and emphasized that many hopes other than that of Israel were fulfilled by Christ's coming.

Father Makary El Souriany of the Coptic Church proposed the

entire deletion of references to Israel in view of the special political problems vexing the Near East. He said the World Council must not single out one nation for special concern.

Bishop Lilje drew attention to thought given the present text by members of the Assembly who knew the possible political implications. References were to ancient Israel or to Israel scattered abroad, not to Israel as a single state. The Assembly would have to face up to the New Testament evidence and not retreat from any political implications involved.

The Archbishop of Canterbury, on a show of hands, declared Father Makary's proposed change not to be favoured.

Dr. Leslie Cooke suggested a transposition of paragraphs to allow for a strong and joyful conclusion with the words "but our hope is sure."

The point was referred to the drafters.

Pastor Niemöller supported Professor von der Gablentz in not regarding a society where "efforts" are made as a sign of hope. He said the coming of Christ was not the greatest of signs but utterly different from all the rest in character.

Bishop Newbigin asked whether adoption of Professor Torrance's amendment implied that the Assembly would also wish a more positive emphasis on Christ's return in glory in the Assembly's message. It seemed that the request for a more ringing note of joy could only mean that the Message Committee should be more specific in this respect than it had so far thought. He also wished to record his agreement with Professor Wingren concerning the use of the word "sign."

Bishop Lilje summarized the discussion. He said that, as a first step, the Advisory Commission's report was prepared by twenty-five of the most brilliant minds; a second step, embodied in the statement, was a summary of the discussion of the main theme groups. The third step was the present discussion. In some ways it had been most helpful, notably in elucidating the contents of such specific terms as "sign" and in relating ultimate to present hope. The sections on Israel would need re-examination. At the same time he questioned whether justice and concern for human dignity could not be considered as signs of Christ's presence, in view of the parable of the gospel. He assured the Assembly that its discussion would be given full consideration in redrafting.

Second Discussion

The second discussion was directed toward a new draft of the statement, presented by Bishop Lilje.

Archbishop Michael read a statement on the main theme on behalf of the Orthodox delegation (see page 329).

Bishop Bereczky, speaking for the Hungarian Delegation on the main theme, referred to the hopeful and expectant preparations undertaken for the Assembly by congregations in his country. He said the hopes expressed were not unfulfilled and that the Amsterdam promise "we intend to stay together" had never been forgotten in Hungary, but kept by God's loving help. Evanston gave real hope for going forward. He said Hungary looked forward in the near future to a meeting of a World Council group in that country. Facilities would be offered for a meeting of churches from East and West in full freedom. He asked the Assembly's love and prayer in this good cause. Hungary expressed esteem for the World Council and desired to develop the main theme and sub-themes in witness and study. He thanked the Assembly for the love that had been shown and asked attention to the testimony of Hungarian Protestantism.

Bishop Lilje announced that all the positive expressions of opinion on the statement on the main theme document had been incorporated in some form.

The Archbishop of Canterbury explained that the revised statement was open for immediate amendment, but no longer for radical revision.

The Bishop of Durham spoke to the content of the report of the Advisory Commission and the statement. He said the Orthodox Church was not alone in radical criticism. It was extraordinary that the report of the Commission did not begin with Creation nor properly treat the relation of hope to the vision of God and holiness. He was apprehensive about reception of the report and felt unable to recommend it unreservedly to the clergy. It ill bore comparison with "the glorious statement from the Orthodox Church."

Mr. George Goyder suggested the report of the Commission was lukewarm about the Second Coming, and contended that concern about the time of Christ's return was a necessary Christian state of mind.

Mr. George Chacko (youth consultant, India) made certain

suggestions concerning insertion in the statement on the main theme of sentences describing the "responsible society."

Mr. Charles Taft reluctantly indicated that he could not accept the statement as it stood and believed he spoke for the laity. He particularly objected to references to the Jewish people, which were an addition to the report of the Advisory Commission. Such statements should not be foisted on a minority which did not agree with them. He did not believe that these references were "the way to start a mission to the Jews." They would jeopardize relations of the members of the Assembly with their Jewish friends. He asked the secretary, in the event of a vote, to record his disagreement.

The Rev. Kenneth Henderson said he spoke as a Christian humanist. He believed a note should be struck which would give the laity "more self-confidence," and that a summons to action was deeply needed.

Third Discussion

Bishop Lilje presented a further series of proposals concerning the statement on the main theme.

Dr. Fry stated that the Steering Committee recommended that the statement on the main theme be sent, together with the Advisory Commission's Report, to the churches.

Bishop Nygren said that there was no necessity for an introductory statement from the Assembly; there was not sufficient consensus.

Bishop Lilje, in reply, said he did not wish to oppose Bishop Nygren but he warned the Assembly that a common word on Christian hope was expected of it. A weak impression would be made if the headlines should say, "Assembly fails to reach agreement on Christian hope." If the Assembly was prepared to face such a consequence he saw no reason why Bishop Nygren's proposal should not be accepted.

Professor Torrance said he preferred Bishop Nygren's proposal to acceptance of the statement as it stood. Nevertheless he asked for patience from the Assembly in accepting amendments to the statement. He would be horrified if at this stage in the Assembly nothing positive could be said on the main theme. It would mean a failure in the Assembly's work.

Dr. Meyer said the Assembly had lost sight of the great

achievements of the report in bringing the churches back from human plans and opinions to the Word of God and in turning from church-centredness to Christ. He said that if these achievements were not endorsed the Assembly would fail.

Dr. Fry then put Bishop Nygren's motion, which was lost on a show of hands.

Dr. Audeh regretted the necessity to draw attention again to the reference to the Jews. He asked whether Christ was less the hope of all peoples than of one and said he did not believe the Assembly wished to make the task of churches in the Near East more difficult. He read a telegram from Dr. Charles Malik disclaiming any suggestion that political events at present befalling the Jews were associated with the fulfilment of Christian hope.

Dr. Atiya said he was impelled to speak out of loyalty and expedience. He wished to be loyal to the World Council but was persuaded it would be a disservice to the cause of the World Council in the Near East to mention Israel. Nor would mention of Israel be historically expedient at the present time.

Dr. Berkhof, opposing the amendment, said he did not want to offend, but had to say that Jesus Christ was born of Israel as fulfilment of the promises God gave to His people. There were no political implications in such a statement. Chapters 9–11 of the Epistle to the Romans meant that Christians looked to Israel in a special spiritual sense.

Dr. Fry put the vote for the amendment seeking elimination of the reference to Israel. It was adopted by 195 votes to 150.

Dr. Yochum then proposed a second amendment to eliminate language about "signs" and speak in simpler and more readily comprehensible terms on this subject.

Mr. Taft said he favoured this change.

Dr. Wagner spoke against deletion since it would take out the note of joy about signs of hope visible in the daily life of men and women here and now. The manifestations in question were not tokens but signs of God's living presence.

Following this discussion, the Steering Committee was authorized to present a further draft of the statement at a subsequent meeting.

Fourth Discussion

Bishop Oxnam was in the chair.

Dr. Fry outlined the procedure. He introduced both the

statement as amended in the light of previous discussion, and the judgment of the Steering Committee that the major difficulty observed in the Assembly concerning the Hope of Israel should become the subject of further study under the Central Committee's guidance.

Bishop Oxnam said he believed the statement was now a representative document and would be acceptable to the Assembly.

The statement was then approved.

Dr. Fry read the resolution asking the Central Committee to arrange further study on the Hope of Israel, which was adopted:

> In view of the major divergence of views revealed in the action of the Assembly amending the Statement on the Report of the Advisory Commission on the Main Theme by omitting all references to " the New Testament concepts of the ultimate fulfilment of God's promises to the people of Ancient Israel," the Steering Committee is convinced that this is the type of issue that calls for further study and ecumenical conversation, and therefore proposes that the Central Committee be instructed to make suitable arrangements for such study and conversation on this subject.

Professor Sittler presented a statement signed by a number of delegates which expressed the conviction that the Christian hope included the hope for the conversion of Israel (see Appendix 5).

Bishop Oxnam received the statement for purposes of record.

DISCUSSION ON THE MESSAGE

The Assembly appointed a Message Committee at its first plenary session. The Committee reported towards the end of the Assembly after careful work carried on in close touch with the Main Theme Co-ordinating Group, the Sections and the Steering Committee. There was no discussion following the first presentation of the Message, but a special hearing was held, at which the Message Committee heard comments from members of the Assembly and made alterations in its draft accordingly. The revised draft was then presented to the Assembly, discussed in plenary session and adopted. The following comments do not record recommended changes in wording, but do present a summary of the substantive points made in the discussion.

Bishop Newbigin introduced the revised draft of the Message. In doing so he drew attention to the addition of one sentence to the ninth paragraph. He then read the text of the Message as it stood.

Mr. Louden welcomed the Message as moving and impressive, but believed it could be improved. A message should be urgent, personal and fresh. The present text was too long and too much a summary. A message which could be read in ten minutes would be better for parishes. He proposed shortening under four headings: (1) greetings to the churches; (2) Christ the hope of the world; (3) the contents of the sixth paragraph concerning the ecumenical task; (4) closing questions.

Professor Michalko, speaking for the Czech Evangelical Churches, expressed heartfelt thanks and joy at the possibility of attending the Assembly. He spoke of the brotherly welcome extended and urged that western churches visit eastern Europe. At the same time he expressed gratitude for the contents of the Message.

Dr. Baillie said he found the Message both beautiful and appropriate. He raised certain points of detail to ensure more felicitous expression.

Pastor Boegner hailed those who had given hours of time to the Message. He believed the opening should be less theological—more simple and concrete. He felt there was too much in the first part of the Message, but was consoled by its quality as a whole.

Bishop Newbigin said the Drafting Committee felt that abbreviation, as advocated by Mr. Louden, would demand a fresh Message.

Mr. Louden's amendment was then put and lost.

Professor d'Espine said that the end of the third paragraph contained the only allusion to the substance of the personal Christian hope anywhere in the Message. An insertion of Christ's words: "He who believes in me, though he were dead, yet shall he live" would convey to the man in the street a personal hope of eternal life.

Bishop Newbigin said the point had been considered and omitted because it was desired not to make the Message too long. The implication of what was already there would have to suffice.

Pastor Maury said he used English to try to express what was deep in his heart. All the first part of the Message, though close to the gospel, could pass quite by those outside the Church. Even the assurance affirmed in the fifth paragraph did not meet the need of the multitude of terrible sufferers among mankind. "We are too comfortable," he said. "We must be *with* the hopeless." M. Maury asked that his utterance be heard as a true "cri du coeur."

Baron van Tuyll asked for the addition of a few words about helping the needy. He said that these could be placed in the fifth paragraph and refer to obligation towards our neighbours, all those who, like the refugees, are in need of the prayer and sacrificial help of the churches.

Professor Torrance said he spoke for others including Professor Schlink, Bishop Nygren and Mr. Louden. They believed that the fifth paragraph suggested only a favourable final judgment and smacked of "securitas" in the worst sense. Surely this was not intended. The paragraph needed redrafting.

Bishop Newbigin, commenting on the points raised, said he felt Pastor Maury's point very deeply. There was an attempt to put what he had said in the fourth paragraph, but "good courage" must be stressed. The Committee would be thankful for any concrete change M. Maury could suggest. He further said that Baron van Tuyll's proposed allusion to obligations towards one's neighbour presented difficulty since it singled out the need of the refugee. Professor Torrance's comment raised difficulties because it would be hard to discriminate between believers and non-believers in making an affirmation about judgment. The last judgment *is* obviously a judgment of Christ, and His words apply to what we have, and have not, done.

The Reports of the Sections

The Report of Section I

FAITH AND ORDER: OUR ONENESS IN CHRIST AND OUR DISUNITY AS CHURCHES

Received by the Assembly and commended to the Churches for study and appropriate action with the request that the Churches report the results of their study and action to the Central Committee

"Christ in you, the hope of glory" (Col. 1: 27)

Introduction

1. We speak as those who have met together in the World Council of Churches and have known for a fact that we have been given a "oneness in Christ," in spite of our "disunity as churches."

This oneness is no mere unity of sentiment. We become aware of it because it is given to us by God as the Holy Spirit reveals to us what Christ has done for us. In this report we have tried to make clearer what we believe about this given unity, in the prayer that if we, and the churches from which we come, strive earnestly to lay hold upon the meaning of that which is already given, the Spirit of God will open our eyes to still deeper understanding, and our hearts to still fuller enjoyment of the unity which is ours in Christ.

To that end:

First, we speak together with one mind and in accordance with the witness of the New Testament, of the oneness of the Church, as grounded in the whole work of Christ, as growth into the fulness of Christ and as partially realized even in our present divided state.

Secondly, we speak of our disunity as churches as partaking of that disobedience over which Christ has won His victory, granting us even in our disunity some foretaste of our ultimate unity in Him.

Thirdly, we speak of some of the consequences for us, in the obedience of faith, as we meet together in His saving Name to beg Him to fulfil His unifying work in us.

I. Our Oneness in Christ

A. *Christ's Unifying Work*

2. The New Testament conceives of the unity of the Church, not as sociological, but as having its essential reality in Christ Himself and in His indissoluble unity with His people (Acts 9: 4ff.; 1 Cor. 12: 12; Jn. 15: 1f.). Hence we must still ask Paul's question about division in the Church: "Is Christ divided?" (1 Cor. 1: 13), and assert with the Apostle the indestructible unity that belongs to the Church in Christ. Christ is the *one* Lord who represents and gathers to Himself the *many* of redeemed humanity, and it is therefore He alone who makes the many to be one in the Church (1 Cor. 12: 12; Eph. 1: 10, 22; cf. Jn. 14: 20; 17: 4ff.; 1 Cor. 6: 16f.).

3. The New Testament speaks in many ways of the relationship of Christ and His people to describe their unity in Him. The Church is many members in one body (1 Cor. 12: 12); the several members are subject to the one Lord as Head of the body (Eph. 1: 22; 4: 15; 5: 23; Col. 1: 18; 2: 19); the Church is His bride, to be united to Him, the bridegroom (Mk. 2: 19; Rev. 19: 7; cf. Mt. 22: 2ff.; 25: 10f.; Lk. 12: 36; Eph. 1: 22ff.) the faithful are His people (1 Pet. 2: 9f.; Col. 3: 12; Rom. 11: 2, 11f., 32); He is the new temple in whom true worship is offered (Jn. 2: 19ff.; cf. 4: 21ff.) or the one building of which the believers constitute living stones (1 Pet. 2: 5; Eph. 2: 20; cf. 1 Cor. 3: 9); He is the vine, of which we are the branches (Jn. 15: 1ff), or the shepherd whose flock we are (Jn. 10: 1ff.).

4. The New Testament thinks of the one life of the Church as deriving from the whole Person and work of Jesus Christ as Saviour and Lord. The Church's unity is grounded in His taking of our nature upon Him; in His own words and works by which the power and life of His kingdom were manifested; in His calling

of men into the fellowship of His kingdom, and in the appointing of the Twelve to share in His messianic ministry and work; in His passion and death, where sin was finally conquered and the power of divisiveness defeated; in His resurrection, where He manifested the new man unto whom we all grow (Eph. 4: 11ff.), in whom all human divisions are done away (Gal. 3: 28); in His ascension and heavenly reign, by which all history is brought under His authority; in His outpouring of the Holy Spirit on the whole Church at Pentecost, which gives to each subsequent baptismal rite its deepest significance; and in His promise to come again as the triumphant and glorious king. Through the indwelling Spirit, the Comforter, who leads the Church into all truth, the unity of the Church even now is a foretaste of the fulness that is to be because it already is; therefore, the Church can work tirelessly and wait patiently and expectantly for the day when God shall sum up all things in Christ.

B. *The Oneness of the Church in its Earthly Pilgrimage*

5. From the beginning the Church has been given an indissoluble unity in Christ, by reason of His self-identification with His people. But the Church has never realized the fulness of that unity. From the beginning discord has marred the manifested unity of Christ's people (Lk. 22: 24ff; Mk. 10: 35ff.) Thus we may speak of the oneness of the Church in its earthly pilgrimage as a growth from its unity, as given, to its unity, as fully manifested (Eph. 4: 3, 13). In this way we may think of the Church as we are able to think of the individual believer, who may be said at one and the same time to be both a justified man and a sinner (*simul justus et peccator*). In each Christian there is both the "new man" who has been created and yet must be put on daily (2 Cor. 5: 17) and also the "old man" who has been crucified with Christ and yet must be daily mortified (Col. 3: 1–5). So the Church is already one in Christ, by virtue of His identification of Himself with it (Jn. 14: 20; 15: 1–5) and must become one in Christ, so as to manifest its true unity (Eph. 4: 11–16) in the mortification of its divisions.

6. Christ of His love and grace has given His Church such gifts as it needs for its growth from unity to unity. The gifts are severally and together none other than Christ Himself, but each has its place and its function in the life of the Church as it strives

to give obedience to its Lord. Christ has given His Spirit, which is the bond of peace and love, and the guide to all truth. He has given apostles, prophets, evangelists, pastors and teachers, that the unity of the body may be continually built up. He has given the Scriptures, the preaching of the Word, Baptism and Eucharist by which the Church proclaims the forgiveness of sins and by which, in the power of the Holy Spirit, faith is quickened and nourished. He has given the Church the gift and power of prayer, by which the Church can plead both for its own unity and for the reconciliation of men to God and to one another. He has given it faith and hope and love, that in its own life a new divine unity shall be manifest in deeds, and that its service to the world shall be both a manifestation of unity and a summons to it.

7. The New Testament, therefore, testifies to us that the Church shares in the life both of this world and of that which is to come. Indeed the Church's life is encompassed by a "great cloud of witnesses" (Heb. 12: 2)—and the Church must never forget that its citizenship is really there, in the heavenly places (Eph. 2: 6). Its responsibilities must be discharged in this present world, but it must never become conformed to the world.

8. Thus the fellowship (*koinonia*) that the members of the Church have is not simply human fellowship; it is fellowship with the Father and with His Son Jesus Christ through the Holy Spirit and fellowship with the saints, in the Church triumphant. In all the Church's life there is being manifested not simply the activity of mortal men, but the life of the whole Church, militant on earth, triumphant in heaven, as it has its unity in the one Lord of the Church, who is its life.

9. But all this cannot be asserted without understanding that the unity given to the Church in Christ, and gifts given to the Church to help and enable it to manifest its given unity, are not for the sake of the Church as an historical society, but for the sake of the world. The Church has its being and its unity in the "Son of Man, who came not to be ministered unto, but to minister and to give his life a ransom for many." The being and unity of the Church belong to Christ and therefore to His mission, to His enduring the Cross for the joy that was set before Him. Christ wrought "one new man" for us all by His death, and it is by entering into His passion for the redemption of a sinful and divided world that the Church finds its unity in its crucified and risen Lord.

C. *The Oneness of the Church Partially Realized*

10. Jesus Christ has given to His Church the gift of Himself and thereby the means of corporate life. These gifts were given not solely to the Church of New Testament days, nor are they reserved for the Church in some ideal state which ought to exist but unhappily does not. We acknowlege these gifts as being in a real sense present possessions.

11. It would be ungrateful to a merciful God if we did not speak now of those gifts which assure us that the undivided Christ is present amongst us, pouring His life into us all, in spite of our divisions.

12. We all wait upon one Father, through the one Holy Spirit, praying that we may be ready to hear and obey when He takes of the things of Christ and shows them to us. We all read the Holy Scriptures and proclaim the gospel from them in the faith that the Word speaking through them draws us to Himself and into the apostolic faith. We all receive His gift of Baptism whereby, in faith, we are engrafted in Him even while we have not yet allowed it fully to unite us with each other. We all hear His command to "do this" and His word "This is my body . . . this is my blood" in the Sacrament of the Eucharist, even whilst our celebration of the Lord's Supper is not yet at one Table. We all receive a ministry of the Word and Sacraments, even whilst our ministries are not yet recognized by all and not understood in the same sense. We all are called to be imitators of Christ and to follow Him in moral obedience as we confess Him before men even though we are still unprofitable servants.

13. As we have come to know each other better in the World Council of Churches, we have come to appreciate the immense range of common practice and intention which we share. The *fact* of our common (though diverse) use of these gifts is a powerful evidence of our unity in Christ and a powerful aid to reminding us that unity lies in His work and not in our own achievements. We have also discovered that the old confessional divisions are being criss-crossed by new lines of agreement and disagreement.

14. We give thanks to our Father for these evidences that our unity in Christ is a present reality, both in the World Council of Churches and in relation to other Christians whose fellowship we do not as yet fully enjoy. But the very fact that, in every case, our

benefit from these mercies in marred by our separation from each other, compels us now to examine seriously how it is that our disunity as churches contradicts our unity in Christ.

II. Our Disunity as Churches

15. Only in the light of the oneness of the Church in Christ can we understand the difference between diversity and division in the Church, and their relation to sin. There is diversity which is not sinful but good because it reflects both the diversities of gifts of the Spirit in the one body and diversities of creation by the one Creator. But when diversity disrupts the manifest unity of the body, then it changes its quality and becomes sinful division. It is sinful because it obscures from men the sufficiency of Christ's atonement, inasmuch as the gospel of reconciliation is denied in the very lives of those who proclaim it.

16. Divisions in the Church have been caused and are perpetuated, to a large degree, by sincere concern for the gospel. Some believed that others were departing from the God-given structure and faith of the Church by unwarrantable claims and unfounded doctrines. So came the schism between East and West. Some believed that God had called them to such reformation of the faith and order of the Church as would restore it to its primitive purity. They found their work could not be completed within the framework of Roman Catholicism; thus came the separate churches of the Reformation. Some believed that the faith must indeed be reformed but within the framework of ancient and historic episcopacy. So the Anglican and Old Catholic communions became separated both from Rome and from many of the Reformed churches. Some believed that the established churches of their day would not give free course to the Word of salvation. So the older free churches and the Methodist connexion felt themselves forced to adopt independent church orders. Similar acts of conscientious obedience to the will of God have likewise resulted, even if unintended, in breaches of Christian fellowship in doctrine, sacraments and order. God in His mercy has used such decisions to save souls, to build up communities who worship Him, and to preserve or recover aspects of His truth. All this we can and must say. But He has also given to us today a fresh awareness of the sin which characterizes the divided state which we have

inherited. We shall never, in this life, escape from our sinfulness, but we can repent of sin when it is revealed to us. Even when we have done that which we thought it right to do, we must remember that we are culpably implicated in sin not wholly of our own making and cannot dissociate ourselves from the sin of division. Confession of oneness with Christ carries with it confession of solidarity with our brethren in sin.

17. We ask each other whether we do not sin when we deny the sole lordship of Christ over the Church by claiming the vineyard for our own, by possessing our "church" for ourselves, by regarding our theology, order, history, nationality, etc., as our own "valued treasures," thus involving ourselves more and more in the separation of sin. The point at which we are unable to renounce the things which divide us, because we believe that obedience to God Himself compels us to stand fast—this is the point at which we come together to ask for mercy and light. So what we believe to be our "faithfulness" must bring us together at the foot of the Cross. The Cross tells us that where the dividing power of sin was most manifest, there God has gained the victory. By the same Cross He is able to make all things to work together for good—even our divisions. By planting the Cross of Christ in the midst of our divisions we believe He will overrule all their sin and make them serve His purpose of unity.

18. Concretely, this means that when churches, in their actual historical situations, reach a point of readiness and a time of decision, then their witnessing may require obedience unto death. They may then have to be prepared to offer up some of their accustomed, inherited forms of life in uniting with other churches without complete certainty as to all that will emerge from the step of faith. Otherwise, acts of apparent re-union might be merely acts of calculated self-aggrandizement and a betrayal of the true calling of the Church. But when churches have been ready in this sense "to die with Christ," they have found that He who raised Jesus from the dead is faithful and powerful still.

19. It is certain that the perfect unity of the Church will not be totally achieved until God sums up all things in Christ. But the New Testament affirms that this unity is already being realized within the present historical order. By the power of His resurrection, Christ has granted this grace to His Church even now, and the signs of His work are discernible to him who has eyes to see.

In the upheavals of the present hour, Jesus Christ is gathering His people in a true community of faith and obedience without respect for existing divisions.

We must not assume that the divisions which now separate Christians from one another correspond to those which Christ brings about in times of tribulation. Still less can we think that they will coincide with the separation finally to be made by the Son of Man. In this eschatological perspective all our human divisions are provisional.

III. The Action of Faith

20. Christ has made us one by breaking down walls of partition. We are nevertheless disunited as churches. How are we to act in the obedience of faith and hope in our one Lord?

21. At least we all ought to be united in thinking of our divisions with repentance: not the repentance we may expect of others, but that which *we* undertake ourselves—cost what it may— even when others are unwilling to follow. True repentance is the acknowledgment before God that we have sinned so as to be caught in the net of inexplicable evil and rendered unable to heal our divisions by ourselves. But we cannot in sincerity and truth repent of our various understandings of God's will for His Church, unless the Spirit Himself reveals that our understandings have been in error. Penitence cannot be hypocrisy. Neither can it truly be expressed without desire for forgiveness and amendment of life.

22. All of us as members of churches believe that we have been entrusted by God with certain elements of the one Church of Christ which we cannot forfeit. But at least we in the World Council of Churches are committed to a fellowship in which we are ready to bring our convictions under scrutiny in the presence of our fellow Christians and in the presence of the living Christ. In common we seek to know the judgment of the Word of God upon these convictions as to any error which may be involved in them.

23. Together we suggest the following ways in which, being both united and divided, we all must seek to be obedient:

(i) In thanking God joyfully for the actual oneness He has given us in the World Council of Churches, we must try to understand the theological implications of this ecumenical fact and to implement it in the concrete relations of neighbour churches. With the Lund Conference on Faith and Order, we ask the churches "whether they should not act together in all matters except those in which deep differences of conviction compel them to act separately." We do not minimize the deep differences separating some churches. Nor do we ignore the numerous attempts to unite churches and the achievements of such reunion. In the World Council of Churches we still "intend to stay together." But beyond that, as the Holy Spirit may guide us, we intend to unite. "The World Council of Churches is not. . . . a Super-Church."[1] Hence we do not ask the World Council of Churches to initiate plans for union, but to keep providing occasions for honest encounter between divided Christians.

24. (ii) We must all listen together in the midst of our disunity to our one Lord speaking to us through Holy Scripture. This is a hard thing to do. We still struggle to comprehend the meaning and authority of Holy Scripture. Yet whenever we are prepared to undertake together the study of the Word of God and are resolved to be obedient to what we are told, we are on the way toward realizing the oneness of the Church in Christ in the actual state of our dividedness on earth. In this connection we need also to study together the significance of Christian tradition and our various traditions, as reflected in liturgy, preaching and teaching.

25. (iii) We must consider frankly the influence of social and cultural differences upon the matters of faith and order which cause divisions, and also perceive how the events and developments of current history make disunity a most urgent question.

26. (iv) We must speak the truth in love with one another and practise that love towards those with whom we disagree (Eph. 4: 15, 25). Sometimes this involves us in judgments which fellow Christians cannot recognize as being made in love. At other times, we are so conscious of both the sin and the cultural conditioning with which all our judgments are infected that we are tempted to be more tolerant than truth allows.

27. (v) We must learn afresh the implications of the one Baptism for our sharing in the one Eucharist. For some, but not for all, it follows that the churches can only be conformed to the

[1] See "The Church, the Churches, and the World Council of Churches," W.C.C. Central Committee, Toronto, 1950.

dying and rising again in Christ, which both Sacraments set forth, if they renounce their eucharistic separateness. We must explore the deeper meaning of these two sacramental gifts of the Lord to His Church as they are rooted in His own redeeming work.[1]

28. (vi) We must seek to acknowledge beyond the bounds of our own church each ministry that preaches the gospel of reconciliation as a means whereby Christ performs His saving deeds. Especially need we to discover the meaning of the ministry of the laity for Christian unity.

29. (vii) We must bear witness together to the gospel of Him who has already overcome our sins and divisions and who graciously uses sinners as His servants. Our divided witness is a necessarily defective witness, and indeed a scandal in the face of the non-Christian world. We have scarcely begun to work out the essential connection between "mission" and "unity." Our Lord's own prayer (Jn. 17: 21f.) must become our own, not only on our lips but in our lives.

30. (viii) The measure of our concern for unity is the degree to which we pray for it. We cannot expect God to give us unity unless we prepare ourselves to receive His gift by costly and purifying prayer. To pray *together* is to be drawn together. We urge, wherever possible, the observance of the Week of Prayer for Christian Unity, January 18–25 (or some other period suited to local conditions) as a public testimony to prayer as the road to unity.

31. We cannot discern all that will be disclosed to us when we look to Him who is the Head of the body and affirm our oneness in Him. We know that we shall be changed, but wherein we shall be changed we cannot know until, in the act of faith and self-denial, we are given to discern, through crucifixion and resurrection, the lineaments of the one true Body of Christ which our sinful dividedness obscures from ourselves and from the world. Rejoicing in the grace which has been bestowed upon us in His various gifts even in our sin and separateness, we here set our hope on our one Lord Jesus Christ, who comes to take control over our divided and broken estate and to heal it by His grace and power. At Amsterdam we said that we intend to stay together. He has kept us together. He has shown Himself again as our Hope. Emboldened by this Hope, we dedicate ourselves to God anew, that He may enable us to grow together.

[1] Cf. Lund Report, Chapter V.

DISCUSSION ON THE REPORT ON FAITH AND ORDER

Dr. Van Dusen was in the chair.

Archbishop Brilioth, presenting the report, said that its theme summed up the central ecumenical problem. An outstanding contribution of the Lund Conference to the doctrine of the Church had been to point to its close connection with Christology. In the Working Paper this idea was set forth very forcefully. The main structure of the Working Paper, which seemed indicated by the theme, had been retained in the report, but expressed in a simpler and less theological language. Part I (C) was new; and in Part II an attempt had been made to distinguish as closely as possible between diversity and division. This Assembly could not say the final word or offer a solution acceptable to everybody. All we could hope to do was to move a step forward in the understanding of our mysterious unity and the tragedy of our divisions. He hoped that the Assembly would be able to commend the report to the churches for study and appropriate action, and ask the member churches to report their reactions to the Central Committee.

The Bishop of Armidale, commenting on the report as a whole, said that the impression left upon the mind was static. There was a desire for real movement. Even phrases such as "We intend to stay together" could convey introverted self-consciousness. There was room for the churches to study not only one another's convictions but also their own in the light of the Scriptures. By remaining on the surface and avoiding the depths the Church tended to be its own self-conscious guarantor. There was a call to the churches to read the Bible as the eschatological community of the Messiah.

Archbishop Michael read the following statement on behalf of the Orthodox delegates:

THE DECLARATION OF THE ORTHODOX DELEGATES CONCERNING FAITH AND ORDER

As delegates of the Orthodox Church participating at this Assembly of the World Council of Churches, we submit the following statement concerning the report of Section I.

1. We have studied the document with considerable interest. It falls into three parts: the first contains an able exposition of the

New Testament doctrine of the Church. The organic character of the Church and her indissoluble unity with Christ are adequately stressed in the document. We feel that this at least provides fruitful ground for further theological elaboration. The second and third parts of the document deal with the divided state of Christendom and suggest practical steps toward union. It is our conviction that it does not follow logically and consistently from the first part and indeed if we do actually accept the New Testament doctrine of the Church we should come to quite different practical conclusions which have been familiar to us Orthodox for centuries. The whole approach to the problem of reunion is entirely unacceptable from the standpoint of the Orthodox Church.

2. The Orthodox conception of church unity implies a twofold agreement:

(a) The whole of the Christian Faith should be regarded as one indivisible unity. It is not enough to accept just certain particular doctrines, basic as they may be in themselves, e.g. that Christ is God and Saviour. It is compelling that all doctrines as formulated by the Ecumenical Councils, as well as the totality of the teaching of the early, undivided Church, should be accepted. One cannot be satisfied with formulas which are isolated from the life and experience of the Church. They must be assessed and understood within the context of the Church's life. From the Orthodox viewpoint, re-union of Christendom with which the World Council of Churches is concerned can be achieved solely on the basis of the total, dogmatic Faith of the early, undivided Church without either subtraction or alteration. We cannot accept a rigid distinction between essential and non-essential doctrines, and there is no room for comprehensiveness in the Faith. On the other hand, the Orthodox Church cannot accept that the Holy Spirit speaks to us only through the Bible. The Holy Spirit abides and witnesses through the totality of the Church's life and experience. The Bible is given to us within the context of Apostolic Tradition in which in turn we possess the authentic interpretation and explication of the Word of God. Loyalty to Apostolic Tradition safeguards the reality and continuity of church unity.

(b) It is through the Apostolic Ministry that the mystery of Pentecost is perpetuated in the Church. The Episcopal Succession from the Apostles constitutes an historical reality in the life and structure of the Church and one of the pre-suppositions of her unity through the ages. The unity of the Church is preserved through the unity of the Episcopate. The Church is one Body whose historical continuity and unity is also safeguarded by the common faith arising spontaneously out of the fulness (*pleroma*) of the Church.

3. Thus when we are considering the problem of Church unity we cannot envisage it in any other way than as the complete restoration of the total faith and the total episcopal structure of the Church which is basic to the sacramental life of the Church. We would not pass judgment upon those of the separated communions. However, it is our conviction that in these communions certain basic elements are lacking which constitute the reality of the fulness of the Church. We believe that the return of the communions to the Faith of the ancient, united, and indivisible Church of the Seven Ecumenical Councils, namely to the pure and unchanged and common heritage of the forefathers of all divided Christians, shall alone produce the desired reunion of all separated Christians. For, only the unity and the fellowship of Christians in a common Faith shall have as a necessary result their fellowship in the sacraments and their indissoluble unity in love, as members of one and the same Body of the one Church of Christ.

4. The "perfect unity" of Christians must not be interpreted exclusively as a realization at the Second Coming of Christ. We must acknowledge that even at the present age the Holy Spirit dwelling in the Church continues to breathe in the world, guiding all Christians to unity. The unity of the Church must not be understood only eschatologically, but as a present reality which is to receive its consummation in the Last Day.

5. It is suggested in the report of the section that the road which the Church must take in restoring unity is that of repentance. We recognize that there have been and there are imperfections and failures within the life and witness of Christian believers, but we reject the notion that the Church herself, being the Body of Christ and the repository of revealed Truth and the "whole operation of the Holy Spirit," could be affected by human sin. Therefore, we cannot speak of the repentance of the Church which is intrinsically holy and unerring. For, "Christ loved the Church and gave Himself for it, that He might sanctify it and cleanse it in the washing of water and the word, that He might

present it to Himself as a glorious Church, not having spot or wrinkle or blemish or any such thing, but that it should be holy and without blemish" (Eph. 5: 26–27).

Thus the Lord, the only Holy One, sanctified His Church for ever and ordained that her task be the "edification of the saints and the building of the body of Christ." Her holiness is not vitiated by the sins and failures of her members. They cannot in any way lessen or exhaust the inexhaustible holiness of the divine life which from the Head of the Church is diffused throughout all the body.

6. In conclusion, we are bound to declare our profound conviction that the Holy Orthodox Church alone has preserved in full and intact "the faith once delivered unto the saints." It is not because of our human merit, but because it pleases God to preserve "his treasure in earthen vessels, that the excellency of the power may be of God." (2 Cor. 4: 7).

Dr. Van Dusen indicated that suitable use would be made of Archbishop Michael's important declaration.

Oberkirchenrat Schmidt described the report as being well balanced, but suggested the omission of certain sections implying that acts of intercommunion were a desirable expression of the churches' present unity. He did not wish to vote in this matter against his own confession.

Archbishop Brilioth expressed the willingness of the drafting committee to consider rephrasing to meet the point.

Oberkirchenrat Hübner was concerned that biblical phrases such as "crucified and risen with Christ," which were applied to individuals in their original contexts, were here transferred to the Church. He objected also to transfer by analogy of the phrase *simul justus et peccator*.

Dr. Marsh (speaking for the Drafting Committee) said that such analogies were considered helpful, but that a re-examination would be undertaken with a view to modifying the words and maintaining the sense.

A vote taken at this stage indicated that a majority favoured the wording as set out.

Canon Hartford asked that the end of Section I (C) of the report be modified to stress the importance of moral obedience in witness. He said that this would render the section more meaningful to the laity.

Archbishop Brilioth expressed readiness to confer to meet the point.

Pastor Puffert, referring to Section I (C), asked that a sentence concerning the celebration of the Lord's Supper read "not *yet* at one Table."

Archbishop Brilioth accepted the change.

The Bishop of Durham asked for the omission of the last four sentences of the Report as they stood, so that the closing words would be "grace and power," rather than "we intend to grow together." He believed this would strengthen the ending.

Principal Nørgaard warned against passing a judgment anywhere in the Report on what the forefathers of the churches had done. He further argued that to believe the churches could be made perfect in unity was to place too big a demand on credulity.

Professor Prenter associated himself with those who claimed the New Testament did not speak of churches dying. He further claimed that the step of faith towards deeper unity implied not only readiness to lose some of what was our own, but readiness to receive from others.

Professor Nikolainen proposed that the phrase "obedience unto death" as applied to churches be replaced by some phrase such as "The churches must be prepared to surrender their ways of living by uniting with other churches of similar confession."

Professor Eenigenburg contended that words in the second paragraph of Section II implied that division itself was necessarily sin. One could conclude that to get rid of sin was to get rid of division, and to get rid of division was to get rid of sin. "Is this true?" he asked. He then suggested an alternative less sweeping formulation.

The Drafting Committee accepted Prof. Eenigenburg's suggestion.

Professor T. M. Taylor asked that the second paragraph of Section III be altered to permit of a distinction between divisions due on the one hand to human frailty and on the other to the guidance of the Holy Spirit. This should be supplemented by a plea that room be left for deeper and fuller insight into God's truth.

The proposed change was approved by the Drafting Committee and the Assembly.

Dr. Birkeli hoped that the fourth paragraph of Section III would be strengthened by inserting an actual quotation concerning the World Council's disavowal of any intention to be a Super-Church.

Dr. Hampton Adams urged that a further way of obedience be added to those enumerated in Section III, namely the growing practice of "passing beyond traditional bounds to another denomination" in order to maintain religious unity within families.

Mr. Coles urged that the reference to Christian tradition in the description of the second "way of obedience" in Section III should be strengthened by specific insertion of the Reformation doctrines concerning the preaching and teaching office of the Church.

Professor Wingren sought a modification in (v) among the "ways of obedience" in Section III. He thought references to "dying and rising" in the part concerning eucharistic unity could force Orthodox representatives and some Anglicans into an uncongenial position.

Principal Moses proposed the insertion of more reference to the Church's mission in certain parts of the report.

Archbishop Brilioth agreed that the point was well taken but said that it had been duly met in the work of Section II and elsewhere in the Assembly.

Mr. LeQuesne proposed the words "Let us go forward together as God shall direct" in the closing sentence. He was inclined to agree with the Bishop of Durham's move for deletion, but would press for his form of words if the Bishop's were not accepted. He believed the language as it stood suggested growth into a single organization, an idea unacceptable to Baptists.

Dr. Visser 't Hooft said that a complete redraft of that paragraph was desirable.

Professor Mehl, in reply to the Bishop of Durham, explained the meaning of the last sentence in the Report. It showed that the churches bound themselves together for the future (1) to face new emerging problems concerning questions such as tradition and the unity in Christ given by Baptism; (2) to face the necessary and happy "confusion" inseparable from setting out together without knowing exactly where they would be led by looking to Christ. "Expect to be led where Abraham was led," Professor Mehl said.

Mr. Robison said that he disagreed with both the Bishop of Durham and Mr. LeQuesne. The last words of the report were acceptable to a united church, because such a church understood from experience that not organization but organism was involved.

Mr. McLuskey suggested that the last sentence nevertheless lacked strength. The intention of the churches to stay together was not irrelevant, but more was required than intention. Unqualified use of the word almost suggested pride. He proposed the form "We dedicate ourselves to God anew, that we may grow together."

Dr. Nelson said that Mr. McLuskey had provided a clue towards satisfactory re-wording. He proposed (for the drafters) "We dedicate ourselves to God anew, that He may enable us to grow together."

Dr. Van Dusen then put the Bishop of Durham's motion, which was lost. He put Mr. LeQuesne's motion, which was also lost. He put the proposal of the Drafting Committee, which was adopted. The entire report was received.

The Report of Section II

EVANGELISM: THE MISSION OF THE CHURCH TO THOSE OUTSIDE HER LIFE

Received by the Assembly and commended to the Churches for study and appropriate action, with the request that the Churches report the results of their study and action to the Central Committee.

I. The Evangelizing Church

1. Jesus Christ is the gospel we proclaim. He is also Himself the Evangelist. He is the Apostle of God (Heb. 3 : 1) sent to the world to redeem it. As the Father sent Him so He sends us. He calls us and we must obey. He sends us and we must go.

2. We were hopeless about life and our place in it; He has given us hope and filled our life with meaning. We were hopeless in our sin, unable to do the right; Christ has given us hope. We are hopeless in our suffering and distress; we have seen our affliction turned into blessing by His grace and used for the furtherance of His glory. We are hopeless about the final outcome of the human

story, in distress about the futility of our own efforts; Christ has given us hope. We were hopeless in face of death, trembling between the fear of annihilation and the fear of future punishment, but Christ having overcome the sharpness of death has opened to us the gates of the Kingdom.

3. Who are the "we" who have hope not only for themselves but for all the world? The people of God, the Church of Christ on earth. For the Church is the community which is able to say this "we" in truth. Indeed, called from heaven and answering on earth, set by God as the sign and sharer of the life and work of Jesus Christ, the Church's very existence is a miracle of grace. To evangelize is to participate in His life and in His ministry to the world.

4. This ministry is the ministry of the risen and ascended Christ: Christ as He is today. It is the ministry of God become man, by which God's Kingdom is come among men. It is the ministry of Christ's life on earth by which God is revealed as the Father. It is the ministry of His death on the Cross by which the sin of the world is taken away. It is the ministry of His resurrection by which the powers of death and evil have been decisively defeated. It is the ministry of the heavenly Intercessor who does not will that any should perish. It is the ministry of the coming Christ by whose mercy and judgment the world is governed even now.

5. In and by this ministry the Church lives in the power of the Holy Spirit whose work enables and confirms its testimony. He changes the lives of sinful men and they, forgiven and restored to their true heritage as God's children, are being gathered together against the day of Christ's return in power. They are called by Him to be witnesses of His gospel. We have, alas, to confess with shame that we have all too often failed our Lord by the feebleness of our testimony and the slackness of our zeal. Nevertheless, where the gospel has found true lodgment in men's hearts, they have been inspired with compassionate desire to share it with their fellows. The love of Christ constrains them through their understanding of His death for all men. It impels them, in loving gratitude to Him to whom alone they owe their salvation, to share with others the unspeakable benefits they have themselves received, so that all may enter into the joy of the Lord.

6. Therefore, whether it meet success or failure, closed doors or

open doors, the Church in its work of evangelism is delivered from bondage to visible results. The gospel is preached because the Lord is risen and the age of the Messiah begun and "He must reign until He has put all enemies under His feet." Meanwhile we await the full disclosure of His kingly glory. Nevertheless He has not left His people at any time without some sign that He is at work victoriously, nor are such signs lacking in the time in which we now live. Thus is the Church enabled to find its joy in simple obedience to the divine call.

II. The Evangelistic Dimension

7. The people of God are in this world as the Church, and they are never alone with their Lord in isolation from the world. It is the *world* which He came to save. Without the gospel the world is without sense, but without the world the gospel is without reality. Evangelism is no specialized or separable or periodic activity, but is rather a dimension of the total activity of the Church. Everything the Church does is of evangelizing significance. Through all the aspects of its life the Church participates in Christ's mission to the world, both partaking of the gospel and seeking to communicate it. Evangelism is the place where the Church discovers itself in its true depth and outreach.

8. But this witness of the Church to its Lord is weakened by our faithlessness—not least by our divisions. Therefore will the Church deal with these divisions with holy impatience, and passionately strive for unity. Unity is destroyed where there are confessional antagonisms, nor will unity of faith and life among Christians be achieved except as churches increasingly work together to bring the gospel to the whole world. Also, wherever Christians find themselves separated by caste, class, racial or other barriers, they will boldly cross them, manifesting Christ's solidarity with the whole of mankind. In a divided world they will fulfil Christ's ministry of peace, manifesting in their own life the new mankind which has begun in Jesus Christ. Wherever they encounter social injustice, they will do battle for its redress, bearing witness to the restoration of humanity in Christ.

9. These truths, however, have frequently remained platitudes to which we have paid lip service, while we ourselves rest in self-satisfaction and sloth.

10. What then are the concerns of evangelism? One is surely so to proclaim the gospel that it will transform the groupings and patterns of society in which men and women are involved, to the end that human institutions and structures may more nearly conform to the divine intention, and respect the limiting prerogative of God. We who think ourselves converted to the Christian gospel, and who have indeed entered into many of its blessings, should beware lest whole areas of our thought and outlook remain unregenerate, so that it is after all not the whole gospel to which we have been converted. No man is fully regenerate until he has brought every thought into captivity to the obedience of Christ.

11. Still another aspect of evangelism is the attempt to bring people into the full life of the Church as expressed in a local congregation; for an isolated Christian, if such were possible, would be in a tragic state.

12. But underlying these concerns of evangelism is the bringing of persons to Christ as Saviour and Lord that they may share in His eternal life. Here is the heart of the matter. There must be personal encounter with Christ. It is not enough to present Him merely as an example to follow. The gospel proclaims a living Christ. Just as to remain with Him is the mark of Christian experience, so to bring men to meet Him is the purpose of all evangelism. For on his relationship to God in Christ depends the eternal destiny of every man.

III. COMMUNICATING THE GOSPEL

13. We must remember that evangelism is God's work in which we are His agents. It is not our work, and therefore we must wait upon Him in prayer and in meditation upon His holy Word, that we may learn what He would have us do, and so be able to say, "It seemed good to the Holy Spirit and to us." Through His guidance we must seek lines of effective communication with those outside the Church's life, and be prepared to face the demands which the proclamation of the gospel makes upon us.

14. We must recognize that the first requisite for communicating the gospel is to be possessed by the transforming power of Jesus Christ. As we witness to it, so do we also live by it. If it stops with us, it begins to fade in us. The second requisite is that we must love our neighbour as he is, even as Christ has loved us.

He must feel that we understand him and that he can trust us. By some form of acceptance and helpfulness he must come to feel that we truly care for him.

15. The Church which God uses to communicate the gospel is a fellowship, a *koinonia*, drawn and held together by the love of Christ through the power of the Holy Spirit, and by the need and desire of its members to share this experience with each other, and to draw those outside into that *koinonia*. The evangelizing Church will offer this gift in its preaching and teaching; in its acts of worship and administration of its sacraments; through the individual and group witness of its members; by leading its people to base their life upon God's Word used in personal and family devotions; by fostering small fellowships; and by works of social service.

16. Although no strategy of communication is itself a guarantee of success, communication with those outside the life of the Church makes the following demands:

17. Firstly, there must be encounter with the world. The Church must break out of its isolation and introversion, meeting the individual where he is with the compassion and comprehension of Christ. While this initial demand applies to all evangelism, it is particularly relevant to workers and intellectuals, many of whom are conspicuously outside the life of the Church. No social group lies outside the orbit of the compassion of Christ.

18. Secondly, there must follow the speaking of a word which is intimately related to the problems of the individual in his world. We must let every man know that he is of inestimable worth in the sight of God. There are times of personal crisis when the relevant word can only be the good news of the loving compassion of God in Jesus Christ. In addressing the worker, the word must be related to his social condition and aspirations; and the word cannot be spoken to the intellectual unless we make it clear that in the Church's message there is a cogent and coherent view of life.

19. Thirdly, too often our words have been impotent because they have not been embodied in works of service, compassion and identification. It is not enough for the Church to speak out of its security. Following our incarnate and crucified Lord, we must live in such identification with man, with his sin, his hopes and fears, his misery and needs, that we become his brother and can witness from his place and condition to God's love for him. Those outside the Church make little distinction between faith and works.

20. Fourthly, in order to possess the power to evangelize, the Church must nourish its life on the Bible. To recover for current thought the great biblical concepts is one of the pressing needs of evangelism. In the communication of the gospel the Bible occupies a unique and central place. The Bible speaks to all, provides a common language for the Church, transcending our divisions. The translation and distribution of the Holy Scriptures is an inescapable task of the evangelizing Church.

IV. Exploring Frontiers

A. *Renewal of the Inner Life*

21. The first area of evangelism is our own inner life. When Jesus gave us the solemn and joyous commission to be His witnesses, He commanded us to wait for the power of the Holy Spirit. This does not mean that we should delay our mission until we become perfect. As we seek to communicate our faith to others, we are inwardly renewed and forced back upon the resources of the Spirit. This is equally true of the congregation in its corporate witness.

B. *The Witnessing Laity*

22. The laity stand at the very outposts of the Kingdom of God. They are the missionaries of Christ in every secular sphere. Theirs is the task to carry the message of the Church into every area of life, to be informed and courageous witnesses to the will of our Lord in the world. To this end they will need training and guidance. Such training involves instruction in the content of the Christian faith and in the significance of that faith for obedience and witness in the different contexts of lay life. This kind of training will require the services both of ministers and of experienced laymen.

C. *Christian Education*

23. One of the most important areas of evangelism is that of childhood and youth. Every new generation requires the fresh presentation of the gospel. Among the most important methods of Christian nurture are Sunday schools, youth programmes, Bible fellowships, discussion groups and, most of all, Christian training in the home.

D. *Chaplaincies*

24. New forms of specialized ministries are appearing. Because they are more fluid and indigenous, they enable the Church to penetrate structures and groups partially or wholly outside its life. In them the ecumenical approach of the churches working together can achieve what the various denominations acting separately can never bring to pass. Among such chaplaincies are those to hospitals, prisons, the armed forces, industry, the universities and schools.

E. *Parish Experiments*

25. Traditionally the Church's congregational life has been based on the family and on the geographical area. Where this is breaking down, it is urgent that the Church come to life in small neighbourhoods, e.g. in "street or house churches" where neighbours, church and non-church, gather to think and pray, with the help of the minister, about their work and leisure, and thence enter the Church's continuing life. Such fellowships often cut across denominational boundaries.

26. But in many parts of the world today the determining context of a person's life is not where he lives but where he works. The companionship of those with whom he works largely determines the framework of his beliefs and attitudes. What has been and is still true of village life in Asia or Africa, where decisions are decisions of the group, is now true in many social environments in the West also. It has become imperative, therefore, that the gospel be addressed to the group as well as to the individual. Where this has been done successfully, the result has been the emergence of a Christian community whose locus is the factory, the mine, the office, the waterfront, the university. When a Christian community emerges and when this community seeks to express its life and faith in worship and witness, its members form to all intents and purposes a Christian congregation.

27. Such developments raise questions about the adequacy of traditional forms of parish life, and about the co-operation of the churches, since the groups are often interdenominational. They also raise questions about the role of the minister and about the way in which he should identify himself with the group which he seeks to lead to faith in Jesus Christ.

28. We would urge the churches to give serious thought to

those questions, for they point to a challenge which the new form of society in our technical age makes to the present social structure of parish life.

F. *Media of Mass-Communication*

29. Literature and the arts play an increasing part in the shaping of men's outlook; but we also face today the overwhelming impact of the cinema, radio and television, as well as the greater perfection of posters, newpapers and magazines. The result is that the convictions and decisions of individuals in many countries are reached under the pressure of a common mental climate which these media of mass communication tend to create. Hence the Christian Church must use these same media: for it is essential that Christianity, the questions it asks and the answers it offers, should permeate the general consciousness, if the ground is to be prepared for individual decision for Jesus Christ. In many countries the churches can make full use of these opportunities only if they are prepared to work together.

30. There are dangers in the use of these media. When the gospel is secularized, vulgarized or diluted into an easy alternative to facing the demand of God for a personal response, it does much harm. The main means by which the Holy Spirit brings men out of passive looking and listening into personal commitment to Christ in His Church is personal meeting with a living Christian. Yet religious broadcasts and films, and Christian messages in the daily press, and in tracts, can do much to preserve channels of communication for the gospel.

31. Religious material for broadcasting should be of the best quality and should by no means be confined to services of worship. In our day, Christians in many parts of the world have numerous opportunities for following up religious broadcasts in casual conversation and discussion, since such broadcasts reach great numbers who are not committed members of any church.

G. *A Trained Ministry*

32. Because of its importance in the life of the Church, serious thought should be given to a more realistic training of the ministry, including provision for the service of theological students in industry and agriculture, and the addition of social studies and field work to the curriculum.

V. Non-Christian Faiths

33. The renascence of non-Christian religions and the spread of new ideologies necessitate a new approach in our evangelizing task. In many countries, especially in Asia and parts of Africa, these religious revivals are reinforced by nationalism and often present themselves as effective bases for social reform. It is not so much the truth of these systems of thought and feeling which makes appeal, but rather the present determination to interpret and change oppressive conditions of life. Therefore they confront us not only as reformulated creeds but also as foundations for universal hope. Such hope is based on man's persistent desire to be master of his own destiny. The gospel hope, on the contrary, does not rest upon what man can do for himself but on God's promise, in judgment and mercy, finally to fulfil His purposes.

34. The Christian knows and believes that in Jesus Christ God has given to man the full and only-sufficient revelation of Himself. "There is none other name given under heaven by which we must be saved." The Christian will proclaim the gospel as God's judgment upon all human quests and questionings. But in his approach to men of other faiths he will humbly acknowledge that God has "left not himself without witness." Wherever he finds light he will not try to quench it but bear witness to Jesus Christ, the true Light—"the light which lighteth every man."

35. The ambassador of Christ is primarily concerned not with the faith that a man professes, though he should understand it with sympathetic insight, but with him as he really is, a sinner like himself and one for whom Christ died. This means that the first step in evangelism must always be not that of controversy but of identification and alongsidedness.

36. In our task of evangelism among the adherents of non-Christian religions we must claim the whole truth of the Christian gospel. But we must always bear in mind that there are human elements in our witness to it which stand under the judgment of God. The gospel is greater than any particular human testimony to it. It is also the ultimate standard of God's judgment on every aspect of our response to His light and truth. There is always the danger, in the case of both the Christian and the non-Christian, of limiting the gospel to his own understanding of it. In our missionary effort we must always measure our conformity to the gracious

will of God by the gospel, assured that, as we pray, the Holy Spirit will lead us into all truth. Also, only as we are willing to put our life and witness under the constant judgment of our Lord, and have been enriched by the fruits of evangelism, can we guard against this danger, and bear witness to the gospel in ever-increasing measure.

37. The proclamation of the gospel and every argument to commend it must be accompanied by the demonstration of its transforming power. The gospel is not the emergence of a new ideal in man, but the entrance of a new power from God into the world. It must, therefore, be proclaimed in the context of power in action. The seeds of the Kingdom are not words and arguments but the children of the Kingdom themselves, scattered and sown in the field of the world.

38. Finally, since the gospel is the lifting up of the cross of Jesus Christ as the sole hope of mankind, He asks His witnesses to walk the way of the cross, in complete self-sacrifice and faithfulness unto death.

VI. Come, Lord Jesus

39. The Church partaking through the Holy Spirit in the life of its Head is assured of the fulfilment of His work. The messenger of the unlimited grace of Christ looks towards the consummation of the Kingdom in which His redeeming love shall have achieved its full intention. How thoughtlessly they speak who say, "Where is the promise of His coming? For ever since the fathers fell asleep, all things have continued as they were from the beginning of all creation." To them the answer has been given, "The Lord is not slack concerning his promise, as some men count slackness, but is long-suffering to us-ward, not willing that any should perish, but that all should come to repentance." The time of expectation is the time of evangelism, even as the time of evangelism is the time of expectation. For He who comes as our Judge is also our Redeemer.

40. The tragedy of the world is that it knows no judge, no lord of history. To the Church it is given to know that man is not condemned to an endless succession of meaningless nights and days, to never completed toil, to uncomforted mourning or ever-disillusioned hoping. It possesses, or rather is possessed by, the hope of a glorious fulfilment.

41. In this hope we are saved and by it we live, considering "the sufferings of this present time not worthy to be compared with the glory which shall be revealed in us." The time of evangelism will not last for ever; it will be succeeded by the time of the Kingdom fulfilled. The good news will not remain for ever a promise made: it will become a promise kept. The gospel will not be the knowledge of the privileged few: it will be revealed to all. Seeing in a glass darkly will not be our ultimate vision of God: we will know even as we are known until we say, "We are complete in Him."

42. Therefore are Christians under constraint to declare this hope to the world until the consummation of the Kingdom and the coming of the King.

DISCUSSION ON THE REPORT ON EVANGELISM

First Discussion

The Bishop of Chichester presided.

Bishop Raines introduced the draft report.

Mr. Urwin rose to speak with regret against acceptance of the report. He said people would not be stirred by it to go forth as "flaming evangelists." He made three major criticisms:

1. The text nowhere indicates the magnitude of the remaining task before the Christian community;

2. There is no adequate analysis of the special needs of scientific intelligentsia, alienated workers, other great world religions, or the sore-hearted and spiritually needy;

3. There was no fresh advance in techniques of evangelism.

Bishop Raines replied that these three factors had been amply covered in the preparatory survey and were more summarily and implicitly mentioned in the present report.

Principal Chandran said that the first two paragraphs were an inadequate introduction to a good report. Something more positive was needed than a reiteration of the words "hopeless" and "hope." Our hopelessness was not our own, but had been revealed to us by Christ. He proposed an amendment to meet these points.

Dr. Niles (responding for the Section) said that the additional points in Mr. Chandran's amendment were already embodied in other paragraphs. A transposition of this material would involve a change in the structure of the document. He hoped the present structure would be retained. Although Jesus Christ showed the full extent of human hopelessness it was true that St. Paul had said men were "finding hope" even before Christ's coming.

Prof. Torrance sought an amendment embodying a more precise account of the motive of evangelism. He said that in the New Testament the motive was more objectively set forth. He gave a form of words to cover the point involved.

Oberkirchenrat Schmidt moved for the deletion of words in paragraph 3 which might suggest that the objective factors of Word and Sacrament in the life of the Church were of small importance.

Canon Naylor said that a very important point had been omitted in the 23rd paragraph dealing with Christian education. He asked that mention be made of the need for definite Christian education in day schools.

The Section indicated that it would be prepared to embody an allusion to this need but would qualify the insertion by saying that if did not favour the exclusive rights of any one church in the field.

Dr. Baxter sought inclusion of the mention of evangelism by the making of speeches in cinemas, and the opportunities provided by Christian festivals.

Bishop Raines, in reply, said that inclusion of one such specific reference would open the way for too many others. Other literature issued by the World Council would in time provide for such points but the amendment was not acceptable.

Dr. Reuben Nelson, referring to Canon Naylor's contention, said he was disturbed, as an American, at the uncritical acceptance by the Assembly of Canon Naylor's speech. He said that in the United States, Protestants were struggling to provide for religious teaching of some kind while trying to prevent the erection of barriers between religious and racial groups.

Bishop Raines said the point would be safeguarded when a re-draft was submitted.

Dr. Preston Roberts further pressed for inclusion of "communicant and catechetical groups within the Church" among agencies of Christian education to be enumerated.

Mr. Taft further drew attention to the fact that Christian education in day schools raised a difficult issue in the United States. In view of many sharp divisions even within Protestantism it was impossible to reach a decision acceptable to the Assembly. Though he personally supported the sense of the amendment he thought its insertion undesirable.

Bishop Raines said the controversial character of the change was now apparent. He suggested that reference to schools be dropped.

Bishop Oxnam said the matter was of fundamental importance. If it was contended that Christian education should become part of the public educational system, could not Jews, Muslims, and others make the same request? It was better to drop the proposal than attempt to re-draft it.

Dr. Van Dusen said the Assembly had become involved at this point in an intra-American discussion. There were Americans who welcomed Canon Naylor's amendment. The matter was not one of procedure but of principle. Was God significant for the educational process or not? He moved to refer the question to the Drafting Committee for further conference.

Pastor Westphal asked that the appeal not to neglect the cinema as a medium of mass communication should be put differently. He asked that it be said that the Church may use mass media rather than *must* use them. The Church was not bound to use the world's means of communication.

Bishop Raines said the committee believed the Church *should* use these media and therefore was not willing to accept the amendment.

Professor Tindal, referring to paragraph 32 on the training of the ministry, said it would be regrettable if the implication was that training was chiefly for the pulpit. He said that training in intercession and pastoralia was important. He asked that the point be met and that agriculture be added to the mention of industry.

Mrs. Fisher said she rose with diffidence. She was afraid that Dr. Niles might get up and tell her that her point was covered in "paragraph so and so." She added, however, "I do not think it is !" She drew attention to the home as a centre of Christian influence and said it had not been adequately mentioned.

Bishop Raines explained that this point had not been included because it was a concern of the Section on the Laity. The Drafting Committee would compare notes with other groups in the Assembly and would insert the point if it had not been covered elsewhere.

Professor Surjit Singh (consultant) said that the paragraph of the report concerning identification might suggest as it stood a divorce between Christian theory and practice. This was a serious matter in environments where Christianity was in conflict with ideologies professing unity of theory and practice.

The report of the Section was received as a whole, subject to re-drafting.

Second Discussion

Bishop Raines said that the drafters felt that the situation in public schools was so different in different countries that mention of the issue would do more harm than good. It was therefore recommended that special study of the question be undertaken on the initiative of the Central Committee for report to a subsequent assembly or other World Council meeting.

The Bishop of Armidale said it was strange that a document on evangelism did not mention "evangelistic missions." There should be some recognition of this still effective method of communicating the gospel. He moved a short form of words to meet the deficiency.

Bishop Raines said that a number of such suggestions had come forward. It had not been felt wise to burden the document even by special mention of the Kirchentag. The Committee was therefore not ready to accede to the Bishop of Armidale's amendment.

Mr. McLuskey asked leave to speak further on Christian education in schools. He felt that the discussion on the question tended to be dominated by the American situation. Many would be unhappy to see left out of account the critically important role of the school. At least it should be said that specific attention was being given to the question. The importance of the school would thus be recognized.

Canon Naylor said the matter had not been introduced to embarrass the United States, but indeed as a result of concern felt in Canada at the influence of the American system on Canada's schools.

Dr. Niles said the issue should be discussed quite apart from the report of the Section.

Bishop Pickett asked leave to speak because the problem had been discussed as though America only were involved. The issue was alive and explosive in India and Pakistan, where it appeared in reverse, since Christian churches there did not want Christian children taught Islam in government schools.

The question was put to the vote, and *it was agreed* to refer the problem (as above) to the Central Committee, giving notice to the churches that this action had been taken.

The report as a whole was received.

THE REPORT OF SECTION III

SOCIAL QUESTIONS: THE RESPONSIBLE SOCIETY IN A WORLD PERSPECTIVE

Received by the Assembly and commended to the Churches for study and appropriate action, with the request that the Churches report the results of their study and action to the Central Committee.

INTRODUCTION

1. Christian social responsibility is grounded in the mighty acts of God, who is revealed in Jesus Christ our Lord. He has created the world, and all time is embraced within His eternal purpose. He moves and acts within history as the ever-living God. The centre of world history is the earthly life, the cross, and the resurrection of Jesus Christ. As has been affirmed in the Report on the Main Theme, in Him God entered history decisively, to judge and to forgive. In Him are revealed the present plight of man, and the end toward which the world is moving.

2. He has established with men a living relationship of promise and commandment in which they are called to live in faithful obedience to His purpose. The promise is the gift of abundant life as children of God for those who hear and follow the divine call. The commandment is that men should love God and their neighbours. In the call to responsible social action, the promise and the commandent of the righteous and loving God require us to recognize that in every human being Christ Himself comes to claim our service. Responding to God's love in Christ, and being aware of His final judgment Christians will act responsibly. The call to social righteousness is sustained by the sure hope that the victory

is with God, who in Christ has vanquished the powers of evil and in His own day will make this victory fully manifest in Christ.

3. Man and all the powers of this world are under the sovereignty of their Maker who calls men in families, societies, nations and all human groups to responsibility under Him. From Christ men receive the direction for their service, the obligation to share heartily in the world's work and daily tasks, and the responsibility to seek a better social and political life. Our hope in Christ enables us to know that there are limitations set upon every human ideal and achievement, so that we never make an idol out of any social cause, institution or system. Moreover, because our hope is in Christ, we are saved from frustration where our efforts to influence public opinion or social action are seemingly in vain and we are saved from despair when all human hopes collapse.

4. The churches have come to realize more fully that they have a duty to society as part of their mission in the world. The scope of this mission is defined in the inclusive reports of this Assembly, but its relation to the responsible society is the assignment of this report.

5. Our hope in Christ does not offer technical answers or specific solutions which statesmen and experts have not found. But in the context of Christian faith we gain new insights into our dilemmas and ways to overcome them. In all the specific tasks with which this report deals we attempt to give expression to that hope.

I. The Meaning of the Responsible Society

6. The first Assembly of the World Council of Churches at Amsterdam coined the term "The Responsible Society." It was stated that the responsible society is a society "where freedom is the freedom of men who acknowledge responsibility to justice and public order and where those who hold political authority or economic power are responsible for its exercise to God and to the people whose welfare is affected by it."

7. "Responsible society" is not an alternative social or political system, but a criterion by which we judge all existing social orders and at the same time a standard to guide us in the specific choices we have to make. Christians are called to live responsibly, to live in response to God's act of redemption in Christ, in any society, even within the most unfavourable social structures.

8. This report will deal mainly with large-scale institutions. But the realization of a responsible society must be achieved in small groups as well as in large. Human living acquires meaning and depth only in relations with other persons, and since an individual can have direct and close contact only with a limited number of people, the art of social living has to be learned in small groups.

9. The most fundamental of these is the family. For this reason the churches must give strong warning against the widespread disruption of family life. The family itself needs to be protected; for this the witness of the Christian family is all-important. More attention should be given to the conditions which cause the forcible separation of families and every effort should be made to reunite those who have been separated. For right development into responsible adulthood, children need security and love, and the discipline which family life pre-eminently secures. Disintegration here is closely related to disintegration in the larger groupings of society. In predominantly non-Christian countries, the building of a Christian family life implies in some cases a rupture with old non-Christian family systems. The specifically Christian attitude toward the family should be clarified within different cultural circumstances in order to strengthen the community life of Christians in its most elemental form.

10. But the family is not the only group in which man can practise the art of living as "little men in big societies." There is often in modern life a family egotism which hinders social responsibility rather than furthering it. We are called to serve in other communities also. People co-operating in the same work or in the same factory should form nuclei of human relationships in a technical world; for young people teamwork and co-operation with friends sometimes provide the best opportunities for learning the art of living together; where in some parts of the world the village community or tribal group still offers a protection for human relations, they should be preserved and adapted to modern circumstances.

The Christian congregation itself should be a visible centre of community and a base for local social responsibility. Its worship should be discernibly relevant to the total life of the society in which it is set. It must break down those barriers within its own life which deny fellowship so that it may begin to show in its action a solution to the real problems troubling the local community. It should also be concerned with the possibilities of renewing personal life through the corporate life of small groups. And it must, equally with the family, beware of egotism that prevents its sharing in the wider life of the Church or of the community as a whole.

A. *The Structure and Function of the State*

11. The Oxford Conference on Church, Community and State in 1937 gave the following definition of the function of the state with regard to justice: "Since we believe in the Holy God as the source of justice, we do not consider the state as the ultimate source of law, but rather its guarantor. It is not the lord but the servant of justice. There can be for the Christian no ultimate authority but very God."

12. True justice is dynamic and its forms must vary to meet changing needs. Those who seek it should be made sensitive by love to discover such needs where they have been neglected. Justice involves the continuous effort to overcome those economic disadvantages which are a grievous human burden and which are incompatible with equal opportunity for people to develop their capacities. Justice requires the development of political institutions which are humane as they touch the lives of people, which provide protection by law against the arbitrary use of power, and which encourage responsible participation by all citizens.

13. In recent years the churches have had to give fresh thought to the nature and functions of the state. No one form of government has a universal claim on Christians, but any political system must include some elements without which it tends to become an oppressive tyranny. For these, Christians should work by active participation in political affairs. In some situations where it may at present seem impossible to work directly for them, the Christian has chiefly the obligation to do what he can to defend other persons against particular acts of cruelty and injustice.

14. Christians should work for the embodiment of the responsible society in political institutions by emphasizing the following:

(*a*) Every person should be protected against arbitrary arrest or other interference with elementary human rights.

(*b*) Every person should have the right to express his religious, moral, and political convictions. This is especially important for those who belong to minorities.

(c) Channels of political action must be developed by which the people can without recourse to violence change their governments.

(d) Forms of association within society which have their own foundations and principles should be respected, and not controlled in their inner life, by the state. Churches, families, and universities are dissimilar examples of this non-political type of association.

15. The Oxford statement applies in the following way to the function of the state with regard to social justice in economic life. While the state is sometimes the enemy of freedom, under many circumstances the state is the only instrument which can make freedom possible for large sectors of the population. The state is not the source of social justice, but it must be its guardian, ready if necessary to accept responsibility to counteract depression or inflation and to relieve the impact of unemployment, industrial injury, low wages, and unfavourable working conditions, sickness, and old age. But in doing so the state remains the servant not the lord of social justice. Therefore we must warn against the danger that the union of political and economic power may result in an all-controlling state. In contradistinction to actions of the state it is the task of the non-governmental sectors in economic life to be the guardian of responsible private action in society. But within the private sector, both employers and employees in all their varied organizations in their turn are the servant, and not the lord, of freedom and welfare. When necessary in the public interest, the state must intervene to prevent any centre of economic or social power which represents partial interest from becoming stronger than itself, for the state alone has the power and the authority under God to act as trustee for society as a whole.

16. At all stages of political development and in the face of all the problems noted here, a Christian community must act as a conscience for the nation and ceaselessly remind all who hold power of God's purpose for the nation and of God's judgment upon their use of power.

B. *Problems of Economic Life*

17. *New Trends.* One of the most important features of the modern world is the way in which society has increasingly taken

the control of economic affairs out of the sphere of "automatic responses." Full employment policies, the spread of state action in economic life, and the growing economic power of organized groups of employers, employees, farmers, and professional people have brought great changes in the highly industrialized countries.

18. The need for inter-governmental co-operation in economic affairs accompanies the increase in domestic state action. In some areas, such as Europe, social reconstruction and supra-national integration go hand in hand and challenge many old political and economic ideas. At the same time, the priority given to full employment policies in many countries strengthens tendencies towards economic self-sufficiency and can threaten international economic co-operation.

19. The new emphasis on state initiative and international organization in the development of economic life has been accompanied by a fresh recognition of the importance of relative freedom in enterprise and of the regulating role of the price system. Many socialists have come to appreciate the importance of the private sector of the economy and the necessity for the energetic, enterprising, and expert business man as well as being aware of the dangers of centralized government.

20. *New Problems.* These developments suggest that disputes about "capitalism" and "socialism" disguise the more important issues in the field of economic and social policy. Each word is applied to many different social forms and economic systems. It is not the case that we have merely a choice between two easily distinguishable types of economic organization. Private enterprise takes many shapes in different countries at different stages and in different parts of one economy and is profoundly affected by the forms of government regulation. The operations of the state in business also take various forms, such as post offices run by government departments, supply of electric power or gas by local authorities, and national or state public corporations. In all types of economy there is to be found a variety of forms; there is no one pattern that is universally valid. There are also various types of co-operative organization. In some countries the "welfare state" or the " mixed economy" suggests a new pattern of economic life; others may be regarded as "capitalist," but the capitalism of today is very different from the capitalism of even twenty or thirty years years ago. The concrete issues in all countries concern the newly

evolving forms of economic organization, and the relative roles of the state, organized groups and private enterprises.

21. *The Church's Role*. The Church is concerned with economic life, because of God's concern for human beings who work to produce goods and services, who use them, and for whom business exists. The Church cannot uncritically support any particular form of organization as it exists in any particular country, but should be especially concerned with the following moral implications of economic life:

(*a*) State action in recent years has taken many new forms. The state must do those things for the economy that private industry cannot do properly, such as planning for urban development, stimulating industrial expansion and soil conservation, some types of large-scale industrial and agricultural research, and guidance of the distribution of industry. But state action needs to be decentralized, limited, and adaptable. The Christian should be ready to welcome fruitful new experiments, whether in the field of state action, private business or co-operative endeavour.

(*b*) Efficient production is important as well as fair distribution. Much Christian social thought in the past has tended to ignore the former and stress primarily the latter. Laziness and waste are sins before God no less than selfishness and greed.

(*c*) The churches have been properly critical of monopolistic practices, and of the effects of many irresponsible business practices on people and society generally. But they also need to understand and lay stress on the valuable contribution which the skilled executive has to make to society, irrespective of the form of ownership or organization. At its best the business system has provided incentives for the responsible initiative and hard work which produce economic progress, and has embodied the wisdom of decentralized decisions and widely distributed power. These are virtues needed in any system.

(*d*) The churches must never fail to recognize that the worker should have a status in society which accords with his responsibilities and his human dignity. Much has been done in recent years, but Christians are too ready to forget how much needs to be done, even in countries where social security and re-distribution of income and power have gone far.

(*e*) One of the most important economic roles is that played by the world's farmers. In some countries they have met urgent needs by extraordinary advances in productivity. For the feeding of increasing populations with a better diet, radical changes in farming methods will have to be carried through in many other countries, but always with due regard to the human consequences. The churches should recognize the justice of the farmer's demand for a reasonable measure of security of income; but even as they advance their legitimate demands for justice, farmers must resist the temptations to exhaust the soil, to exploit those who work for them, or to take unfair advantage of the consumers.

22. There are a number of places where our Christian concern for society makes us uneasy about the existing situation or where there is a demand for positive action.

(a) We can never forget the warnings in the Bible about the dangers to the rich man. In our day these warnings must be applied to the temptations facing everyone in a rich society. The tendencies to create unlimited wants, to over-emphasize material values and to appeal to motives of social pride, envy and lust, stimulated by irresponsible salesmanship and advertising, are dangerous and need curbing.

(b) Not only increased production but a stronger regard for equity in the distribution of wealth and income is also required. At the same time such factors as the place of incentive and the desire to avoid regimentation necessitate a measure of inequality in modern economic life. But every society should recognize the extent to which great contrasts between rich and poor destroy fellowship and undercut the political institutions of a responsible society.

(c) The churches have a duty to promote adequate assistance on the national and international level for children, the sick, the old, the refugees and other economically weak groups, by means of church organizations, voluntary societies, and local or national governments. It is the duty of the Christian to work for improved national or local welfare legislation and for the provision of adequate medical care. It may also be his duty to fight against any tendency for the state to monopolize social welfare activity.

(d) Serious problems arise from the great importance of organized groups, such as trade unions and associations of employers, farmers or professional people. Christians can bear witness that these groups must be responsible to the whole of society, that their leadership must be responsible to their members, and that the members must participate responsibly in the organization.

We welcome the role of responsible trade unions in fighting exploitation and promoting a humane environment for workers, and also the growing co-operation between labour and management to increase the material resources available for human welfare.

(*e*) Christians have a duty to bring to the attention of their governments that national policies have effects on the lives and welfare of peoples in other countries. National economic and political stability, justice, freedom and peace are dependent upon world economic and political stability. National and international policies are far more closely inter-related than ever before. Excessive barriers to trade can create economic crises elsewhere. The greater the economic power, the larger is the responsibility in this field. The richer countries particularly must remember that one test of their policies is their effect on the underdeveloped areas of the world.

II. The Church in Relation to Communist–Non-Communist Tension

23. The conflict between communists and non-communists affects the political and economic life of nearly every nation in the world, and creates divisions even within the Church regarding the right attitude toward communism. Only as Christians work for social justice and political freedom for all, and rise above both fear and resentment, will they be fully able to meet the challenge of this conflict. It is our concern for the brother for whom Christ died that should impel us to fulfil our obligations in the face of this conflict. In this way Christians living in different parts of our divided world may contribute to the creation of the necessary conditions for different systems to live side by side. This concern of Christians does not alter the mission of the churches to bear witness in the face of all atheistic and self-righteous ideologies.

24. The churches at Oxford and Amsterdam indicated the various points of conflict between the Christian faith and Marxist ideology and totalitarian practice.[1] We wish to reaffirm this state-

[1] At Amsterdam the churches referred to the following points of conflict: 1. "The communist promise of what amounts to a complete redemption of man in history; 2. the belief that a particular class by virtue of its role as the bearer of a new order is free from the sins and ambiguities that Christians believe characteristic of all human existence; 3. the materialistic and deterministic teachings, however they may be qualified, that are incompatible with belief in God and with the Christian view of man as a person, made in God's image and responsible to

ment about these basic conflicts, as well as to stress that the growth of communism is a judgment upon our modern societies generally for past or present indifference to social injustice, in which the Church is also involved.

25. In one form or another the conflict about communism has important consequences for the political and economic life of nearly every nation. In some regions of the world, especially in Asia, Africa and Latin America, communism has strong appeal. Here poverty, misery, the newly aroused aspirations for freedom and security, doubts as to the effectiveness of democracy, and the tendency of those in power to brand all reforms as communistic, combine to make the promises of communism attractive in spite of the totalitarianism which accompanies it. For many there seems to be no alternative which will bring essential social change quickly enough. There are Christians who think that they can co-operate with the communist movement in their countries because they see it as the way to a new order of material abundance and greater justice. We must ask: "Can communism be an effective instrument for these limited purposes or must we give warning that, where such social and economic methods are introduced, the total communist scheme will come to dominate the minds of men as well as their institutions?"

26. Christians must consider carefully the serious effects the conflict with communism is already producing: for example, the tendencies in democratic societies to lower their standards of civil liberties, and sometimes to strengthen reactionary forces in countries abroad. Preoccupation with the real dangers of subversion in many situations has led to a less widely recognized and more subtle danger to society from those who identify as subversive any unpopular opinions or associations. Enemies of essential human freedom appear on both the political right and the political left and Christians have a duty to strengthen the forces of freedom which fight on both fronts. Yet we must not forget the love due to the neighbour who stands for an ideology which we reject.

27. There is a particular danger that nations will overemphasize the military aspect in their defence against communism

Him; 4. the ruthless methods of communists in dealing with their opponents; 5. the demand of the party on its members for an exclusive and unqualified loyalty which belongs only to God, and the coercive policies of communist dictatorship in controlling every aspect of life."

and fail to see the need for reforms in political, social and econo-mic institutions as an important part of their response to its challenge. These nations can have greater influence on the course of the present world conflict if they show their ability to deal justly with the legitimate aspirations of the dependent peoples, to cope successfully and creatively with their own social problems, and to remain self-critical.

28. It will be the task of the churches to point to the dangers inherent in the present situation: on the one hand the temptation to succumb to anti-communist hysteria and the danger of a self-righteous assurance concerning the political and social systems of the West; on the other hand the temptation to accept the false promises of communism and to overlook its threat to any responsible society.

29. Christians in communist and non-communist countries are called to hold each other in special brotherly concern and prayer across all barriers. Those of us in non-communist lands affirm our unity with these churches in the ecumenical fellowship and the bond of the Spirit, and our confidence in their loyalty to Christ. We rejoice with them in the Christian witness which they make in these new circumstances and seek to understand and affirm our fellowship with them in their temptations and in their Christian hope, for this witness and these temptations are relevant also to our social responsibility. Therefore we are presented with a number of questions which challenge Christians in communist as well as in non-communist countries in different ways. All Chris-tians must wrestle with the following questions which are urgent in a special way in communist lands.

(a) What are the ways, and what is the content of Christian witness in the face of atheistic ideologies?

(b) What is the social significance of the existence of the Church as an inclusive worshipping and evangelistic community? How can the life of the congregation in all its forms, including its pastoral and social work, affect society? How does the Church's teaching ministry relate to state education under a communist regime?

(c) What reforms are necessary in the life and structure of the Church? What are the values and dangers of agreements between Church and state?

(d) At what points can the Church and Christians co-operate with governments in their plans for social reconstruction? What are the limits of this co-operation? How does Christian social responsibility avoid both surrender to communism and the temptations of a negative resistance?

(*e*) What new forms of prophetic ministry are required? How far are public statements by the Church on social questions effective?

(*f*) What Christian witness can church members bear in their daily work? What is the place of suffering in Christian social witness?

(*g*) What, if any, is the Church's responsibility for standards of truth in all fields? For pre-communist social and cultural traditions? What is the relation between a Christian demand and a communist demand for repentance for past social injustices?

30. The following questions are especially urgent for Christians in non-communist countries:

(*a*) What are the special temptations of the Church in a traditional "Christian society"?

(*b*) Does secularism in the non-communist world differ from the materialism in the communist world?

(*c*) What is the content of Christian witness toward the large mass of secularized people? How far is this secularization due to the class nature of the Church and the accommodation of its life and message to bourgeois interests and values? What reforms in the life of the Church are necessary to meet these challenges?

(*d*) How far are the churches in non-communist lands genuinely prophetic in their relation to society and the state?

(*e*) What is the responsibility of the churches in non-communist lands for the cultivation of traditions of freedom and community over against the growing pressure toward social conformity?

III. The Problems in the Economically Underdeveloped Regions

31. Society in Asia Africa, and some parts of Latin America today is characterized by the urge to national self-determination in political and economic matters. There is a growing shift of social, economic and political authority from those persons and institutions who by inheritance or tradition possessed it, to those who exercise it because of the function they perform. The peoples of these countries have awakened to a new sense of fundamental human rights and justice and they are in revolt against enslaving

political, economic, religious and social conditions. There is also the pressure to achieve changes rapidly. All of the processes of social development—increasing productivity, raising standards of living, democratization and the rest—which have taken centuries in the West, demand in these areas to be completed together and within decades. The temptation is to use irresponsible methods of collectivism, whether of the right or of the left, in the desire for rapid results. In such circumstances the Church has the duty to point the way to responsible society and herself to follow it.

32. The Ecumenical Study Conference, Lucknow, India, in December, 1952, presented a number of specific points which can be faced and tackled only as world problems and should be the concern of all the churches.

(a) *Development of political institutions:* Political institutions must be developed which are strong enough to accomplish the needed social and economic changes while extending and promoting fundamental human rights and freedom. It is necessary to re-define democratic political, economic and social values and objectives in the new context of Asian life and in the light of a more realistic understanding of human nature than can be provided by utopian concepts.

(b) *Land reform and rural development:* Absentee landlordism and other unjust forms of land tenure and privilege, not least where the churches themselves are guilty of such practices, must be abolished. At the same time, positive measures should make possible new systems of productive land use and community life. In rural areas, bold programmes of agriculture, rural industry, social education, co-operatives and the provision of rural credit and professional services are urgently needed. The rural community development programme in India recognizes agriculture as a way of life as well as an occupation. The churches can give concrete assistance in this development everywhere.

(c) *Industrial development:* In order to raise standards of living, underdeveloped countries properly insist upon developing industry. Ways should be found of obtaining capital within the country without endangering standards of consumption; technical assistance and foreign capital should be provided without doing violence to social objectives; the roles of the state and public and private enterprise in industry need to be examined in the light of local circumstances; forms of industry which can be integrated in suitable ways with village community life need to be found. In countries where industries are being developed rapidly, e.g. Brazil, India, Japan, Mexico and South Africa, special care should be given to protect new industrial labourers and their families from the dehumanizing factors which often accompany such industrialization.

(*d*) *Population:* Many underdeveloped countries, especially in Asia, are very densely populated in relation to their resources. Redistribution of population nationally and internationally, family planning and birth control are burning questions. The profound ethical, political and social issues which they raise need to be courageously examined and guidance should be given by the churches.

(*e*) *Independence and the responsibilities of interdependence:* A number of the underdeveloped countries have attained national freedom and full sovereignty after a colonial period. There are difficulties in adaptation to an international situation where national sovereignty in political and economic affairs, especially for weaker nations, is necessarily limited by the facts of interdependence. At the same time they need capital from the outside for development and industrialization. The flow of capital from former colonial powers having dried up, they find it difficult to mobilize the necessary capital, since private investors hesitate to enter the scene without specific guarantees, and public funds without political strings attached are hard to procure. Unless the responsibilities of interdependence are clearly defined and accepted by all concerned, this impasse could easily lead to bitterness and a sense of frustration.

33. The churches must be especially concerned with the way in which the present world struggle with its hot and cold wars militates against progress in the social reconstruction of the underdeveloped countries. It is significant for Christians on all continents that the Ecumenical Study Conference at Lucknow gave the following illustration concerning this:

"When American foreign policy is determined primarily by the criterion of anti-communism it generally strengthens conservative and reactionary political groups in the East Asian scene and tends to weaken the forces of healthy social reform. This line is bound to be self-defeating because in the final analysis social and spiritual health is the best answer to communism."

34. Underlying all the problems of the underdeveloped

countries is the need for extension of opportunities for education. Special attention should be given to the training of experts in public administration and technology. The churches have a direct responsibility towards education; especially in the rural areas and with regard to women.

CONCLUSION

35. In all these fields, the real dangers are complacency, lack of imagination, and the dull sense of hopelessness that settles upon those of little faith. World economic and social interdependence involves a new dimension in the task of creating a responsible society, which men will have to face realizing that statistics are only inadequate indications of desperate human need. Upon Christians rests a special responsibility to see the challenge, to press their governments to take the issue seriously and themselves to act sacrificially.

36. Because Jesus Christ is Lord in earth and heaven, the call to responsible social action which God addresses to His Church does not present us with an impossible task. We are not called upon to shoulder the burden of this world, but to seek justice, freedom and peace to the best of our ability in the social order. The Church knows that in obedience and prayer our efforts will bear fruit. For God has called us unto liberty to serve one another by love. "Faithful is he that calleth you, who also will do it."

DISCUSSION ON THE REPORT ON SOCIAL QUESTIONS

First Discussion

Dr. C. L. Patijn introduced the report of the Section and explained that its purpose was to elaborate the meaning of the Responsible Society in more concrete terms, stressing family life, small groups, the responsibility of the state and a new emphasis in economic life. Special reference was made in the second part of the report to tensions between communists and non-communists. Members of the Section were gratified that working agreement could be found in this area. The differences emerging were ethical and theoretical, but not political.

Bishop Peter, speaking to the report in general, explained the Hungarian attitude. He said there were still points of misunderstanding. The world was too divided to be abl: to share fully all the experiences surrounding the discussion of this problem; but, in spite of all difficulties, members of the Hungarian delegation were ready to vote in favour of the document. They did so because it was a good new starting-point on the route to a more complete understanding. The questions in the second part of the report, directed to churches in East and West, were most valuable. The churches must continue their East-West dialogue for the sake of contacts and common witness.

Professor Devadutt said the report required serious editing. In places its meaning was not clear. Moreover, the first part concentrated on industrial problems at the expense of rural problems. There was further need to speak with greater clarity to the industrial worker wherever labour conditions were not good and to the great numbers of plantation workers in countries like India. Paragraph 14 of the report should be amplified to stress the positive role of the state.

Mr. Goyder commended the report as a whole but regretted that there was no mention of the potential irresponsibility embodied in the relation of shareholders to industry. He quoted Deuteronomy and said that God's law applied to the industrial order and that a new theology of industry was needed.

Professor Torrance said that the report did not show how the gospel itself was linked with the actual points later enumerated. He thought the parables of Jesus had many direct and important things to say on this subject.

Professor Mehl said that the French translation gave a false impression of the content of the second sentence. It suggested a mechanical unrolling of history rather than divine rule. He agreed with Professor Torrance that the relation between the theological and the practical parts of the report was not sufficiently clear. It was not that the theme of Christian hope had to be included artificially. The final victory, as in war, had its intense bearing on our present history. He therefore proposed re-drafting with emphasis on the pressure of the coming of the Kingdom.

Dr. Patijn (for the Section) said the text of the first two pages was a draft produced by compromise. Professor Mehl's first objection was based on a mistranslation. What he further said was embodied in a measure in the early part of the report but amendment throughout would be difficult in view of the balance between different emphases on the main theme required to do justice to all points of view.

Professor Mehl's amendment was then put and lost.

Bishop Walls suggested that the churches always had a sense of social duty and that it would be more appropriate to say that they had come to realize this more fully than that they had acknowledged it for the first time.

Dr. William C. Robinson sought amplification of the Amsterdam Assembly's definition of the responsible society to provide for the insertion of "responsibility to God" in the early part of the definition as quoted in the present document.

Dr. Patijn said acceptance of this suggestion was difficult since it would lead to circulation of two texts of the Amsterdam definition, and thus to confusion.

Mrs. Coombs asked that a more positive note be struck in paragraph 9 of the report in referring to the home. It was necessary to find ways within the democratic state in which the family might flourish.

Dr. Bosley sought addition of further points about the family in view of the need to associate the World Council's witness with advances in family welfare.

Principal Cunliffe-Jones proposed a redraft to allow for mention of the congregation at the end of paragraph 8. He considered the congregation a starting-point for work in the family and other small groups.

The Bishop of Armidale drew attention to the phrases concerning the rule of the price system in paragraph 19 of the report. The free movement of prices no longer existed in a pure form in any economy. He therefore suggested some such amendment as "a relatively free price system." It must be indicated that a completely free price system leads to exploitation and then to government intervention and the emergence of black markets. A "mixed" system was preferable.

Mr. Fichter spoke gratefully of the work done in Section III on rural problems but asked for a revision of part of paragraph 21 to stress the importance of the family farm as against mechanization. He said recognition of the need to conserve the soil was also required and that generally church groups should more adequately acknowledge the importance of agriculture. There were too few agricultural people among Assembly participants.

Pastor Lauriol took some exception to paragraph 21 as suggesting that the hungry must wait until tomorrow for relief. The most privileged must make sacrifices today.

The Duke of Hamilton suggested substitution of the word "equity" for "equality" in paragraph 22. He said that the notion of equality could be used for un-Christian ideological ends.

Dr. Patijn replied that "equality" was exactly what was meant. The word "equity" was ambiguous and not acceptable.

After a vote the word "equity" was adopted.

Bishop Dun pointed out that the words "rich man" in paragraph 22 really meant "rich society." He said "I have seldom heard anyone who thought of himself as the rich man to whom this paragraph refers, though I have heard many complain how expensive it is to be rich."

Dr. Patijn said the Section was willing to accept the sense of Bishop Dun's proposal.

The debate on the subject was temporarily adjourned.

Second Discussion

Dr. Van Dusen was in the chair.

Mr. Taft drew attention to the use of the question form in paragraphs 29 and 30. He said the Section now felt it fairly contrasted the situation of churches in communist and non-communist countries. The closing part of the Section's report presented a firm criticism of communism and of other existing systems which was fair, vigorous and relatively complete. He apologized for the length of the report but said restriction within the originally laid down limits was impossible.

Mr. Myung said that ten years' experience in Korea had shown that communism is a world-wide imperialism which intends to attempt to stamp out all religions. It was wrong to compromise at any point with communism. He therefore suggested deletion of the words "co-existence" and "anti-communist hysteria."

Dr. Patijn said the proposed deletions could not be made since they would lead to weakening of the statement. However, he agreed to use the words "living together" (as in the report of Section IV) in place of " co-existence."

Dr. Cragg, commenting on paragraph 24, said that the assumption was that the only major conflict was between Christianity and communism; but fascism survived in various forms and this should be recognized.

Dr. Patijn said that the paragraph in question was on communist–non-communist tensions specifically. Conditions for which Christians should work in the state were set out elsewhere.

Bishop Bayne said that the demand for self-determination may exalt political independence. The Church must distinguish between supporting developments that may lead to tyranny and working for genuine independence with better conditions.

Mr. Harold M. Jackson said that a basic economic rule was self-sacrifice and another was integrity. He proposed certain additions to the report to emphasize these values in connection with borrowing and repayment of money.

Dr. Morehouse took exception to the singling out of the United States for special criticism in respect to its foreign policy. He said that the motive of the policy was not primarily anti-communism and that the point made in paragraph 33 of the report was sufficiently stressed elsewhere.

Dr. Patijn said the section considered the matter to be of great importance in Asia. The point should be made again as explicitly as had been done at the meeting of the Central Committee at Lucknow in 1953.

Dr. Morehouse's proposal was then put and lost.

The entire report was then received, subject to inclusion of the amendments by the Drafting Committee.

The Report of Section IV

INTERNATIONAL AFFAIRS: CHRISTIANS IN THE STRUGGLE FOR WORLD COMMUNITY

Received by the Assembly and commended to the Churches for study and appropriate action, with the request that the Churches report the results of their study and action to the Central Committee

Introduction

1. The Assembly of the World Council of Churches proclaims the Christian hope in an hour of grave international crisis. Social and political systems are in conflict. Opposing ideologies compete

for the minds and souls of men. Rival power blocs imperil the peace of nations large and small. An arms race of unprecedented dimensions casts its ominous shadow over the face of the earth. Natural and human resources, intended by God for the enrichment of society, are diverted to purposes alien to His holy will. Science is conscripted. Hydrogen weapons carry the threat of mass destruction on a scale hitherto unknown.

2. Nations arbitrarily divided by war and the aftermath of war press for the restoration of their unity, as free and sovereign peoples. Millions of God's children are in revolt against economic deprivation, political bondage and social inequality. Other millions of God's children, uprooted from the land of their fathers, seek refuge from the storms by which they are beset. Curtains of disunity and divisiveness create situations of tension around the globe. Nations and peoples whose primary desire is to dwell in peace, live in fear lest they will be destroyed by the conflict of power.

3. This troubled world, disfigured and distorted as it is, is still God's world. He rules and overrules its tangled history. In praying, "Thy will be done on earth as it is in heaven," we commit ourselves to seek earthly justice, freedom and peace for all men. Here as everywhere Christ is our hope. Our confidence lies not in our own reason or strength, but in the power that comes from God. Impelled by this faith, all our actions will be but humble, grateful and obedient acknowledgment that He has redeemed the world. The fruit of our efforts rests in His hands. We can therefore live and work as those who know that God reigns, undaunted by all the arrogant pretensions of evil, ready to face situations that seem hopeless and yet to act in them as men whose hope is indestructible.

4. With this situation before us, and our hope in Christ within us, we commend to the 170 millions of our fellow Christians in the 163 member churches of the World Council of Churches, the following concerns on which the common judgment of Christians should be exercised, with a view to our corporate and individual action in world affairs.

I. The Desire for Peace and the Fear of War

5. Deeply and persistently man longs for peace. He no longer finds any glamour in war; he has tasted the fruit of its insanity and

found it bitter and poisonous. His ideals are mocked, his liberty curtailed, his possessions destroyed, and his future undermined by total war even as its high-sounding goals have eluded his grasp. He is sick of it, and wants to be at peace!

6. Christians everywhere are committed to world peace as a goal. However, for them "peace" means far more than mere "absence of war"; it is characterized positively by freedom, justice, truth and love. For such peace the Church must labour and pray.

7. Christians must also face the fact that such a peace will not be easily or quickly attained. We live in a world in which from generation to generation ignorance of God and rebellion against Him have resulted in greed and an insatiable lust for power. War and its evils are the consequences. Basically the problem is a spiritual one, and economic and political measures alone will not solve it. Men's hearts must be changed. This is always the supreme evangelistic challenge to the Church, although we must confess that our response has been tragically casual and feeble.

8. The development of nuclear weapons makes this an age of fear. True peace cannot rest on fear. It is vain to think that the hydrogen bomb or its development has guaranteed peace because men will be afraid to go to war, nor can fear provide an effective restraint against the temptation to use such a decisive weapon either in hope of total victory or in the desperation of total defeat.

9. The thought of all-out nuclear warfare is indeed horrifying. Such warfare introduces a new moral challenge. It has served to quicken public concern, and has intensified awareness of the urgency of finding means of prevention. War's consequences can no longer seem remote to any individual; all mankind is vulnerable to a disaster from which there may be no escape.

10. The foremost responsibility of the Christian Church in this situation is undoubtedly to bring the transforming power of Jesus Christ to bear upon the hearts of men. Christians must pray more fervently for peace, repent more earnestly of their individual and collective failures to further world order, and strive more urgently to establish world contacts for reconciliation, fellowship and love.

11. Lofty objectives so often invented to justify war cannot conceal the truth that its violence and destruction are inherently evil. Therefore Christians, in their respective countries, must not lend themselves to, but expose, this deceit.

12. It is not enough for the churches to proclaim that war is evil. They must study afresh the Christian approaches to peace, taking into account both Christian pacifism as a mode of witness and the conviction of Christians that in certain circumstances military action is justifiable.

Whatever views Christians hold in respect of these approaches, they must seek out, analyse, and help to remove the psychological and social, the political and economic causes of war. Without forsaking their conviction that all weapons of war are evil, the churches should press for restraints on their use. Christians in all lands must plead with their governments to be patient and persistent in their search for means to limit weapons and advance disarmament.

13. But even this is not enough. An international order of truth and peace would require:

(a) under effective international inspection and control and in such a way that no state would have cause to fear that its security was endangered, the elimination and prohibition of atomic, hydrogen and all other weapons of mass destruction, as well as the reduction of all armaments to a minimum;

(b) the development and acceptance of methods for peaceful change to rectify existing injustices.

14. However, it must be recognized that on the basis of current suspicions and distrust the nations at the moment have reached a stalemate on the issue of control of atomic and nuclear weapons, either through international inspection or by mere resolution. What constructive steps can be proposed in this impasse?

15. We first of all call upon the nations to pledge that they will refrain from the threat or the use of hydrogen, atomic, and all other weapons of mass destruction as well as any other means of force against the territorial integrity or political independence of any state.

16. If this pledge should be broken, the Charter of the United Nations provides for collective action and, pending such international action, recognizes the right of national self-defence. We believe that any measures to deter or combat aggression should conform to the requirements of the United Nations Charter and Christians should urge that both the United Nations and their own governments limit military action strictly to the necessities of international security.

17. Yet even this is not enough. The churches must condemn the deliberate mass destruction of civilians in open cities by whatever means and for whatever purpose. The churches should press through C.C.I.A. and other channels for the automatic stationing of U.N. Peace Commission teams in areas of tension to identify any aggression if it takes place. Christians must continue to press for social, political and economic measures to prevent war. Among these should be the giving of strong moral support for the positive use of atomic power for the benefit of mankind.

18. We must also see that experimental tests of hydrogen bombs have raised issues of human rights, caused suffering and imposed an additional strain on human relations between nations. Among safeguards against the aggravation of these international tensions is the insistence that nations carry on tests only within their respective territories or, if elsewhere, only by international clearance and agreement.

19. Above all, Christians must witness to a dynamic hope in God, in whose hands lie the destinies of nations, and in this confidence be untiring in their efforts to create and maintain an international climate favourable for reconciliation and goodwill. The specific problems and tasks will vary in each country according to circumstances. Civil authorities may be hostile to the Church or even avowed enemies of Christ. We know that the power of the Holy Spirit does work effectively through the witness of faithful and obedient and suffering Christians, and the purposes of God will not be denied but will be fulfilled in His time.

II. Living Together in a Divided World

20. The Assembly believes that an international order conformed to the will of God and established in His peace can be achieved only through the reconciliation which Christ makes possible. Only thus will those transformed attitudes and standards, agreements and practices which alone will ensure lasting peace become possible. Because of their belief in this gospel of reconciliation and their experience of its power, Christians can never accept, as the only kind of existence open to nations, a state of perpetual tension leading to "inevitable" war. On the contrary, it is the Christian conviction that war is not inevitable, because God wills peace.

21. From this it follows that the first responsibility of Christians is to live and work for the reconciliation of men to God and, therefore, as individuals and nations, to one another. Endeavours to secure that nations shall live together in peace on any basis less fundamental than this are always precarious; at any moment they may prove to be but frail expedients in a world which has not yet become subject to the power of the Cross.

22. Nevertheless, the preservation even of these "frail expedients," in a world where Christ's reign is not yet acknowledged, is morally imperative as a minimum condition of international order. Today there is urgent need for this moral imperative to be recognized and acknowledged. The clash of national interests, social systems and ideologies tends to dominate every phase of international life. Hostile propaganda, border incidents and a suicidal competition in arms more deadly than any hitherto used, characterize a situation which is unfit to be described as peace. Over all there moves the spectre of total war. Only as these current tensions are reduced and controlled will time be secured for bringing to bear the deeper and more creative influences of reconciliation.

23. A current political definition of such endeavours is "co-existence." We avoid the use of this term because of its unhappy historical significance and some of its current political implications. "Co-existence" as conceived by Christians cannot imply any willingness to disguise from themselves or others the vast difference which lies between the search for an international order based on belief in Christ and His reconciling work, and the pursuit of aims which repudiate the Christian revelation. There can be no abandonment of the right to assert this fundamental difference and the faith on which it rests.

24. We stand against submission to, engulfment by, or appeasement of, totalitarian tyranny and aggression. We also stand against the exploitation of any people by economic monopoly or political imperialism. In the world community we must stand for the freedom of all people to know the truth which makes men free and for the basic civil liberties of all people to struggle for a higher freedom.

25. Christians claim the right to propagate their faith, by proclamation and persuasion, by example and suffering, just as they uphold the same right for others. Nevertheless, conflicts of

conviction about the origin and destiny of man have long existed within societies essentially peaceful and Christians must continue to condemn totalitarianism as false in doctrine and dangerous in practice. They will be no less firm in continuing to oppose atheistic materialism. Yet however deep the conflict may be it is not necessarily an insuperable bar to living together in a divided world. The same may be said of methods of political and economic organization, whether they be democratic or dictatorial.

26. Such living together does, however, require that certain minimum conditions be met on both sides:

(*a*) A conviction that it is possible for nations and peoples to live together, at least for a considerable period of years.

(*b*) A willingness not to use force as an instrument of policy beyond the existing frontiers. This would not mean the recognition and freezing of present injustices and the unnatural divisions of nations, but it would mean renouncing coercion as a means of securing or redressing them.

(*c*) A vigorous effort to end social and other injustices which might lead to civil, and hence, international, war.

(*d*) A scrupulous respect for the pledged word.

(*e*) A continuing effort to reach agreement on outstanding issues, such as the peace treaties and disarmament, which are essential to a broader stabilization and pacification of relations.

(*f*) Readiness to submit all unresolved questions of conflict to an impartial international organization and to carry out its decisions.

27. These are minimum requirements. This limited form of living together can only be a transitional stage or a point of departure. It must move, through untiring endeavour, beyond these minimum requirements into an order of genuine co-operation. The first move into such an order must surely be in the direction of peaceful competition with growing co-operation. This order will be facilitated and reinforced through the free exchange of persons, culture, information and goods; through common undertakings for relief and human welfare and through the growth of the United Nations as an instrument for peaceful change. Christians must go still farther. They must promote the reconciliation of the nations; they must work for the establishment of justice based on a rule of law, so that a responsible society, grounded in truth, may be possible.

28. For the Christian the ecumenical fellowship of the churches is evidence of progress towards this goal, and of God's use of the Christian Church as one of the foundation stones of world order. Further, by its supra-national character the Church also provides the point of meeting where the search for the truth as it is in Christ in its bearing on all the problems of human society may be pursued in faith and hope as well as in love's creative power.

III. What Nations Owe to One Another

29. The world community has become interdependent. The status of hitherto dependent people has undergone radical change, resulting in entirely new relationships between them and the rest of the world. The older types of colonialism and imperialism are surely dying out, but new forms of imperialism call for vigilance.

30. Nationalism in many countries has been a creative force and has enabled people to win and preserve their freedom; but it displays a tendency to become an end in itself. The self-sufficient attitude of nationalism is an obstacle to international co-operation.

31. The exploitation of one people by another, in any form, is evil and unjustifiable. Those countries which administer non-self-governing territories have a special obligation so to promote the educational, economic, social and political advancement of dependent peoples, that they may be enabled to play their full part in the international community.

32. We welcome the development of international responsibility in place of old colonialism, and the principle of international study and review, exemplified by the United Nations Trusteeship System. While this System is open to abuse, the progress made by Trust Territories under it testifies to its value. Administering authorities should consider placing their non-self-governing territories not yet ready for self-government or independence under the Trusteeship System.

33. The legitimate right of the self-determination of peoples must be recognized. Specific assurance of independence or self-government should be given and administering authorities should take reasonable risks in speeding progress toward this goal.

34. In the new context of our age, relations between peoples hitherto "subject" and "ruling" should be one of partnership and

co-operation. Countries enjoying new political freedom urgently need economic and technical help.

35. The response of more developed countries through expanded international programmes of technical assistance is one of the brightest pages of recent history; but the effort thus far has been small in comparison with the needs of the less developed countries and the resources of those more developed. A progressively sustained effort will for a long time be required and involves mutual responsibilities and benefits which challenge all who co-operate in such endeavours.

36. Many of the politically new nations are old nations with centuries of culture and civilization behind them. In this partnership of sharing they have their own distinctive contribution to make. But for this partnership to be fruitful there is required in nations "young" or "old" a readiness always to learn from one another.

IV. The United Nations and World Community

37. Despite the critical post-war tensions which have divided the international community, the United Nations has made significant contributions to order and justice. Its recurrent meetings have provided opportunities for continuing diplomatic contacts and for peaceful settlement. Major international problems have been brought before the forum of world public opinion in the U.N. General Assembly. An historic Universal Declaration of Human Rights has provided an international standard. In the Expanded Technical Assistance Programme the U.N. and Specialized Agencies have served as a centre for harmonizing the actions of states for human welfare.

38. Yet the weaknesses of the United Nations, which reflect the divisions within the international community, are also clear. Little or no progress has been made toward world disarmament or the creation of an international police force. On many other questions effective action has been frustrated by the deadlocks of the cold war. Too often issues have been viewed solely on the basis of narrow self-interest, rather than on the basis of merit. While the United Nations stands and grows, the international crisis deepens.

39. The brief history of the United Nations has been one of growth and development and if it is to live it must continue to

grow. The United Nations can become more comprehensive in its membership. The world organization can grow through more loyal and responsible use of the charter provisions by the members. At many points charter commitments are neglected or by-passed through unilateral action. Again, the U.N. can grow through the evolution of powers inherent in the Charter or delegated to it by common consent.

40. A further method by which the United Nations can develop is through revision of the Charter. While the common moral convictions essential for major improvement of the Charter are not now apparent, it is important that a dynamic concept of the world organization be kept alive and that the U.N. structure be subjected to periodic review. After taking into due consideration the experience and accomplishments of the U.N. and the U.N.'s growth and development under the present Charter, a review conference should try to determine the organic and structural requirements of the U.N. for carrying out programmes dealing with universal enforceable disarmament, human rights, greatly expanded technical assistance, and more rapid development of self-government in colonial areas. On the basis of its study, if a review conference finds charter changes to be advisable and necessary, the appropriate charter amendments can then be recommended for ratification by the nations.

41. A related issue is the continued development of regional organizations for collective self-defence and the pursuit of common interests. The Council of Europe and the Organization of American States provide the major examples. In all such regional arrangements, including those existing arrangements which have not been formally announced, there are potential benefits and potential dangers.

42. Regional groupings notably those for economic and cultural co-operation are a natural reflection of the cultural, economic and historical ties which link the nations of a given area in a regional community. They also reflect in part the failure of the nations to organize a sure global security through the U.N. Despite the potential danger to international peace and security seen in regional associations, they have a valid place in a co-operative world order, provided:—

(a) They are clearly defensive in character and military actions are subject to collective decision;

(*b*) They are subordinate to and reinforce the aims of the Charter of the United Nations;

(*c*) They serve the genuine mutual interests and needs of the peoples of the region.

43. Regional associations which meet these requirements can strengthen the world organization by reducing threats to peace and by lessening the number of international questions thrust before the world forum. Christians have an obligation to measure regional groupings by the interests of the world community.

44. One of the fundamental principles of international community in the U.N. Charter is that of the "sovereign" equality of states, great and small. This principle is again and again in danger of being disregarded by the Great Powers, not merely through efforts to dominate, but also through efforts to impose a type of organization on the community of nations. Christians, therefore, should stand firmly for the respect and protection of the essential rights of smaller nations.

V. The Protection of Human Rights

45. A call for the protection of human rights is all the more insistent in this age when, in various parts of the world, totalitarianism—based on ideologies sometimes atheistic and sometimes under the guise of religion—oppresses the freedom of men and of institutions and denies those God-given rights which are His will for all men. A system of justice which defends the rights and dignity of the human person is fundamental. Denials of religious freedom and other rights against which the churches have repeatedly raised voices of protest, are signs of the moral sickness of the world. The struggle for the essential freedoms of man as defined in the Universal Declaration of Human Rights is the struggle for peace. The World Council of Churches' current study and support of the right of conscientious objection, as authorized by the Central Committee in 1951, is a necessary step in the direction of national and international action for its protection. Meanwhile, as far as possible the churches should plead for just judgment and humane treatment of those who know themselves called to this personal witness for peace.

46. The proclamation of international standards in the Declaration of Human Rights, and efforts to provide international

safeguards through Covenants on Human Rights with effective implementation reflect an awakening international conscience.

47. The importance of attempts to secure international legal safeguards for human rights is not diminished by the obstacles. The fundamental concern of the churches, however, is to promote mutually recognized rights in the ethos and practices of society. International covenants offer a valuable means to this end, but there are limits to what can be achieved through such means. International law is more often the fruit than the source of community. To build a strong defence of human rights requires vigorous, broad and persistent educational efforts. Christian education can make an important contribution here.

48. The love of God for man lays upon the Christian conscience a special measure of responsibility for the care of those who are the victims of world disorder. By governmental action and by international co-operation, as well as by the direct effort of the churches, measures should be taken for the relief of refugees, migrants, still un-repatriated prisoners, civil and military, and similar groups of suffering and oppressed men and women, whatever their origin, race or religion. More important still than their relief is a just and permanent solution of their problem.

VI. TOWARDS AN INTERNATIONAL ETHOS

49. Underlying the more obvious barriers to a genuine world community is the lack of a common foundation of moral principles. At the root of the most stubborn conflicts is the failure of governments and peoples to treasure any common set of guiding principles. Attempted settlements involving differing ideologies are essentially unstable and tend to produce new frictions, not only because of political differences but also because of underlying differences as to moral values.

50. The world of nations desperately needs an international ethos to provide a sound groundwork for the development of international law and institutions. This requires not only attempts to find wider areas of common moral understanding, but also efforts to bring the guiding principles of international life into greater harmony with God's will. Christians should urge statesmen to devote more attention to this fundamental task. In order to do this with authority Christians must be clear in their own

understanding of the essential principles. This can be done only by sustained study. Tentatively, we advance the following considerations:

(*a*) All power carries responsibility and all nations are trustees of power which should be used for the common good.

(*b*) All nations are subject to moral law, and should strive to abide by the accepted principles of international law, to develop this law, and to enforce it through common actions.

(*c*) All nations should honour their pledged word and international agreements into which they have entered.

(*d*) No nation in an international dispute has the right to be sole judge in its own cause or to resort to war to advance its policies, but should seek to settle disputes by direct negotiation or by submitting them to conciliation, arbitration or judicial settlement.

(*e*) All nations have a moral obligation to ensure universal security and to this end should support measures designed to deny victory to a declared aggressor.

(*f*) All nations should recognize and safeguard the inherent dignity, worth and essential rights of the human person, without distinction as to race, sex, language or religion.

(*g*) Each nation should recognize the rights of every other nation, which observes such standards, to live by and proclaim its own political and social beliefs, provided that it does not seek by coercion, threat, infiltration or deception to impose these on other nations.

(*h*) All nations should recognize an obligation to share their scientific and technical skills with peoples in less developed regions, and to help the victims of disaster in other lands.

(*i*) All nations should strive to develop cordial relations with their neighbours, encourage friendly cultural and commercial dealings and join in creative international efforts for human welfare.

51. The churches must, therefore, see in the international sphere a field of obedience to Jesus Christ. They cannot agree that it falls outside the range of His sovereignty or the scope of the moral law. Their first duty is to fulfil their calling to manifest the Kingdom of God among men. Their fellowship must be a bond of union among all, a bond both more patient and more resistant than any other. The Church must seek to be the kind of community which God wishes the world to become. By virtue of its calling it must act as a redemptive suffering fellowship in the form

and manner of its Lord Jesus Christ. Within it differences of sex, class, nation, colour or race are to become a source of mutual enrichment, and not of rivalry or antagonism. Its members must rise above the limitations of nationalism to a truly ecumenical outlook. It must carry into the turmoil of international relations the real possibility of the reconciliation of all races, nationalities and classes in the love of Christ. It must witness to the creative power of forgiveness and spiritual renewal.

52. All these things the churches must do as an essential part of their evangelistic task. But they can never be content with words. Through the life, service and sacrifice of their members, they must make their contribution to justice and peace, to the improvement of human conditions and to the care of the needy and of the refugee. They must serve humbly the needs of the less developed peoples. In persecution and oppression they still can witness to the spiritual freedom which their members enjoy, and which no human authority can take away. Thus they will testify, both by deed and word, to the hope which Jesus Christ has brought to the world.

VII. THE CHURCHES AND SPECIFIC INTERNATIONAL TENSIONS

53. Because this statement has painted a tempestuous scene with a broad brush it must not be assumed that the churches are indifferent to particular international tensions. The reverse is the truth. The churches' work is likely to be effective only when they direct themselves to the causes of friction and to friction itself as, when and where they arise.

54. Even to agree on a limited list of places of friction would be almost impossible. They are very numerous and those that seem trivial to some loom up as vital to others. And these questions are often so complex and in the course of long negotiation vary their character so considerably that it would be difficult for the Assembly to speak confidently and unanimously about them. Further, agreed pronouncement by the Assembly on particular issues would almost certainly have to be in broad and general terms. But international conflicts, large and small, do not yield to broad generalizations.

55. It is for this among other reasons that the churches and bodies in the World Council of Churches and the International

Missionary Council have established the Churches' Commission on International Affairs to give heed to these issues. It is therefore important that councils, federations and groups of churches should develop and make full use of their own committees or commissions on international affairs. In this way they may express the minds of the churches on international relations, increase their influence in the search for positive solutions, and seek to build up an enlightened and effective Christian public opinion on international affairs.

DISCUSSION ON THE REPORT ON
INTERNATIONAL RELATIONS

Sir Kenneth Grubb, in moving reception of the report, drew attention to the omission of reference to specific "sore points" in the modern world. He said that if one were included all would have to be included. These points had been remitted to the C.C.I.A. for continued attention. The second part of the report dealt with nuclear weapons. He paid tribute to the spirit and temper of pacifist friends during discussions on this subject. The middle parts of the report dealt with "living together" in a time of uneasy peace.

A supplementary appeal to the nations had been drafted to cover much the same ground as Part II of the Section's report, but it would be presented separately to the Assembly.

The content of the Section's report could be sub-divided into:—

1. An analysis of the crisis;
2. Immediate practical measures;
3. Foundations for a happier order tomorrow.

Dr. Surjit Singh expressed deep sympathy with the whole report with the exception of Part VII, on which he deferred comment.

Dr. Bosley asked whether the concern by some members of the Assembly had really been made explicit in the report. He advocated insertion in paragraph 11 of the words "the Christian churches confirm that mass destruction of civil populations must be condemned as evil for whatever reason and whatever the means employed."

Sir Kenneth Grubb said acceptance did not seem possible in view of the difficulty in defining an open city. The drafters were willing to find a form of words.

Dr. Devadutt suggested that a pledge not to use atomic and other weapons against the territory or independence of other states might be misinterpreted. Should any such means sometimes be used, for instance, to end unlawful occupations?

Sir Kenneth Grubb said that the reference was to peace time and the deletion of the words from "against" onwards in paragraph 15, as suggested by Dr. Devadutt could not be accepted.

Dr. Devadutt's amendment was then put and lost.

Dr. ten Doornkaat, speaking of paragraph 45, said that a clearer statement of the human rights of conscientious objectors was required. The churches should seek justice for conscientious objectors because their stand is based on testimony as well as principle. The strong words spoken at Oxford and Amsterdam should be strengthened.

Sir Kenneth Grubb accepted the amendment in substance.

Dr. Surjit Singh expressed opposition to paragraphs 49 and 50. The proposed basis of an international ethos as set out here was sub-Christian. The role of the Church as suffering servant and redemptive remnant should be stressed.

Dr. George Thomas suggested that sub-section 5 should include a word to indicate that all nations are morally bound to resist aggression.

The sense of the proposed change was accepted.

Mr. Urwin had put forward, in his absence, a suggestion that in the last sentence of the report it should be indicated that the public opinion to be influenced was *Christian* public opinion.

Dr. Kagawa was granted leave to speak as a consultant, and made three points:

1. The membership of the United Nations should be extended with a Charter as under revision;

2. Inter-Christian co-operative unions are needed;

3. Atomic energy is harmful to our enemies and ourselves and negotiations should take place concerning destruction of atomic weapons.

Sir Kenneth Grubb, in reply, said that:

1. Charter revision was already mentioned as desirable;

2. Christian co-operative unions were a matter for Section III rather than Section IV;

3. The Section was not able to modify statements concerning atomic weapons.

The motion for the reception and commendation of the report as amended was put and adopted.

RESOLUTIONS ON INTERNATIONAL AFFAIRS

Adopted by the Assembly
Note: See also Report of the Committee on the Department of Inter-Church Aid, page 233.

RESOLUTION I

AN APPEAL FROM THE WORLD COUNCIL OF CHURCHES

God is the God of justice and peace, and the Lord of history. He calls us all to repentance. It is in obedience to Him, and through the eyes of our Christian faith, that we look at the problems of this troubled world.

It is not our purpose in the present statement to pass judgment on past actions. We seek rather to contribute to a new spiritual climate in which a fresh start can be made by all governments and peoples.

The world is so broken up and divided that international agreement seems remote at the moment. Everywhere fear and mistrust prevail. The very possibility of good-neighbourly relations between nations is denied.

We believe that there are two conditions of crucial importance which must be met, if catastrophe is to be avoided:

1. The prohibition of all weapons of mass destruction; including atomic and hydrogen bombs, with provision for international inspection and control, such as would safeguard the security of all nations, together with the drastic reduction of all other armaments.

2. The certain assurance that no country will engage in or support aggressive or subversive acts in other countries.

We believe that a sound international order is possible only to the extent that peace, justice, freedom and truth are assured.

We are convinced that peace will be gravely endangered so long as the armaments race continues, and so long as any nation seeks to extend its power by the threat or use of military force.

To meet the demands of justice, whether in a particular nation, or in the assistance of peoples in underdeveloped countries, is our moral duty. We recognize that progress in raising the standard of living in underdeveloped countries is discouragingly slow; and that increasing sacrifice on the part of richer nations is essential. Freedom means man's opportunity to realize his worth in God's sight, and to fulfil his God-given destiny. All nations have a duty to secure for their citizens the right to criticize or approve, as conscience dictates. Moreover fear and suspicion cannot be replaced by respect and trust unless powerful nations remove the yoke which now prevents other nations and peoples from freely determining their own government and form of society. Freedom and justice in their turn depend upon the steady proclamation of truth. False propaganda, whether to defend a national policy or to criticize the practice of another government will increase international tension and may contribute to war.

The World Council of Churches bears witness to Christ as the Hope of the World. In the strength of that hope, and impelled by the desire to help in the relief of present tensions, it makes the following appeal:—

1. We appeal to the governments and the peoples to continue to speak to one another, to avoid rancour and malice, and to look for ways by which fear and suspicion may be removed.

2. We appeal to the governments and the peoples also to devote their strength and their resources to meeting the peaceful needs of the citizens of their countries, and above all to a determined common effort to secure a decent standard of living among poorer and underdeveloped countries.

3. We appeal to the statesmen and the leaders of public opinion and the press to refrain from words and actions which are designed to inflame enmity and hatred.

4. We appeal to the representatives of the churches in those countries between which tension exists to visit one another, so that they may gain a better understanding of one another, and of the countries in which they live, and thus strengthen the bonds of fellowship, and promote the reconciliation of the nations.

5. We appeal to the churches to bid their members recognize their political responsibilities, and also to ask Christian technicians and administrators to find a vocation in the service of U.N. Agencies engaged in meeting the needs of economically

and technically underdeveloped countries, thus bringing a Christian temper of love and understanding to bear upon the immensely difficult task of mutual assistance in the encounter of different cultures.

6. We appeal to all members of all churches to unite in a common ministry of reconciliation in proclaiming Christ as the Hope of the World, in intercession for one another, and in mutual service.

7. Finally, we call upon all Christians everywhere to join in prayer to Almighty God, that He will guide the governments and the peoples in the ways of justice and peace.

RESOLUTION II

That the Central Committee be requested to appoint a delegation or delegations (i) to communicate the foregoing statement to the member churches of the World Council of Churches, (ii) to take such steps as seem most suitable with a view to the presentation of the same statement to the churches not related to the World Council of Churches, including the churches in U.S.S.R. and in other lands, (iii) to invite these churches to consider ways in which they might communicate the statement to the governments of their countries.

RESOLUTION III

The World Council of Churches, at its Second Assembly in August 1954, records its concern and sorrow over the continuing sufferings and disabilities of fellow Christians in many parts of the world.

It knows that the Assembly is incomplete because the World Council cannot communicate with many churches over whose life and testimony a veil of silence has been forcibly drawn. We assure these fellow Christians and those who stand with them of our prayers and we earnestly look forward to the day of freedom and reunion.

Christians must stand together with all who, in the struggle for freedom, suffer pain and trial. We thank God for the steadfastness of our fellow Christians who, in trial and tribulation, gave so much—even their lives—for Christ's sake and for ours, and we humbly pray that we may not be unworthy of their sacrifice.

The Assembly also deeply regrets that in certain countries from which information can be gathered with reasonable accuracy, Christians are suffering many disabilities and even violence; and human rights and liberties, albeit acknowledged in official protestations, have in practice been denied.

To all such the Assembly extends the assurance of the prayers of its member churches, that those who are absent from its fellowship may be sustained by the presence of Christ. The World Council will continue to work for a new day of fellowship and liberty of witness.

We thank God that His Church is worthy to follow its Lord in suffering.

We rejoice—with our brethren who suffer in the faith—in that fellowship in Christ which nobody and nothing can destroy. We know that their fidelity and ours will prevail.

RESOLUTION IV

Having received representations regarding a number of specific and serious cases of religious persecution and repression, this Assembly of the World Council of Churches reaffirms previous declarations regarding religious liberty and expresses its grave concern regarding the situation in a number of lands and continents. It also calls attention to the statement on religious freedom in the United Nations' Declaration of Human Rights. The Assembly instructs its officers and the Commission of the Churches on International Affairs to continue to use every effort in representations to the governments concerned and, where they are involved, the religious authorities; and appeals to its member churches to make direct representations in certain cases and to continue in prayer for those suffering from persecution and repression.

DISCUSSION OF RESOLUTIONS ON INTERNATIONAL AFFAIRS

Sir Kenneth Grubb introduced the resolutions of the Section, and drew attention to the appeal to the nations prepared by a sub-committee under the guidance of the Bishop of Chichester. He moved the reception and adoption of this document.

The Bishop of Chichester explained the desire of the Section that some clear statement should emanate from the Assembly in view of the disturbed state of the world. He explained that Dr.

Malik, Dr. Sayre, M. Philippe Maury, Mr. Potter, and Dr. Nolde had been with him in its drafting.

Bishop Sobrepena proposed an insertion appealing to leaders of Christian organizations to resist undue religious discrimination and persecution.

Sir Kenneth Grubb said the Section believed such an addition would disturb the unity of the Appeal. Attention might be given to improving the third resolution to be put forward by the Section to incorporate such a concern.

Professor Alivisatos sought inclusion of material on human rights and more particularly the right of self-determination.

Pastor Niemöller suggested that the implication that the arms race would continue could paralyse effective action for peace. He asked that certain words in the first paragraph read "Peace will be utterly endangered."

Sir Kenneth Grubb asked whether "seriously endangered" was acceptable.

Pastor Niemöller said it was.

Bishop Ward asked why the statement specifically included reference to approaching the U.S.S.R. Could the reference be modified to allude to all lands?

Sir Kenneth Grubb indicated that the Drafting Committee would be opposed.

Dr. Zigler expressed appreciation of the statement on behalf of the Church of the Brethren. He sought closer definition of the words "mutual service" with a view to calling on youth to give their lives for their fellows.

Sir Kenneth Grubb said that the Drafting Committee wished to insert a qualification concerning international control of nuclear energy, to read "with provision for international inspection and control such as would safeguard the security of all nations."

The Assembly adopted the addition.

The Bishop of Chichester expressed the hope that the Assembly would not agree to Professor Alivisatos' proposed amendment. There was already sufficient reference in the report of the Section to human rights and self-determination. The proposed addition would introduce a somewhat alien note into a part of the statement where churches were asked to visit one another.

Professor Alivisatos' amendment was then put and lost.

Resolutions I and II from the Section were then adopted.

Bishop Smemo, speaking to the third resolution, said that it did not deal enough with human suffering. A direct outspoken word of encouragement to suffering Christian brethren was necessary. He therefore moved a stronger alternative resolution.

Dr. Poling, a fraternal delegate, spoke in support of the resolution and for the "dead, imprisoned and missing."

Bishop Sobrepena agreed with Bishop Smemo and urged that the insertion he had pressed earlier be made in the third resolution.

Pastor Maury expressed preference for the first formulation.

Mr. Coles wished to strengthen the third paragraph of the resolution by a reference to persecution undertaken by "tyrannical churches."

Bishop Barbieri urged that after the reference to countries where persecution was rife, Spain and Columbia be specified.

The proposals of Bishop Sobrepena, Mr. Coles and Bishop Barbieri were all put and lost.

Dr. Visser 't Hooft urged that all suggestions be referred back to the Drafting Committee with power to act.

The suggestion was adopted, and the resolution accepted on this understanding.

THE REPORT OF SECTION V

INTERGROUP RELATIONS: THE CHURCHES AMID RACIAL AND ETHNIC TENSIONS

Received by the Assembly and commended to the Churches for study and appropriate action, with the request that the Churches report the results of their study and action to the Central Committee.

Note: Both the Report of the Section and the Resolutions from the Section were received by the Assembly without substantive debate. A statement by delegates from the Dutch Reformed Church in South Africa appears on p. 328.

I. THE STATE OF THE WORLD

1. Everywhere there is restlessness in the world. This is due in great part to the hunger of millions of people for status and

recognition, for a meaning for both life and work, and for a fuller share of the fruits of the earth.

2. The impact of technically advanced civilization on all parts of the world has affected every country, for good or ill. Now a new phase has been entered, with the struggle of disadvantaged peoples of many races to participate fully in the opportunities and responsibilities of society.

3. While the advance and emancipation of any people, and the removal of any deprivation under which men, women and children have suffered, are causes of rejoicing for any Christian, impending events are so massive and their approach so swift and the new weapons of war so terrible, that fear and anxiety afflict us all.

4. The hatreds, jealousies and suspicions with which the world has always been afflicted are deepened by racial prejudices and fears, rooted in the sinful human heart and entrenched in law and custom. In some situations men come to accept race conflict as inevitable and lose hope of peaceful solution.

II. The Hope of the World

5. Yet it is the nature of men to seek always for some new ground of hope. Some believe that the solution of the world's racial problems lies in the economic and political re-ordering of society; others that it lies in the pursuit and use of knowledge; others that man must rid himself of dependence on some Greater Being, and look only to himself; others that their safety lies in the power of their race or class or nation.

6. Disadvantaged people have their special and individual hopes, that by education, the achievement of the franchise, and a higher standard of living, they will find the security which they seek, and that justice which is the right of every human being.

7. It is our Christian belief that our Lord is concerned for all just hopes of men but in Himself He offers the hope that transcends them all. The Bible teaches us that God is the Sovereign Creator of all men, and by Him they are sustained and have their being. When He made the world, He saw that it was good. But man by his sin—by his disobedience and pride and the lifting of his arm against his brother—has filled it with division and distrust.

8. What is the Christian hope in this disunity? It is Jesus Christ,

who revealed God as Father and who died for all men, reconciling them to God and to each other by His Cross. From every race and nation a new people of God is created, in which the power of the Spirit overcomes racial pride and fear. So far from being without hope or purpose, God's people now as new creatures are co-workers with Him, and are filled with joy, and assured His final victory.

9. So to us is given the gift of sharing in and working for the Kingdom even now. Assured that the final victory is Christ's, we can work actively, continually repentant and continually forgiven, for that reconciliation which we believe to be God's will.

III. THE CALLING OF THE CHURCH

10. This is the calling of the Church with regard to race, to witness within itself to the Kingship of Christ and the unity of His people, in Him transcending all diversity. Jesus Christ in His Incarnation and redemptive action restores this unity which from the beginning was God's design.

11. Their calling requires Christians to witness to the Kingship of Christ and the unity of all mankind, and to strive through social and political action to secure justice, freedom and peace for all, as a foretaste of that Kingdom into which the faithful shall be gathered.

12. All churches and Christians are involved, whether they recognize it or not, in the racial and ethnic tensions of the world. But it is in communities where segregation prevails that they face the plainest difficulties and the most challenging opportunities; for such segregation denies to those who are segregated their just and equal rights and results in deep injuries to the human spirit, suffered by offender and victim alike.

13. The great majority of Christian churches affiliated with the World Council have declared that physical separation within the Church on grounds of race is a denial of spiritual unity, and of the brotherhood of man. Yet such separations persist within these very churches, and we often seek to justify them on other grounds than race, because in our own hearts we know that separation solely on the grounds of race is abhorrent in the eyes of God.

14. We seek to justify such exclusion on the ground of difference of culture, or on the ground that a residential pattern of segregation necessitates it, or on the ground that the time is not

yet ripe. We even say that we are willing to abandon all separations, but must retain them because so many others are unwilling to abandon them. We often make use of the unregenerateness of the world to excuse our own.

15. The Church is called upon, therefore, to set aside such excuses and to declare God's will both in words and deeds. "Be not conformed to this world, but be ye transformed by the renewing of your mind, that ye may prove what is that good, and acceptable, and perfect, will of God." We believe it to be the will of God that such proof in word and deed now be given.

IV. Repentance and Obedience

16. Many churches and many Christians have striven to be obedient to God's will in matters of race; for every such obedience we give our thanks, both for God's power and His servants' faithfulness. Increasingly racial and ethnic barriers are breached in the life of the churches. But it is the most obedient who would best understand the need of all churches and Christians for deep repentance that they are so largely conformed to the world's compromises. This same world watches any denial of human brotherhood, and is not deceived. This is an especial time of testing for the faith that we all live and have our truest being in God the Father, whose children we are in Christ and whose redemptive love enables us to treasure all men as brothers.

17. But we need to repent of something far deeper than our disunity and our offences. We need to repent of our separation from God, from which these spring, and of our feeble grasp of the truth of the gospel. To us is given power to become the sons of God and to be every one members one of another.

18. True repentance is followed by a new assurance of God's power and a new obedience, and this new assurance fills Church and man with hope. Our faith is renewed that love is indeed God's power: churches and nations and men may rebel against it but never can prevail.

19. Therefore the problems of race, difficult as they are, insoluble as they sometimes appear to be, provide for Christians an opportunity for obedience, and for a deeper understanding that bond and free, Jew and Gentile, Greek and barbarian, people of every land and continent, are all one in Christ.

20. If Christian obedience leads to suffering, that is part of the price. For the Lord of all was in Gethsemane in an agony, and His sweat was as it were great drops of blood falling down to the ground; but He endured the cross, despising the shame, for the joy that was set before Him.

21. When we are given Christian insight the whole pattern of racial discrimination is seen as an unutterable offence against God, to be endured no longer, so that the very stones cry out. In such moments we understand more fully the meaning of the gospel, and the duty of both Church and Christian.

V. THE TASK OF THE CHURCHES[1]

22. Racial and ethnic fears, hates and prejudices are more than social problems with whose existence we must reckon; they are sins against God and His commandments that the gospel alone can cure. To the Church has been committed the preaching of the gospel; to proclaim "the healing of the nations" through Christ is verily her task. The gospel has a power of its own, which manifests itself despite the shortcomings of the churches.

23. It is, however, only when the churches come to Christ in penitence and obedience, and receive from Him His cleansing, that they receive from Him authority to proclaim His will with the voice of prophecy. Never should they cease to search themselves and to declare and repent their disobedience, especially in those multi-racial countries where they proclaim the noblest principles, yet are in their own practice largely conformed to the principles of this world. Equally is it the duty of those few churches which have given segregation the status of a principle, to search themselves continually whether their theology is not the child of fear, and meanwhile to test every application of segregation by the standard of Christian love.

24. The churches have this two-fold duty, to obey and to proclaim the word of judgment, to repent and to call to repentance. It is their task to challenge the conscience of society; if there is no tension between the church and society, then either the

[1] This section of our report is both complementary and supplementary to Chapter IV of the *Ecumenical Survey on Intergroup Relations*. In considering the task of the churches, we would begin by calling attention to Section C in that chapter, in which there is set out an illustrative list of specific activities in which churches may engage.

society is regenerate or the church is conformed. Yet it also has a duty to create and to keep open every possible line of communication between people, between political opponents, between people of differing views, cultures, races, languages, between the conservative and the venturesome.

25. The churches have a special duty toward those of their members who feel called to challenge actively the conscience of society, and who thus offend against custom, and incur loneliness and suffering. It is a great duty of the Church to offer its love and fellowship, and even its admonition in the light of the gospel, to all who strive to be obedient whatever the world's opinion. It is chastening to remember how often both churches and parents have been estranged from their children who tried in obedience to do what they were taught.

26. The duty of the Church is not accomplished when it has given its support to its more adventurous sons and daughters. It also has a duty to alert all its members to the nature and scope of their responsibilities, to help them to carry out their duties, and to stand by them when they do. So would the frequent loneliness of Christian action be tempered, the unity of Christian fellowship affirmed, and its members made to feel not helpless, but confident in the face of great events. It is hard to overestimate the importance of this comforting and strengthening role of the Church.

27. As part of its task of challenging the conscience of society, it is the duty of the Church to protest against any law or arrangement that is unjust to any human being or which would make Christian fellowship impossible, or would prevent the Christian from practising his vocation. Some of its members may feel bound to disobey such law. The Church does not contemplate lightly any breaking of the law, but it recognizes the duty of a Christian to do so when he feels that he has reached that point where the honour and glory of God command him to obey God rather than man. In so doing, the Church must point out the possible consequences of such action and the consequent necessity for spiritual discipline according to the gospel.

28. The Church of Christ cannot approve of any law which discriminates on grounds of race, which restricts the opportunity of any person to acquire education to prepare himself for his vocation, to procure or to practise employment in his vocation, or in any other way curtails his exercise of the full rights and

responsibilities of citizenship and of sharing in the responsibilities and duties of government. While it can find in the Bible no clear justification or condemnation of intermarriage, but only a discussion of the duties of the faithful in marriage with partners of other religions, it cannot approve any law against racial or ethnic intermarriage, for Christian marriage involves primarily a union of two individuals before God which goes beyond the jurisdiction of the state or of culture.

29. A minister of the Church should advise young people, when preparing them for the grave responsibilities of intermarriage, both of the potential richness of such marriages and of the painful consequences in some situations, which consequences are often caused by the hardness of men's hearts and by cultural differences. There is no evidence that the children of such marriages are inherently inferior, and any treatment of them as such should be condemned.

30. The churches are not alone in their concern for the welfare of society and the need for resolving the tensions within it between racial and ethnic groups. Many international agencies are at work in this field and in nearly every country there are governmental, civic and private bodies that are devotedly using their resources—often including expert knowledge—in the solution of these problems. It is impossible to generalize on the nature and scope of the churches' co-operation with these agencies. Amongst them there are those which accuse the churches and their members of being preachers of love, but lukewarm in their passion for justice, slow in action, and afraid of public opinion and unpleasant consequences. The courage of some of these bodies, and the success of some of their experiments, often put the churches to shame. On the other hand some churches feel that co-operation with these bodies is impossible because of their political or other views. Where such co-operation seems impossible, despite a common aim, the churches should take action of their own. Every congregation should concern itself with action in this field of racial and ethnic tensions in society, seeking continually opportunities to make its contribution.

31. What good grounds for hope there are in the ecumenical movement that gives to our divided churches an opportunity to speak with more certain voice on the problems of the world, and to exercise greater influence in its affairs. In a world in which

national and international problems are complicated by the facts of race and colour, there are great grounds of hope in the existence of Christians of every nation whose supreme loyalty is to Christ their Lord. A great duty lies upon us all to reject utterly any claims of racialism or nationalism that are incompatible with our faith, to extend fellowship to those at whose hands we may have suffered, and to forget hurts of the past. Out of such love and generosity, new hope can be born.

32. And what hope there is in the existence of so many Christians amongst peoples whose whole way of life was changed by the expansion of western civilization into their countries! In the very situations in which some of the greatest tensions exist, they will help their fellow Christians, in humble obedience to God, to form a right judgment upon problems in which judgment has hitherto been so confused.

33. We are concerned here with our hopes for the peace and unity of all mankind, but what greater hope there would be if only our Christian unity were achieved, a unity transcending the ethnic and racial differences of all believers. That is our urgent and immediate task; when it is accomplished how great the further contribution that we might make.

34. Has any greater challenge ever been presented to the Church? If not, then no greater opportunity has ever been offered it. And this opportunity is, simply, to be the creative instrument of our God of love in a restless and changing world and the faithful servant of our Lord who is its hope.

RESOLUTIONS ON INTERGROUP RELATIONS

Adopted by the Assembly

RESOLUTION I

The Second Assembly of the World Council of Churches declares its conviction that any form of segregation based on race, colour or ethnic origin is contrary to the gospel, and is incompatible with the Christian doctrine of man and with the nature of the Church of Christ. The Assembly urges the churches within its membership to renounce all forms of segregation or discrimination and to work for their abolition within their own life and within society.

In doing so the Assembly is painfully aware that, in the realities of the contemporary world, many churches find themselves confronted by historical, political, social and economic circumstances which may make the immediate achievement of this objective extremely difficult. But under God the fellowship of the ecumenical movement is such as to offer to these churches the strength and encouragement to help them and individuals within them to overcome these difficulties with the courage given by faith, and with the desire to testify ever more faithfully to our Master.

From its very beginning the ecumenical movement by its very nature has been committed to a form of fellowship in which there is no segregation or discrimination. The Assembly of the World Council of Churches rejoices in this fact and confirms this practice as the established policy of the Council.

RESOLUTION II

This Second Assembly of the World Council of Churches recognizes that one of the major problems of social justice in situations involving racial and ethnic tensions is that of securing for all the opportunities for the free exercise of responsible citizenship and for effective participation by way of franchise in both local and central government activity. It commends this matter to the attention of all Christian people for such action as, under God, they may be led to take in order to secure the solution of this problem.

RESOLUTION III

While the questions of the Christian approach to the Jews and of anti-semitism present certain problems in the realm of racial and ethnic tensions, this Section was, by its terms of reference, precluded from giving attention to them. It nevertheless reaffirms that anti-semitic prejudice is incompatible with Christian faith, and it recommends to the Central Committee that the study of anti-semitism be pressed forward in conjunction with the International Committee on the Christian Approach to the Jews.

RESOLUTION IV

The Second Assembly recommends to the Central Committee that, in consultation with the International Missionary Council, it make structural provision for an organization, preferably a department, giving assistance to the constituent churches in their efforts to bring the gospel to bear more effectively upon relations between racial and ethnic groups. Such organization should provide leadership and assistance not only in (*a*) continuing study of the problems of inter-group relations, especially of racial and ethnic tensions; (*b*) exchanging information on the matter of racial and ethnic groups and on the positions and work of the churches; and (*c*) producing and distributing reports and educational materials to increase concern and understanding with regard to these matters in the constituency of the Council; but should also be the means whereby the various contributions of the rich cultural heritages of the groups within the Council's constituency may stengthen the life and witness of all the churches and of this Council as a whole.

THE REPORT OF SECTION VI

THE LAITY:
THE CHRISTIAN IN HIS VOCATION

Received by the Assembly and commended to the Churches for study and appropriate action, with the request that the Churches report the results of their study and action to the Central Committee.

I. THE MINISTRY OF THE LAITY

1. The title of this report is here taken to signify Christian vocation in the sphere of daily work. The Assembly of the World Council of Churches at Amsterdam in 1948 declared: "Only by the witness of a spiritually intelligent and active laity can the Church meet the modern world in its actual perplexities and life situations. Since one of the hard facts of the present time is that millions of people think of the Church as floating above the modern world and entirely out of touch with it, the importance of this simple pronouncement cannot easily be overestimated." Since 1948 much has been done by the churches and by pioneering groups within them to rediscover the role of the laity as the Church's representatives in the world. In different lands an

awakening sense of the responsibility of the laity is attested by such developments as the Kirchentag, Evangelical Academies, the Christian Frontier, the "Christian and his Daily Work" movement, the concern for Christian stewardship, Aktines, Zoe and many similar enterprises.

2. Clergy and laity belong together in the Church; if the Church is to perform her mission in the world, they need each other. The growing emphasis in many parts of the world upon the function of the laity since the Amsterdam Assembly is not to be understood as an attempt to secure for the laity some larger place or recognition in the Church, nor yet as merely a means to supplement an overburdened and understaffed ordained ministry. It springs from the rediscovery of the true nature of the Church as the People of God. The word "laity" must not be understood in a merely negative way as meaning those church members who are not clergy. Though not yet fully articulated, a more positive understanding of the ministry of the laity is gaining acceptance. The phrase "the ministry of the laity" expresses the privilege of the whole Church to share in Christ's ministry to the world. We must understand anew the implications of the fact that we are all baptized, that, as Christ came to minister, so must all Christians become ministers of His saving purpose according to the particular gift of the Spirit which each has received, as messengers of the hope revealed in Christ. Therefore in daily living and work the laity are not mere fragments of the Church who are scattered about in the world and who come together again for worship, instruction and specifically Christian fellowship on Sundays. They are the Church's representatives, no matter where they are. It is the laity who draw together work and worship; it is they who bridge the gulf between the Church and the world, and it is they who manifest in word and action the Lordship of Christ over that world which claims so much of their time and energy and labour. This, and not some new order or organization, is the ministry of the laity. They are called to it because they belong to the Church, although many do not yet know that they are thus called.

3. But no attempt is here made to find an unexceptionable definition of the term "laity." "Layman" and "laity" are used to indicate those members of the Church, both men and women, who earn their livelihood in a secular job and who therefore spend most of their waking hours in a "worldly" occupation (not

excluding housewives). This is what distinguishes them in a sociological sense from the clergy and from full-time church-workers. Accordingly, the theme of *work* is prominent in this discussion, not because it is the only aspect of life in this world, but because it is a very important one and one which has not received from the churches the attention it deserves, although some important attempts to redress this situation have been made. God calls the whole Church to a life of faith, obedience, service and worship; this is the meaning of Christian vocation in the teaching of the New Testament. Every Christian has a vocation in this biblical sense. In modern usage, however, the term is frequently employed to mean "occupation" or "profession"; and, though we cannot prevent this secular use of a great biblical word, we shall here use "vocation" in the Christian meaning of God's call which comes to each member of His household, the Church. The principal object of this discussion is, therefore, to make clear the true meaning of Christian vocation in all the occupations or professions in which Christian lay-folk engage.

II. THE PRESENT SITUATION:
CHRISTIAN FAITH AND DAILY WORK

4. Today many people are asking whether Christianity has any relevance to their daily work. They feel that there is a gulf between the Church and its worship and their workaday lives. Both Christians and non-Christians are aware of this gulf and are concerned with it. It would appear that in comparison with the Church's effort to teach the application of the gospel to the life of the family and to personal relations, the effort to apply the gospel to the world of work has been relatively slight. The following reasons may be mentioned as accounting for the gulf that seems to exist between the faith and worship of many lay people and the work which they do during the week:—

(*a*) The old local community in which men used to work and spend their leisure, make their homes and offer their worship has in many places disappeared as a result of industrialization. Many do little more than sleep in their "parish," while they spend their working hours, and often their leisure also, in another environment. It is small wonder that the clergy have little contact with their parishioners at work and know little of the conditions, stresses and fellowship of the working group. Many people no longer worship with their work-fellows but with a quite different group. Unless the Church is embodied in the laity who know Christ as the hope of the world, the parish has little chance of coming into direct contact with the world of work.

(b) In lands which were once "Christendom," the Church through its clergy controlled great areas of human life which today stand altogether outside the Church's realm. The old order cannot, and many Christians would say should not, be restored; nevertheless, the resultant separation of Church and world has made it difficult for many people to see the relation between the two. Because they do not understand their ministry as laity, they are often misled into narrowly religious ways or else are carried into an unconscious acceptance of secular viewpoints. There are often no visible distinctions between the Christian's hopes and purposes and his work and those of unbelievers.

(c) The gulf is widened when current evaluation of different kinds of work is accepted by Christians. Thus academic or highly skilled work is over-valued, despite the fact that from a Christian standpoint the most menial work possesses a high dignity; and this still happens even in a day in which society itself is in many lands overthrowing this outdated scale of values. In some parts of the world Christians who have received a higher education, when they cannot find the kind of work which they accept, will refuse other forms of work out of a defective sense of the true dignity of work. On this subject the Church should have much to teach to its own members.

(d) Though it is right to stress the importance of work as God's ordinance for human life, it happens in some places that an idol is made out of work. Work is not the whole of life, and when men make it their chief object in living, they are prevented from coming into right relationships with God and with their fellow-men.

(e) Certain inherited false views of work are still in some places effective in dividing the Church from the working world. There is a tendency in some sections of church life to be interested in man only as a soul to be saved without regard to his physical, mental and social welfare. Work is accordingly viewed only as a field for evangelism, a sphere of opportunity for personal witness. While, of course, the Christian layman will miss no suitable occasion for bearing his testimony to the truth, he will regard his job as itself a matter in which he may directly serve his Lord. He will bear witness not only with his lips but by the quality of his workmanship; he will do his work as "unto his Master in heaven." A right understanding of the doctrine of Creation will remind him that God has given to man an awesome capacity to change the face of nature by his work; the wonderful achievements of man in his work must neither be ignored nor regarded as manifestations of his sinful pride.

III. The Christian Understanding of Work

5. This gulf between the Church and the life of the world can be bridged by those who have a Christian view of work. Certain aspects of work may be distinguished. In real life they overlap, and there is an element of each in all work.

(a) In one aspect work is the necessary ordering of daily life so that human needs may be fulfilled and as such work begins every morning in farm, factory and home. Such work can under good conditions become a source of profound satisfaction, but it has often become a drudgery which has led to futility and despair. In either case, and perhaps especially in the latter, Christians will find strength in the confident hope that this world will be consummated in the Kingdom of Christ. Obedience to the divine ordinance of work, doing one's work not as men-pleasers but as unto our Master in heaven, is a deliverance from the frustration of men's efforts; it bears the assurance that all honest toil derives meaning from this final consummation. Earthly success will not be the highest standard by which Christians judge their daily work. While they will want to insist that work receives a decent and just recompense, adequate for the worker and his dependants, Christians yet know that, whatever may be its reward in this life, their labour is not in vain in the Lord.

(b) Furthermore, all honest work is service rendered to society. Even amongst those who are not Christians, this truth is often recognized and is a source of gratification. When it is ignored and men think only of their rights and not of the service which they may render to the community, they violate their own nature; increased production or higher rewards become ends in themselves. When this happens the very rewards of work, greater wealth and increased leisure, are wasted in selfish enjoyments which bring no benefit to society at large. The relevance of the Christian teaching about service to one's neighbour is obvious here. Every human being, worthy or unworthy, becomes one's neighbour, and the Christian rejoices that in his work he may thus, however feebly, reflect the goodness of God, who causes His sun to shine and His rain to fall on the just and the unjust alike.

(c) Implanted in all men is a desire to create new forms of being and of value, and it is in the work of the very few that this power of creation is seen at the highest level. These are the individuals who transform the face of nature, change men's view of the world, and create new forms of value—the great philosophers, scientists, artists, poets, craftsmen, and so on. If we speak of the work of such men as creative, we must do so with the utmost circumspection, since it is all too easy for men in their pride to say to themselves, "ye shall be as gods." The biblical writers use the word "create" only of God, never of men, and they shrink from speaking of man's work as creative. This kind of work becomes demonic in its mighty achievements as soon as men trust in their own power to re-create the world by means of their scientific and technical skill. Yet, properly understood, man's spontaneous joy in the creative element in work is a sign of that freedom for which creation longs and of the truth that man shall subdue the earth and have dominion over it. That his freedom and dominion are achieved only in Christ and His "new creation" is the profound biblical truth to which all human "creative" aspiration points, even though men often do not know this.

6. God is not only the Creator of the world, He is also its Redeemer. The Church of Christ is the sphere of God's redemptive work, the new creation which is destined to renew the old. Every member of the Church, and therefore every layman, is called by God to witness to the reality of this new creation, that is to the redemptive work of Christ, in all his work and words and life; this is the meaning of Christian vocation in secular affairs. Every situation in daily life provides an opportunity to respond to this call of God. In this way the Church through the laity becomes the leaven in the lump, the constant sign at the centre of the world's affairs of the divine mercy and admonition.

7. Of course, serious conflicts will arise as Christians seek to relate their divine vocation to their daily work. Duties towards dependants, fellow-workers and society, frequently conflict with

one another. Work that is socially harmful or which thwarts the worker's sense of craftsmanship is an offence to the awakened conscience, as is also work that is relentless drudgery. The use of machinery has abolished much (though not all) back-breaking toil in industrialized areas. But it has as yet hardly affected vast agricultural communities in other parts of the world, where Christians also have to learn to serve God in their work, even while that work is still largely drudgery. Moreover, the use of machinery has created problems as well as solved them.

8. There is special need for Christian consideration of some of the new problems in a highly organized industrial society. For example, in such societies today the making of decisions passes into the hands of the few at the top of the organization, unless strenuous attempts are made to devolve control. Furthermore, many important decisions are not personal decisions based on personal responsibility, but group decisions based on group responsibilities. Both the company director and the trade unionist act as members of a group. The individual Christian will make his voice heard, and a group decision is reached on a basis of compromise. He is not of course always or necessarily at variance with the group. The difficulty arises from the fact that the churches are still working only with an ethic of individual responsibility and have not yet thought out the ethics of group responsibility.

9. Another matter to which the attention of Christians should be directed is the way in which work brings men into new forms of association with their fellows. The working group often becomes a real community in which effective bonds of loyalty, fellow-feeling and mutual interest are engendered. Hence it happens that a working community in this sense may become opposed to the wider community around it as it seeks to promote its own ends; or perhaps it may be exploited by the state in its effort to subordinate the individual and to reduce man to the status of a worker and nothing more. Here again it is necessary that the traditional concern of Christian ethics with personal morality should be widened so that the insights of Christian faith may be brought to bear upon this important problem of group behaviour. The working community must be seen to be neither an end in itself nor a means to the ends of the state; and its true status and character must be defined in the light of the Christian understanding of man.

10. Because work is a divine ordinance for human life, there is an obligation upon society to provide all its members with opportunity to work. Unemployment is not only a problem for economists but for all Christian people; the Christian view of the nature of work lays upon the laity the duty of promoting measures which will ensure the opportunity of all those who wish to work to secure employment. Similarly, the Christian will sometimes judge in the light of his Christian understanding that the structure of his occupation should be changed. His divine calling may enable him to transcend the framework of secular society, but if he is to transform it he must associate with his fellows in a united struggle to improve working conditions. Labour unions, farmers' groups, professional associations and the like, can be organs through which a Christian layman may serve God's purpose as truly as he serves it in what is conventionally recognized as "church work." The Christian should work within such groups, or in the political party which he deems to be the most useful in combating social ills, and in this effort he is sustained by his hope in Christ. While he accepts at its full weight the fact of sin in all human ideals and achievements, he will not give way to apathy because of his Christian hope; nor will he share the despair of those who have not this hope but are conscious of their insignificance in face of the vast processes which they seem powerless to change or bend to righteous ends. The Christian will hold firmly to the fact of Christ as the hope of the world, and he will therefore view the resources of nature not as so much raw material to be used entirely as man wills, but as God's gifts to be used responsibly in the light of this Christian hope concerning the end for which all things were made.

11. Thus, all human life and work are transformed by hope in Christ. All work honestly done, whether undertaken for the sake of earning a livelihood, or for the sake of the community, or out of spontaneous joy in creative effort, has genuine value and meaning in the purpose of God. Regarded solely from the standpoint of this world, the work which men do is of transient worth; even man's most enduring achievements must one day pass away. But regarded from the standpoint of hope in the coming Kingdom of Christ, every act of obedience to God's law possesses abiding significance and worth.

IV. THE MINISTRY OF THE LAITY: HOW CAN IT BECOME EFFECTIVE?

12. The time has come to make the ministry of the laity explicit, visible and active in the world. The real battles of the faith today are being fought in factories, shops, offices and farms, in political parties and government agencies, in countless homes, in the press, radio and television, in the relationship of nations. Very often it is said that the Church should "go into these spheres"; but the fact is, that the Church is already in these spheres in the persons of its laity.

13. So far, although in varying degrees, our churches have failed to give their members the support they need to make them effective representatives of the Church in their working life. Millions of men who know they belong in the world and speak its language and who are also faithful church members are still looking for the Church that will stand beside them as they work. Only if our churches succeed in being with their laity in the struggles of our present world will the laity in their turn become genuine representatives of the Church in areas of modern life to which otherwise the Church has no access. An immense opportunity is open to the churches in the world through their laity not to be seized for ecclesiastical domination but for Christian witness. But this opportunity for witness can only be seized if there is a change of emphasis and of prevailing atmosphere in many churches.

(a) Churches can become preoccupied with their own internal organization programmes and activities to such an extent or in such a manner that they fail to grasp the importance of Christian witness in and through secular organs of society and to encourage their members to participate fully in them. The Christian who, for example, throws himself into the social and political struggle should be actively encouraged and considered a gain, not a loss, to the Church.

(b) There is need to change the atmosphere which strikes the newcomer so forcibly in many churches, the atmosphere of an old-fashioned, middle-class culture, now radically changed in society but surviving in the Church. A tendency to choose the lay leadership of a congregation from among white-collar workers often prevents others, especially young industrial workers, from feeling at home in the Church.

(*c*) It is often thought in the Church that the clergy are the only ones who are obliged to walk worthily of their Christian calling wherever they may be. From the laity a lower standard is tolerated or even expected. The clergy have their appointed function in the Church, the ministry of Word and Sacraments. God calls men to this ministry, and every Christian needs to ask whether it is to this ministry or to the ministry of the laity that God's call comes. But on clergy and laity alike God lays the demand for total commitment to Him. The ministry of the laity should mean nothing less than this total commitment of all man's time, deeds and possessions.

14. Many people are conscious that they are ill-equipped for their task of ministry. The following suggestions are put forward with a view to equipping them for their task.

(*a*) In churches with many recent converts, basic Christian teaching in the faith, in prayer, worship and Bible reading is the first task, proceeding step by step with Christian witness and obedience in the home and daily work. Even in long-established congregations it cannot be taken for granted that such basic instruction is unnecessary. An active and organized laity could be a menace if it were not well instructed in the essentials of Christian faith and life.

(*b*) Among the laity there will be those who by reason of their devotion and gifts hold positions of responsibility and influence amongst the rank and file of church members. It is of especial importance that they should be able to bring the truths of Christian doctrine to bear upon the lay experience of life and work in the world. Theology is not for clergy only; it must be accessible to lay people in a form which they recognize as relevant and essential to their proper task.

(*c*) The clergy need a better acquaintance with present-day working society, both by study and experience, in order that they may help their laity and follow them with their prayers. Some theological seminaries have already made notable progress in this respect.

(*d*) The home should become a place where children grow up to regard work and occupation as a sphere of Christian vocation. In it children can learn to recognize God's voice and obey Him when He calls. Parents need to learn in the Church Christian attitudes toward work and vocation, and teach them to their children in place of the prevailing worldly standards of "getting on" or "keeping up with the Joneses." Christian youth organizations should reinforce this teaching by helping young people to choose their occupations in the light of Christian teaching about vocation.

(e) Any emphasis on the ministry of the laity means not only training but a special kind of pastoral care. Laymen and women should be encouraged to use the pastoral gifts that many of them possess. Mutual care of members by each other as well as by the clergy is needed in the Church. Christians have many natural opportunities for the pastoral care of neighbours, workmates and others.

(f) Christians from the same or related occupations should have some opportunity to meet occasionally. In fellowship with Christians in similar work they can study and discuss common concerns, including problems of the structure of their occupation, in the light of Christian faith. This practice is spreading to many parts of the world, taking different forms. In many instances the single parish is not large enough to draw people together in a specialized way and a regional and ecumenical basis serves the purpose better. There is room for more experiment and for a wide interchange of experience between the many associations, groups and cells of laity, residential colleges, and "Evangelical Academies." These, along with other specific activities such as lay retreats, conferences and consultations are rapidly growing in number and scope.

15. The Church is sent into the world as a ministering community, not only in the sense that the parts serve each other, but that all serve the world. Here we see the relevance of the main theme of the Assembly to the subject under discussion. Christ died for the whole world, and a deep conviction that this was so would make the Church the bearer of hope to the world. The Church would become outward-going both in evangelism and in daily service through work.

16. Our world is characterized by unprecedented technical, organizational and scientific achievements and at the same time by disillusionments, cynicism and fear of final self-destruction. The Church must not become an escape for those who do not dare to look such a world in the face. The Church cannot offer men security in this world, but because she preaches the Cross and Resurrection of Jesus Christ, she brings hope to men. It is for this reason that Christians can never abandon the world.

RESOLUTIONS ON THE LAITY
Adopted by the Assembly

RESOLUTION I

We commend this report to the churches in the hope that they will make it a part of their thinking and encourage adventurous experiments.

RESOLUTION II

We commend this report to those engaged in such experiments in order to strengthen their efforts and to draw their attention to certain criteria which may help them and to certain dangers which they may encounter.

RESOLUTION III

We commend this report to organizations of lay men and women in the Church asking them to consider how their activities can be co-ordinated so as to contribute to a better realization of the ministry of the laity in the Church and in the world.

RESOLUTION IV

We recommend that the World Council of Churches continue the study of the Christian understanding of work, begun before Evanston, and that it be jointly undertaken by the Department of Church and Society and the Department of Laity.

RESOLUTION V

We recommend that the Central Committee provide for the adequate staffing of the Department of Laity and that the Central Committee take care that it remain a flexible instrument able to assist, by every possible means, the emergence of a true ministry of the laity.

DISCUSSION ON THE REPORT ON THE LAITY

The Bishop of Chichester was in the chair.

Dr. Kathleen Bliss outlined the argument of the report. She drew attention in particular to its analysis of the gulf between the Church and the world. The laity were conscious that when they moved from the workaday world to the Church they left one set of concepts and took up another. If the theologians were left to themselves, the laity soon remarked that the work the theologians were talking about was not what they recognized as the work they did every day, and that they could not follow the theological language. If the laity alone took the lead it became a question whether by beginning at the sociological end they could ever arrive at the real challenge of the gospel. Laymen and theologians must learn to work together. The Church in the modern world needed to see itself as interpenetrating the world, as having its home wholly in Christ, and precisely because of that, wholly in the world whose only hope Christ is.

Dr. Reinold von Thadden presented a statement on the Kirchentag in Germany, describing the spiritual encounter in the meetings between large numbers of lay men and women from both East and West. He emphasized the relationship between the work of the World Council for the laity and the united endeavours of the German churches in the Kirchentag.

Professor Torrance offered two reflections and a suggestion. He said that (1) there were conflicting views concerning the meaning and function of the laity; (2) the document as a whole was too analytical and not sufficiently constructive. He thought the excellent early theology of the report should have been followed up by more emphasis on the corporate priesthood of believers, at which point there was much in common between Calvin and Chrysostom. He therefore suggested that the ministry of the laity might profitably be described in future in terms of the prophetic, kingly and priestly offices.

Miss van Asch van Wyck said that the report claimed not to define a layman, then went on to try to do so. Its tentative definition omitted housewives and those not gainfully employed. A change of wording would remove the impression that these categories were negligible.

Dean Pope said the phrase "earthly success will not be the standard" might suggest that the churches are pressing the workers to be content with their lot. He moved a consequent amendment, which was accepted by the Drafting Committee and embodied in the text.

Professor Wingren asked what was the relation between headings (*a*) and (*c*) in section II. Hope was mentioned in connection with (*a*) but not (*c*), which might imply that Christian hope becomes an opiate for the people. Moreover to speak, as the report did, of a power of creation seen in the work of a very few was unbiblical romanticism. He moved that the part in question be rewritten to distinguish between different forms of work in relation to hope and creation.

Professor Richardson, replying for the Drafting Committee, said that although hope and creation were not uniformly mentioned, their presence was implied. The Committee would give the point some attention nevertheless.

Mr. Taft moved two amendments in section III. Each was designed to meet the need for integrating the theology behind the report and its specific application.

The Chairman indicated that all the amendments proposed in section III would be appropriately inserted.

Mr. Winton asked for the addition of words explaining that the motives of the Church in entering into relations with the trade unions were not ecclesiastical.

Dr. Bliss drew attention to a disclaimer of ecclesiastical intentions in section III of the report. The drafters were prepared to say that the Church had no axe to grind, but not specifically to refer to trade unions.

Dr. Blake objected to words in section IV discouraging "over-participation" by the laity in church activities. He felt that the tone of the part in question was too negative, and that it was only necessary to say that churches fail to appreciate the non-ecclesiastical activities of some of their members.

Dr. Bliss said the drafters were prepared for some re-writing, but were not willing to remove the suggestion of over-participation in certain aspects of church life.

Dr. Blake's amendment was then put and carried.

The report as a whole was received.

Dr. Bliss put the three resolutions of the Section as a single proposition. The resolutions were carried.

The Report of the Central Committee to the Assembly concerning the Structure and Functioning of the Council in the Period following the Second Assembly

Note:

(i) *The Assembly received the Report of the Central Committee on Structure and Functioning, subject to amendment in detail during its subsequent deliberations.*

(ii) *The divisional and departmental working committees made certain proposals which were subsequently incorporated by the Assembly in the text of the Report.*

(iii) *The Report as here printed is in its final form.*

(iv) *The text of the Report as circulated to the delegates can be found in the Assembly Work Book, pages 10 to 50.*

PREAMBLE

This report sets out the proposals which the Central Committee wishes to submit to the Assembly regarding the structure and functioning of the World Council of Churches in the period following the Second Assembly.

A. ORIGIN OF PROPOSALS

In its report to the First Assembly at Amsterdam in 1948, the Committee of the Assembly on Programme and Administration recommended that the detailed plans for the organization of the World Council of Churches should be approved in principle and referred to the Central Committee for further consideration. In making this recommendation, the Committee recognized that experience was needed before clear judgments could be reached regarding the organization of the World Council and that the first period must in many respects be regarded as experimental. The

Central Committee at its meeting at Rolle, Switzerland, in August 1951, therefore decided to set in motion a detailed study of the experience of the first few years with a view to preparing for submission to the Second Assembly detailed and carefully considered proposals for the structure and functioning of the World Council of Churches in the period following that Assembly. The Central Committee appointed a Committee on Structure and Functioning "to evaluate the structure and review the procedures of the World Council and to report to the Central Committee, with a view to the preparation of a full report of the Central Committee to the Second Assembly." The following were appointed to the Committee:

> Dr. Leslie E. Cooke (Chairman)
> Dr. Alphons Koechlin
> Dr. Carl Lund-Quist
> Dr. Pierre Maury
> The Rev. R. David Say.

The Central Committee also nominated as advisers to the Committee:

> The Rt. Hon. Ernest Brown
> Dr. Samuel McCrea Cavert
> Dr. W. J. Gallagher
> Sir Kenneth Grubb
> Bishop H. Høgsbro
> Bishop H. Lilje
> Bishop S. K. Mondol
> Principal T. M. Taylor.

During the ensuing eighteen months the Committee held three meetings, each of two or three days' duration, and also presented draft reports to the Executive Committee at its meetings in February 1952 at Lambeth and in August 1952 at Nykøbing. The Committee then presented its draft report to the meeting of the Central Committee at Lucknow in December 1952/January 1953. The Central Committee amended the report at certain points and then adopted the report as a whole and agreed that the Committee on Structure and Functioning be asked to continue its work and to report to the meeting of the Central Committee before the Assembly.

The Committee of Structure and Functioning held two further meetings of three days, and two days, duration respectively and then reported again to the Executive Committee at its meeting at Bossey in August 1953. It then held one further two-day meeting at which its report was prepared for final presentation to the Executive Committee meeting at Frankfurt in February 1954. The Executive Committee approved the report and agreed that it should be circulated to all who should receive Assembly documents.

B. Status of this Report

The status of this report at the time of its circulation is thus that it has the approval of the Executive Committee and that an earlier draft, not differing greatly from the present report, was considered and approved by the Central Committee. The report in its present form will receive final consideration by the Central Committee at its meeting immediately prior to the Assembly and the Central Committee will decide at that meeting with what comments it wishes to present the report to the Assembly.

C. Scope of Report

An attempt has been made to cover the whole field of activity of the World Council of Churches while observing the following principles:

(a) that no recommendations may be made which involve changes in the constitution but that changes in the rules may be recommended where necessary;

(b) that the provisions laid down at Amsterdam concerning the organization are not binding, since this report is intended for presentation at the Second Assembly;

(c) that as far as possible, proposed changes in organization should be made within the present budgetary limitations.

The report is presented in four parts:

Part 1. General Report divided into the following sections:

    I. The Structure of the Governing Bodies
    II. Communication with the Member Churches
    III. The External Relationships of the World Council of Churches

IV. Divisional and Departmental Structure
V. Committees and Commissions
VI. Nomination Procedure for Officers and Members of Committees
VII. Financial Provisions
VIII. Office Organization and Administration.

Part 2. Proposed Statements of Aims and Functions of the proposed Divisions and Departments.

Part 3. Proposed Revisions of the Rules of the World Council of Churches (partly consequent on the proposals in Part 1 of the report and partly independent thereof).

Part 4. Conclusion.

PART 1—GENERAL REPORT

I. THE STRUCTURE OF THE GOVERNING BODIES

A. THE ASSEMBLY

Since there has been only one Assembly of the World Council of Churches and that of a unique character, it is felt that there is insufficient experience and evidence to warrant any proposals for major change in the form and constitution of the Assembly. The Central Committee at Toronto decided to increase the number of delegates and not to repeat the Amsterdam provision for the presence in the Assembly of an alternate to each delegate. The Committee recalls to the attention of the Second Assembly that a decision should be taken by that body as to the date of the Third Assembly and that the constitution provides that the Assembly "shall ordinarily meet every five years."

B. PRESIDIUM

The Presidium has, in the opinion of the Committee, proved a valuable part of the organization of the World Council of Churches. The Committee submits the four following recommendations concerning provisions to be added to the rules regarding the constitution of the Presidium, and suggests that the nomination of its members be subject to the provisions outlined in section VI of this report on Nomination Procedure:

(1) that a maximum of six be fixed for the number of Presidents;

(2) that a President shall be ineligible for immediate re-election when his term of office ends;

(3) that the term of office of a President shall end at the adjournment of the next Assembly following his or her election;

(4) that the President or Presidents shall be entitled to attend the Assembly with full right of speech even if not appointed as delegates by their churches.

C. CENTRAL COMMITTEE

It is the Central Committee which acts on behalf of the Assembly and which, between meetings of the Assembly, is the authoritative body of the World Council of Churches. It therefore seems important that the status and responsibility of the Central Committee should be preserved and enhanced. Close attention has therefore been given to the procedure of the Central Committee, the duration of its meetings and its sub-committee structure.

It is felt that the practice of considering one or more main issues of the ecumenical movement at each meeting—e.g. "The Calling of the Church to Mission and Unity" and "The Role of the World Council of Churches in Time of Tension" at the Rolle Meeting—has proved to be of real value.

Clearly there are two sub-committees of the Central Committee which must be regarded as permanent features of every Central Committee meeting—the Finance Committee and the Nominations Committee.

On the other hand, it is considered that there has been inadequate consideration of the Executive Committee's Report and that undue time has been taken in receiving oral reports from departments. It is further considered that the Central Committee will act more effectively if matters of policy arising either from reports or in the course of the Central Committee's discussions are referred to a Reference Committee or Committees. Such Committees would report to a plenary session of the Central Committee.

The following recommendations are therefore submitted:

1. that the report of the Executive Committee to the Central Committee covering the work done by the Executive Com-

mittee since the previous Central Committee meeting, shall be given greater importance in the agenda of the Central Committee; that the report of the General Secretary be, however, retained and cover the activities of the Council and a general review of the most important developments in the church situation throughout the world;

2. that divisional reports to the Central Committee be in future circulated in writing and be in the hands of Central Committee members at least one month before each meeting;

3. that a motion for the reception of each report shall be included in the agenda of the Central Committee thus providing an opportunity for questions to be raised on the written reports or on any other matters concerning the work of the division in question;

4. that it shall not be the rule in future that every division or department shall report orally to each meeting of the Central Committee but the Central Committee may call for an oral report from any division or department if it sees fit to do so;

5. that the Central Committee shall normally meet for eight days from a Tuesday night to a Wednesday night;

6. that the Central Committee shall have the following sub-committees:

(a) Finance Committee (a standing committee),

(b) Nominations Committee (newly appointed at each meeting),

(c) Reference Committee or Committees (appointed as needed at each meeting) to advise the Central Committee on any other questions arising which call for special consideration or action by the Central Committee;

7. that the practice of taking one or more main issues for consideration at each Central Committee meeting has proved highly creative and profitable and be continued;

8. that it should be recommended to the Assembly that the Central Committee should be kept in existence until its report has been received and discharge has been given.

9. In the event that the Chairman and/or Vice-Chairman of the Central Committee shall not be appointed as delegates to the Assembly by their churches, they shall be entitled to attend the Assembly as consultants.

It is further recommended that recommendations 6, 8, and 9 above shall be incorporated into the Rules of the World Council of Churches (see Part 3 of this report[1]).

D. THE EXECUTIVE COMMITTEE OF THE CENTRAL COMMITTEE

The mandate of the Executive Committee was not clearly defined at Amsterdam. Experience has shown that the Executive has had to carry a considerable amount of responsibility, and on one occasion at least has found it necessary to issue a statement in the form of a letter to the churches concerning public affairs. The pattern of procedure in the Executive has been similar to that in the Central Committee, which has meant a considerable amount of duplication.

The fact that hitherto the Chairman of the Executive Committee has also been Chairman of the Central Committee has meant that the Executive Committee report has been given from the Chair of the Central Committee. This represents a situation which could limit the freedom of discussion in the Central Committee.

Experience has shown that there has been clear advantage in having as members of the Executive persons closely connected with the work of certain divisions or departments, since from their own knowledge they have been able to focus the attention of the Committee on salient matters concerning those divisions or departments. Other reports have suffered in the Executive Committee from lack of personal contact on the part of members of the Executive with the activities covered by the reports.

It has become apparent that while a meeting of the Executive Committee before the Central Committee is imperative, there would be advantages in an arrangement whereby the Executive should meet for a short time after the Central Committee so that the implementing of Central Committee decisions should not be left entirely in the hands of staff of the World Council without opportunity of further consultations and advices.

In the light of these considerations it is recommended:

1. that the present provision of the Rules that "the Chairman of the Central Committee shall also be the Chairman of the

[1] This part of the report (the Rules of the World Council of Churches), appears in its amended form as Appendix 12.

Executive Committee" (Rule V 1 (c))[1] be left unchanged, but that during the reports to the Central Committee of the Executive Committee and of the General Secretary, the Chair shall be taken by a member of the Presidium;

2. that the functions of the Executive Committee at present defined as follows: "The Executive Committee shall carry out the decisions of the Central Committee. It shall meet ordinarily twice a year" (Rule V 2) shall be re-defined in the following terms:

"The Executive Committee is a committee of the Central Committee appointed by it and responsible to it. The Executive Committee shall, between meetings of the Central Committee, carry out the decisions of the Central Committee and implement the policy laid down by it. It shall meet ordinarily twice a year. The Executive Committee shall have no authority to make decisions on policy except that in circumstances of special urgency it can take provisional decisions. It may only issue public statements under the provisions laid down in Rule IX 4. It shall have power to appoint heads of departments provisionally but such appointments shall be subject to confirmation by the Central Committee. It shall supervise the operation of the budget and have power to impose limitations on expenditure if necessary."

3. that certain members of the Executive Committee shall be given assignments of interest in specific fields of World Council work, without any particular executive or administrative responsibility for that work;

4. that the Executive Committee shall meet normally twice a year. It shall meet for two days before each meeting of the Central Committee and may also hold a one-day meeting after the Central Committee, if considered necessary on any occasion;

5. that there should be no power for the appointment of substitutes for members of the Executive Committee unable to attend meetings and that this shall be explicitly stated in the Rules. The Executive might, however, wish use to be made of the power granted to the officers "to invite others to attend a meeting of the Executive Committee for consultation, always

[1] References are to the Rules as they appear in the official Report of the Amsterdam Assembly, *The First Assembly of the World Council of Churches*, London, SCM Press, 1949, pages 202–213.

having in mind the need of preserving a due balance of the confessions and of the geographical areas" (Rule V 1 (d)).

It is not thought desirable to recommend that a quorum should be fixed in the Rules for meetings of the Executive Committee; it is felt that flexibility is needed on this point. It is, however, recommended that it should be understood that at the request of any member, the number of members present when any particular decision is taken shall be recorded in the minutes.

As to the relative claims of continuity and change in the membership of the Executive Committee, it is considered that neither complete continuity nor complete change is desirable and that no limitation of the Central Committee's choice should be imposed.

II. COMMUNICATION WITH THE MEMBER CHURCHES

A. DIRECT COMMUNICATION

The problem of communication has arisen in several ways; the response of the churches to communications from the Secretariat of the World Council of Churches is disappointing; the variety of documents issued from Geneva is sometimes bewildering; and the relative authority of each document not clearly defined. No communication with the churches is more effective than the personal visitation by World Council staff, especially by the General Secretary, and the proposed arrangements for divisional and departmental structure are designed to make such visitation possible in greater measure than in the past.

As regards written communications, it is recommended:

1. that it be re-affirmed that the World Council must maintain direct communications with the member churches, their committees and boards;

2. that where a member church agrees:

(*a*) communications relating to important policy questions shall be sent to the chief executive of a church;

(*b*) World Council divisions or departments shall communicate directly with the offices and departments of a church responsible for the corresponding fields of work;

3. that documents should bear a clear indication of their authority, e.g. reports of conferences should bear a clear indication that their conclusions are not World Council conclusions.

B. RELATIONS WITH NATIONAL COUNCILS

Rulings governing the relations of the World Council of Churches with national councils were adopted by the Central Committee at its first meeting immediately following the Amsterdam Assembly. Developments over the subsequent period have demonstrated the significance of national councils in relation to the World Council of Churches and it is considered desirable that appropriate provisions should now be introduced into the Rules. The revised Rules which are suggested below have been discussed and approved by the Joint Committee of the I.M.C. and the W.C.C.

It is therefore recommended:

(i) that the present clause under Rule X be left unaltered but be given the sub-heading: "1. International Missionary Council";

(ii) that there be added to Rule X a new clause reading:

2. *National Councils*

(*a*) The World Council, recognizing that national councils of churches or national Christian councils have been established in a number of countries for purposes of fellowship and co-operation with one another and for the promotion and support of ecumenical activities and other common interests within their own area, shall invite selected national councils to enter into working relationships as associated councils.

(*b*) The purpose of such working relationships shall be to help national councils in their work and to encourage them to help the World Council of Churches in the promotion of ecumenical activities in the area concerned and in the furthering of the plans and policies which the Central Committee has laid down for the various divisions and departments of the Council.

(*c*) These councils shall be regularly designated to receive invitations to send a fraternal delegate to the Assembly and a consultant to the Central Committee (in accordance with Section VII ii of the Constitution).

(*d*) Opportunity shall be provided at the time of any meeting of the Assembly or Central Committee for the representatives of national councils to meet together for mutual consultation.

(*e*) While the World Council retains the right to deal with its member churches directly, no action shall be taken by it which would disturb any already existing fellowships or ecumenical organization within a nation or region.

(*f*) Any member church which prefers to have direct relationships with the World Council in any field of work can have such direct relationships.

(*g*) The following criteria, among others, shall be applied by the Central Committee in selecting national councils for these working relationships:

(i) that the national council accept the Basis of the World Council of Churches or express its willingness to co-operate on that Basis;

(ii) that there be prior consultation with the member churches of the World Council in the area concerned;

(iii) that there be prior consultation with the International Missionary Council in the case of national councils which are members of that body;

(iv) that the membership of the national council consist wholly or to a large extent of churches which hold membership in the World Council of Churches;

(v) that the national council have an interest in the work of the World Council of Churches and be willing to work for that Council;

(vi) that the national council give evidence of stability and have a staff with time to devote to World Council concerns.

(*h*) In the case of countries where national missionary councils exist, whether integrated in or associated with national councils of churches or independently, the Central Committee may invite such a national missionary council to send a fraternal delegate to the Assembly and a consultant to the Central Committee.

C. WORLD CONFESSIONAL ASSOCIATIONS

It may be noted with satisfaction that almost all world confessional associations have gone on record as wishing to support the ecumenical movement, and it is suggested that the General Secretary shall arrange for informal consultations from time to time, with three or four representatives from each association, to discuss the implementation of that desire and other common problems. There is provision in the Constitution (paragraph VII) for the representation at sessions of the Assembly and of the Central Committee of such world confessional associations as may be designated by the Central Committee, but the status of such representatives is not fully defined and it is therefore recommended:

that there be added to Rule X a further new clause reading:

3. *World Confessional Associations*

Such world confessional associations as may be designated by the Central Committee shall be invited to send fraternal delegates to the Assembly, and consultants to the Central Committee.

III. THE EXTERNAL RELATIONSHIPS OF THE WORLD COUNCIL OF CHURCHES

A. INTERNATIONAL MISSIONARY COUNCIL

The Amsterdam Assembly agreed that the words "in association with the International Missionary Council" should be part of the general description of the World Council of Churches and also approved the continuation of a Joint Committee with the I.M.C. to which all questions with regard to collaboration between the two bodies should be referred. Fruitful progress has been made over the first six years in giving substance to this "association." At the time of the Amsterdam Assembly, the I.M.C. and the W.C.C. had created a joint organ in the Commission of the Churches on International Affairs and were considering the possibility of establishing a joint office in East Asia. In the period since Amsterdam, a Joint Secretary for East Asia has been appointed and the World Council Department of Inter-Church Aid and Service to Refugees has been given responsibility for the co-ordination on behalf of the two bodies of emergency inter-church aid and relief outside Europe. The Joint Committee is further recommending that there should be one Division of

Studies which should serve both the I.M.C. and the W.C.C. and should include three World Council Departments for Faith and Order, Church and Society and Evangelism, and one I.M.C. Department of Missionary Studies, and also that steps should be taken to ensure closer ties in public relations and information. It is further recommended that the Joint Committee, which has increasingly become an effective instrument for dealing with matters of common concern, should be strengthened in its membership and provided with a full-time secretary so that it may be still better equipped to develop further the association between the I.M.C. and the W.C.C. The relationships between the two bodies are set out more fully in the report of the Joint Committee on pages 322–327.

B. UNITED BIBLE SOCIETIES

There have been close and cordial relationships with this body since its inception. At present there is a member of the U.B.S. staff working at the World Council of Churches headquarters in close co-operation with the Secretariat for Evangelism. In view of the vital importance of the promotion of Bible distribution and Bible reading for the life of the churches and for the ecumenical movement, it is recommended that these relationships should be developed and encouraged.

C. OTHER DESIGNATED ECUMENICAL ORGANIZATIONS

At present the Central Committee has fraternal representation from the World's Committee of Y.M.C.A.s, the World's Y.W.C.A., the World's Student Christian Federation and the World Council of Christian Education and Sunday School Association. All these bodies are members, along with the World Council of Churches, of the World Christian Youth Commission, which carries out an important piece of co-ordination in the field of youth work. Further, relations between the Youth Departments of the W.C.C.E. and the World Council of Churches are particularly close and cordial; indeed the two Departments share the majority of their committee members and hold their committee meetings at the same time.

Relationships with these four organizations are not confined to the youth field and it is therefore recommended that regular discussions between the general secretaries and *ad hoc* consultations on specific questions of common interest should be encouraged.

IV. DIVISIONAL AND DEPARTMENTAL STRUCTURE

When considering the departmental structure of the World Council of Churches, it must be remembered that the World Council is an organism rather than an organization. The present structure of the World Council is the result of a series of responses made to a series of stimuli. As a new need has become manifest so the Council has sought to meet it by developing a new piece of organization. Co-ordination and integration have been achieved at the personal level rather than by strategic planning. One result of this is that the World Council has developed too many departments whose secretaries live in a constant tension between field and office work while at the same time they seek to meet the demands made upon them to effect cross-representation between the departments. An immense burden rests upon the General Secretary and the organization inevitably suffers during his necessary absences from Geneva.

There would appear to be no single integrating principle under which the existing departmental organization is subsumed and there is a serious lack of liaison between the departments and the Central Committee. The suggested changes in structure are designed in the belief that if they are adopted the whole position will be improved.

The main changes involved in the proposals set out below are a strengthening of the General Secretariat and the creation of two new divisions bringing together departments which have certain common functions to perform.

It is recommended that there shall be four Associate General Secretaries, three of whom will be responsible for a division and the fourth for the Commission of the Churches on International Affairs. One Associate General Secretary will be the Deputy General Secretary who will act for the General Secretary in his absence. In addition to their special responsibilities, the Associate General Secretaries shall share with the General Secretary responsibility for the life of the World Council of Churches as a whole. The General Secretary and the Associate General Secretaries, together with the Directors of Finance and Administration and of

Information, will provide at the centre of the organization a central secretarial group capable of discussing the whole work of the Council and co-ordinating its activities. The Executive Secretary of the New York office and the East Asia Secretary will, when available, sit with this secretarial group.

The centralizing of the Secretariat in Geneva, which to some, at first sight, may seem undesirable, will make possible greater personal contact of the chief executives of the World Council with the constituency. Personal visits to the churches by the chief executives of the World Council are of the greatest value and importance. The adoption of the present proposals will make possible a representation by them to the churches not only of those details which are their personal responsibility but of the total concerns of the World Council of Churches. Those contacts will be made with less interruption of the work of the central offices and with less anxiety for the executives themselves who at present, when they are abroad, know that essential tasks in Geneva are being generally neglected.

The principle underlying the proposed divisional and departmental structure is *that the Principle of Integration must be Unity of Function.*

There can of course be no complete and absolute differentiation between the proposed divisions nor would such differentiation be desirable. On the other hand, there is need for definition of the areas of operation and at the same time provision must be made for the fullest possible co-ordination.

In the light of these considerations the Committee believes that the organization of the W.C.C. should be reconstructed upon a divisional basis, each division being constituted so as to bring together departments which have certain common functions to perform.

A division will, therefore, be the organ for putting into effect a particular part of the policy of the World Council. It will be an entity in the World Council organization having freedom to initiate policy and take action in its own field although it will do so in relation to the other divisions and subject to the Assembly and Central Committee, whose total policy it is the responsibility of the General Secretariat to administer and direct.

The division, besides operating as an entity in itself, will work through departments to which will belong the responsibility for study and action in certain specified fields. The grouping of the departments and divisions will make possible strategic planning of departmental work and integration of departmental activities. The departments will also have freedom to initiate projects, prepare programmes and take action in their own fields, subject to the general policy of the division itself.

It is proposed that each division shall have a divisional committee and shall operate under the supervision of an Associate General Secretary. Each department will have a working committee and a director or executive secretary.

It is also proposed that the committee membership shall be such as to establish a direct relationship between the divisional and departmental committees and the Central Committee.

The departments will therefore be integral parts of the division in which they have their place, and thus will have the benefit of co-operation and planning. The division and its Associate General Secretary will serve the departments in keeping them in close touch with the policy of the World Council and the General Secretariat. While the report to the Central Committee on a department's work will normally form a part of the division's report, the departments will, if occasion arises, have opportunity to present particular concerns direct to the Central Committee.

The divisions may, with the sanction of the Central Committee, create new departments to meet needs, or effect re-arrangements within the existing departmental structure.

This arrangement will call for recognition by the departmental committees and by the departmental secretaries themselves, that the departmental secretaries are not only members of the World Council staff to whom departmental responsibilities have been entrusted, but that they are also members of a divisional team under the immediate leadership of the Associate General Secretary and that the divisional committees may assign tasks to them in the working of the divisions as a whole, in addition to those which belong to them as departmental secretaries.

The Committee is of the opinion that an organization such as this, which provides for both a unified committee and secretarial relationship is most likely to effect that integration of the organization of the World Council which is the immediate need.

It is therefore recommended:

A. That there shall be three divisions:

(i) *The Division of Studies*

This Division shall co-ordinate all work of a study nature. Within the Division there shall be departments for Faith and Order, Church and Society and Evangelism, each with at least one full-time secretary. Provision has also been made in the committee structure for a close liaison between this Division and the Ecumenical Institute, especially with regard to study conferences. The decisions made by the World Conference on Faith and Order at Lund took account of a number of recommendations made by the Committee on Structure and Functioning and have made possible the integration of the work of Faith and Order into the structure of the World Council. The Joint Committee of the I.M.C. and the W.C.C., at its meeting in January 1954, agreed to recommend that the Division of Studies of the World Council should also be the Division of Studies of the I.M.C. and should include a Department of Missionary Studies, of which the Research Secretary of the I.M.C. should be Executive Secretary. This recommendation was approved by the Executive Committee of the World Council at its meeting in February 1954 and will go forward to the meetings of the Ad Interim Committee of the I.M.C. and the Central Committee of the World Council which will be held shortly before the Second Assembly (see Report of Joint Committee on pages 322–327).

(ii) *The Division of Ecumenical Action*

This Division shall be concerned with helping the churches to make their membership of the World Council a practical, living reality. It shall include the Ecumenical Institute, including the Graduate School of Ecumenical Studies, the Youth Department, the Department on Co-operation of Men and Women in Church and Society and the Department on Work for the Laity. Through the work of these Departments, and through other means which may from time to time be chosen, the Division will aim at building up ecumenical consciousness and understanding. It shall not be primarily concerned with making known the activities of the World Council, but with promoting activities within the churches which are ecumenical in character. The Ecumenical Institute is included in this Division because it is an essential experimental ground for ecumenism, where new groupings and new methods of approach are being tried out. At the same time the Ecumenical Institute shall have a special relationship to the Division of Studies since it is pre-eminently a place where ecumenical study and action are being fruitfully related for the benefit of the World Council as a whole as well as for the member churches.

(iii) *The Division of Inter-Church Aid and Service to Refugees*

This Division, which already exists within the present structure, helps the churches to fulfil their obligations to help one another and also to give help to groups in special need such as the millions of refugees in the world today. It shall be responsible for all work of the World Council in the field of inter-church aid and service to refugees, including the new responsibility for emergency inter-church aid and relief, in the name of both the I.M.C. and the W.C.C., in countries outside Europe. It will collaborate with the C.C.I.A. in public representations on behalf of refugees and other suffering groups.

B. That there shall be a commission appointed jointly by the World Council and the International Missionary Council:

The Commission of the Churches on International Affairs

This Commission already exists and no change in its structure or relationship to the World Council is proposed. (The Executive Committee of the C.C.I.A. meeting at Willingen in July 1952 considered this question and decided that no major change of structure was needed.)

C. That there shall be two departments both directly responsible to the General Secretary:

(i) *The Department of Finance and Administration*

This Department shall be responsible for providing for all of the divisions and departments of the World Council all financial, accounting, and general services. It has a clear responsibility to relieve the General Secretary, as far as possible, of administrative work. It shall be headed by a director and shall have an adequate staff of departmental secretaries.

(ii) *The Department of Information*

This Department shall be responsible for making known the activities of the World Council through the church and secular press and other media and for the press offices at the time of meetings. It shall also serve the churches by providing them with news about the life of their sister churches. It shall be responsible for the co-ordination of all publications issued by the World Council. Since its task is to interpret the work of the World Council, the Director of this Department should be a man with a knowledge of the ecumenical movement and the churches, who will be able to give leadership to the Department. He must be supported by an adequate staff of departmental secretaries. With safeguards to ensure that publicity, especially promotional publicity concerning inter-church aid and refugee work should not be hampered, the information service of the Department of Inter-Church Aid shall be included in the Information Department, under the control of the Director. The Joint Committee of the I.M.C. and W.C.C., at its meeting in January 1954, welcomed a suggestion that the I.M.C. should use the facilities of the new Department of Information and this suggestion, which was approved by the Executive Committee of the World Council in February 1954, will go forward to the meetings of the Ad Interim Committee of the I.M.C. and the Central Committee of the World Council which will be held shortly before the Second Assembly (see Report of Joint Committee on pages 322–327.)

D. That there shall be regional representation of the World Council in two areas:

(i) *The New York Office*

An office was established in New York because of the large group of member churches in the U.S.A.—at a long distance from Geneva—with which relations have to be maintained, and because of the importance of New York as a point of contact with extensive missionary and ecumenical interests.

The New York office is under the general supervision of the Central Committee and directly responsible to the General Secretary. It is proposed that its staff include the following, subject to review from time to time by the Central Committee:

1. *Executive Secretary in the U.S.A.*, appointed by the Central Committee.

The Executive Secretary shall:

(*a*) have oversight of all of the activities of the New York office;

(*b*) maintain continuous liaison with the General Secretary in Geneva on all matters of policy and interpret World Council policies to the American public;

(*c*) serve the three Divisions—Interchurch Aid, Studies (including Faith and Order), Ecumenical Action—and the Departments of Information and of Finance and Administration in their relations with the churches in the U.S.;

(*d*) co-operate with the office and staff of the C.C.I.A. in New York;

(*e*) be a member of the staff executive group of the Council and meet with the General Secretary and Associate General Secretaries whenever practicable;

(*f*) render such service as may be required to the U.S. Conference for the World Council of Churches.

2. *Associate* (*or Assistant*) *Executive Secretary*—as may be found desirable—appointed by the Executive Committee.

The Associate (or Assistant) Executive Secretary shall:

(*a*) assist the Executive Secretary in discharging the general duties of the New York office;

(*b*) carry special responsibility for such phases of the programme as the General Secretary and the Executive Secretary in the U.S.A. may assign.

3. *Secretary of the Youth Department.*

This Secretary shall be a part of the regular staff of the Youth Department and be under its direction in all matters of programme and policy, and under the administrative supervision of the Executive Secretary in the U.S.A.

Other members of the New York staff, if deemed necessary by the Executive Committee (for example, for service in finance and publicity) may be appointed by the General Secretary and the Executive Secretary in the U.S.A.

(ii) *Secretariat for East Asia*

This Secretariat, which serves both the World Council and the I.M.C., was set up following the Bangkok Conference at which it was requested that the East Asia Secretary should be an Asian Christian and should have "official membership and status in the secretariat of the I.M.C. and the W.C.C. and that his budget should be included jointly in the secretarial budgets of the I.M.C. and W.C.C." It was further suggested at that conference that he should "give his full time to visiting churches and Christian councils in East Asia, helping the churches to share more fully their thought and experience, with a view to strengthening the churches in their evangelistic task in East Asia, and establishing closer contact than at present exists between the East Asian churches and councils and the world-wide movement of the Church." Experience over the last few years has fully justified the existence of this Secretariat. It is therefore recommended that there should be a Secretary for East Asia who should be a full staff member of the W.C.C. and should when available sit in with the General Secretariat.

It should be noted here that it is not recommended that a W.C.C. office should be maintained in London. The British Council of Churches, which has had a working relationship with the World Council of Churches since its inauguration, is willing to accept responsibility for the financial and administrative work at present done by the London office, and it is felt that there is now no justification for the maintenance of the W.C.C. office there.

V. COMMITTEES AND COMMISSIONS

The following recommendations regarding divisional and departmental committees are in the main an application to committee procedure of the proposals in section IV of this report on divisional and departmental structure. It is recommended that, with the exception of recommendation (2 c), they should be incorporated in the rules of the World Council of Churches.

It is recommended that:

1. There shall be a small committee for each division whose responsibility shall be to carry out the aim of the division. It shall be responsible for the preparation and presentation to the Central Committee of the reports on the division's work.

2. Divisional committees shall be appointed by the Central Committee as follows:

(a) For the Division of Studies and the Division of Ecumenical Action, the committees shall consist of three persons who are not members of any departmental working committee within the division, plus the chairman and one other member of each departmental working committee within the division. One of the two representatives of each departmental working committee must be a member of the Central Committee. For the purpose of co-ordination, the Division of Studies should be represented by one or two members on the Committee of the Division of Ecumenical Action and vice versa.

(*b*) For the Division of Inter-Church Aid, the committee shall consist of seven members, at least two of whom shall be members of the Central Committee.

(*c*) The exceptional position of C.C.I.A. was recognized and no change is suggested in respect of its committee structure, but it is recommended that at least two members of the Executive Committee of the C.C.I.A. shall be drawn from the membership of the Central Committee.

Departmental secretaries shall normally be present at the meetings of divisional committees.

3. There shall be working committees for each department appointed by the Central Committee and responsible for the preparation of departmental programmes for submission to the divisional committees and for the execution of the programmes. The chairmen of departmental working committees shall be *ex officio* members of the appropriate divisional committees. Departmental working committees shall have power to call in *ad hoc* consultants as needed on particular problems. In the case of the Ecumenical Institute, its Board shall be regarded as the working committee. Normally a working committee shall consist of fifteen members at least one of whom shall be a member of the Central Committee. In the interest of closest possible co-ordination of the Department on Evangelism and the Department of Missionary Studies, the working committees of these Departments shall meet together from time to time.

Some departments have constitutions which have been approved by the Central Committee. In some measure those constitutions are superseded by the statements of aims and functions set out in Part 2 of this report; in certain cases they also provide for committees with titles different from those proposed in this report. The Constitution of Faith and Order adopted by the Lund Conference in August 1952 was drafted after consultation with the Committee on Structure and Functioning and no change in the status of the Faith and Order Commission is suggested. C.C.I.A. is in a special position as a semi-autonomous body created by and with a constitution approved by the I.M.C. and the W.C.C. and there appears to be no occasion to revise its constitution. It is further suggested that the Youth Committee and the Annual Consultation of the Department of Inter-Church Aid and Service to Refugees, provided for in the constitutions of those two Departments, shall continue to exist, in addition to the departmental or divisional committees. It is recommended that all departments, other than Faith and Order and C.C.I.A., which have constitutions shall be directed to redraft them under the title of "Departmental Bye-laws," incorporating the statements of aims and functions as adopted by the Assembly and adopting the terminology of the Structure and Functioning Report as adopted by the Assembly, and shall submit the revised departmental bye-laws to an early meeting of the Central Committee after the Assembly.

VI. Nomination Procedure for Officers and Members of Committees

In an international body made up of churches of various nations and confessions, the task of securing fair and adequate representation is of paramount importance. The present nomination procedure has been reviewed, taking into account previous decisions. There would appear to be need for a tightening up of procedure and a clear definition of responsibility.

The following recommendations are therefore submitted:

1. That no change be made in the present provision in the Rules concerning the Nominations Committee of the Assembly, namely:

(1) At an early session of the Assembly, the Assembly shall appoint a Nominations Committee, on which there shall be appropriate confessional and geographical representation of the membership of the Assembly.

(2) The Nominations Committee in consultation with the officers of the World Council and the Executive Committee

shall draft proposals concerning (*a*) the President or Presidents of the World Council of Churches and (*b*) a list of persons proposed for membership on the Central Committee.

(3) The President or Presidents shall be *ex officio* members of the Central Committee and of the Executive Committee.

(4) The Nominations Committee shall present its proposals to the Assembly for its acceptance or revision.

(5) It shall be open to any six members of the Assembly acting together to put forward in writing other proposals.

(6) Election shall be by ballot unless the Assembly shall otherwise determine.

2. That the rule regarding the Nominations Committee of the Central Committee, reading as follows:

(2b) For this purpose it shall appoint a Nominations Committee of not more than four persons, who shall bring before the Central Committee one or more names for each office. Any member of the Central Committee may make alternative proposals.

should be revised to read:

The Central Committee shall appoint a Nominations Committee which shall:

(*a*) nominate individuals to the Central Committee for the offices of Chairman and Vice-Chairman or Vice-Chairmen of the Central Committee.

(*b*) nominate individuals for election as President, if between Assemblies need arises for such appointments, under the power conferred on the Central Committee by the Constitution and Rules.

(*c*) nominate the members of the Executive Committee and divisional committees and departmental working committees.

3. That the following new paragraph should be added to the Rules: In making nominations, the Nominations Committees of the Assembly and the Central Committee shall have regard to the following principles:

(*a*) the personal qualifications of the individual for the task for which he is to be nominated;

(*b*) fair and adequate confessional representation;

(*c*) fair and adequate geographical representation;

and shall satisfy itself as to the general acceptability of the nominations to the churches to which the nominees belong.

In applying the principles (*b*) and (*c*) above to the nomination of members of the divisional committees and the departmental working committees, the Nominations Committee shall consider the representative character of the combined membership of all such committees.

VII. FINANCIAL PROVISIONS

Under the proposed new structure, each division will have an expenditure budget sub-divided into sections covering:

(*a*) the expenses of its Associate General Secretary and any other central staff and other divisional expenses;
(*b*) the expenses of each department within the division.

On the basis of proposals made by divisional committees, the General Secretariat, assisted by the Department of Finance and Administration, will prepare for submission to the Finance Committee of the Central Committee, a consolidated budget for the operations of the World Council of Churches as a whole.

The divisional committee will have power to vary the allocations of the total budget as between the various headings within the budget at its discretion, provided that the authorized total be not exceeded and the policy of the division be thereby advanced.

VIII. OFFICE ORGANIZATION AND ADMINISTRATION

After consideration, it was concluded that an enquiry into the internal office organization could not profitably be undertaken until after the establishing of a revised structure by the Evanston Assembly.

PART 2—PROPOSED STATEMENTS OF AIMS AND FUNCTIONS OF THE PROPOSED DIVISIONS AND DEPARTMENTS

The Central Committee submits to the Assembly the following draft statements of the aims and functions of each of the divisions and departments proposed in Part 1, Section IV of this report. It will be recalled that in Part 1, Section V it is recommended that these statements should be incorporated in departmental bye-laws, which should be submitted for approval to an early meeting of the Central Committee after the Assembly and that such departmental bye-laws should supersede the constitutions which are at present in force for certain World Council departments, but not the constitutions of the Faith and Order Commission nor of the Commission of the Churches on International Affairs.

I. Division of Studies

The *aim* of the Division shall be to serve the churches by promoting ecumenical studies on the fundamental issues of their faith and life, so that they may increasingly think together, advance in unity, render common witness and take common action in the social and international field.

The *functions* of the Division shall be:

(i) to work out the policy and determine the programme of studies concerning questions which are of crucial importance for the life of the churches and of the ecumenical movement as a whole;

(ii) to be responsible for and to plan studies in preparation for the Assemblies and other major meetings of the World Council;

(iii) to co-ordinate and to help to plan studies which are required by the work of other divisions;

(iv) to serve as a clearing house for studies undertaken in and by the churches;

(v) to provide background information on trends of thought and life about which the churches need to be informed;

(vi) to co-ordinate the studies undertaken by the Departments on Faith and Order, Church and Society, and Evangelism;

(vii) to advise the churches about actions resulting from the studies.

Note.—The Joint Committee of the I.M.C. and the W.C.C., at its meeting in January 1954, agreed to recommend that the Division of Studies of the World Council should also be the Division of Studies of the I.M.C. and that the I.M.C. should adopt, with appropriate modifications arising from the difference in constituent membership, the above statement of the Aims and

Functions of the Division. This recommendation was approved by the Executive Committee of the World Council at its meeting in February 1954 and will go forward to the meetings of the Ad Interim Committee of the I.M.C. and the Central Committee of the World Council which will be held shortly before the Second Assembly (see Report of Joint Committee on pages 322–327).

A. DEPARTMENT ON FAITH AND ORDER

The *aim* of the Department shall be to draw the churches out of isolation into conference about questions of faith and order.

The *functions* of the Department are stated as follows in paragraph 3 of the Constitution of the Faith and Order Commission:

(i) to proclaim the essential oneness of the Church of Christ and to keep prominently before the World Council and the churches the obligation to manifest that unity and its urgency for the work of evangelism;

(ii) to study questions of faith, order and worship with the relevant social, cultural, political, racial and other factors in their bearing on the unity of the Church;

(iii) to study the theological implications of the existence of the ecumenical movement;

(iv) to study matters in the present relationships of the churches to one another which cause difficulties and need theological clarification;

(v) to provide information concerning actual steps taken by the churches towards reunion.

B. DEPARTMENT ON CHURCH AND SOCIETY

The *aim* of the Department shall be to serve the churches by the study of problems arising out of their mission in and to society.

The *functions* of the Department shall be:

(i) to select for recommendation to the Division the crucial problems of society about which the churches should declare their common mind and take action including (in consultation with C.C.I.A.) such basic problems of international life and inter-racial relations as require long-range study;

(ii) to study in the light of the Christian faith, and together with competent persons from different churches and walks of life, relevant problems in this field;

(iii) to disseminate the results of such studies;

(iv) to keep the churches informed about important developments in society;

(v) to acquaint the churches with the action taken by other churches in this field;

(vi) to assist other divisions or departments in relating their activities to society.

C. DEPARTMENT ON EVANGELISM

The *aim* of the Department shall be to serve the churches by promoting ecumenical study and consultation on the evangelistic calling and task of the churches.

The *functions* of the Department shall be:

(i) to keep prominently before the World Council, all its divisions and departments and its member churches, the importance of the Church's evangelistic and missionary obligation and its call to unity;

(ii) as and when requested, to help churches in activities of common witness and evangelism;

(iii) to undertake studies concerning the method and content of the evangelistic approach of the Church toward those outside its life;

(iv) to collect and circulate to the churches information on effective approaches to evangelism.

D. DEPARTMENT OF MISSIONARY STUDIES

Note.—The following is the suggested statement of Aims and Functions for the Department, which will be submitted to the Ad Interim Committee of the I.M.C. (see above, page 199–200).

The *aim* of the Department shall be the furtherance of the world mission of the Church. To this end it shall seek to initiate and co-ordinate studies and enquiries regarding the missionary task of the churches.

The *functions* of the Department shall be:

(i) to study the emergence and growth of "younger churches" and the relationship of the work of the missionary societies to such churches;

(ii) through such studies to help churches and missionary societies in the formulation of mission policy;

(iii) to undertake, within the resources available to it, such special studies as may be requested by the member councils of the I.M.C.;

(iv) to promote and co-ordinate studies of the missionary task of the Church;

(v) through publication of the results of special studies and by other means available, to provide churches and missions with information regarding developments of special importance in the field of missionary thinking.

II. Division of Ecumenical Action

The *aim* of the Division shall be to serve the churches by promoting the growth of ecumenical consciousness amongst their members, by relating ecumenical knowledge and experience to the whole life of the churches and by working for the renewal of the churches through active ecumenical encounter.

The *functions* of the Division shall be:

(i) to work out policies and methods which will enable the World Council to achieve these aims, and in particular to help in ensuring the participation of local congregations in the life of the ecumenical movement;

(ii) to co-ordinate the plans of the Ecumenical Institute, the Youth Department, the Department on Work for the Laity, and the Department on Co-operation of Men and Women in Church and Society;

(iii) to guide the four Departments in the carrying out of their activities so as best to achieve the aims of the Division;

(iv) to help the churches to relate ecumenical thinking to Christian education in all its aspects;

(v) to foster co-operation between the World Council and other organizations in so far as this will further the aims of the Division;

(vi) to serve as a clearing-house for experiments and new methods of ecumenical education and consultation.

A. ECUMENICAL INSTITUTE

The *aim* of the Ecumenical Institute shall be to serve the churches as a centre of ecumenical study and teaching, worship, and experience, where men and women may deepen their understanding of questions affecting the unity, renewal and witness of the Church.

The *functions* of the Ecumenical Institute shall be:

(i) to hold educational courses for a wide variety of individuals and groups within the churches with a view to the development of ecumenical consciousness at every level;

(ii) to arrange for consultations of representatives of the same professions or occupations with a view to studying the fundamental assumptions of a given profession and the Christian witness of individuals within it, and, in co-operation with the Department on Work for the Laity, to help in co-ordinating work done in this realm by national groups;

(iii) to arrange study conferences of lay experts and theologians on problems which call for pioneering in thought and action on the part of the churches or of the ecumenical movement as a whole;

(iv) to provide through the Graduate School of Ecumenical Studies a thorough grounding in the history, objectives, and problems of the ecumenical movement for senior students, pastors and members of theological teaching staffs and to help them to undertake specialized studies on ecumenical subjects;

(v) to co-operate with the Department on Work for the Laity, the Department on Co-operation of Men and Women in Church and Society, and the Youth Department, so that all work in this field may be integrated;

(vi) to co-operate with the Division of Studies in those activities of the Institute which are relevant to the work of that Division.

B. YOUTH DEPARTMENT

The *aim* of the Youth Department is, within the general policy of the Division of Ecumenical Action, to keep before the churches their responsibility for the evangelization of young people and their growth in Christian faith, to keep before young people their responsibility to play their part in the ecumenical movement and especially in the World Council of Churches, to create ecumenical fellowship among Christian young people and to strengthen the youth work of the churches in all parts of the world.

The *functions* of the Department are:

(i) to enable the youth of all churches to meet, to learn about one another, and so to share their faith in Christ in relation to the whole of life;

(ii) to encourage young people to participate fully and responsibly in the life and witness of their own churches and of the World Council of Churches;

(iii) to interpret the aims and work of the World Council of Churches and the ecumenical movement to youth leaders and young people;

(iv) to offer young people the means of expressing active ecumenical concern through spiritual and material aid:

for churches and national councils wishing to establish or develop youth work; in emergency situations affecting young people; by sponsoring international inter-confessional service projects and encouraging national initiative in setting up such projects;

(v) to encourage the participation of young people themselves in the formulation of policy and the direction of activity in youth work at the local, national, regional and world levels;

(vi) to provide opportunities for the churches to examine together the needs of youth and to advise each other about policy, programme and activities leading to Christian commitment and growth of young people in Christian faith and life;

(vii) to provide opportunities for fellowship and exchange of experience among church youth leaders;

(viii) to co-operate with world Christian youth organizations in ecumenical activities of common concern.

C. DEPARTMENT ON CO-OPERATION OF MEN AND WOMEN IN CHURCH AND SOCIETY

The *aim* of the Department shall be to help the churches to work towards such co-operation between men and women as may enable them both to make their full contribution to church and society.

The *functions* of the Department shall be:

(i) to promote among men and women, through the Division of Studies, and directly, the study of questions affecting the relationship, the co-operation, and the common service of men and women in the churches and in society;

(ii) to help women to make their contribution to the total life of the churches and at the same time to encourage the churches to accept the contribution of women to a fuller extent and in more varied ways;

(iii) to foster an ecumenical outlook in women's organizations in the various churches and countries, to promote co-operation among them and to secure their participation in the ecumenical movement as a whole;

(iv) to advise and co-operate with the Ecumenical Institute, the Department on Work for the Laity, the Youth Department, and any other ecumenical body on the work of the Division of Ecumenical Action;

(v) to keep actively in touch with other divisions of the World Council of Churches and with other bodies whose work may have a bearing on the work of the Department.

D. DEPARTMENT ON WORK FOR THE LAITY

The *aim* of the Department on Work for the Laity shall be to keep before the churches their responsibility for helping the laity to serve their churches and to witness before the world, to strengthen work for the laity in the churches, to promote fellowship between church-related organizations of laity throughout the world, to foster ecumenical understanding among the laity.

The *functions* of the Department shall be:

(i) to assemble and disseminate information about developments in work for the laity in different countries;

(ii) to consult with national institutes and organizations for the laity on topics requiring study, and to arrange for the ecumenical consideration of these topics;

(iii) to provide a news bulletin, surveys, bibliographies and particular studies as may be required;

(iv) to arrange for regional conferences of the laity;

(v) to arrange for the visitation of laity in different countries by persons able to advise on the development of work for the laity and to stimulate new experiments;

(vi) to co-operate with the Ecumenical Institute, the Department on Co-operation of Men and Women in Church and Society, the Youth Department and the Division of Studies in all matters concerning the work of this Department.

III. Division of Inter-Church Aid and Service to Refugees

The *aim* of the Division shall be to further, on an ecumenical basis, the renewal of the churches through practical help which churches may render one another, through the relief of human need, and through services to refugees.

The *functions* of the Division shall be:

(i) to provide, on the basis of mutual study and consultation, a total strategy of Inter-Church Aid and Service to Refugees in which the initiatives and programmes of all churches and national committees can be related to one another, and thus be given maximum usefulness;

(ii) to secure and disseminate information about the needs of the churches and of refugees, and also about the gifts and services which may be made available to meet these needs;

(iii) to find contributions to meet requests;

(iv) to suggest projects and spheres of need which might be neglected and should receive attention;

(v) to operate, at the request of the churches, such services as may best be carried out co-operatively, e.g. for refugees;

(vi) to receive and administer such gifts, whether earmarked or unearmarked, which churches and other bodies place at its disposal;

(vii) to co-operate with the I.M.C. on terms mutually agreed, and to report to its officers and governing committees on all matters concerned with Emergency Inter-Church Aid and Relief in countries outside Europe.

IV. Department of Information

The *aim* of the Department shall be to make the policies of the World Council of Churches known and understood, to provide and disseminate news of its activities, and to inform the churches about each other's life.

The *functions* of the Department of Information, under the supervision of the General Secretary, shall be:

(i) to carry out the information policy of the World Council;

(ii) to issue general publicity material about the World Council of Churches and to supervise departmental publicity;

(iii) to represent the World Council in relation to the church press and the general press and to issue all press releases in the name of the W.C.C. and its divisions;

(iv) to provide such information and article services as will help the churches to be well informed about the life of other churches and about the ecumenical movement as a whole;

(v) to prepare publicity material for those divisions or departments which require the services of the Department for this purpose;

(vi) to work out a general policy concerning the regular publications of the W.C.C., to co-ordinate such publications, and to give guidance to those who are responsible for their preparation and presentation;

(vii) to co-operate with other agencies in the fields of radio, television and film, and to help to ensure the intelligent use of these media by the churches.

V. Department of Finance and Administration

The *aim* of the Department shall be to provide the World Council and its divisions and departments with financial, accounting and general services needed, and to assist the General Secretary in certain specified fields of administrative responsibility.

The *functions* of the Department shall be:

(i) to maintain the books of account, to supervise expenditure in relation to budgets and approved levels of expenditure and to prepare all financial reports and the annual accounts;

(ii) in consultation with the General Secretariat and the divisions and departments, to prepare draft budgets and to collect the contributions of member churches to the general budget;

(iii) to make all payments and operate all bank, postal cheque and cash accounts, both in relation to the General Budget and to the Division of Inter-Church Aid and Service to Refugees, and to supervise all salary and pension payments, keep salary records and administer the salary scales for office staff;

(iv) to operate the following general services at Geneva headquarters: mail, telephone, telegrams, insurance, cyclostyle, maintenance, heating and lighting of buildings, provision of office furniture and supplies and the purchase and transportation of all supplies needed;

(v) to undertake specific responsibilities at the request of the General Secretary, particularly in connection with the organization and administration of Assemblies and meetings;

(vi) to administer the properties of the World Council of Churches.

PART 4—CONCLUSION[1]

The Central Committee believes that if the recommendations made in this report are adopted, the structure and functioning of the World Council of Churches will be improved and strengthened. It will be observed that one objective has been to provide for an increased involvement of the representatives of the churches, not only in responsibility for the World Council of Churches but in its actions and life. On the other hand, the proposals regarding the General Secretariat and divisional and departmental structure should enable increased personal communication and visitation of the member churches by the executives of the World Council.

The recommendations involve a revision of the structure but increased staff is needed only at the following two points. The creation of a Department of Information was envisaged by the first Assembly but was not found possible in the first period; the proposals in this report represent merely a drawing together into one department of activities which have been carried on in the first period and the appointment of a director to co-ordinate and direct the work. The report also suggests the creation of a Department on Work for the Laity to continue within the framework of the General Budget the important work which for the past few years has been carried on under the Service Programme of the Department of Inter-Church Aid.

It must be recognized that the World Council of Churches is still young and for that reason an endeavour has been made to retain flexibility so as to permit the Central Committee and the Executive Committee to act in response to changing situations. It should also be noted that the decisions which may be taken by the Assembly on the basis of the recommendations made in this

[1] Part 3 of the recommendations of the Central Committee on Structure and Functioning contained the old Rules with suggested amendments in parallel columns. In the present volume the Rules are printed as amended by the Second Assembly (see Appendix, p. 337).

report, cannot become fully effective until 1955. In the judgment of the Central Committee, the proposals in this report should not be regarded as final and there may well be need for a further review of the structure and functioning of the World Council to be undertaken by the Third Assembly in the light of further experience.

DISCUSSION ON STRUCTURE AND FUNCTIONING

First Discussion

The Bishop of London called attention to an entirely new principle invoked by the Committee in suggesting that the presidents of the World Council should be ineligible for re-election. He said no reason had been given for the enunciation of the new principle and that its consequences could be disastrous. Some presidents had given valued service and should certainly continue. He said he did not speak on a personal basis, but that the removal of some members of the presidium whose influence for the World Council in their own countries was strong might prove highly undesirable.

Mr. Charles P. Taft expressed embarrassment in speaking contrary to Dr. Wand, a member of his own communion. In view of the fact that Assemblies of the World Council of Churches are held only every five or six years, the Council should try to have a truly representative presidium. The proposed arrangement would spread the representative character of the presidents' offices, and continuity could be preserved by electing ex-presidents to the Central Committee, where they could vote and be even more influential.

Dr. P. Bersell asked that the Assembly should not "tinker with the present provisions concerning the presidium." He said many hoped the time would come when the World Council would have only one president but that the present men had gained prestige for the World Council.

Dr. Willem F. Golterman welcomed the proposal to enable more churches to give good presidents to the Council, but doubted whether so much discontinuity was good. Why should not three of the presidium of six resign at each Assembly; or, alternatively, a rule about the filling of vacancies could provide for the Central Committee to vary the presidium's composition.

Dr. Eugene C. Blake spoke in favour of the proposal and said that it was more desirable that a variety of member churches compose a presidium than that it should be thought of as a panel of *kinds of churches*. The presidium should rotate equally among all the churches and be truly representative of them all.

Mr. Charles T. LeQuesne asked whether the departmental bye-laws might be held under the terms of the report as legally superseding the constitution of the Commission on Faith and Order. He further asked whether the provision requiring departmental programmes to be submitted to divisional committees applied to Faith and Order.

Dr. Leslie Cooke, replying to Mr. LeQuesne, said that the word department had been used with the clear understanding that some departments, and notably Faith and Order, would work under their existing constitutions. Thus, the Faith and Order department would work under its Commission. The point was worthy of further elaboration during the Structure and Functioning Committee's "hearing." No question of subordination is anticipated as arising within the outlined structure.

Second Discussion

Dr. Franklin Clark Fry (in the chair) called the meeting to order and explained the procedure.

Dr. Leslie Cooke formally moved the resolution for the adoption of the report of the Committee on Structure and Functioning. In doing so he acted for the Central Committee and explained that the resolution would involve amendment of the rules as set out in Part 3 of the report and inclusion of minor amendments accepted during the Committee's "hearing" on the previous day. Adoption of the report would be subject to budgetary provision.

The Rev. R. D. Say spoke as a member of the Structure and Functioning Committee to second Dr. Cooke's motion. He reminded the Assembly of certain considerations. The Structure and Functioning Committee was concerned that the World Council of Churches should be an effective instrument in "helping the ecumenical movement to move." The Committee desired effective relations between the Council and its constituent churches and looked forward to the increasing participation of all the churches in its work. Efficiency and the best use of money were also desirable in order that the Council reflect present conditions under which many member churches worked. The above requirements might be met by:

1. Strong central direction;
2. Flexibility of movement;
3. Effective outward and backward communication.

The "hearing" had approved the report's three main recommendations concerning structure, staffing and external relationships.

Mr. Say then alluded to the presidium. He said the present proposal was one of six considered by the Central Committee since 1952 and outlined the alternatives. The reasons for the present proposal were:

1. That the World Council should be both geographically and confessionally representative;
2. That the office of president was representative and not administrative and continuity was not therefore vital;
3. That the confessional and geographical balance could best be preserved by an entirely new selection at each Assembly.

There would be real regret in some places at such a decision, but the World Council now drew its membership from 163 churches and 48 countries. The trend was away from dependence on great personalities and towards a day when each church would have a real stake in the Council's life and work. The proposal was a stage along this road.

Dr. Fry drew attention, from the chair, to the procedure concerning amendments embodied in rule 14 of the Council.

Dr. Kathleen Bliss drew attention to the position of the Director of the Ecumenical Institute, in the new plan. She foresaw a "threat of subordination" in that the Institute was one department within the Division of Ecumenical Action. The Institute was equally linked with Evangelism and Studies. Annual expenditure on its work was the largest single item on the World Council's budget. The office of Director was very important. The present Director was a man of high calibre, and his successor should be equally so. Though the aim of the plan is co-ordination, any coming Director seeing it would be led to anticipate subordination. The Institute was a living pulse for the ecumenical movement. Dr. Bliss hoped the future of Bossey would be referred back to the Structure and Functioning Committee for further consideration.

Dr. Fry, explaining procedure from the chair, said that the report would be adopted section by section and that Dr. Bliss should bring a concrete proposal at the relevant point.

Dr. Leslie Cooke, for the Central Committee, reminded Dr. Bliss and the Assembly that the chart did not imply precedence or subordination.

The report was then submitted and adopted with amendments, in sections, the discussion being as follows:

Canon R. K. Naylor spoke on the question of retirement of the presidium. He said that their complete simultaneous withdrawal might lead to confusion.

Archbishop Brilioth said that if the new rule on the presidium were carried against a small but determined minority this would be regrettable. He saw weighty reasons against the rule. It may limit the freedom of action of the Assembly in relation to the presidium. A system of rotation would have been better. He asked leave to move the deletion of the words "a president shall be ineligible for immediate re-election when his term of office ends."

Leave was granted.

Bishop Oxnam, speaking to answer Archbishop Brilioth's points, opposed the deletion. He said that the presidency was not an administrative but a representative office. Committees and staff preserve necessary continuity for the Council. A retiring president may be elected to the incoming Central Committee. Qualified leaders were available. Failure to adopt the Central Committee's resolution could drive a wedge into the Council. If only some presidents retire both churches which are not chosen and individuals not elected may be offended. Without offence to his colleagues in the presidium he could see that there was danger in having too many presidents who were over seventy. The adoption of the new rule did not imply its inflexibility. Archbishop Brilioth's amendment would tend to fix the present pattern and was therefore itself an inflexible rather than a flexible measure. Bishop Oxnam urged, therefore, that a president should not succeed himself.

Dr. Bersell said that it was really effectively shown that the presidium was not administrative. Presidents had helped establish the Council's influence and acted valuably in an advisory capacity, but the fate of the World Council did not depend on any one man. The Central Committee's plan would make complete rotation of all offices in the presidium mandatory. He favoured the original proposition because it left the Assembly free to determine even the number of presidents.

Dr. Douglas Horton spoke for the recommendation and against the amendment. He said the Council could still alter such a decision later, but must decide the issue on the higher ground of principle, not the lower ground of personal affection and loyalty.

The Bishop of Armidale asked whether the new provision for the presidium could become retrospective, in the sense that the present presidents would be no longer presidents when their terms of office ended. Could they then be renominated for another five years at least at the present Assembly? He said that great names and figures carry weight on "the outskirts of the world."

Dr. Fry then ruled that the proposal was to be immediately operative.

Dr. Benjamin Mays spoke in favour of the new proposal on the presidium. He said it would be dangerous if it were not adopted, because presidents would then be too long in office. There was no dearth of leadership. More countries and communions could participate in representative office.

Mr. F. Larudy spoke as representing the smallest (Iranian) church in membership. He said that many small churches joining the World Council in the future would be encouraged locally by knowing they could be even within the presidium.

Dr. Fry then put Archbishop Brilioth's amendment which was lost.

Following approval of further sections of the report (subject to budgetary revision) Dr. Bliss introduced her proposal for the future of the Ecumenical Institute.

Dr. Visser 't Hooft said that it would be undesirable for the Assembly at this stage to create uncertainty as to whether the Ecumenical Institute should be related to the Division of Ecumenical Action.

Dr. Bliss then successfuly moved that the Central Committee be asked to review the status of the Director of the Ecumenical Institute with power to make necessary alterations at this point.

The remainder of the report was adopted. The Assembly proceeded to confirm consequent changes in the Council's Rules.

Dr. Visser 't Hooft said that the aims and functions of departments as set out in the report should be subject to modification in detail on the advice of the Assembly Committees on World Council business.

Canon Hartford, speaking of the integration of Faith and Order into the new plan, said that it must be remembered that Faith and Order had a specific function in reminding the World Council that no mere loose federation is the goal of the Christian world. The functions of Faith and Order had been safeguarded in the new arrangement but the spirit in which they are interpreted is important.

Part 2 of the report, setting out aims and functions of divisions and departments, was adopted, with the understanding that the approval given was general and not necessarily detailed.

Bishop Nichols questioned the use of the term "main confessions" in the provisions of the new rules covering the Nominations Committee.

Dr. Fry interpreted the phrase as implying "wide representation" rather than implied status.

Dr. Cooke asked the Commission to insert under the rules for the Nominations Committee of the Central Committee that it should also nominate the Executive Committee. He foreshadowed an amendment to make this possible.

Part 3 of the report of the Committee of Structure and Functioning was then adopted with the insertion of amendments remitted from the "hearing," subject to insertion of Dr. Cooke's foreshadowed amendment on the Executive Committee.

The Reports of the Assembly Committees

THE REPORT OF
THE COMMITTEE ON GENERAL POLICY

Adopted by the Assembly

Note: The Report of the Committee on General Policy was adopted without substantive debate.

I. The Basis

A. The committee has taken note of the action of the Central Committee as recorded on page 51 of the Work Book and calls attention to the fact that as a result of this decision no proposal for a change in the Basis is before the Assembly at this time.

B. The committee reports to the Assembly that the Church of Norway has submitted a proposal for amending Article I of the Constitution so that it will read as follows:

The World Council of Churches is a fellowship of churches which, in accordance with Holy Scripture confess our Lord Jesus Christ as God and Saviour.

This proposal was received too late to be considered by the Second Assembly, since Article VIII of the Constitution requires that notice of any proposed amendment must be sent to the constituent churches "not less than six months before the meeting of the Assembly." The proposal will be studied carefully by the Central Committee which will report thereon to the Third Assembly.

C. The committee recommends to the Assembly approval of the draft statement on purpose and function of the Basis as found on pages 52 and 53 of the Assembly Work Book (see Appendix 1).

D. The committee notes that the Arminian Church in Holland (Remonstrant Brotherhood) has withdrawn its request for a change in the Basis because it desires to further an informal theological discussion on the Basis rather than to promote a constitutional decision.

II. Amendments to Articles III and VI of the Constitution

In order to adapt the Constitution of the World Council of Churches to the new situation created by the acceptance of the new constitution of Faith and Order by the Lund Conference and by the Central Committee, the General Policy Committee recommends to the Assembly:

1. That in Article III—Functions—of the Constitution of the World Council of Churches the following words be dropped:

In matters of common interest to all the churches and pertaining to Faith and Order, the Council shall always proceed in accordance with the basis on which the Lausanne (1927) and Edinburgh (1937) Conferences were called and conducted.

2. That in Article VI—Appointment of Commissions—of the Constitution of the World Council of Churches the following words be dropped:

There shall be a Faith and Order Commission which shall conform to the requirements of the Second World Conference on Faith and Order, held at Edinburgh in 1937, as follows:

(i) That the World Council's Commission on Faith and Order shall, in the first instance, be the Continuation Committee appointed by this Conference.

(ii) In any further appointments made by the Council to membership of the Commission on Faith and Order, the persons appointed shall always be members of the churches which fall within the terms of the Faith and Order invitation as addressed to "all Christian bodies throughout the world which accept our Lord Jesus Christ as God and Saviour."

(iii) The work of the Commission on Faith and Order shall be carried on under the general care of a Theological Secretariat appointed by the Commission, in consultation with the Council and acting in close co-operation with other secretariats of the Council. The Council shall make adequate financial provision for the work of the Commission after consultation with the Commission.

(iv) In matters of common interest to all the churches and pertaining to Faith and Order, the Council shall always proceed in accordance with the basis on which this Conference was called and is being conducted.

(v) The World Council shall consist of official representatives of the churches participating.

(vi) Any Council formed before the first meeting of the Central Assembly shall be called Provisional, and the Assembly, representing all the churches, shall have complete freedom to determine the constitution of the Central Council.

and that in Article VI the following clauses be substituted for those which are thus removed:

There shall be a Faith and Order Commission of which the following shall be the functions:

(i) To proclaim the essential oneness of the Church of Christ and to keep prominently before the World Council and the churches the obligation to manifest that unity and its urgency for the work of evangelism;

(ii) To study questions of faith, order, and worship with the relevant social, cultural, political, racial, and other factors in their bearing on the unity of the churches;

(iii) To study the theological implications of the existence of the ecumenical movement;

(iv) To study matters in the present relationships of the churches to one another which cause difficulties and need theological clarification;

(v) To provide information concerning actual steps taken by the churches towards reunion.

The Commission shall discharge these functions in accordance with a constitution approved by the Central Committee.

In invitations to world conferences on Faith and Order, it shall be specified that such conferences are to be composed of official delegates of churches which accept Jesus Christ as God and Saviour.

The notice of this amendment was sent to the churches in 1953 as required by the Constitution (Article VIII).

III. INTERPRETATION OF
ARTICLE VIII OF THE CONSTITUTION

The question was raised as to the interpretation of Article
VIII of the Constitution which has to do with amendments and
reads as follows:

> The Constitution may be amended by a two-thirds majority
> vote of the Assembly, provided that the proposed amendment
> shall have been reviewed by the Central Committee, and notice
> of it sent to the constituent churches not less than six months
> before the meeting of the Assembly. The Central Committee
> itself, as well as the individual churches, shall have the right to
> propose such amendment.

The committee therefore suggests that this Article be interpreted to mean that the sending to the constituent churches of the
notice of a proposed constitutional amendment is the responsibility of the General Secretariat and should be mandatory, unless,
as a result of review by the Central Committee or for any other
reason, the member church making the proposal should withdraw
it more than six months before the meeting of the Assembly.

IV. RELATIONS WITH THE
INTERNATIONAL MISSIONARY COUNCIL

A. The committee recommends to the Assembly acceptance of
the report of the Joint Committee of the World Council of
Churches and the International Missionary Council as contained on pages 54–8 of the Assembly Work Book and the
adoption of the recommendations contained therein (see pp. 322–
327).

B. The Committee on General Policy in recommending
acceptance of the report of the Joint Committee notes with deep
appreciation the resolutions of the Ad Interim Committee of the
International Missionary Council in July 1954, advising the
World Council of Churches of its approval of the report and in
addition expressing a sense of necessity to press on to further ways
and means by which "the inseparable oneness of mission and
unity" may be more convincingly demonstrated in the life of the
I.M.C. and the W.C.C. The resolutions of the I.M.C. also recom-

mend "that the two bodies continue to think and work together in such a way as to give even closer and more dynamic expression to their 'association' with one another (and) that with a deep sense of urgency and under the guidance of the Holy Spirit they should strive to reach a consummation in which the churches which compose the W.C.C. and the councils which compose the I.M.C. would sponsor and promote unitedly the world mission of the church." The committee does not, however, understand or intend this statement to imply any judgment regarding the structure of any united organization that may eventually emerge.

The Assembly will hear with gratitude that these resolutions not only authorize the implementation of the proposal to establish a secretariat for the Joint Committee but provide for budget resources to meet the I.M.C.'s share of the cost of such an office.

While approving the continuation of the regional secretaryship in East Asia, the Ad Interim Committee of the I.M.C. communicates its sense of the necessity to extend the policy of regional secretaryships to such regions as Africa, the Middle East, Latin America, the West Indies, etc., and advises that it will instruct its officers and representatives on the Joint Committee to keep this matter under constant review, looking toward action as soon as agreed plans and resources permit.

V. Policy with regard to Public Pronouncements

The committee recommends that the Assembly record its judgment that the rules governing the issuance of public statements as formulated in the Central Committee's report on Structure and Functioning (see pp. 174–214) adopted on 17th August, 1954, afford adequate guidance for the present.

The committee further recommends that whenever a public statement has been issued by the Central Committee in accordance with these rules, it be promptly communicated to the responsible officials of all member churches, with a request that it be brought to the attention of the churches and with an intimation that comments on it would be welcome.

VI. The Third Assembly

A. The committee recommends to the Assembly that the date and place of the Third Assembly be left to the decision of the

Central Committee but that this Assembly express the judgment that the Third Assembly should be held not earlier than 1960.

B. The committee recommends to the Assembly that the number of members of the Third Assembly be set at five hundred (500) and that the Central Committee be authorized to increase or diminish this number by not more than twenty (20) per cent.

C. The committee recommends to the Assembly that it express satisfaction with the distribution of seats in this Assembly.

VII. REPORT OF THE CHAIRMAN OF THE CENTRAL COMMITTEE AND THE GENERAL SECRETARY

This committee takes special notice of the report of the Central Committee and the statement by the General Secretary made during the early meetings of the Assembly.

We commend the General Secretary for compelling us to think through the answer to the sharply penetrating questions which his report posed. Did we go too far? Did we undertake too much? Has the World Council lost its momentum? Have we made real progress in church unity? These questions demand imaginative thinking and the committee suggests that the churches of the Council urge study of them in congregations throughout the world.

Likewise we express appreciation to the Bishop of Chichester for his interpretation of the spirit in which the Central Committee works. He drew aside the curtain for a bit and revealed a genuine ecumenicity at the vital centre of all World Council planning and activity.

It would be desirable that all members of the World Council Secretariat be named and thanked individually, but this is an obvious impossibility. This committee recommends that the Assembly record its gratitude in general to all members of the staff for the contribution made to the progress of the Council.

We must, nevertheless, single out two persons for special commendation, the Bishop of Chichester whose wisdom, gentleness, and firmness, whose steady courage and unremitting patience have been stamped upon the entire life of the World Council, and the General Secretary, Dr. Visser 't Hooft, for leadership that combines breadth of understanding and depth of conviction in a measure that accomplishes seemingly impossible tasks.

THE REPORT OF THE
COMMITTEE ON THE DIVISION OF STUDIES

Adopted by the Assembly

I. Approval of Whole Scheme of Division of Studies

The Committee expresses its conviction that the Division of Studies with its four departments as set forth in the General Report on Structure and Functioning and as further described in the documents for the working committees, is of extreme value for the work of the W.C.C. and I.M.C. to serve the churches by promoting ecumenical studies on the fundamental issues of their faith and life, so that they may increasingly think together, advance in unity, render common witness, and take common action in the social and international field. The Committee is particularly convinced that the new relationship between the Research Department of the I.M.C. and the Division of Studies of the W.C.C. is an important step forward in the direction of closer association between the two bodies.

A. *The Committee* RECOMMENDS *to the Assembly to adopt the documents for the working committees as far as they concern the Division of Studies as a general guide for the work of this Division. (See Appendix 2 in addition to the Report of the Joint Committee of the I.M.C.-W.C.C. See pp. 322–327.)*

B. *It further* RECOMMENDS *that the following three points be incorporated in this general guide:*

1. All studies undertaken should be aimed at serving the cause of the *whole* ecumenical movement and of the *whole* church.

2. While recognizing the relative independence of each department, their *interdependence* too should be realized in all ways possible in the actual process of study work.

3. In view of the comparatively small staff and the limited funds at the disposal of the Division of Studies, the Divisional Committee and the staff should constantly aim at devising the *greatest economy* in using the available resources.

C. *General theme*

There was considerable discussion of the question whether all studies of the Division of Studies might be carried out in relation to a general theme and whether this general theme should be "The Mission of the Church into the World," emphasis to be put on its christological interpretation and an ecumenical biblical approach. This general theme was not meant as a separate topic for study but rather as an indication of the direction in which the various study projects should be undertaken. The Committee was unable to come to a clear decision as to the advisability of such a general theme, the main objection being that a general theme might restrict the flexibility of departmental studies.

It is therefore RECOMMENDED *that the content of the discussion be reported to the Divisional Committee, final decision to be taken by the Central Committee.*

II. Approval or Alterations of the Study Programme

The sub-committees discussed at length the study programmes outlined on pp. 61–5 of the Assembly Work Book. A number of changes and additions were suggested and accepted by the working committee (see Appendix 3). They will be submitted to the Division of Studies for consideration and incorporation in the general guide for the work of the Division. A special study should be added to the Department of Church and Society on the Christian understanding of work, jointly with the Department of the Laity.

The Committee RECOMMENDS *that the question of priorities in the study programmes should be left to the decision of the committees of the Division of Studies.*

Three changes in the wording of the general report relating to the work of the Division of Studies were suggested, namely:

A. In the section on the Department of Evangelism (Report of Structure and Functioning, Part 2, 1, C, i) the text should read as follows: ". . . to keep prominently . . . member churches, the importance of the Church's evangelistic and missionary obligation and *its call to unity*", and

B. An addition should be made under Part 2, 1, "vii. To advise the churches about actions resulting from the studies."

C. In Part 2, 1, B, ii, to change the last part to read ". . . walks of life, relevant problems in this field," deleting the last part "as have . . . by the divisional committee."

III. Correlation:
Ecumenical Institute—Division of Studies

In the interest of better co-ordination of all study work undertaken under the auspices of the W.C.C. and of establishing a more organic relationship between studies and teaching,

The Committee RECOMMENDS *that the Central Committee give special consideration to the need of correlating the study programme of the Division of Studies and of the Ecumenical Institute in accordance with the principle set forth in the Report on Structure and Functioning, Pt. I, IV, A, i.*

IV. Co-operation and Joint Studies

Realizing that the study work of the various departments will have to be done in closest contact and mutual consultation between the responsible bodies and workers, the Committee discussed at some length the principles which should govern such collaboration and consultation.

A. *The Committee* RECOMMENDS *that in all study enterprises undertaken by two or more departments in close co-operation it should be determined which department is to be mainly responsible instead of setting up joint committees; and that in instances in which it is not clear which department should be responsible, the decision should be made by the Divisional Committee.*

B. Answering the first question contained in Part 4, B, 3, of the Assembly Work Book (see Appendix 2), *the Committee* RECOMMENDS *closest possible co-ordination of the work of the Department of Evangelism and of the Department of Missionary Studies. The Committee* RECOMMENDS *further that the following passage be inserted at the proper place in Part 1, V, 3, (Report on Structure and Functioning): "In the interest of closest possible co-ordination of the Department on Evangelism and the Department of Missionary Studies, the working committees of these Departments shall meet together from time to time."*

C. *The Committee* RECOMMENDS *that the Department on Evangelism and the Department of Missionary Studies co-operate with the proposed joint committee of the I.M.C., W.C.C. and United Bible Societies, in the work of that committee.*

D. *The Committee* RECOMMENDS *to add at the end of Part I,*

V, 2 (a), Report on Structure and Functioning "For the purpose of co-ordination the Division of Studies should be represented by one or two members on the Committee of the Division of Ecumenical Action and vice versa.

V. STAFF AND MEANS

In order to accomplish the proposed large study programme, the sub-committees and the Working Committee felt that the staff and means as envisaged according to the proposed Budget are not adequate.

In particular the Committee RECOMMENDS:

A. *East Asia Secretariat*

1. *The appointment of an assistant secretary to the Division of Studies, who would be associated with the East Asia Secretariat and who would be responsible to the Division of Studies for the promotion of studies in East Asia.*

2. *That a small representative advisory committee on studies in East Asia be constituted in consultation with the East Asia Secretariat and that additional financial provision for its meeting once a year be made in the budget of the Division of Studies.*

3. *That periodical East Asia study consultations along the lines of the one held at Lucknow, India, in 1952 be made possible by the Division of Studies.*

B. *Evangelism*

The Committee expresses its judgment that the Department on Evangelism would need more staff time than one secretary can give. It would also need a stenographer with ability to read in more than one language so that she can read the documents that come to the Department on Evangelism and to some extent be able to correlate them.

The Committee RECOMMENDS *that the present budgetary provision as shown in the Work Book, p. 88 (Note: See Report of Committee on Finance) be increased*

1. *to provide for the staff as requested above,*

2. *to provide for the holding of an annual major international study conference on evangelism,*

3. *to provide for adequate help to be given for evangelistic studies being done on a regional basis.*

C. The Committee discussed and found acceptable the proposal to have a joint secretary between the C.C.I.A. and the Division of Studies who would work primarily with the Department of Church and Society on questions of mutual concern to the Division of Studies and C.C.I.A. The Committee RECOMMENDS accordingly.

D. The Committee is aware that the proposed study programmes will require very considerable facilities for the translation of memoranda, printed papers, and other documents, and therefore RECOMMENDS *that provision for the needed staff be made in the budget.*

VI. RESOURCES OUTSIDE THE STAFF OF THE DIVISION OF STUDIES

Both because of the large scope of the proposed study programme and because these studies are undertaken on behalf and in the service of the churches, *the Committee* RECOMMENDS *that additional resources and personnel be sought, and particularly*

A. *that the W.C.C. ask the churches to put at the disposal of the Division of Studies from time to time scholars interested in ecumenical studies and to bear as much of the cost thereof as they are able to do,*

B. *that the attention of the churches be drawn to the necessity of carrying out specific ecumenical studies on a regional basis,*

C. *that the theological faculties be approached also by the Division of Studies with regard to particular study topics for which one or the other professor might be specially equipped,*

D. *to draw the attention of theological faculties, seminaries and professors to the unique facility that students desiring to write a thesis for a degree might work on topics contained in the study programme of the Division of Studies and thus aid the ecumenical studies.*

VII. EVANSTON FOLLOW-UP

A Sub-Committee of the former Study Department Committee submitted to the Committee of the Division of Studies a number of proposals regarding the follow-up work of the Evanston Assembly. (See Appendix 3).

The Committee ENDORSES *these proposals and* RECOMMENDS *to the Assembly that appropriate action be taken.*

DISCUSSION ON THE REPORT ON
THE DIVISION OF STUDIES

Dr. Meyer presented seriatim the sections and the report of the Committee on the Division of Studies.

Dr. Fry suggested that where projects outlined require budget support, the Central Committee should be asked to provide the funds required only as resources were forthcoming.

Dr. Payne asked what would be the first call on such resources if the money should be available.

Dr. Meyer said his Committee did not feel it should establish priorities but should leave their determination to the Central Committee.

Professor Tiga expressed joy and gratitude for the recommendation that an East Asia study secretary be appointed. He suggested that a small representative advisory committee should assist such a secretary.

The report of Committee II was then adopted.

THE REPORT OF THE COMMITTEE ON THE DIVISION OF ECUMENICAL ACTION

Adopted by the Assembly

GENERAL REVIEW

The Assembly's Working Committee on Ecumenical Action has endeavoured within the time limitations of our meetings to review the work of the four existing departments assigned to us, and the plan for their grouping in a new Division of Ecumenical Action as provided for in the Report on Structure and Functioning of the World Council.

It is our conviction that the four departments under consideration correspond to needs widely recognized or calling for recognition in our member churches. All of us wish to express our indebtedness to their heavily burdened staffs for the devotion and ability they have brought to our common cause. Let us not forget that the whole executive staff of these four far-reaching undertakings will number only nine persons.

1. *The Ecumenical Institute* is a unique institution within the framework of the Council. It provides an opportunity for leaders, clerical and lay, from many churches and nations to live together, to worship and study together. It is an essential instrument of the Division of Studies, and for consultations and conferences essential to the work of other divisions and departments. It is an exploratory and creative centre for all our shared concerns for the renewal and mission of the Church. The closely related Graduate School of Ecumenical Studies gives promise of offering the opportunity for the training of highly competent leadership in ecumenical thought and action, which can have wide influence in the years ahead.

2. *The Youth Department* has increasingly served the churches by introducing young people to the ecumenical movement through personal contacts, conferences and participation in the life of the World Council. It has encouraged the development of youth work in new areas. Through the department's work camp programme and through the mutual aid programme known as World Youth Projects, young people of all confessions and continents are seeking to express in practical terms their faith in the oneness of the Church and its world-wide task. They have found in the ecumenical movement evangelistic power. To continuance of such service this department is rightly directed.

3. *The Department on Work for the Laity* has in its first years established through visitations and correspondence, ecumenical contacts with more than two hundred lay groups, organizations and institutes all over the world; has published a bulletin entitled *Laymen's Work*; has organized the European Lay Conference; has contributed to the establishment of the American Lay Conference; and has developed an index of lay leaders, and organized courses and conferences for various groups of the laity. We heartily endorse the continuance of its work along these lines.

4. *The Department on the Co-operation of Men and Women in Church and Society*, formerly the Commission of the Life and Work of Women in the Church, is concerned with certain quite special problems of dislocation and unbalance in the life of the Church, now seen as urgent in many areas, but which we dare hope may prove to be transitional. Its task is to promote among *men and women* the study of questions affecting the co-operation and the common service of men and women in the churches and in society.

It seeks to help women to make their contribution to the total life of the churches, and to urge the churches to enable and stimulate women to share fully in the opportunities and responsibilities of church membership. In view of the strength of women's organizations in many countries and churches, this Department is inevitably called upon: (1) to foster an ecumenical outlook among them; (2) to encourage their participation in the ecumenical movement as a whole, and (3) to provide for women church members information on the life and work of women in churches everywhere and to encourage contacts between them. We commend this Department to the confidence and support of the Assembly, until its task shall have been substantially fulfilled.

5. Turning now to the new *Division of Ecumenical Action*, in which these departments have been grouped, your working committee fully recognizes the advantages in terms of more effective administration and correlation of the new structural arrangement. We are not satisfied with the name of the Division, and we think that there are some tendencies to over-elaboration and artificiality in the plan resulting from a commendable effort to put on paper a tidy and rational scheme. We do not advise any attempt at this time to alter the structure or to revise the definition of the aim and functions of the Division. But we are confident that the Central Committee will view the scheme as somewhat provisional and experimental and as subject to revision in the light of experience with its workings. In particular, we suggest the departmental committees be strongly maintained (in conjunction with the Divisional Committee) on account of the diverse and distinctive tasks of the four departments.

More Detailed Recommendations

I come now to the specific recommendations made by the working committee. They are divided into (I) recommendations made through the Assembly to the member churches, (II) recommendations to the Assembly, and (III) recommendations made through the Assembly to the Central Committee. Other recommendations which primarily concern separate departments have been noted and will be referred directly to the departmental committees and staff for consideration and action.

I. RECOMMENDATIONS THROUGH THE ASSEMBLY TO THE MEMBER CHURCHES

A. *General*

1. The member churches should be asked to review most carefully their own administrative structures to make sure that within each church adequate *provision is made for co-operation* with the different departments of the World Council of Churches, with the corresponding departments in national councils of churches, and with neighbouring churches.

2. The member churches should be reminded that *ecumenical education* is not one particular activity within the life of a church, but concerns the life of the Church in all its activities including preaching and teaching on major doctrines.

3. The member churches should be asked to give attention to the urgent question of the *approach of the churches*, severally and jointly, *to industrial workers*.

B. *Concerning Various Departments*

Youth Department

4. Churches and mission boards should be asked to give earnest consideration to the development of *new patterns of co-operative ecumenical youth work* in different parts of the world.

Department on Work for the Laity

5. The member churches should be asked to note the fact that the department is not concerned with lay *men* only, but with the laity, i.e. *lay men* and *lay women* generally.

Department on Co-operation of Men and Women in Church and Society

6. The member churches should be asked to recognize *the seriousness of the problem of the co-operation of men and women* in various areas of church life, and to seek ways in which this problem can be solved so that both men and women can give their full contribution to the life of the Church. It should be recognized that these are not questions for women only, but for men and women to consider together.

Ecumenical Institute

7. The member churches should be asked to take note of the importance of the *Graduate School of the Ecumenical Institute*, and be urged to explore ways of encouraging and financing the enrolment of selected mature students in the Graduate School.

8. The member churches should be asked to note that the Ecumenical Institute provides unusual *opportunities for following up special problems and concerns* which have been the subjects of ecumenical gatherings and conferences held elsewhere.

9. The member churches should be asked to note that the Ecumenical Institute will continue to provide many courses and conferences of great value in *developing ecumenical consciousness* among members of the churches.

II. RECOMMENDATIONS TO THE ASSEMBLY

Youth Department (see Report on Structure and Functioning, Part 2, 2)

10. The statement of *aim* and *functions* should be accepted as satisfactory.

Department on Work for the Laity (see Report on Structure and Functioning, Part 2, 2)

11. The question of the name of this Department is referred to the Central Committee.

12. The statement of *aim* and *functions*, with the addition to the *aim* of the words "to foster ecumenical understanding among the laity," should be accepted as satisfactory.

Department on Co-operation of Men and Women in Church and Society (see Report on Structure and Functioning, Part 2, 2)

13. The statement of *aim* and *functions* should be accepted as satisfactory subject to a number of changes not involving questions of principle which are referred to the Central Committee.

Ecumenical Institute (see Report on Structure and Functioning, Part 2, 2)

14. The statement of *aim* and *functions* should be accepted as satisfactory.

III. RECOMMENDATIONS THROUGH THE ASSEMBLY TO THE CENTRAL COMMITTEE

A. *General*

15. The Central Committee should consider how the World Council might help the member churches to make *better use of delegates to ecumenical conferences* and meetings, and of visitors of other churches, for the ecumenical education of their membership especially at the local level.

16. The Central Committee should consider the possibility of an investigation by the World Council in co-operation with the W.C.C.E. and other interested bodies of means of assisting the churches in providing *ecumenical education for boys and girls under eighteen.*

17. The attention of the Central Committee should be drawn to the exceptional difficulty of *departments to which only one member of staff is assigned,* in carrying out the services required of them, especially visitation of the churches.

18. The Central Committee should consider ways and means whereby the Council might respond to the widespread and serious demands from the churches for help in *study and action concerning family life.*

19. The Central Committee should consider whether and how the World Council could give more assistance to the churches in promoting *ecumenical prayer and worship.*

20. The Central Committee should be asked to continue the practice of inviting observers from the *world Christian organizations* to sit in with the various departmental and divisional committees of the Council with which they have some concern, and to welcome reciprocal invitations.

B. *Concerning Departments*

Department on Co-operation of Men and Women

21. The Central Committee should be asked to note the departmental sub-committee's strongly expressed opinion that at present the work of this Department should be *kept distinct* from that of the Department on Work for the Laity.

Ecumenical Institute

22. The Central Committee should be asked to make an early study of the possibility that *regional institutes* on parallel lines should be brought into existence, so that church members in all parts of the world may have the opportunity to share in consultations, conferences, and courses of the type now available at Bossey.

23. The Central Committee should regard the *provision for staff* for the Ecumenical Institute now made in the budget (see Report of the Committee on Finance) as the absolute minimum necessary if the Institute is to be able to do the work committed to it.

24. The Central Committee should recognize that a high degree of flexibility is necessary in operating the provisions of the new divisional structure of the World Council, in order that the closest possible co-ordination of the Institute with a wide variety of the Council's activities outside the Division of Ecumenical Action should be preserved and fostered, and that the Institute itself may have the freedom for initiative and imagination which is necessary for its work.

25. In particular it is recommended that the Central Committee should be asked to note the need for the Institute in consultation with the General Secretariat, to retain (a) freedom of direct communication with the churches, (b) freedom in making proposals for the recruitment of staff, and (c) freedom in planning travel by the staff of the Institute.

DISCUSSION ON THE REPORT OF THE COMMITTEE ON THE DIVISION OF ECUMENICAL ACTION

The report was presented by Bishop Dun, who said that the work of the Committee had been complicated by the number of tasks before the Division in relation to the size of the budget. The whole complex undertaking would have to be directed by an executive staff of only nine persons. The need for further financial provision was therefore imperative.

Dr. Cooke moved that the title of the Department on Work for the Laity be referred to the Central Committee for further consideration.

Dr. Meyer, referring to the place of the Ecumenical Institute in the Division, moved that the word "relationship" in the third of the recommendations made concerning the Ecumenical Institute should be replaced by the words "closest possible co-ordination."

Bishop Dun said the change was acceptable. It was duly made by the Assembly.

THE REPORT OF THE COMMITTEE ON THE DIVISION OF INTER-CHURCH AID AND SERVICE TO REFUGEES

Adopted by the Assembly

Note: The Report of the Committee on Inter-Church Aid and Service to Refugees was adopted without substantive debate.

I. BASIS

"Inter-Church Aid" is based on the teaching of Scripture and the practice of the apostolic church. The Christian Church, which is the Body of Christ in the world, in obedience to her Lord seeks to "do good unto all men, especially unto them who are of the household of faith" (Gal. 6: 10), being reminded that "the body is one, and hath many members . . . and if one member suffer, all the members suffer with it" (Cor. 12: 12, 26).

II. PRINCIPLES

1. Inter-Church Aid has become a permanent obligation of the World Council of Churches. By accepting the privilege of sharing in this work the member churches bear witness to their hope in Christ and manifest the reality of the fellowship and wholeness of the Church. The World Council of Churches through the Division of Inter-Church Aid and Service to Refugees concerns itself with the renewal and strengthening of the life of the churches, with programmes of material aid in the case of ongoing emergency situations such as those of refugees, war victims, and with emergency relief and rehabilitation in situations of sudden disaster and natural catastrophe.

2. The relationships in the field of Inter-Church Aid can only be sustained by mutual trust and confidence among the churches. Every church is responsible for its own area and its own members. Christian love and compassion, however, impel churches to suggest and initiate assistance to other churches. The Division at all times seeks to co-operate with non-member churches or other bodies working on similar principles.

III. Policies and Programme of the Division

1. The Committee finds itself in agreement with the aims and functions already stated as follows (see Report on Structure and Functioning, Part 3, 3):

The *aim* of the Division shall be to further, on an ecumenical basis, the renewal of the churches through practical help which churches may render to one another, through the relief of human need, and through service to refugees.

The *functions* of the Division shall be:

(*a*) to provide, on the basis of mutual study and consultation, a total strategy of Inter-Church Aid and Service to Refugees in which the initiatives and programmes of all churches and national committees can be related to one another, and thus be given maximum usefulness;

(*b*) to secure and disseminate information about the needs of the churches and of refugees, and also about the gifts and services which may be made available to meet these needs;

(*c*) to find contributions to meet requests;

(*d*) to suggest projects and spheres of need which might be neglected and should receive attention;

(*e*) to operate, at the request of the churches, such services as may best be carried out co-operatively, e.g. for refugees;

(*f*) to receive and administer such gifts, whether earmarked or unearmarked, which churches and other bodies place at its disposal;

(*g*) to co-operate with the International Missionary Council on terms mutually agreed, and to report to its officers and governing committees on all matters concerned with Emergency Inter-Church Aid and Relief in countries outside Europe.

2. In the light of the above functions the Division shall provide for:

(*a*) consultation with world confessional associations on giving within the same church family and continual emphasis on the need for inter-confessional giving;

(*b*) an increased service of information and publicity;

(*c*) a system of identifying gifts and interpreting the meaning of Inter-Church Aid;

(*d*) visitation and personnel exchanges;

(*e*) attention to the needs of minority churches;

(*f*) aid to churches through loans as well as gifts;

(*g*) health services;

(*h*) a theological scholarship programme;

(*i*) a theological literature programme;

(*j*) experimental and pilot projects.

3. In the light of the new agreement with the International Missionary Council, the programme of the Division in Asia and Africa is concerned for the time being with emergency inter-church aid, emergency relief, and refugee services. The Division should therefore continue to develop its responsibilities for areas of need such as: Japan, Korea, Hong Kong, Indonesia, Indo-China, Pakistan, India, the Near East, and Kenya, and other situations where such needs arise.

4. Providing supplies for people in need is an expression of the Church's compassion and, therefore, comes within the scope of the Division's work. The Division shall appraise needs, stimulate and co-ordinate the action of both contributing and distributing churches, and where necessary provide administration. In discharging the Christian duty to meet the emergency needs of those who lack food, clothing, shelter or medical care, relief is given on the basis of human need, in the name of Christ. Every effort shall be made to distribute in all countries where there is human need, provided that such distribution shall be under the auspices or with the approval of the churches, and that the church origin of the gifts shall be clearly stated.

The Division shall:

(*a*) encourage a continuing effort on the part of the contributing churches to meet the programmes of the distributing churches in all areas of need;

(*b*) offer and be prepared to co-ordinate the programmes of the member churches and their inter-church agencies or bodies in the Church's two-fold responsibility of providing and distributing supplies, including the present abundance of certain food commodities made available by the people of the United States through American church relief agencies;

(*c*) devise within its framework a plan on a world-wide scale and specifically with reference to Asia and other non-European areas for the ecumenical approach and co-ordination of the contribution and use of supplies.

5. The Division may co-operate with governmental or inter-governmental agencies wherever such co-operation furthers the Division's purpose and affords opportunities for ensuring Christian guidance of secular sources of aid.

IV. Service to Refugees and Migrants

1. The World Council of Churches reaffirms its deep concern for the millions of refugees who represent in 1954 an even greater claim upon the Christian churches than confronted them at Amsterdam in 1948 when its First Assembly resolved to:

give high priority to work for the material and spiritual welfare of refugees; and appeal to its member churches in countries capable of receiving any settlers, both to influence public opinion towards a liberal immigration policy and to welcome and care for those who arrive in their countries.

2. The World Council of Churches should:

(*a*) urge upon the United Nations and its member governments the need for continuing and maximum support for the United Nations High Commissioner for Refugees and particularly for financial support to his programme of integration and emergency relief (see the letter of the U.N. High Commissioner which is appended);

(*b*) call upon governments to support the Inter-Governmental Committee for European Migration both by membership of that body and by generous provision of immigration opportunities for refugees and to maintain their financial support to such agencies as the United Nations Relief and Works Agency for Palestine Refugees, the United Nations

Korean Reconstruction Agency, or other agencies as may be needed;

(*c*) press for the conditions which will make possible the repatriation of those refugees who wish to return to their homes;

(*d*) negotiate with the authorities involved to secure the reunion, in accordance with their wishes, of families now separated.

(*e*) maintain and extend its service to refugees and migrants in Europe, the Near East, and Asia, especially in Japan and Hong Kong and other areas where refugee needs may arise;

(*f*) keep before the member churches the need for providing resettlement opportunities for refugees within their local communities;

(*g*) ensure that the spiritual needs of refugees are adequately provided for and continue to hold all refugees within the fellowship of prayer.

EXTRACT OF LETTER FROM THE HIGH COMMISSIONER FOR REFUGEES

"It seems to me to be one of the greatest achievements of the Christian churches in recent times that they have started increasingly to translate their faith and their hope into terms of practical programmes and projects in fields in which they bear responsibility. I do not think that I have any right to compare, but I would be surprised if there were any field in which the Christians have achieved so much as they have in the field of the refugee problem. During my travels I have met the programmes of the World Council and of the Lutheran World Federation literally everywhere and I have the greatest admiration for those men and women who, with unflagging courage and belief in what they are doing, fight day by day for the solution of a problem which is still with us and unfortunately will remain with us for many years to come.

Over the borders which separate freedom from oppression refugees come every day walking into the unknown with a poor little bundle on their shoulders. They have been led to believe that the free world will restore their basic rights and their human dignity. They come to us with confidence and hope and the one thing which Christians cannot afford to do would be to let them down. Fortunately so far they never have, but it is human nature to get tired of a problem as the years go by and it is therefore indispensable to remind people of goodwill time and again that there is still a task ahead as long as the problem has not been really solved."

THE REPORT OF THE COMMITTEE ON THE DEPARTMENT OF INFORMATION

Adopted by the Assembly

Note: The Report of the Committee on the Department was adopted without substantive debate.

I. THE NATURE AND FUNCTION OF THE NEW DEPARTMENT

The decision to implement the proposal for the establishment of a Department of Information for the World Council, at the present Assembly, is to be warmly welcomed. The plan set out for the Department by the Committee on Structure and Functioning presents an adequate foundation for its general development.

The Department is to open ways for Christ's entry into the world through the churches. The quality of its work will, to some extent, be a measure of our readiness to become part of the total mission for which our churches have been brought together in the World Council. The co-ordination of resources made possible by the Assembly's action should be conceived as requiring more than efficient technical processes. The Department should seek a distinctive "style" and way of dealing with its problems so as to be of service to all parts of the Council's structure and to the member churches in interpreting the ecumenical movement.

In all forms of information, it should be the aim of the Department to render theological and other technical vocabularies intelligible, without dilution and distortion.

The Department should also aim at securing as well as providing information, and it should endeavour to reach people outside the churches.

In the sense that radio and television are in themselves part of a new technique of communication, they provide a specific instance where the Department's work is to be viewed as more than the furnishing of information.

II. Meeting a Variety of Needs

The primary problem before the Department is clearly that it is meant to be an agency to facilitate the processes whereby the World Council of Churches may become real both to the rank and file membership of its constituency and to people who at present take little or no notice of the Church. The task of providing information to help meet this need is obviously long and difficult. Whatever media are used should be regarded as instruments in the hands of people whose long-range endeavour is face-to-face, and much more fully personal, communication. While there is already a good deal of fundamental material concerning the World Council's structure and purpose, much more remains to be done in the way of stressing the practical programmes, activities and personalities of the Council, since these have human appeal. Co-operation with all divisions and departments is essential; at this point the Department of Information is to be the servant and adviser of the Council. Inclusion of Inter-Church Aid publicity within the functions of the Department is to be welcomed, because the story of Inter-Church Aid is spectacular, and inseparable from a true understanding of the character of ecumenical fellowship.

The penetration of language barriers must also be a concern especially in such important smaller language areas as Scandinavia, and in the case of Spanish. Other needs are indicated as the present report proceeds.

III. Present Publications and Future Policy

A measure of flexibility in assessing the value of current publications and providing for the future should be preserved as the Department's work is discussed by the Central Committee. It is agreed, however, that there should be no sense of competition as between the World Council and its member churches in determining the content of material sent out. In the World Council of Churches it is true that "the churches do it but the Council helps to make it possible." In this sense the two emphases are interdependent. The Council is to be represented, as in the past, in its character as a means of common action and service.

The *Ecumenical Review* is excellent for its purpose and does not require to be supplemented by a popular publication with the same scope. Steps should be taken to advertise it more widely and extend its circulation. The format of the Review should be kept under discussion.

The *Ecumenical Press Service* has fulfilled important functions for the bodies that sponsor it, but the time has arrived for a careful re-examination of its form and purpose. It is suggested that the possibility of semi-monthly rather than weekly publication should be examined, that the basic information thus provided be supplemented by rapidly sent out news releases as required, that background supplements fuller than hitherto be included in the regular issues, that format and layout be revised, and that a drive for improved circulation be undertaken with a view to gradual elimination of the annual deficit. If it proves financially possible, the free list should be gradually extended, especially among participants in Assemblies of the World Council. Editions in three languages should be continued and a further edition in Spanish seems desirable.

Consultation with Dr. Rajah B. Manikam, Joint East Asia Secretary of the World Council of Churches and the International Missionary Council, might well lead to the publication of a periodical East Asian Newsletter or a supplement to the *E.P.S.*

The series of fourteen brochures available at the Assembly mark a commendable new departure in colourful and well-written illustrated descriptions of the World Council's actual achievements. In view of the fact that resources are now available as a result of the gathering of photographs, more similar publications seem called for. Drafts of forthcoming publications should be prepared where possible in English, French and German and sent to countries in the three main language areas for significant local adaptation.

If it proves possible to publish materials in Spanish (and this seems called for, upon examination of the present situation in Latin America), there is a strong case for doing the work in Geneva. An alternative and less satisfactory method would be by local translations and adaptations. Mission boards might be asked whether they have funds to help in the development of a Spanish translation service.

A simple popular booklet on the World Council, to supplant

all existing shorter handbooks, should be made available after the Evanston Assembly. It should include an account of the Council's future plans, contain pictures and conclude with specific points for action by individual readers.

The publications of particular divisions and departments of the World Council are a natural concern of the Department of Information and it is hoped that divisional and departmental officers will seek the advice of the Information staff in preparing material.

IV. RELATIONSHIPS OF THE DEPARTMENT

Direct communication with member churches is a first call on the Department's resources for disseminating information. The official heads or designated executive officers of the churches should receive specimens. Ecumenical committees or other designated agencies should then be provided with quantities. Provided this direct communication is safeguarded in the first instance, the Department should be free to work through national ecumenical bodies, local councils of churches, interested ministers and clergy, theological seminaries, organizations for men, women, and youth, and the church press. In countries where member churches are preponderantly in the majority of the population, the appropriate world confessional alliances may be consulted on questions of public relations; for instance, in Scandinavia it might prove convenient to incorporate ecumenical information in publications in the national languages as they go out from the Lutheran World Federation.

The International Missionary Council will be using the Department's services. For this purpose regular conferences with officers of the I.M.C. must be undertaken. Missionary bodies can provide valuable material for departmental use.

National Christian councils throughout the world are valuable allies. They should be consulted and assisted, where they so desire, to devise their own methods of distribution and deputation work on the World Council's behalf. Advice on methods of distribution may also be given to member churches requiring it.

Opportunities such as Whitsunday, the Octave of Prayer for Christian Unity and the Women's World Day of Prayer should be used for special publicity.

V. Consultations and Training Courses

The Department can act as a central point of reference for meetings between workers in public relations, radio and television, journalism and related fields. The work of such groups should be interpreted to the churches, and regional meetings of collaborators may be held in various parts of the world. Such meetings could become training courses. Conferences already held at Bossey for journalists and in connection with the inauguration of the World Committee for Christian Broadcasting have set the stage for future experiments.

VI. Radio and Television

It is impossible to stress too sharply the importance of these media for the Department's future. Co-operation between Christian agencies at this point is essential because of the skills required and the costs involved. The Department cannot be a producing agency to any large extent, but should certainly be a stimulating and collecting agency. The entire staff must be aware of the promise and urgency of church use of these media. Contact must be maintained by cross-representation on the World Committee for Christian Broadcasting. Radio is a first priority because it gives access at present to the widest of all publics. The task in television is to pioneer its right use in the ecumenical context. It is very much to be hoped that member churches may second specialists for a period as supported members of the departmental staff. In the opinion of the Committee, the appointment of a full-time staff member concerned with radio and television is already highly desirable and will shortly become imperative, even if this means a redistribution of staff responsibilities. Meanwhile, resources of film and sound recordings should be built up to aid writers, producers, and directors, and everything possible should be done to build on the foundations laid by the Committee on Films, Radio and Television at the Evanston Assembly.

VII. Audio-Visual Materials

The sound film at present being made at the Evanston Assembly should be widely distributed in collaboration with the Department, with provision for alternative sound tracks in different languages. Sets of kodachrome slide sequences with accompanying script may be distributed internationally as an experiment. Good black and white film strips of the Assembly and of other World Council meetings and activities may also be prepared experimentally in Geneva.

Short films are expensive, but if they can be underwritten in advance on a basis acceptable to the financial officers of the World Council, it should be possible to produce one film each year. The expenditure would be justified even then, only if a film is to be or outstanding quality.

Extension of all types of photographic services is strongly recommended.

VIII. The Press: Services and Relationships

Flexibility must be shown in meeting the needs of both church and general press, which should be cultivated together. All releases should be carefully planned as concerns format, local colouring and suitability, use of local styles, personal contacts with editors and journalists, and intelligent "prewriting." Factual releases are better than fully written out articles. The frequency of releases must be a matter of discretion but advance notice to the recipient is advisable. A clipping service will help in assessing the value of materials sent out. National and local correspondents should be appointed to aid in gathering news. Editors of church papers may be induced to co-operate in sending advance airmail copies of material for publication from their own papers. The existing library of ecumenical biographies should be extended and sent for filing to national agencies. The Department may help bridge the East-West division by providing more full and detailed information about sister churches elsewhere.

IX. Departmental Administration and Budget

It is the considered opinion of the Committee that a budget of $35,000 is unlikely to prove adequate for the work of the Department as set out in the Work Book. The developments which the Committee believe to be necessary in the field of radio and television would require further substantial increases of this sum. It is fundamental to the understanding of the Department's work that its progress should indirectly be of service to the Council's finances as a whole.

The precise division of labour between the Director and the three secretaries should be at the discretion of the General Secretariat and the Director, but all staff members will need to gain all-round experience and think of communication as a single problem.

The pattern of committee work for the Department should be left open pending some experience of its actual functioning. However, appointment of fully competent advisory committees in at least Europe and America seems indicated. The arrangement in the New York office may be worked out by conference between the Executive Secretary in the United States and the Department.

Resolutions for Presentation to the Assembly

Moved *that* a further function of the Department be added to the functions as set out on page 32 of the Assembly Work Book (see Report on Structure and Functioning, Part 2, IV) to read as follows:

(*vii*) to co-operate with other agencies in the fields of radio, television and film, and to help to ensure the intelligent use of these media by the churches.

Moved *that* the Assembly congratulate the Committee on Press and Broadcasting on the arrangements made for the reporting of the Evanston Assembly, and request the presentation of a report with recommendations arising as a basis for similar work to be undertaken by the Information Department in connection with future ecumenical meetings.

THE REPORT OF THE COMMITTEE ON FINANCE

Adopted by the Assembly

Your Committee on Finance takes pleasure in presenting its report to the Assembly for its approval. The Committee has met five times and has had the benefit of reports from two sub-committees which were asked to deal with problems better handled in smaller and specialized groups. Although the time allotted for the work of this Committee was short and the items of business needing attention were many and important, it was possible to examine all the matters suggested in the agenda which appeared on pages 84 and 85 of the Work Book, plus additional items brought to its attention by other committees of the Assembly. There was general discussion and participation by the members of the Committee and the report was unanimously approved as follows:

I. Revenue and Expenditure in the "First Six Years"—General Budget

The Committee examined the report on revenue and expenditure in the document *The First Six Years*, the audited accounts for the year 1953 and the Balance Sheet as at 31st December 1953, and received supplementary, detailed information and explanations, and agreed to RECOMMEND:

(*a*) that the Assembly receive and approve the report on operations on the General Budget for the five years 1949-1953, noting that the additions to reserves called for by the Amsterdam Assembly had been provided and that expenditure had in each year been kept below revenue, so that the accounts had each year been closed with a small surplus, and

(*b*) that the Assembly express gratitude to the retiring Central Committee, its Finance Committee, and the Chairman of the Finance Committee, Bishop Oxnam, as well as to the Director of Finance and Administration and his staff for their skill and fidelity during this first difficult period of the life of the World Council of Churches and

(*c*) that the Assembly note the publication of the volume *A History of the Ecumenical Movement*, edited by Dr. Ruth Rouse and Bishop Stephen Neill, and under the History Committee chaired by Dr. Adolph Keller, and express its appreciation to the Disciples of Christ, whose generous gifts for this purpose made possible this important project.

II. RESERVES, INVESTMENT POLICY AND CASH POSITION

The Committee reviewed the reserves of the World Council of Churches as reported on pages 83–5 of *The First Six Years* and received supplementary information concerning certain smaller reserves not mentioned in that document, and noted that:

(i) the General Reserve as at 31st December 1953 was S.f. 526,322.09 or about $123,000;

(ii) there is a small special reserve which at 31st December 1953 amounted to S.f. 92,418.91 or about $21,600, which will probably be needed by the Central Committee for 1955 expenses, since revenue will inevitably lag because all member churches will not be able to implement their undertakings for increased support in time for payment next year;

(iii) on 31st December 1954, the General Reserve for the Ecumenical Institute at Bossey will be approximately $50,000;

(iv) there are a number of other smaller reserves, arising from designated gifts for special purposes or created for special needs, e.g. eventual repairs to properties and fluctuations in value of investments;

(v) the General Reserve and the Bossey Reserve have been invested in Switzerland in bonds bringing an average annual income of approximately 3 per cent;

(vi) the Division of Inter-Church Aid and Service to Refugees will shortly be in an embarrassing cash position. The Service to Refugees conducted in 1953 an operation costing in total about $2½ million and does not have an operating fund to provide the finances needed for an operation of this size. It is the practice of the World Council to use, temporarily, cash resources belonging to one division or department to carry on the work of another, provided that the Central or Executive Committee is satisfied that the budget of such a department is in actual balance between assured revenue and approved programme. But the total resources of the World Council are no longer sufficient to provide an adequate operating fund for the Service to Refugees.

In the light of these several facts, the Committee therefore RECOMMENDS:

(*a*) that the Assembly approve the continuance of the policy of building up the General Reserve by annual allocations from revenue until in the judgment of the Central Committee or a subsequent Assembly, an adequate General Reserve has been established;

(b) that the Assembly ask the Central Committee to investigate whether or not it may be desirable, as an insurance against inflation, to invest some part of its permanent reserves in equities;

(c) that the Assembly approve the plan of retaining approximately $50,000 as a special reserve for the Ecumenical Institute in view of the large properties at Bossey and the type and scope of its programme (this will mean that the whole support of the Institute will in future necessarily come from current revenue);

(d) that the Assembly give approval for a request to be made from the Department of Inter-Church Aid and Service to Refugees to member churches for the provision of an operating fund for the Service to Refugees, by either (i) an advance payment against future contributions to the Service Programme or (ii) special non-recurring gifts.

III. DEPARTMENT OF INTER-CHURCH AID AND SERVICE TO REFUGEES

The Committee examined the report in *The First Six Years* on the operations of this department and received supplementary information and explanations. The Committee noted that the operations of this department largely exceed in cost the total of the General Budget and RECOMMENDS:

that the Assembly approve the continuation of the policy of the Central Committee to depend in the first instance, upon the Administrative Committee of the Department of Inter-Church Aid and Service to Refugees for detailed examination and administrative control of the Service Programme.

IV. COMMISSION OF THE CHURCHES ON INTERNATIONAL AFFAIRS

The Committee received a statement of the proposed post-Evanston budget of C.C.I.A. and Dr. Nolde informed the Committee of the plans for C.C.I.A. on which the budget was based. The Committee noted with approval the great volume of work being done on the limited budget and was satisfied as to the need for the contribution of $55,000 per annum from W.C.C. to C.C.I.A. which has been included in the model budget for the post-Evanston period.

V. United States Conference for the World Council of Churches

Your Committee was informed of the reasons for which the Central Committee has each year considered the budget of the United States Conference and fixed a maximum level for the budget and RECOMMENDED:

> that the Central Committee be authorized to continue to fix a maximum level for the budget of the U.S. Conference for the W.C.C.

VI. Revenue and Expenditure on the Evanston Assembly Budget

The Committee was informed that sufficient revenue had been raised for the central World Council budget of $267,500 for the Evanston Assembly and for the originally approved public relations budget of $40,000. It appeared assured that expenses on the central budget would not exceed the budget total of $267,500. Authority had been granted by the Executive Committee in February 1954, for an increase in the public relations budget; exact expenses were not yet known but might exceed the $40,000 by as much as $25,000 and the necessary additional revenue was not yet assured. There was, however, good reason to hope that sufficient further support could be secured to ensure that the Assembly budget would close without deficit. The symphony concert at Ravinia Park was organized by the World Council as a self-supporting event, expenses were about $7,500, and even if ticket sales to the public do not entirely cover expenses, the deficit will not be more than $200–$300. The Committee had been informed that, in addition to the above-mentioned budgets, the Evanston Committee of One Hundred had raised a local budget of about $30,000 and that expenses for the Soldier Field event which was organized jointly by the Church Federation of Greater Chicago and the U.S. Conference for the W.C.C., had amounted to about $75,000 and had been entirely covered by contributions from those who secured tickets or from other contributions. Furthermore, a number of member churches had provided substantial indirect help by financing the travel of representatives from distant and economically weak member churches. The Committee RECOMMENDS:

that the Assembly express its gratitude and appreciation to all those who by their labours and gifts had enriched the programme of the Assembly.

VII. MODEL BUDGET FOR THE POST-EVANSTON PERIOD

The Committee reminds the Assembly that the actual budget for the W.C.C. for 1955 and subsequent years will be fixed by the new Central Committee.

It should be noted that the model budget which the Committee is about to recommend provides neither a ceiling nor a floor but establishes the cost relationships and priorities of programme with average indications of cost for the various parts of that programme. For example, the figures in the Work Book, on pages 88–91, appear on the surface to indicate that a severe cut is proposed for the Division of Studies. Actually, this is not so, for your Committee is assured that the work carried on in the past, with the modifications already approved by this Assembly in its adoption of the Report of the Committee on Structure and Functioning, is provided for in the model budget.

The Committee took as its first directive for the establishment of the budget, the Report of the Structure and Functioning Committee as it has already been approved by this Assembly. It calls to the attention of the Assembly that the various committees on W.C.C. business all believe that additional money and staff would enable the departments or divisions under their responsibility to accomplish more and better work. Unfortunately, after examination of these requests for additions, which would have totalled more than $50,000, and after conferences with representatives of the churches as to possibilities of revenue, it has not been possible to respond favourably to those appeals.

Your Committee has consulted with representatives of many churches from all over the world and is gratified to report that these consultations justify the Committee in recommending a budget calling for income from churches of $420,000, which must be compared with the actual 1953 income of $311,000—an increase of $109,000 or clearly over one third. In view of the concern shared by all our churches that the financial support for the World Council should be provided more equitably by all the member churches and all parts of the world, it is even more gratifying to note that the estimates on which this budget is based indicate that contributions from churches other than those in the United States will amount, when the present estimates are realized, to 50 per cent more than those churches were able to contribute in 1953.

Lest we fall into the error of thinking that this revenue is already assured, let the Assembly understand that it will not be provided unless the delegates to this Assembly return to their churches with enthusiasm and determination to rise to this new opportunity. Full mutuality in the World Council requires that every church shall participate in the support of the Council. The revenue estimates likewise require that every church shall increase its giving against the giving of those other churches which are contributing generously rather than those whose contributions they may consider to be lagging.

It must be said that the Finance Committee was told that the income of $420,000 is not quite fully assured, at the writing of this report. The accepted objectives add to some $6,000 less than that total. Furthermore, official response and action accepting the increase is yet to be taken in most churches and it is an unhappy fact that some churches will not be able to take action in time to increase their contributions in 1955. Nevertheless, your Committee felt reasonably assured that the revenue figure proposed in the following budget is realizable, provided that the churches will respond in the spirit of their representatives at this Assembly.

The expenditure side of the budget recommended by your Committee provides for the programme proposed on pages 88 and 89 of the Work Book (see Appendix 4, pp. 320, 321, which presents the summary figures) plus:

(a) an additional $5,000 for the C.C.I.A., as desired by the Central Committee;

(b) $10,000 for contingencies which your Committee considered an essential additional provision;

(c) $1,500 to raise the W.C.C. share of the cost of the Joint

Far East Secretariat of I.M.C. and W.C.C. from one third to one half of the total, and $3,000 to cover one half of the cost of a secretary for the Joint Committee of I.M.C. and W.C.C. These increases were called for in the report of the Joint Committee (see p. 322) which report was approved by the committee on General Policy. Hence, your Committee agreed to recommend:

that the Assembly approve the model budget for the post-Evanston period the details of which are set forth on pages 85–93 of the Work Book (see Appendix 4), plus the additions noted above, giving a total budget as follows:

Revenue:

From Churches	$420,000
From Department of Inter-Church Aid and Service to Refugees	21,000
	$441,000

Expenditure:	$441,000

VIII. Continuing Action by the Central Committee

In view of the unmet requests reported by other committees on World Council business for strengthening the staff and increasing the work of all divisions and departments, your Committee finally RECOMMENDS:

that the Central Committee be authorized to continue to seek from all the member churches a proper proportion of support for the work of the World Council and, if income allows, to initiate such advances in programme as in its judgment are the most pressing and promise to be the most fruitful.

Discussion on the Report of the Finance Committee

Dr. Blake presented to the Assembly the report of the Finance Committee, first reading or summarizing sections 1–6 of that report. The Assembly received with applause recommendation 1 (b) and the recommendation on item 6, expressing gratitude in the first instance for the conduct of financial operations in the first six years, and in the second place for all the help received in connection with the Evanston Assembly. Dr. Blake then drew attention to the fact that items 7 and 8 were the most important and read that part of the report in detail. He then moved the adoption of the report of the Finance Committee and the recommendations contained in it.

Bishop Fuglsang-Damgaard paid tribute in the name of the member churches in countries other than the U.S. to the generosity of the American churches during this initial period of the life of the World Council. He recalled that post-war conditions had made it impossible for many churches to contribute or to contribute adequately during the early years, but expressed the determination of the member churches in countries other than the U.S.A. to strive to take a fuller share in the next period.

Professor Tindal asked for a modification of the recommendation under item VIII which, in his opinion, in its original form appeared to give *carte blanche* to the Central Committee to increase the budget. He felt that there was more urgent need for the churches to equip themselves to make maximum use of the material prepared by the World Council than for the World Council to undertake increased work. Dr. Blake agreed to re-draft the recommendation in the light of Professor Tindal's suggestion.

THE REPORT OF THE COMMITTEE ON THE COMMISSION OF THE CHURCHES ON INTERNATIONAL AFFAIRS

Adopted by the Assembly

Note: The Report of the Committee on the Commission of the Churches on International Affairs was adopted without substantive debate.

The Committee held three meetings. In the light of the working papers before it and of reports orally presented, it reviewed the work of the C.C.I.A. with particular reference to:

the organization of the Commission;
the bases of its work and actions;
the areas of its substantive concern;
the extent and limits of its selected points of representation.

The Committee was unanimous in endorsing and approving the work of the Commission and its officers in the six years under review in so far as it had developed.

In studying the future policy and programmes of the Commission the Committee was of the opinion that the work of the Commission is of such strategic importance that it must not only be maintained, but substantially developed.

The Committee was made aware that the present budgetary figures did not adequately represent the real cost of the Commission's current operations and that such additional funds as the second Assembly may vote would no more than correct this misleading position.

These financial limitations notwithstanding, the Committee expressed the view that the work of the Commission was of such paramount importance and its proper development so urgent that the churches should be urged to give it the highest priority in their financial planning.

In particular the Committee decided to recommend:

I. That the urgency and international significance of the problems of Europe were such as to require much more specific attention and study than they have hitherto received. Recognizing that the failure to meet this need was due primarily to lack of manpower, the Committee urged that an additional staff appointment—a European—should be made to meet this situation.

II. That the increasing importance of Asian action and opinion in international affairs emphasizes the comparative inactivity of the churches in Asia in international action and representation and calls for the early appointment of an officer—an Asian—responsible for Asia and for the mobilization of concerted action by the churches in Asia.

III. The Committee was of the opinion that the two appointments recommended above were also necessary as they would provide a much needed redress of the present Anglo-Saxon predominance in the composition of the Commission's staff.

IV. The Committee recognized that neither of these additional appointments would be possible without increased financial contributions from the member churches or interested groups within them and that in any case they should not take precedence over the need for relief to the existing staff in its present workload. It also suggested that, as one method of easing the man-power problems of the Commission, particularly as regards national representation, consideration be given to the use of *ad hoc* representatives and sub-commissions.

V. The Committee recognized that in regard to practical issues that have arisen, the officers of the Commission have already evolved a most satisfactory technique of analytical and fact-finding study. At the same time the Committee decided that the whole subject of study both in relation to major world issues and to the theological bases of the Commission's work required increased attention.

Issues that were regarded as in need of urgent study included "An International Ethos," "Religious Liberty and Proselytism," "The Background of UNESCO," "The Application by Governments of the Principle of Reciprocity, particularly in the Admission of Missionaries," "The Problem of Germany," "Issues in the Near East" and "An Asian Security Pact."

On the question of theological study there was considerable discussion as to both need and method and varying views were expressed as to the bearing which such study would have on the Commission's approach to the practical issues which it is called upon to face. The Committee agreed to emphasize the need for study, particularly in order to define the Christian bases of action, directions to be followed and the limits of competency, but it was of the opinion that the present restricted resources of the Commission necessarily confine its bases of action to practical wisdom and that, failing help from elsewhere, it could not, at this time and with its present staff, develop a full theological basis for its programme.

VI. The Committee gave consideration to the dangers of overlapping and the possibilities of co-operation, notably in the field of study, between the Commission and the departments of the World Council of Churches dealing with social questions and with racial and inter-group relations. The Committee expressed concern that assignments to the Commission should be limited by the distinctive purpose for which it was established. It recommended that the Officers of the Commission should consult with Officers of the World Council of Churches and the International Missionary Council as to the most economical and fruitful methods of co-operation in these related fields.

VII. The Committee was unanimously of the opinion that the

two-way principle on which the Commission works would be still further strengthened by closer and more regular contact with national commissions. To this end it recommended more extensive travel by officers of the Commission for liaison with national commissions and suggested that such visits could usefully be the occasion for regional conferences of church leaders and for the training of churchmen in Christian responsibilities in international affairs.

VIII. The Committee recognized the need for a more intensive programme of publicity and education, but reluctantly agreed that present commitments and financial limitations necessarily made this a long-term objective except in so far as assistance can be immediately forthcoming from the World Council of Churches' new Department of Information.

RESOLUTION FOR PRESENTATION TO THE ASSEMBLY

Resolved:

that the Assembly adopt the report of Committee VII and, subject to concurrent action by the International Missionary Council, the Commission of the Churches on International Affairs be authorized to implement the proposals therein as the required resources become available.

The Report of the Credentials Committee

Adopted by the Assembly

The members of the Committee appointed to examine credentials have assumed that they were concerned only with those of full members of the Assembly, that is those who are entitled to vote as duly accredited delegates representing the various churches in membership with the World Council, and not with consultants, fraternal delegates, accredited visitors, and youth representatives who have no vote.

They have considered the credentials presented and find them all in order in accordance with the rule in Section V (i) of the Constitution, which says that the Assembly shall be composed of official representatives of the churches or groups of churches adhering to the World Council and directly appointed by them.

Two questions have been raised as to the interpretation and application of the Rule. In two cases a delegate has been asked to represent two or more churches closely related and of similar faith and order. To illustrate, our distinguished colleague, Professor Alivisatos of Athens, has been appointed as delegate not only by the Church of Greece, to which he belongs, but also by the Church of Cyprus. This shows that the island which gave St. Barnabas to the Christian Church still has the good sense to be worthily represented by one who bears an honoured name throughout Christendom.

Your Committee feel that ideally all member churches should be represented by delegates who belong to them and are in the fullest way acquainted with their life, problems, views and aspirations. But we realize that this may be difficult for some churches remote from the meeting-place of the Assembly, which have scanty financial resources, or cannot find among their members those who have the time and opportunity to travel a great distance. We consider it would be wrong to disfranchise them under such conditions and appreciate that the only way for them to be represented at all, and to make their membership of the Council effective, is to appoint from outside their membership, and we consider that each church should be allowed to appoint such a delegate as it may be able to approve with confidence.

We recommend therefore that a delegate be permitted to represent more than one church if he is properly accredited by each of them; and, further, that when votes are reckoned by churches (as for example in the admission of new member churches) he should be entitled to vote in behalf of each; but that when votes of individuals are counted, as usually on a motion after discussion in the Assembly, he should have only one vote.

The other question arises from the late substitution of a delegate for another. Nothing is said in the Constitution concerning the latest date when names of delegates may be received by the World Council office. It would be hard to make a satisfactory rule since death, illness or some other unavoidable cause, may create at the last moment a gap which can be filled to the advantage of the Assembly as well as to the church concerned.

No problem arises when the substitute is appointed by his church or some duly authorized committee or person designated by it and the usual form is sent in.

But your Committee feel that last-minute substitutions, even from among accredited visitors, should not be allowed unless any such substitution is authorized through the usual church channel of communication, or by a delegation or leader who has been definitely appointed to make it and the authorization made known to the World Council office through the appropriate channel.

In receiving delegates it is felt that the Council should act only on the instructions of the churches communicated through the normal intermediaries. We do not think it is enough, for example, for another delegate, whatever his ecclesiastical standing, to say on his own initiative, "*A* cannot come and I think *B* should take his place." Such an appointment might subsequently be repudiated by the church concerned with embarrassing and unhappy consequences.

We recommend therefore that no delegate be recognized as such unless he has been appointed by the governing body of his church, or by some body or person authorized by it, after due notice of such authorization has been sent to the World Council office.

The Credentials Committee would through the Assembly ask all churches to see that in future the three credential forms supplied by the Council Secretariat be used as directed, one for each delegate returned to Geneva as soon as possible, one retained for purposes of record by the church, and one presented by the appointed delegate at the time of registration. This will save the staff of the Council a good deal of work and avoid uncertainty as to the standing of a few of the Council's members.

The Report of the Nominations Committee

The Nominations Committee presents the following report to the Assembly. In presenting its report, the Committee calls attention to the fact that care has been taken to follow faithfully the rules of procedure governing the action of the Committee, adopted by the Assembly 17th August 1954. These rules provide that "the maximum number of presidents shall be six" and that "in making nominations, the Nominations Committee shall have regard to the following principles:

(*a*) the personal qualifications of the individual for the task for which he is to be nominated;

(*b*) fair and adequate confessional representation;

(*c*) fair and adequate geographical representation;

and shall satisfy itself as to the general acceptability of the nominations to the churches to which the nominees belong."

The Nominations Committee takes pleasure in proposing to the Assembly that the Bishop of Chichester be elected an Honorary President of the World Council of Churches. In proposing this, the Committee recommends strongly that the Assembly should decide that the Bishop of Chichester be requested to continue to serve the World Council by giving it the full benefit of his activity and counsel, and that he be invited to attend the meetings of the Executive and Central Committees with full rights of participation. The Nominations Committee makes this proposal in grateful recognition of the thirty-five years of pioneering work given by the Bishop of Chichester to the ecumenical movement.

The Committee is pleased to make the following proposals for the Presidium:

The Very Rev. Principal John Baillie, *British Isles*
Bishop Sante Uberto Barbieri, *South America*
Bishop Otto Dibelius, *Europe*
The Most Rev. Metropolitan Juhanon, *Asia*
The Most Rev. Archbishop Michael, *Eastern Orthodox*
The Right Rev. Henry Knox Sherrill, *North America*.

The Nominations Committee has sought to follow the detailed instructions set forth in Part 3, Section V, of the Rules in its choice of nominees for the Central Committee. The statements which follow will serve to point up the rules of procedure which underlie the proposals as presented:—

I. The confessional representation of the Central Committee, as proposed, is as follows:

Anglicans	11
Baptist	4
Congregational	4
Coptic	2
Disciples	1
Lutheran	16
Methodist	10
Old Catholic	1
Orthodox	12
Orthodox Syrian	1
Reformed	16
Salvation Army	1
United	10
Brethren	1
Total	90

II. The geographical distribution of the nominees to the Central Committee are:

North America	22
Europe	22
United Kingdom & Eire	10
Eastern Orthodox	12
Asia	12
Africa & Latin America	6
Australia & New Zealand	5
International	1
Total	90

III. Twenty-three of the nominees, if approved by the Assembly, will be continued from the Central Committee elected at Amsterdam. Sixty-seven new nominees are being proposed.

The Nominations Committee presents the accompanying list of nominees for the Central Committee.

It is further proposed that the Chairman of the International Missionary Council, which is "in association with" the World Council, be invited to sit with the Central Committee at all sessions.

It is our understanding that Dr. John R. Mott shall continue as Honorary President of the World Council of Churches, to which honorary position he was elected in 1948 in just recognition of his long and distinguished leadership in the world-wide movement of co-operation among the churches.

CENTRAL COMMITTEE OF THE
WORLD COUNCIL OF CHURCHES

Professor H. Aharonian
Professor H. Alivisatos
The Rev. J. A. Do Amaral
Archbishop Athenagoras of Thyateira
Dr. A. S. Atiya
Dr. Eric Baker
Mrs. F. O. Bennett
Dr. H. Berkhof
Dr. P. O. Bersell
Dr. Eugene C. Blake
Mrs. K. Bliss
The Rev. J. R. Boyd
Professor P. Bratsiotis
Archbishop Y. Brilioth
The Rev. C. B. Brink
Mrs. Frank Brooks
Dr. George W. Buckner
The Archbishop of Canterbury, Dr.
    G. F. Fisher
Bishop Jan Chabada
The Bishop of Christchurch, Dr.
    A. K. Warren
Archimandrite Parthenios Coinidis
Archimandrite Ieronimos Cotsonis
Archimandrite James Coucouzis
The Rev. P. K. Dagadu
The Rev. G. P. David
Bishop L. De Mel
Professor H. C. W. d'Espine
Bishop Angus Dun
Dr. A. Eeg-Olofsson
Professor G. Florovsky
Dr. Franklin Clark Fry
Bishop Hans Fuglsang-Damgaard
Mr. B. J. Hartwell

Professor V. Herntrich
Professor J. L. Hromadka
Professor Basil Ioannidis
Dr. J. H. Jackson
The Metropolitan of Philadelphia,
    James
Mrs. Ernest Jarvis
The Bishop of Johannesburg, Dr.
    R. A. Reeves
Canon W. W. Judd
Dr. Enkichi Kan
Dr. M. Kozaki
Principal Robert B. Lew
Bishop Hanns Lilje
Mrs. Margit Lindstrom
Dr. Ralph W. Lloyd
Dr. Charles Malik
The Bishop of Malmesbury, The Rt.
    Rev. I. S. Watkins
Bishop William C. Martin
The Rev. C. Mataheru
Dr. Pierre Maury
Bishop G. J. F. May
Mr. Francis P. Miller
Dr. Reuben E. Nelson
Bishop J. E. L. Newbigin
Bishop D. Ward Nichols
Principal C. M. Nicholson
Dr. M. Niemöller
Dr. W. Niesel
Prof. A. T. Nikolainen
Bishop G. Noth
Bishop G. Bromley Oxnam
The Bishop of Salonica, Panteleimon
Professor L. Pap

Mr. Charles Parlin
Mr. Rajaiah D. Paul
Dr. Ernest A. Payne
The Rev. Korah Philipos
Inspector T. C. Poincenot
Dean Liston Pope
Pres. Nathan M. Pusey
Archbishop Andreas Rinkel
Professor Harold Roberts
The Rev. C. D. Ryan
Dr. Henry F. Schuh
The Bishop of San Francisco, John Shahovskoy
Commissioner V. G. Simpson

The Rev. K. Sitompul
Bishop Johannes Smemo
Bishop E. C. Sobrepena
Mrs. Leslie Swain
The Archbishop of Sydney, Dr. H. W. K. Howell
Dr. Andrew Thakur Das
The Bishop of Harrar, Theophilos
Professor W. S. Tindal
Bishop Lajos Vetoe
Dr. R. Von Thadden
Dr. James E. Wagner
Dr. M. R. Zigler

DISCUSSION ON THE FINAL PRESENTATION OF THE REPORT OF THE NOMINATIONS COMMITTEE

Note.—Previous presentations of the Report are described on pp. 49 and 50 above.

The Archbishop of Canterbury in the chair explained that in the unavoidable absence of Dr. Moreland the Rev. R. D. Say would present the report.

Mr. Say expressed regret that Dr. Moreland was unable to conclude his task but said the final decisions had Dr. Moreland's approval. He moved immediately for the election of the Bishop of Chichester as an honorary president.

The Bishop of Chichester was unanimously elected and the Assembly stood to applaud.

Mr. Say drew attention to the rules concerning nomination and election and said the Nominations Committee was satisfied that the names brought forward for the office of President met all requirements. The Committee had carefully considered the desirability and possibility of nominating a lay person for President, especially bearing in mind the contribution of "the incomparable Sarah Chakko." The one person approached had declined to serve and the Committee favoured retaining the six names already before the Assembly.

Professor d'Espine as the person responsible for the motion to seek ways of adding a lay person to the presidium asked that it be clear this was a question of principle, not of personalities. The persons now named had the complete confidence of those who had moved in this direction. It was only necessary that the Council be aware of the vital importance of participation by laymen and women in the Council's leadership.

The Archbishop of Canterbury then put the resolution for election of the six nominees which was carried.

Mr. Say drew attention to certain errors in the analysis of the nominations for the Central Committee as grouped in confessions and regions. He reported that Canon Greenslade had expressed a desire not to serve and reported the replacement of his name by that of the Bishop of Johannesburg, Dr. R. A. Reeves. He indicated that the list as now set out included seventeen unordained persons, six women, and increased representation from Asia, from Australasia, and from within Orthodoxy. Many alternative suggestions made by individual members of the Assembly had been examined but only one change, as already reported, had been judged necessary.

Mr. Say moved that the chairman of the International Missionary Council be asked to sit with all meetings of the Central Committee, and his motion was carried.

One further motion, that Dr. John R. Mott be asked to continue as honorary president with the assurance of the Council's "unfailing affection and gratitude," was carried.

The Nominations Committee report was approved.

The List of Those Present

DELEGATES

AUSTRALASIA
Methodist Church of Australasia
Grimmett, The Rev. Ian H.
Havea, The Rev. John
Lew, The Rev. R. B.
Williams, The Rev. Colin

AUSTRALIA
Church of England in Australia and Tasmania
Booth, The Most Rev. J. J., Archbishop of Melbourne
Mowll, Mrs. H. W. K.
Mowll, The Most Rev. H. W. K., Archbishop of Sydney
Moyes, The Rt. Rev. J. S., Bishop of Armidale
Housden, The Rt. Rev. J. A. G., Bishop of Rockhampton
Henderson, The Rev. Kenneth
Littleton, Mr. T. G.
Congregational Union of Australia
Dixon, The Rev. Lyall
Ryan, The Rev. C. Denis
Federal Conference of Churches of Christ in Australia
Williams, Principal Edwin L.
Presbyterian Church of Australia
Davidson, Mr. Gordon
Peter, The Rev. J. F.
Watson, The Rev. Alan C.

AUSTRIA
Evangelische Kirche A.u.H.B. in Oesterreich (Evangelical Church of the Augsburgian and Helvetic Confessions)
May, Bishop D. G.
Schneider, Prof. Lic. Dr. Erwin

BELGIUM
Union des Eglises Evangeliques Protestantes de Belgique (Union of Protestant Evangelical Churches of Belgium)
Fagel, Pastor Pieter

BRAZIL
Igreja Metodista do Brasil (Methodist Church of Brazil)
Amaral, The Rev. do Joao Augusto

CANADA
Churches of Christ (Disciples)
McCully, The Rev. O. W.

CANADA—*continued*
Church of England in Canada
Carrington, The Most Rev. Philip, Archbishop of Quebec, Metropolitan
    of the Province of Canada
Judd, The Rev. Canon W. W.
Martin, The Rt. Rev. H. D., Bishop of Saskatchewan
Naylor, The Rev. Canon R. K.
Presbyterian Church in Canada
Coles, The Rev. Stuart
Jackson, Mr. H. M.
United Church of Canada
Cragg, The Rev. G. R.
Harland, The Rev. H. G.
Nicholson, The Very Rev. C. M.
Robison, Mr. Ivan C.
Scott, The Rev. A. A.
Ward, Miss Anne
Yearly Meeting of the Society of Friends
Haslam, Mr. Fred

CEYLON
Methodist Church in Ceylon
Niles, Mrs. D. T.

CYPRUS
Church of Cyprus
Alivisatos, Professor H.

CZECHOSLOVAKIA
Ceskobratska Cirkev Evangelicka (Evangelical Church of Czech Brethren)
Hajek, Dr. Victor
Hromadka, Dr. J. L.
*Evangelicka Cirkev A.V.Na Slovensku (Evangelical Church in Slovakia, Augsburgian
Confession)*
Chabada, Bishop Jan
Michalko, Dr. Jan
Ref. Cirkev Na Slovensku (Reformed Christian Church in Slovakia)
Varga, Bishop Emerich

DENMARK
Baptist Union of Denmark
Norgaard, The Rev. Johannes
Den Evangelisk-Lutherske Folkekirke i Danmark (Church of Denmark)
Fuglsang-Damgaard, Bishop H.
Hoffmeyer, Bishop C. J. Skat
Langhoff, Vicar Johannes
Soe, Professor Niels H.
Sveistrup, Mr. P. P.

EGYPT
Coptic Orthodox Church
Atiya, Dr. Aziz Sorial
Makary El Souriany, Rev. Father
Saleeb Sorial, Rev. Father

ETHIOPIA
Ethiopian Church
Theophilos, His Beatitude Abouna, Bishop of Harrar
Degou, Rev. Abba Gabre-Egziather
Lemma, Mr. Ato Mengstou

FINLAND
Suomen Evankelis-Lutérilainen Kirkko (Evangelical Lutheran Church of Finland)
Gulin, Bishop E. G.
Hallsten-Kallia, Miss Armi
Nikolainen, Prof. Aimo T.
Pinomaa, Prof. Lennart
Yloenen, The Rev. Reino

FORMOSA
Tai-Oan Ki-Tok Tiu-Lo Kau-Hoe (Presbyterian Church in Formosa)
Hwang, The Rev. Chang-Hui

FRANCE
Eglise Evangélique Luthérienne de France (Evangelical Lutheran Church of France)
Poincenot, Dr. Philippe
Eglise Réformée d'Alsace et de Lorraine (Reformed Church of Alsace and Lorraine)
Mehl, Professor Roger
Eglise Réformée de France (Reformed Church of France)
Boegner, Pastor Marc
Burgelin, Professor Pierre
Maury, Pastor Pierre

GERMANY
Altkatholische Kirche in Deutschland (Old Catholic Church in Germany)
Küppers, Dr. Werner
Evangelische Brueder-Unitat (Moravian Church)
Renkewitz, Dr. H. G.
Evangelische Kirche in Deutschland (Evangelical Church in Germany)
Lutheran Delegates
Beste, Landesbischof D.
Herden, Oberkirchenrat Günter
Herntrich, Oberkirchenrat D. Volkmar
Hübner, Oberkirchenrat Dr. F. C. W.
Kinder, Dr. Ernst
Leidig, Gewerkschaftssekretâr Peter-Kristian
Lilje, Landesbischof Hanns
Metzger, Oberkirchenrat D. Wolfgang
Meyer, Missionsdirektor Dr. H.
Nold, Frau Liselotte
Noth, Landesbischof Lic. Gottfried
Peters, Landesjugendpastor H. H.
Schlink, Prof. E.
Schmidt, Oberkirchenrat Lic. W. F.
Spiegel-Schmidt, Pastor Friedrich
Weeber, Dr. R.
Wester, Bischof D. Reinhard
Zimmermann, Vizepräsident Walter

GERMANY—*continued*
Reformed Delegates
Fokken, Dr. B.
Leitz, Dr. Franz J. P.
Niesel, Pastor D. Wilhelm
Obendieck, Prof. Dr. Harmannus
Puffert, Landespfarrer Heinrich
Schwarzhaupt, Oberkirchenrätin Elisabeth
United Delegates
Bourbeck, Dr. Christine
Brennecke, Missionsdirektor P. Gerhard
Dibelius, Bischof F. K. O.
Dietze, Prof. C. von der
Gablentz, Prof. O. H. von der
Herrmann, Diakonisse Gertrud
Jacob, Generalsuperintendent D. Günter
Kreyssig, Dr. Lothar
Niemöller, Kirchenpräsident D. M.
von Thadden-Trieglaff, Dr. Reinold
Wilm, Präses D.
Winterhager, Pfarrer Jürgen

GOLD COAST
Presbyterian Church of the Gold Coast
Clerk, The Rev. Carl Henry

GREECE
Ekklesia Tes Ellados (Church of Greece)
Alivisatos, Professor H.
Bonis, Professor Constantin
Bratsiotis, Professor Panayotis
Cotsonis, Archimandrite Ieronimos
Ioannidis, Professor Basil
Karmiris, Professor Johannes
Konidaris, Professor Gerassimos
Moraitis, Professor Cimitrios
Siotis, Professor Marcus
Trakas, Professor John
Trempelas, Professor Panayiotis
Evangelical Church of Greece
Hadjiantoniou, Rev. G. A.

HUNGARY
A Magyarorszagi Evangelikus Egyhaz (Lutheran Church of Hungary)
Dezséry, Bishop Laszlo
Vetoe, Bishop Lajos
A Magyarorszagi Reformatus Egyhaz (Reformed Church of Hungary)
Bereczky, Bishop Albert
Pap, Dr. Laszlo
Peter, Bishop John

ICELAND
Evangelical Lutheran Church of Iceland
Fridriksson, The Rev. Bragi Reynir

INDIA

Church of India, Pakistan, Burma and Ceylon
 De Mel, The Rt. Rev. H. L.
 Lash, The Rt. Rev. W. Q.
 Mukerjee, The Most Rev. A. N.
Church of South India
 Chandran, The Rev. Russell
 Jacob, The Right Rev. C. K.
 John, Mr. M. J.
 Newbigin, The Right Rev. J. E. L.
 Paramasami, Miss A. K.
 Paul, Mr. Rajaiah D.
Federation of Evangelical Lutheran Churches in India
 Devasahayam, Mr. M.
 David, The Rev. G. Paul
 Paulus, Rao Saheb Dr. T. S.
 Tiga, The Rev. J. J. P.
 Tudu, Mr. M. M.
Mar Thoma Syrian Church of Malabar
 Mar Chrysostom, The Rt. Rev. Philipose
 Mar Theophilus, The Rt. Rev. Alexander
 Mar Thoma, The Most Rev. Metropolitan Juhanon
Orthodox Syrian Church of Malabar Catholicate
 Eapen, Dr. C. T.
 Mar Philoxinos, The Rt. Rev. Daniel
 Philipos, The Rev. Father K.
 Samuel, The Rev. P. S.
 Samuel, The Rev. Father V. C.
United Church of Northern India and Pakistan
 Bhatty, Dr. E. C.
 Thakur Das, Dr. Andrew
 Yohan-Masih, The Rev. Kenneth

INDONESIA

Geredja Kalimantan Evangelis (Church of Kalimantan)
 Kiting, Mr. Chr.
Gredja Masehi Indjilli di Minahassa (Church of Minahassa)
 Tulung, The Rev. Johan Emiel
Gredja Masehi Indjilli di Timoer (Protestant Church of Timor)
 Abineno, The Rev. J. L.
Hoeria Kristen Batak Protestant (Batak Church Sumatra)
 Hutagalung, Mr. Sutan
 Siahaan, Ds. Gustav
 Sitompul, Ds. Karimuda
Geredja Geredja Kristen Djawa di Djawa Tengah (Javanese Christian Churches)
 Probowinoto, The Rev. B.
Geredja Protestant Maluku (Church of the Moluccas)
 Mataheru, The Rev. C.

IRAN

Synod of the Evangelical Churches of North Iran
 Larudy, The Rev. Feizollah

ITALY
Chiesa Evangelica Metodista d'Italia (Evangelical Methodist Church of Italy)
Sbaffi, Pastor Emanuele
Chiesa Evangelica Valdese (Waldensian Church)
Ricca, Dr. Albert

JAPAN
Nippon Kirisuto Kyodan (Church of Christ)
Kozaki, The Rev. Michio
Murata, The Rev. Shiro
Oishi, The Rev. Shigeharu
Nippon Sei Ko Kwai (Anglican Church in Japan)
Kan, Prof. W. E.

KOREA
Korean Methodist Church
Lew, Bishop Hyungki J.
Presbyterian Church of Korea
Kim, The Rev. Hyun Chung
Myung, The Rev. H. S.

LEBANON (SEE ALSO SYRIA)
Union of the Armenian Evangelical Churches in the Near East
Aharonian, Professor Hovhannes

NETHERLANDS
Algemene Doopsgezinde Societeit (General Mennonite Society)
Golterman, Dr. W. F.
Evangelisch Lutherse Kerk (Evangelical Lutheran Church)
van Heest, Pastor J. P.
Nederlands Hervormde Kerk (Netherlands Reformed Church)
Berkhof, Dr. H.
Emmen, Dr. E.
Patijn, Dr. C. L.
van Tuyll van Serooskerken, Baron F.L.S.F.
van Veen, Dr. Jan M.
Oud-Katholieke Kerk (Old Catholic Church)
Rinkel, Archbishop Andreas
Remonstrantse Broederschap (Arminian Church)
van Gelder, The Rev. N.
Hommes, The Rev. T. G.

NEW ZEALAND
Associated Churches of Christ in New Zealand
Haddon, Dr. A. L.
Church of the Province of New Zealand (Church of England)
Sullivan, The Very Reverend M. G.
Warren, Mrs. A. K.
Warren, The Rt. Rev. A. K.
Wilson, Mr. L. H.
Woods, Mr. A. Marsden
Congregational Union of New Zealand
Cunliffe-Jones, The Rev. H.
Davies, Mrs. Maynard

NEW ZEALAND—*continued*
  Methodist Church of New Zealand
    Chrystall, The Rev. B. M.
    Hailwood, The Rev. C. O.
  Presbyterian Church of New Zealand
    Bennett, Mrs. F. O.
    Salmond, The Rev. J. D.
    Winton, The Rev. F. W.

NORWAY
  Norske Kirke (Church of Norway)
    Berggrav, Bishop Eivind
    Birkeli, Dr. Frietjov
    Hansson, Mr. Kristian
    Smemo, Bishop Johannes
    Wikborg, Mr. Erling

PHILIPPINE ISLANDS
  United Church of Christ in the Philippines
    Martinez, Mr. Florentino
    Sobrepena, Dr. Enrique C.

SOUTH AFRICA
  Church of the Province of South Africa
    Inman, The Rt. Rev. T. G. V.
    Reeves, The Rt. Rev. R. A.
  Methodist Church of South Africa
    Hunt, The Rev. J. Wesley
    Rist, The Rev. H. W.
  *Ned. Hervormde of Gereformeerde Kerk Van Zuid-Afrika in Transvaal (Dutch
      Reformed Church of South Africa in Transvaal)*
    Brink, The Rev. C. B.
    Landman, The Rev. W. A.
  Nederduits Hervormde Kerk van Afrika (Dutch Reformed Church of Africa)
    Oosthuizen, The Rev. A. J. G.

SPAIN
  Iglesia Evangelica Española (Spanish Evangelical Church)
    Gutierrez-Marin, Prof. Manuel

SWEDEN
  Svenska Kyrkan (Church of Sweden)
    Anrup, Rector Nils Erik
    Brilioth, Archbishop Yngve
    Bromander, Mr. Axel
    Kempe, Mr. Ragnar
    Lindstam, The Rev. Sten Ingemar
    Lindstrom, Mrs. Margit
    Nygren, Bishop Anders
    Wingren, Professor G.
  Svenska Missionsfoerbundet (Mission Covenant Church of Sweden)
    Eeg-Olofsson, Dr. Ansgar
    Engstrom, Mr. Olle

SWITZERLAND

Christkatholische Kirche der Schweiz (Old Catholic Church)
Frei, Pastor Hans
Schweizerischer Evangelischer Kirchenbund (Swiss Protestant Church Federation)
ten Doornkaat, Pastor H.
d'Espine, Professor H.
Ferrari, Pastor E.
Koechlin, Dr. A.
Kuenzi, Dr. A.

SYRIA (SEE ALSO LEBANON)

Greek Orthodox Patriarchate of Antioch
Khouri, Archimandrite Elias
Malik, Dr. Charles
Evangelical Synod of Syria and Lebanon
Audeh, The Rev. Farid

THAILAND

Church of Christ in Thailand
Taiyong, The Rev. Leck

TURKEY

Oecumenical Patriarchate of Constantinople
Athenagoras, Bishop of Elaia
Athenagoras, Archbishop of Thyateira
Bobrinsky, Count Boris
Ezekiel, Bishop of Nazianos
Gennadios, Metropolitan of Helioupolis
Konstantinidis, Dr. Chrysostomos
Michael, Archbishop
Papaioannou, Archimandrite Jacques
Repanellis, Archimandrite Maxime
Stephanou, Archimandrite Eusebius
Vernik, Father Igor

UNITED KINGDOM AND EIRE

Baptist Union of Great Britain and Ireland
Aubrey, Dr. M. E.
Champion, The Rev. Leonard George
Hubble, The Rev. Gwenyth
LeQuesne, C. T., Esq., Q.C.
Payne, Dr. Ernest A.
Churches of Christ in Great Britain and Ireland
Robinson, Dr. William
Church of England
Bell, The Rt. Rev. G. K. A.
Bliss, Dr. Kathleen
Clark, O. W. H., Esq.
Coombs, Mrs. Eric
Fisher, Mrs. G. F.
Fisher, The Most Rev. Geoffrey
Goyder, George, Esq.
Greenslade, The Rev. Canon S. L.

UNITED KINGDOM AND EIRE—*continued*

Church of England—continued
Grubb, Sir Kenneth
Herklots, The Rev. Canon H. G. G.
Ramsey, The Rt. Rev. A. M.
Raynes, The Rev. R. R. E.
Say, The Rev. R. D.
Tomkins, The Rev. Canon O. S.
Wand, The Rt. Rev. J. W. C.
Watkins, The Rt. Rev. I. S.
Whitbread, Humphrey, Esq.
Wilkins, F. B., Esq.

Church of England—Missionary Dioceses
Baines, The Rt. Rev. H. W.
Beecher, The Rt. Rev. L. J.
Craske, The Rt. Rev. F. W. T.
Houghton, The Rev. J. C.
Peach, The Rev. S. J. E.
Stanway, The Rt. Rev. Alfred
Stewart, The Rt. Rev. W. H.
Stradling, The Rt. Rev. L. E.

Church of Ireland
Elliott, The Very Rev. R. C. H. G.
Hartford, The Rev. Canon R. R.

Church of Scotland
Baillie, The Very Rev. Principal John
Baxter, Dr. W. J.
Dougall, Dr. J. W. C.
Hamilton and Brandon, The Duke of
Jarvis, Mrs. E. D.
Louden, The Rev. R. Stuart
McLuskey, The Rev. J. Fraser
Tindal, The Rev. Professor Wm. S.
Torrance, The Rev. Professor T. F.

Church in Wales
Jones, The Rt. Rev. John C.
Witton-Davies, The Very Rev. C.

The Congregational Union of England and Wales
Chamberlain, The Rev. Elsie
Cooke, Dr. Leslie E.
Davies, Dr. J. Trevor
Hartwell, B. J., Esq.
Marsh, The Rev. Principal John

The Congregational Union of Scotland
Calder, The Rev. James M.

The Episcopal Church in Scotland
Hannay, The Most Rev. T.

The Methodist Church
Baker, Dr. Eric
Easton, The Rev. Wilfred
Farrar, Sister Dorothy H.
Jessop, Professor Thomas E.
Roberts, The Rev. Colin A.

UNITED KINGDOM AND EIRE—*continued*

The Methodist Church—continued
Roberts, The Rev. Prof. Harold
Shearer, The Rev. W. Russell
Urwin, The Rev. E. Clifford

The Methodist Church—Overseas Areas
Dagadu, The Rev. P. K.
Didier, The Rev. Atherton

Methodist Church in Ireland
Plunkett, The Rev. H. W.

Presbyterian Church of England
Richardson, The Rev. J. M.

Presbyterian Church in Ireland
Boyd, The Rev. James Rowland
Davey, The Rev. R. R.

Presbyterian Church of Wales
Davies, The Rev. T. J.
Thomas, The Rev. D. R.

United Free Church of Scotland
Forrester-Paton, John, Esq.

U.S.A.

African Methodist Episcopal Church
Greene, Bishop S. L.
Jordan, Bishop Fred D.
Nichols, Bishop D. Ward
Reid, Bishop Frank M.

African Methodist Episcopal Zion Church
Medford, Bishop H. T.
Walls, Bishop William J.

American Baptist Convention
Dahlberg, Dr. Edwin T.
Derbyshire, Dr. George
Gezork, President Herbert
Hodge, Mrs. Maurice B.
Morikawa, Dr. Jitsuo
Nelson, Dr. Reuben E.
Parsons, Mr. Edwin W.
Porter, The Rev. W. H.
Skoglund, Dr. John E.
Squires, Professor J. Duane
Swain, Mrs. Leslie
Torbet, Dr. Robert G.

American Evangelical Lutheran Church
Nielsen, The Rev. Holger O.

American Lutheran Church
Ewald, Dr. A. H.
Haefner, Dr. A. E.
Menter, Dr. N. A.
Schuh, Dr. Henry F.
Yochum, Dr. H. L.

U.S.A.—*continued*

Augustana Evangelical Lutheran Church
Benson, Dr. Oscar A.
Bersell, Dr. P. O.
Eliufoo, Mr. Solomon
Lund, Dr. Wendell

Christian Methodist Episcopal Church
Hamlett, Bishop J. Arthur
Stewart, Bishop Luther

Church of the Brethren
Baugher, The Rev. Norman J.
Zigler, Dr. M. R.

Congregational Christian Churches of the United States of America
Bennett, The Rev. Prof. John C.
Coe, Dr. Albert B.
Crossen, Mrs. Robert J.
Graham, Mr. Walter A.
Gray, Dr. Arthur D.
Hangen, The Rev. Emerson G.
Hargrove, Miss Margaret
Horton, Dr. Douglas
Jones, Mr. S. Guernsey
Lyman, Professor Mary Ely
Pope, Dean Liston
Wilson, Dr. Arthur E.

Evangelical and Reformed Church
Dearborn, Professor Donald C.
Herbster, Dr. Ben M.
Mueller, Dr. John W.
Schroeder, President Frederick W.
Stanger, Dr. Robert C.
Wagner, President James E.

Evangelical United Brethren Church
Baughman, Dr. L. L.
Epp, Bishop George Edward
Gilbert, Dr. Janet
Heck, President J. Arthur
Mueller, Dr. R. H.
Warner, Bishop I. D.

Holy Apostolic Catholic Church of the East (Assyrians)
Lamsa, Mr. George M.
Rehana, The Rev. Issac

International Convention of Disciples of Christ
Adams, Dr. Hampton
Buckner, Dr. George Walker, Jr.
Cook, Dr. Gaines M.
Fiers, Dr. A. Dale
Finegan, Professor Jack
Osborn, Professor G. Edwin
Sadler, Dr. M. E.
Tobias, The Rev. Robert T.

U.S.A.—*continued*

International Convention of Disciples of Christ—*continued*

Welch, Mrs. Rosa Page
Welsh, The Rev. W. A.
West, Dr. R. Frederick
Wyker, Mrs. James D.

The Methodist Church

Arrington, Mrs. Paul
Bosley, Dr. Harold A.
Bowen, Bishop John Wesley Edward
Brashares, Bishop Charles W.
Brooks, Mrs. Frank G.
Brown, Dr. G. Alfred
Chubb, Dr. James
Clair, Bishop Matthew W., Jr.
Claxton, Mr. Alvie Jacob
Clemens, Dr. Norman W.
Corson, Bishop Fred Pierce
Harrell, Bishop Costen J.
Harris, President M. L.
Harris, Dr. Thomas Summerfield
Holloway, President Fred G.
Holt, Bishop Ivan Lee
Howard, Professor Charles G.
Kennedy, Bishop Gerald
Ledden, Bishop W. Earl
McKee, Dr. Stanley S.
Martin, Mrs. John E.
Martin, Bishop William C.
Medlock, Dr. Melvin K.
Moore, Bishop Arthur J.
Moreland, President J. Earl
Olson, Dr. Oscar T.
Oxnam, Bishop G. Bromley
Palmquist, Dr. Theodore H.
Parlin, Mr. Charles C.
Phillips, Bishop Glenn R.
Raines, Bishop Richard C.
Richardson, President Harry van Buren
Smith, Dr. John Owen
Sockman, Dr. Ralph W.
Ward, Bishop Ralph A.
Wilkins, The Rev. John R.

The Methodist Church—*From Other Parts of the World*

Barbieri, Bishop Sante Uberto
Hagen, Bishop Odd
Pickett, Bishop J. Waskom
Sigg, Dr. Ferdinand
Valencia, Bishop José
Wunderlich, Bishop Friedrich

Moravian Church in America (*Northern Province*)

Stocker, Dr. F. P.

U.S.A.—*continued*

Moravian Church in American (Southern Province)
Spaugh, Dr. R. Gordon

National Baptist Convention, U.S.A., Inc.
Cunningham, Dr. E. Luther
Dudley, Dr. George W.
Gordon, The Rev. Maxie S.
Horne, The Rev. Henry Preston
Jackson, Dr. J. H.
Kilgore, Dr. Thomas
Mays, Dr. Benjamin E.
Ross, Mrs. M. O.
Wilson, Dr. W. L.

Polish National Catholic Church of America
Grochowski, Prime Bishop Leon
Rowinski, The Very Rev. F. C.

Presbyterian Church in the United States
Cunningham, The Rev. John R.
Hopper, Mrs. W. H.
Miller, Mr. Francis P.
Robinson, Dr. William C.
Stitt, Dr. David L.

Presbyterian Church in the United States of America
Barnes, Dr. Roswell P.
Beck, The Rev. J. Wendell
Black, Mrs. Howard
Blake, Dr. Eugene Carson
Cassat, Dr. David B.
Davies, Mr. Richard L.
Emmons, Dr. Peter K.
Frank, President Robert Worth
Harris, Dr. W. Glen
Lloyd, President Ralph W.
Rooks, Dr. Shelby
Salsbury, Mrs. J. R.
Van Dusen, President Henry P.
Wright, Dr. Paul S.

Protestant Episcopal Church
Bayne, The Rt. Rev. Stephen F., Jr.
Brinker, The Rt. Rev. Howard R.
Budzanoski, Mr. Michael
Chapman, Mrs. Alfred M.
Dun, The Rt. Rev. Angus
Kelley, The Very Rev. Alden D.
Kennedy, The Rev. James W.
Morehouse, Mr. Clifford P.
Pennybacker, Mrs. Percy V., Jr.
Pusey, President Nathan
Sherrill, The Rt. Rev. Henry Knox
Stebbins, Mrs. Edwin Allen
Taft, Mr. Charles P.
Wedel, The Rev. Canon Theodore O.

U.S.A.—*continued*
  Reformed Church in America
    Dykstra, Dr. D. Ivan
    Eenigenburg, Prof. Elton M.
  Religious Society of Friends:
    Five Years Meeting of Friends
    Purdy, Dr. Alexander C.
    Rees, The Rev. Russell E.
    General Conference of the Society of Friends
    Roberts, Dr. Preston T., Jr.
    The Religious Society of Friends of Philadelphia and Vicinity
    Haviland, Mr. J. Bernard
  Romanian Orthodox Episcopate in America
    Barbulescu, The Rev. Father Victor
  Russian Orthodox Greek Catholic Church in North America
    Borichevsky, The Rev. Vladimir S.
    Czap, Mr. Ivan Michaelson
    Florovsky, The Very Rev. Georges
    Shahovskoy, The Rt. Rev. John
  Seventh Day Baptist General Conference
    Hansen, The Rev. Clifford
  Syrian Antiochian Orthodox Church (Archdiocese of New York and All North America)
    Khouri, Archimandrite Ellis
  United Evangelical Lutheran Church
    Jersild, President Hans C.
  The United Lutheran Church in America
    Conrad, Dr. F. L.
    Fry, President Franklin Clark
    Gladfelter, Dr. Millard E.
    Herman, Dr. Stewart Winfield
    Knubel, Miss Helen M.
    Lesher, Dr. Royal E.
    List, Mr. Erwin H.
    Lotz, The Rev. Albert W.
    Scherer, Dr. J. J., Jr.
    Sittler, Dr. Joseph
    Stoughton, Dr. Clarence C.
    Witzeman, Mrs. L. A.
  The United Presbyterian Church of North America
    Miller, Dr. J. Kenneth
    Taylor, Dr. Theophilus Mills

WEST AFRICA
  The Church of the Province of West Africa
    Coote, The Rt. Rev. R. N.

WEST INDIES
  Anglican Church of the West Indies
    Burton, The Rt. Rev. Spence, Bishop of Nassau
    Knowles, The Rt. Rev. Donald R., Bishop of Antigua

YUGOSLAVIA
Reformed Christian Church of Yugoslavia
Agoston, Mrs. Sandor

OTHER CHURCHES
Lithuanian Reformed Church
Dilys, Pastor Paul
Esthonian Evangelical Lutheran Church
Hinno, Propst Aleksander
Salvation Army
Bates, Commissioner Claude
Dahya, Colonel Joseph
McMillan, Mrs. Commissioner Donald
Orsborn, Mrs. General Albert
Segawa, Colonel Yasowo
Simpson, Commissioner Gordon

CONSULTANTS

Anderson, Miss Leila, *Protestant Episcopal Church*
Anderson, Mr. Paul B., *Protestant Episcopal Church*
Arbuthnot, The Rev. Charles, *Presbyterian Church in the U.S.A.*
Ariga, Dr. Tetsutaro, *Church of Christ in Japan*
Arnold, Dr. Alice, *Schweizerischer Evangelischer Kirchenbund*
van Asch van Wijck, Miss C. M., *Netherlands Reformed Church*
Baez-Camargo, Professor Gonzalo, *Methodist Church of Mexico*
Baker, Bishop James C., *Methodist Church*
Barfoot, The Most Rev. W. R., *Church of England in Canada*
Barker, Mr. Edwin, *Church of England*
Barnes, Miss Lilace Reid, *Presbyterian Church in the U.S.A.*
Bartlett, P. W., Esq., *Society of Friends*
Batty, The Rt. Rev. F. de W., *Church of England in Australia*
Bell, The Rev. Edwin A., *American Baptist Convention*
Bergendoff, Dr. Conrad, *Augustana Lutheran Church*
von Bismarck, Mr. Klaus, *Evangelische Kirche in Deutschland*
Bragg, Mrs. J. D., *Methodist Church*
Busia, Dr. K. A., *West African Methodist Church*
Calhoun, Professor Robert L., *Congregational Christian Churches of the U.S.A.*
Carleton, Dr. Alford, *Congregational Christian Churches of the U.S.A.*
Carlson, Dr. Edgar M., *Augustana Evangelical Lutheran Church*
Chou, Mrs. Kiyoko Takeda, *Church of Christ in Japan*
Clark, Mr. Elmer T., *Methodist Church*
Demmel, Bishop J. J., *Altkatholische Kirche in Deutschland*
Devadutt, Prof. V. E., *Baptist Church (India)*
Devanandan, Dr. P. D., *Church of South India*
Dudley, Mr. Tilford E., *Congregational Christian Churches of the U.S.A.*
Ellenbeck, Miss Hildegard, *Evangelische Kirche in Deutschland*
Empie, Dr. Paul C., *United Lutheran Church in America*
Farmer, Prof. H. H., *Presbyterian Church in England*
Farris, The Rev. Berlyn, *Methodist Church*
Fichter, Mr. Joseph W., *Methodist Church*
Freudenberg, Dr. Adolf E., *Evangelische Kirche in Deutschland*
Freytag, Professor D. Dr. Walter, *Evangelische Kirche in Deutschland*
Galland, Mr. Valdo, *Schweizerischer Evangelischer Kirchenbund*

Garrison, Professor Winfred E., *International Convention of Disciples of Christ*
Gibson, Miss Henrietta, *Methodist Church*
Goebel, Dr. L. W., *Evangelical and Reformed Church*
Graham, Dr. Frank P., *Presbyterian Church in the U.S.A.*
Greene, Mr. Shirley E., *Congregational Christian Churches of the U.S.A.*
Gregg, Mr. C. C., *Presbyterian Church in the U.S.A.*
Gresham, Dr. Perry E., *Disciples of Christ*
Gruber, Probst D. Heinrich, *Evangelische Kirche in Deutschland*
Hall, The Rev. Cameron P., *Presbyterian Church in the U.S.A.*
Harkness, Professor Georgia, *Methodist Church*
Hauge, Pastor Henrik, *Norske Kirke*
Hayward, The Rev. V. W., *Baptist Union of Great Britain and Ireland*
Hedenquist, The Rev. Goete A. V., *Svenska Kyrkan*
Heinemann, Dr. Gustav W., *Evangelische Kirche in Deutschland*
Hentsch, Mr. Gustav, *Schweizerischer Evangelischer Kirchenbund*
Hoegsbro, Bishop Halfdan R., *Den Evangelisk-Lutherske Folkekirke i Danmark*
Hoffman, Rektor Dr., *Evangelische Kirche in Deutschland*
Horton, Professor Walter, *Congregational Christian Churches of the U.S.A.*
House, The Rev. Francis H., *Church of England*
Howells, Bishop A. W., *The Church of the Province of West Africa (Anglican)*
Hunt, Canon H. R., *Church of England in Canada*
Jackson, Mrs. Clarence P., *African Methodist Episcopal Zion Church*
James, Dr. James Alton, *Methodist Church*
Jenkins, The Rev. Daniel Thomas, *Congregational Union of England and Wales*
Johnson, Dr. F. Ernest, *Methodist Church*
Jones, Mr. Victor, *Methodist Church*
Jullien, Miss Claire, *Eglise Réformée de France*
Kagawa, Dr. Toyohiko, *Church of Christ in Japan*
Kaegi, Prof. Werner, *Schweizerischer Evangelischer Kirchenbund*
Kantonen, Prof. Taito Almer, *United Lutheran Church in America*
Karefa-Smart, Mrs. John, *American Methodist Episcopal Zion Church*
Keller, Prof. Adolph, *Schweizerischer Evangelischer Kirchenbund*
Kitigawa, The Rev. Daisuke, *Protestant Episcopal Church*
Kloppenburg, Oberkirchenrat Pastor H. F. O., *Evangelische Kirche in Deutschland*
Krimm, Dr. Herbert, *Evangelische Kirche in Deutschland*
Krueger, Dr. Hanfried, *Evangelische Kirche in Deutschland*
Kunst, Praelat Hermann, *Evangelische Kirche in Deutschland*
Kyaw Than, Mr., *Burma Baptist Church*
Lauriol, Mr. E., *Eglise Réformée de France*
Leber, Dr. Charles T., *Presbyterian Church in the U.S.A.*
Lee-Woolf, The Rev. J. Philip, *Congregational Union of England and Wales*
Leiper, Dr. Henry Smith, *Congregational Christian Churches of the U.S.A.*
Leung, Dr. S. C., *Church of Christ in China*
Liebenberg, The Rev. F. J., *Ned. Herv. of Geref. Kerk van Zuid-Afrika*
van der Linde, Dr. Hendrik, *Nederlands Hervormde Kerk*
Lombard, Mr. Georges, *Schweizerischer Evangelischer Kirchenbund*
Lugg, Dr. Thomas B., *Methodist Church*
McGaw, Dr. Foster G., *Presbyterian Church in the U.S.A.*
McGiffert, Dr. A. C., Jr., *Congregational Christian Churches of the U.S.A.*
MacLeod, Mrs. W. Murdoch, *Presbyterian Church in the U.S.A.*
McNeil, The Rev. Jesse Jai, *National Baptist Convention, U.S.A., Inc.*
McSwain, Dr. E. T., *Presbyterian Church in the U.S.A.*
Marais, Dr. B. J., *Dutch Reformed Church of South Africa*

Menn, Pastor Wilhelm, *Evangelische Kirche in Deutschland*
Miller, Mr. J. Irwin, *International Convention of Disciples of Christ*
Minear, Dr. Paul S., *Congregational Christian Churches of the U.S.A.*
Moore, Dr. Glenn W., *Presbyterian Church in the U.S.A.*
Moses, Dr. D. G., *United Church of North India*
Mota, Mr. Jorge Cesar, *Presbyterian Church*
Mott, Dr. John R., *Methodist Church*
Muelder, Dean Walter G., *Methodist Church*
Munby, Mr. D. L., *Episcopal Church of Scotland*
Mutchmor, The Rev. J. R., *United Church of Canada*
Nelson, Mr. L. Melvin, *American Baptist Convention*
Niebuhr, Professor Richard, *Evangelical and Reformed Church*
North, Mr. Eric M., *Methodist Church*
Okajima, The Rev. M., *Anglican Church in Japan*
Olsen, Dr. C. Arild, *American Evangelical Lutheran Church*
Paton, Mr. Alan S., *Church of the Province of South Africa*
Platt, The Rev. William J., *Methodist Church*
Prenter, Professor Regin, *Den Evangelislutherske Folkekirke i Danmark*
Ray, The Rev. Canon Chandu, *Church of India, Pakistan, Burma and Ceylon*
Rendtorff, The Rev. C. A. V., *Den Evangelisk-Lutherske Folkekirk i Danmark*
Rendtorff, Dr. Heinrich, *Evangelische Kirche in Deutschland*
Richardson, Professor Alan, *Church of England*
Rueckert, Pastor Norbet, *Evangelische Kirche in Deutschland*
Saito, The Rev. Soichi, *Y.M.C.A., Japan*
Sansbury, The Rev. Canon C. K., *Church of England*
Sargent, Mr. Noel, *Protestant Episcopal Church*
Sayre, Dr. Francis B., *Protestant Episcopal Church*
Schmidt-Clausen, Pastor Kurt, *Evangelische Kirche in Deutschland*
Singh, Professor Surjit, *United Church of North India*
Smith, Dr. Eugene L., *Methodist Church*
Smith, Professor Richard C., *Presbyterian Church in the U.S.A.*
Sommerlath, Dr. Ernst, *Evangelische Kirche in Deutschland*
Stelma, Dr. J. H., *Nederlands Hervormde Kerk*
Stockwell, President B. Foster, *Methodist Church*
Stratenwerth, Dr. Gerhard, *Evangelische Kirche in Deutschland*
Stroh, Pastor Hans, *Evangelische Kirche in Deutschland*
Strong, Dr. Tracy, *Congregational Christian Churches of the U.S.A.*
Symons, Mr. William G., *Methodist Church*
Thimme, Dr. Ephorus, *Evangelische Kirche in Deutschland*
Thomas, Prof. George F., *Protestant Episcopal Church*
Thomas, Mr. M. M., *Mar Thoma Syrian Church of Malabar*
Thomson, Dean James S., *United Church of Canada*
Trinterud, Professor L. J., *Presbyterian Church in the U.S.A.*
Tsu, Bishop Andrew Y. Y., *Anglican Church in China*
Vajta, Dr. Vilmos, *Svenska Kyrkan*
Verkhovsky, Prof. Serge, *Eastern Orthodox Church*
Vogel, Prof. D. Heinrich, *Evangelische Kirche in Deutschland*
de Vries, Dr. E., *Protestant Church in Indonesia*
Waddams, The Rev. Herbert, *Church of England*
Ward, Mrs. Mae Yoho, *International Convention of Disciples of Christ*
Warren, The Rev. M. A. C., *Church of England*
Wedel, Mrs. T. O., *Protestant Episcopal Church*
Wendland, Prof. D., *Evangelische Kirche in Deutschland*

Wentz, Dr. Abdel Ross, *United Lutheran Church in America*
Westphal, Pastor Charles, *Eglise Réformée de France*
Whiting, Dr. Henry J., *American Lutheran Church*
Wolf, Dr. Hans-Heinrich, *Evangelische Kirche in Deutschland*

YOUTH CONSULTANTS

Abe, Miss Ikuyo, *United Church of Christ in Japan*
Bailor, Mr. Max, *United Evangelical Brethren (West Africa)*
Barrett, The Rev. Bernard, *Church of England in Canada*
Beggs, Miss Martha, *Presbyterian (U.S.A.)*
Bhandare, Mr. R. S., *United Church in North India*
Biegert, Mr. John, *Evangelical United Brethren (U.S.A.)*
Brown, Mr. Thomas Kihei, *Congregational (U.S.A.)*
Buason, Mr. Kristjan, *Church of Iceland*
Burns, Miss Pauline, *Church of England*
Burrichter, Miss Lavon, *Evangelical and Reformed (U.S.A.)*
Butterfield, Mr. Michael, *Church of England*
Cesar, Mr. Waldo A. L., *Presbyterian (Brazil)*
Chacko, Mr. George K., *Mar Thoma Syrian Church (India)*
Charlesworth, Mr. Geoffrey, *Methodist Church of Australia*
Clark, Mr. Neville, *Baptist (England)*
Day, The Rev. Duane, *American Baptist*
de Montmollin, Miss Violaine, *Reformed (France)*
Edwards, Miss Ruth, *Disciples (Canada)*
Ely, Miss Rebecca Ann, *Episcopal (U.S.A.)*
Fray, Miss Florence, *United Lutheran (U.S.A.)*
French, Mr. Roderick, *Episcopal (U.S.A.)*
Garrido, Miss Lydia, *Baptist (Philippines)*
Gecau, Mr. Julius, *Anglican (East Africa)*
Grant, Mr. Raymond, S., Jr., *Methodist (U.S.A.)*
Graven, Mr. John, *Orthodox (U.S.A.)*
Harada, Mr. Keiichi, *United Church of Christ in Japan*
Hasler, Mr. Robert, *Reformed (Switzerland)*
Hauge, Mr. Jens G., *Lutheran (World's Student Christian Federation)*
Henderson, Miss Clara, *Society of Friends (U.S.A.)*
Henry, Mr. Kenneth, *Disciples (U.S.A)*
Hjelm, Mr. Norman Arthur, *Lutheran (U.S.A.)*
Istafanous, Rev. Abd-El-Masih, *United Presbyterian (Egypt)*
Jaime, Rev. Angel Luis, *Congregational (Puerto Rico)*
Jason, Miss Hester, *United Church of Christ in the Philippines*
Jenkinson, Miss Sheila, *Church of Scotland (World's Alliance of Y.W.C.A.s)*
Jeppesen, Miss Ragnhild, *Lutheran (Denmark)*
Jeyatheva, Mr. Samuel, *J.D.C.S.I. (Ceylon)*
John, Mr. M. P., *Orthodox Syrian (India)*
Khodr, Mr. George, *Orthodox (Syria-Lebanon)*
Kim, Mr. Chun-Bae, *Presbyterian Church in Korea (World's Student Christian Federation)*
Kirkinen, Mr. Heikki, *Orthodox (Finland)*
Kollias, Mr. Sifis, *Orthodox (Greece)*
Kopp, Mr. Bernard, *Reformed (France)*
Kühnel-Brady, Miss Sigrid, *Evangelical Lutheran (Austria)*
Lange, The Rev. Ernst, *United Evangelical (Germany)*
Langfort, Miss Cristl, *Evangelical Lutheran (Austria)*

Ling, Mr. Kuo-Huang, *Presbyterian* (*Formosa*)
Littmarck, The Rev. Tore, *Swedish Lutheran* (*World's Alliance of Y.M.C.A.s*)
Lønning, The Rev. Per, *Lutheran* (*Norway*)
Lusk, Miss Mary Irene, *Church of Scotland*
McCall, Mr. Kenneth, *Presbyterian* (*U.S.A.*)
McIntyre, Miss Edna, *Presbyterian Church in Canada*
McNeur, The Rev. Ronald, *Reformed* (*New Zealand*)
McRae, Mrs. Ruth, *United Church of Canada* (*World's Student Christian Federation*)
Madany, Miss Hanna Lameece, *Reformed* (*World's Alliance of Y.W.C.A.s*)
Malan, Mr. Leon, *Dutch Reformed* (*South Africa*)
Martin, The Rev. Milton Bruce, *Methodist* (*South Africa*)
Martinez, Mr. Néstor Gordillo, *Methodist* (*Argentina*)
Matthews, Miss Celia, *Church of England*
Metcalf, Mr. William C., *Presbyterian,* (*U.S.A.*)
Meyendorff, Mr. Jean, *Orthodox* (*France*)
Meyer, The Rev. Gerhard, *Reformed* (*Switzerland*)
Miegge, Mr. Mario, *Waldensian* (*Italy*)
Mondlane, Mr. Eduardo, *Swiss Mission* (*Portuguese East Africa*)
Near, Miss Margaret, *Presbyterian Church in Canada*
Nesbitt, Mr. Leroy, *African Methodist Episcopal Church* (*U.S.A.*)
Nettayottin, Miss Praskai, *Church of Christ* (*Thailand*)
Ochsenbein, Miss Ruth, *Presbyterian* (*Spain*)
Palmer, Miss Jean, *United Church of Canada* (*World's Alliance of Y.W.C.A.s*)
Palmer, Mr. Noel, *Society of Friends* (*British West Indies*)
Palmer, Mr. Rufus, *Methodist* (*India*)
Pepys, Lady Paulina, *Orthodox* (*England*)
Peter, Mr. Elia, *Methodist* (*India*)
Piediscalzi, Mr. Nick, *Congregational* (*U.S.A.*)
Potter, The Rev. Philip, *Methodist* (*Haiti*)
Ramaila, Mr. Henry Segoma, *Lutheran* (*South Africa*)
Reeve, Mr. David, *United Church of Canada*
Revel, Miss Myriam Alice, *Waldensian* (*Uruguay*)
Richter, Miss Roswitha, *Lutheran* (*Germany*)
Ricks, Miss Barbara, *Methodist* (*U.S.A.*)
Sandral, Miss Susan, *Presbyterian Church of Australia*
Sapsezian, Mr. Aharon, *Armenian Evangelical* (*Brazil*)
Schlingensiepen, Mr. Gerhard, *Lutheran* (*Germany*)
Schmemann, Fr. Alexander, *Russian Orthodox* (*U.S.A.*)
Scholz, Mr. Friedrich, *Orthodox* (*Germany*)
Shiozuki, Mr. Kentaro, *United Church of Christ in Japan* (*World's Alliance of Y.M.C.A.s*)
Siering, Mr. Walter, *Evangelical United Brethren* (*Germany*)
Soederberg, The Rev. Carl-Ake, *Church of Sweden*
Suhonen, Mr. Niilo, *Evangelical Lutheran* (*Finland*)
Underhill, Miss Beryl E., *Methodist* (*England*)
Van Coeverden, Mr. Huib, *Reformed* (*Netherlands*)
Van de Ven, Mr. J. A., *Old Catholic* (*Netherlands*)
Welch, Miss Barbara Muriel, *Methodist* (*Australia*)
Whisler, Miss Rebecca, *Community* (*U.S.A.*)
Williams, Mr. Lloyd G., *Society of Friends* (*Australia*)
Wissink, Mr. Charles, Jr., *Reformed* (*U.S.A.*)
Zachrisson, Mr. Bertil, *Mission Convenant Church* (*Sweden*)
Zambrano, Rev. Ariel Medina, *Congregational* (*Mexico*)

FRATERNAL DELEGATES

Baptist World Alliance
Ohrn, Dr. Arnold, T.
Friends World Committee for Consultation
Walker, Mr. James F.
International Congregational Council
Berry, The Rev. Dr. Sydney M.
Lutheran World Federation
Lund-Quist, Dr. Carl E.
United Bible Societies
Béguin, Mr. Olivier
World Christian Endeavour Union
Poling, Dr. Daniel A.
World Convention of the Churches of Christ
Bader, Dr. Jesse M.
World Council of Christian Education
Chappel, Mr. Nelson
World Methodist Council
Perkins, The Rev. Ernest Benson
World Presbyterian Alliance
Pradervand, Dr. Marcel
World's Student Christian Federation
Maury, Mr. Philippe
World's Alliance of Y.M.C.A.'s
Limbert, Dr. Paul M.
World's Y.W.C.A.
Roberts, Miss Helen
National Council of the Churches of Christ in America
Ross, The Rev. Dr. Roy
Australian Council for the World Council of Churches
Mackay, Dr. Malcolm
Confederacao Evangelica do Brasil
Smith, The Rev. Wilbur K.
British Council of Churches
Say, The Rev. R. D.
Burma Christian Council
Ah Mya, The Rt. Rev. Francis
Canadian Council of Churches
Gallagher, The Rev. Dr. W. J.
Council of Evangelical Churches of Cuba
Fernandez, The Rev. Raul
Danish Ecumenical Council
Lindqvist, Mr. Kaj Erik
Arbeitsgemeinschaft Christlicher Kirchen in Deutschland (Germany)
Luckey, Dr. Lic. Hans
National Christian Council of India
Mukerjee, The Most Rev. A. N.
Council of Churches in Indonesia
Fransz, Miss A. L.
National Christian Council of Korea
Ho Choon Yu, The Rev.

Malayan Christian Council
  Lee, Canon John
Concilio Evangelico de Mexico
  Velasco, Mr. José O.
Near East Christian Council
  Elder, Dr. E. E.
National Council of Churches of New Zealand
  Bennett, Mr. Jonathan F.
Norwegian Ecumenical Council
  Lier, The Rev. Dr. Alf
Philippine Federation of Evangelical Churches
  Cabotaje, The Rev. F. V.
Association of Evangelical Churches of Puerto Rico
  Marcano, President Hipolito
Confederacion de Iglesias Evangelicas del Rio de la Plata
  Lozada, Miss Jorgelina
Swedish Ecumenical Council
  Johansson, Dr. Harry

OBSERVERS

Anderson, President Theodore W., *Evangelical Mission Covenant Church of America*
Andrey, His Grace Archbishop, *Bulgarian Eastern Orthodox Church*
Bender, Dr. Harold S., *Mennonite Church*
Daane, Dr. James, *Christian Reformed Church*
Dickson, Mr. L. K., *General Conference of Seventh-Day Adventists*
Flower, Dr. J. Roswell, *Assemblies of God*
Fuykschot, Mr. F. T., *International Federation of Workmen's Evangelical Associations*
Grabbe, Father George, *Russian Orthodox Church outside Russia*
Griffin, The Rev. Marvin, *National Baptist Convention*
Hirai, The Rev. Kiyoshi, *Evangelical Lutheran Church in Japan*
Kraan, Dr. K. J., *Gereformeerde Kerken in Nederland*
Lohe, President Max, *United Evangelical Lutheran Church in Australia*
McDormand, Dr. Thomas B., *Baptist Convention of Ontario and Quebec*
Marney, Dr. Carlyle, *Southern Baptist Convention*
Miller, Dean Adam W., *The Church of God*
Moraes, The Rev. Dr. Benjamin, *Presbyterian Church of Brazil*
Nersoyan, The Rt. Rev. Bishop Tiran, *Armenian Church of North America*
Poladian, Bishop Terenig, *Armenian Church*
Rees, Mr. Paul S., *National Association of Evangelicals*
Schiotz, Dr. Frederik, *Evangelical Lutheran Church*
Shelly, Professor Paul R., *Mennonites, U.S.A.*
Sherk, Dr. J. Harold, *Mennonite Church*
Testa, Mr. Michael, *Presbyterian Church of Portugal*
Wilkinson, The Rev. P. S., *National Baptist Convention of America*

SPECIAL GUESTS

Arnaldo, Mr. Salomon V., *U.N.E.S.C.O.*
Creel, Mr. Dana S.
Moornaw, Mr. J. W., *F.A.O.*
Reisner, Mr. John, *F.A.O.*

GUEST SPEAKERS

President Dwight D. Eisenhower
Secretary-General Dag Hammerskjoeld

ACCREDITED VISITORS

AUSTRALASIA
Methodist Church of Australasia
Hayes, Mrs. V. C.
Hayes, The Rev. V. C.
Lew, Mrs. R. B.

AUSTRALIA
Church of England in Australia and Tasmania
Barrett, The Ven. Archdeacon W. R.
Kirby, The Rev. R. F.
Knox, The Rev. D. Broughton
Muschamp, The Rt. Rev. C. E. W.
Royle, Dr. Harold G.
Shevill, The Rt. Rev. I. W. A.
Stocks, Mr. A. W. J.
Congregational Union of Australia
Anderson, The Rev. N.
Davies, Mr. Maynard
Federal Conference of Churches of Christ in Australia
Clark, Mr. H. A. G.
Methodist Conference of Australia
Thomas, Mr. Charles A.
Presbyterian Church of Australia
Heriot, The Rev. Kenneth
Hetzel, Dr. Basil
McCutchan, Mr. Arthur Ingham
Ritchie, Miss C.

AUSTRIA
Evangelische Kirche A.u.H.B. in Oesterreich (Evangelical Church of the Augsburgian and Helvetic Confession)
Sturm, Pfarrer Emil

BRAZIL
Igreja Metodista do Brasil (Methodist Church of Brazil)
Bittencourt, The Rev. Benedito Paul

CANADA
Churches of Christ (Disciples)
Clague, The Rev. Prin. James
Stainton, The Rev. H. Bruce
Church of England in Canada
Brewin, Mr. F. Andrew
Davis, The Rev. Canon A. H.
Hallam, The Rt. Rev. W. T.
Osler, Mrs. Britton
Slater, The Rev. Prin. R. H. L.
Watney, The Rev. Canon D. P.

CANADA—*continued*
  Presbyterian Church in Canada
    McLean, Dr. J. L. W.
    Matthews, Miss Freda E.
    Mulligan, Dr. W. O.
    Wade, Professor D. V.
  United Church of Canada
    Boyce, The Rev. Greer W.
    Chalmers, Dr. R. C.
    Crysdale, The Rev. R. C. S.
    Forster, Dr. H. G.
    Griffith, The Rev. A. L.
    Halpenny, Mrs. J. L.
    Howse, Dr. E. M.
    Legge, Dr. G. W.
    McKillop, Mrs. John
    Switzer, Mr. Gerald
    Turnbull, The Rev. Elgin
    Young, Mr. Ralph C.
  Yearly Meeting of the Society of Friends
    Nelson, Mr. Sterling

DENMARK
  Den Evangelislutherske Folkekirke i Danmark (Church of Denmark)
    Christensen, Mr. Villy
    Hoegsbro, Mrs. Inger
    Thomsen, Mr. J. J.
    Thomsen, Miss Karen Ingrid

FINLAND
  Soumen Evankelis-Luterilainen Kirkko (Evangelical Lutheran Church of Finland)
    Murto, The Rev. Pentti

FRANCE
  Eglise Réformée de France (Reformed Church of France)
    Marchand, Pastor Jacques

GERMANY
  Altkatholische Kirche in Deutschland (Old Catholic Church in Germany)
    Steinwachs, Weihbischof Dr. O.
  Evangelische Kirche in Deutschland (Evangelical Church in Germany)
    Beckmann, Oberkirchenrat Lic. Dr.
    Bender, Landesbischof D.
    Boehle, Pfarrer Th.
    Broelsch, Landesjugendpfarrer
    Burgwitz, Pfarrer Lic. Dr.
    Dibelius, Oberkirchenrat O.
    Ditter, Kaufmann H.
    Drobnitzky, Pfarrer Walter
    Eberhard, Pastor Dr.
    Fokken, Frau Kaete
    Florin, Mr. H. W.
    Freudenberg, Frau A.

GERMANY—*continued*
  Evangelische Kirche in Deutschland—continued
    Grossmann, Frau Martha
    Grueber, Frau Margarethe
    Herntrich, Frau
    Heyne, Pastor Bodo
    Hornig, Bischof D.
    Jochums, Pastor H.
    Krueger, Pastor Erdmann
    Mager, Synodalpraesident R.
    Marquardt, Mr. Georg
    Mehling, Mr. Bodo
    Mueller, Mr. Bernhard
    Niemoeller, Frau E.
    Rautenberg, Praeses D.
    Schlingensiepen, Prof. D.
    Schmidt, Dipl. Ing. Hans
    Schulz, Frau Oberstudiendirektor
    Steuernagel, Mr. Ortwin
    Voll, Predigamtskandidat Dieter
    Wedell, Pfarrer Dr. Hans
    Witte, Superintendent M.
    Wuestemann, Bischof D.

ICELAND
  Evangelical Lutheran Church of Iceland
    Magnussen, The Rev. Peter

INDIA
  Church of India, Pakistan, Burma, and Ceylon
    De Sosa, The Rev. Harold
    West, The Rt. Rev. George
    West, Mrs. George
  Church of South India
    Aaron, The Rev. J. P.
    David, Miss Dora
    Doraiswamy, The Rev. Solomon
    Lazarus, The Rev. Henry
    Muyskens, The Rev. J. D.
    Ratnarajah, The Rev. J. J.
    Rowlands, The Rev. M. A.
    Thomas, The Rev. V. M.
    Thomas, Mrs. V. M.
    Sathyanathan, The Rev. John
  Mar Thoma Syrian Church of Malabar
    Alexander, The Rev. V. V.
    Mathan, The Rev. V.
    Philip, The Rev. K. J.
    Thomas, Mrs. M. M.
  Orthodox Syrian Church of Malabar Catholicate
    Alexander, Mr. V. K.
    Chandrathil, Mr. Mathew K.
    Varghese, Mr. Paul

INDIA—*continued*
  United Church of Northern India and Pakistan
    Dobson, The Rev. Arthur W.
    Hazlett, The Rev. C. H.
    Hivale, Dr. Bhaskar
    Kellas, Dr. John
    Yohan-Masih, Mrs. Kenneth

INDONESIA
  Hoeria Kristen Batak Protestant (Batak Church of Sumatra)
    Sinaga, The Rev. Jetro
  Gredja Kristen di Soelawesi Tengah (Toradja Church)
    Hartojo, The Rev. Oerip

JAPAN
  Nippon Kirisuto Kyodan (Church of Christ)
    De Maagd, Mr. John C.
    Fujita, The Rev. Massanao
    Kanai, Prof. S.
    Kozaki, Mrs. Shizu
    Nakayama, The Rev. S.
    Shinya, Mr. Tokuji
    Takenaka, Mr. Masao
    Vories-Hitotsuyanagi, Dr. Merrell
  Nippon Sei Ko Kwai (Anglican Church in Japan)
    Yanagihara, Bishop Peter S.

KOREA
  Korean Methodist Church
    Song, The Rev. H. K.
  Presbyterian Church of Korea
    Kim, Deacon Jong Whan

NETHERLANDS
  Nederlands Hervormde Kerk (Netherlands Reformed Church)
    Emmen-Aalders, Mrs. C.
    Geurtsen, The Rev. G. J.
    Stelma-Loosjes, Mrs. C. J. E.
    Wesseldijk, Pres. H. J. F.
  Oud-Katholieke Kerk (Old Catholic Church)
    Moleman, Canon Theodorus

NEW ZEALAND
  Congregational Union of New Zealand
    Davies, Mr. Maynard
  Methodist Church of New Zealand
    Goodman, The Rev. G. H.
    Pearce, Mrs. Joy G. S.
    Thornley, The Rev. R.
  Presbyterian Church of New Zealand
    Cree, The Rev. K. S.
    Hubbard, The Rev. John
    Whitelaw, Mrs. A. C.

NORWAY
Norske Kirke (Church of Norway)
Aas, Pastor Ivar
Bonnevie-Svendsen, Dr. C.
Bugge, The Rev. Sten
Hansson, Mrs. Jenny
Hauge, Mrs. Kirsten
Wikborg, Mrs. Dagny

PHILIPPINE ISLANDS
United Church of Christ in the Phillipines
Ambrosio, Mr. Dominador
Dia, Mr. Severo G.

SOUTH AFRICA
Church of the Province of South Africa
Moloi, The Rev. B. J. L.
Tsebe, The Rev. J. B. K.
Presbyterian Church of South Africa
Mzimba, Dr. Livingstone

SWEDEN
Svenska Kyrkan (Church of Sweden)
Arbin, The Rev. Erik
Brilioth, Mrs. Brita
Cederberg, The Rev. Daniel
Hultgard, Mrs. Britta
Johansson, Mrs. Alice
Kempe, Mrs. Ingeborg
Nygren, Mrs. Imgard
Nyrén, The Rev. A. B.
Nyrén, Mrs. Maerta M.
Pernow, Mr. Birger

SWITZERLAND
Schweizerischer Evangelischer Kirchenbund (Swiss Protestant Church Federation)
Buehrig, Miss Margarete
Byland, Mr. Armin
Grin, Professor Edmond

TURKEY
Oecumenical Patriarchate of Constantinople
Demos, Mr. Paul

UNITED KINGDOM AND EIRE
Baptist Union of Great Britain and Ireland
Clifford, The Rev. Paul Rowntree
Grant, The Rev. W. J.
Reeves, Dr. Marjorie
Saunders, The Rev. Jack
Timson, Ernest A., Esq.
Church of Christ in Great Britain and Ireland
Baker, The Rev. William G.

K*

UNITED KINGDOM AND EIRE—*continued*

Church of England
Allen, The Rt. Rev. G. F.
Appleton, The Rev. George
Bell, Mrs. G. A. K.
Bliss, The Rev. R. G.
Campbell, The Rev. J. McLeod
de Blank, The Rt. Rev. Joost
Ducker, The Rev. V. T.
Ducker, Mrs. V. T.
Eaton, The Rev. Canon A. W.
Herklots, Mrs. H. G. G.
Hilton, Miss Beryl
Holmes, Miss E.
Howard, Miss Christian
Ridgway, The Rev. M. H.
Roper, Miss A.
Vodden, Mrs. H. T.
Vodden, The Rt. Rev. H. T.
Wand, Mrs. J. W. C.
Wilkins, Mrs. F. B.

Accredited Visitors from Missionary Dioceses of the Church of England
Arblaster, The Rev. E.
Bailey, The Venerable F. J.
Evans, The Rt. Rev. D. I.
Frank, The Rev. C. N.
Kemp, The Venerable B. H.
Lei, The Venerable K-Y.
Nakhusteen, The Rev. A.
Shammas, The Venerable Adeeb Dolofeet
Stewart, Mrs. W. H.
Thompson, The Rt. Rev. W. J.

Church of Ireland
Herdman, Commander C. A.

Church of Scotland
Baxter, Mrs. W. J.
Cameron, The Rev. G. G.
Dougall, Mrs. J. W. C.
Hamilton, The Duchess of
Harvey, Miss Allison
Macanna, The Rev. R. Clephane
Shaw, The Rev. Geoffrey
Smith, The Rev. Robert
Tindal, Mrs. W. S.

Church in Wales
Jones, Mrs. John Charles
Witton-Davies, Mrs. C.

Congregational Union of England and Wales
Biggs, Miss Dorothy J.
Daniels, Lionel, Esq.
Hartwell, Mrs. B. J.
Janes, The Rev. Maxwell O.

UNITED KINGDOM AND EIRE—*continued*
Congregational Union of England and Wales—continued
   Little, Robert, Esq.
   Northcott, The Rev. Cecil
Congregational Union of Scotland
   Donaldson, The Rev. H. T.
Methodist Church
   Bartlett, Mrs. B. J.
   Crosby, Dr. K. H.
   Davison, The Rev. Leslie
   Morgan, Dr. I.
   Neilson, The Rev. J. Morrison
   Verney, Dr. Douglas
   Wade, The Rev. Wilfred
Methodist Church in Ireland
   Waugh, E. L., Esq.
Presbyterian Church of England
   Slack, The Rev. Kenneth
Presbyterian Church in Ireland
   Boyd, Mrs. J. R.
   Lavery, Miss M. Beatrice
Presbyterian Church of Wales
   Evans, Miss Margaret Nonn

U.S.A.
African Methodist Episcopal Church
   Allen, Bishop A. J.
   Baber, Bishop George W.
   Blakely, Dr. G. Wayman
   Mance, Dr. R. W.
   Ward, Dr. A. Wayman
African Methodist Episcopal Zion Church
   Eichelberger, Dr. J. W.
   Findley, The Rev. J. W.
   Frances, Mrs. M.
   Kyles, Mrs. J. H.
American Baptist Convention
   Adams, Dr. Earl Frederick
   Arey, Mrs. Leslie B.
   Averill, The Rev. Lloyd
   Carlson, Dr. C. Emanuel
   Chastain, Dr. Theron
   Colwell, Mrs. Howard G.
   Diman, Dr. W. A.
   Knapp, Dr. Charles C.
   LeGrand, Mrs. James
   Morong, Dr. Carrol O.
   Morse, Dr. Franklin M.
   Rinck, Miss Suzanne
   Saunders, President Wilbour E.
   Seasholes, Dr. Charles L.
   Straton, Dr. Hillyer H.
   Terrell, Mrs. W. S.
   Wilson, Dr. Jesse R.

U.S.A.—*continued*

American Evangelical Lutheran Church
Jensen, Dr. Alfred
Knudsen, Prof. Johannes

American Lutheran Church
Bodensieck, Dr. J.
Engelbrecht, Dr. A. W.
Fendt, Dr. E. C.
Haas, Miss Dorothy
Ludwig, Dr. L.
Salzmann, Dr. S.
Siefkes, Dr. H. W.

Augustana Evangelical Lutheran Church
Anderson, Dr. O. V.
Carlson, Dr. Martin E.
Hoyer, Dr. H. Conrad
Levander, Prof. Theodore
Lundeen, Dr. Malvin H.

Christian Methodist Episcopal Church
Carter, Mrs. Helen E.
Evans, Dr. Holman W.
Kirkendoll, President Chester A.

Church of the Brethren
Bittinger, The Rev. D. W.
Bowman, Mr. Paul H.
Mallot, Mr. Kenneth

Congregational Christian Churches of the United States of America
Catton, Miss Ione
Dunstan, Dr. J. Leslie
English, Dr. James F.
Evans, Dr. Wilford H.
Gibbons, Dr. Ray
Gregory, The Rev. L.
Houser, Dr. Charles M.
Johnson, Mrs. Charles S.
Jones, Dr. Harold G.
Kahlengberg, Mrs. George
More, The Rev. James H.
Parr, The Rev. C. E.
Russell, The Rev. Galen
Stamp, The Rev. Lloyd R.
Trexler, The Rev. J. M.
Williams, Mrs. Robert G.
Williams, Dean George

Evangelical and Reformed Church
Arndt, Dr. Elmer J. F.
Benchoff, Mrs. Guy A.
Grauer, Dr. Gerhard W.
Helfferich, Dr. R. H.
Herzog, Dr. Friedrich
Partridge, Miss Florence A.
Schmoyer, The Rev. Paul E.

U.S.A.—*continued*

Evangelical and Reformed Church—continued
Szabo, Dr. Stephen
Vassady, Dr. Bela

Evangelical United Brethren Church
Dennis, Bishop Fred L.
Eller, Dr. Paul H.
Heininger, President Harold R.
Heinmiller, Dr. Carl
Roberts, President Walter N.
Showers, Bishop J. Balmer
Stamm, Bishop J. S.

International Convention of Disciples of Christ
Blakemore, Dr. W. B.
Brown, Mr. Carl R.
Dean, Mr. Herman P.
Gaylord, The Rev. Raymond
Jarman, The Rev. W. Jackson
Kleihauer, Dr. Cleveland
Langston, Dr. Ira W.
Lunger, Dr. Harold L.
Morrison, Dr. Charles C.
Richeson, Mrs. Forrest L.
Sawyer, The Rev. Fred D.
Shelton, Dr. O. L.
Smith, Dr. Harlie L.
Stauffer, Mrs. Paul S.
Storey, Mr. R. G.
Stuart, The Rev. George C.
Wood, Dr. Howard Thomas

Methodist Church
Bacon, Dr. C. Clifford
Bertholf, Dr. Lloyd
Blackburn, Dr. H. W.
Boss, The Rev. Charles F., Jr.
Cannon, Professor William N.
Carr, President Harold F.
Carter, Mrs. George W., Jr.
Clary, Dr. George E.
Crossland, Dr. Weldon
Cunningham, Dr. W. Jeff
Curl, Dr. R. Floyd
Denman, Dr. Harry
Dorff, Dr. Earl
Edwards, Dr. K. Morgan
Ellisor, The Rev. J. Thad
Foote, Dr. Edward W.
Garrison, Dr. Edwin A.
Gibson, President Foye G.
Godbold, Dr. Albea
Greene, The Rev. John
Harris, Mrs. Felix
Horton, Mrs. William E., Jr.

U.S.A.—*continued*

Methodist Church—continued

Huggin, Dr. J. G., Jr.
Lewis, Dr. H. H.
Liu, Miss Yu Chen
Long, Mrs. C. C.
McArthur, The Rev. W. A.
McCallum, Mrs. W. H.
McDaniel, Mrs. F. L.
McKibbin, Mr. George B.
Mayfield, The Rev. Robert G.
Mohn, Dr. E. Harold
Morehead, Dr. Connor
Pembroke, The Rev. M. D.
Phelps, Mr. Andrew H.
Phillips, Mrs. Ellis L.
Quimby, Dr. Karl K.
Robinson, Mrs. E. U.
Schisler, Dr. John Q.
Seidenspinner, Dr. Clarence
Slater, Dr. Eugene
Smalley, Professor Stimson R.
Smith, The Rev. Percy F.
Streeter, Mrs. Wallace W.
Thomas, Dr. J. S. Ladd
Throckmorton, Dr. J. Russell
Trott, Dr. Norman L.
Ward, The Rev. A. Dudley
Wilkins, Mr. J. Ernest
Williams, The Rev. C. Fred
Wyatt, Mr. Bige

Moravian Church in America (*Northern Province*)

Bronstein, Mr. J. Paul
Bronstein, Mrs. J. Paul

Moravian Church in America (*Southern Province*)

Allen, The Rev. Walser H., Jr.

National Baptist Convention U.S.A., Inc.

Booker, The Rev. Merrel
Curry, Dr. M. K.
Freeman, Dr. E. A.
Henderson, The Rev. I. H., Jr.
Jackson, The Rev. A. P.
Jordan, Mr. Allen
Means, Mr. Andrew
Pelt, The Rev. Owen D.
Sherrill, The Rev. O.
Stokes, Dr. Olivia Pearl
Washington, Dr. T. R.

Polish National Catholic Church of America

Matla, The Rev. Father Anthony

Presbyterian Church in the U.S.

Farnsworth, Mr. R. A.
Fifield, Dr. Harry

U.S.A.—*continued*

Presbyterian Church in the U.S.—continued
McCutchen, Miss Janie
Overmyer, Dr. Joseph B.
Patterson, Dr. S. J.

Presbyterian Church in the U.S.A.
Albers, Mr. Charles A.
Anderson, The Rev. H. Ray
Bodo, The Rev. John
Kirkland, The Rev. Bryant
Ludwig, Dr. W. Paul
McDowell, Mrs. Charles E.
Meister, The Rev. John W.
Moser, Mr. Paul
Shannon, Miss Margaret
Shuster, Dr. Carroll L.
Spencer, Dr. Donald A.
Visser, Dr. John A.
Walker, Dr. Harold B.
Washburn, Mrs. Howard C.
Wasson, The Rev. S. Carson
Watermulder, The Rev. David
Weber, Mrs. Ralph E.
Wilson, The Rev. Frank T.

Protestant Episcopal Church
Bentley, The Rt. Rev. John B.
Brown, The Rev. W. Don
Burrill, The Rt. Rev. Gerald F.
Cantrill, Mrs. Cecil E.
Clark, The Rev. William H.
Clarkson, Mrs. Francis O.
Coburn, The Very Rev. John B.
Groat, Hon. William B.
Higgins, Dr. H. Ralph
Keeler, The Rt. Rev. Stephen E.
Kuebler, Dr. Clark
Lichtenberger, The Rt. Rev. Arthur C.
Louttit, The Rt. Rev. Henry I.
Nes, Dr. W. H.
Scaife, The Rt. Rev. Lauriston L.
Underwood, Mr. Walter
Wicker, The Very Rev. Norvell E.
Wilmer, Dr. R. H., Jr.
Wolf, Dr. William J.
Zabriskie, Dr. Alexander C.

Reformed Church in America
De Velder, The Rev. Dr. Marion
Dickson, The Rev. Robert G.
Wezeman, Pres. F. H.

Five Years Meeting of Friends
Reynolds, Mr. Wilfred S.
Trueblood, Mrs. D. Elton.
Zelliot, Miss Eleanor

U.S.A.—*continued*
  General Conference of the Society of Friends
    Hubben, Mr. William
  The Religious Society of Friends of Philadelphia and Vicinity
    Brown, Mrs. Thomas
    Stokes, Mrs. S. Emlen
  Russian Orthodox Greek Catholic Church in North America
    Jula, The Rev. Stephen
    Shostah, Mr. Stephen
    Solianka, The Rev. Emilian
  Romanian Orthodox Episcopate in America
    Lazar, The Rev. Father Eugene
    Trifa, The Rt. Rev. Valerian V.
  Seventh Day Baptist General Conference
    Rood, Dr. Wayne R.
  Syrian Antiochian Orthodox Church (Archdiocese of New York and all North America)
    Woolf, The Rt. Rev. Antony
  United Evangelical Lutheran Church
    Girtz, The Rev. J. M.
    Nyholm, Dr. Paul C. E.
  The United Lutheran Church in America
    Baker, Mrs. C. W.
    Endress, Dr. Henry
    Eydt, The Rev. Paul W. H.
    Fischer, Dr. Robert H.
    Flack, Dr. E. E.
    Harkins, Dr. George F.
    Koch, Dr. C. Franklin
    Madsen, The Rev. Frank P.
    Mehlenbacher, The Rev. W. A.
    Moose, Mrs. John B.
    Pointer, Mrs. P. D.
    Robinson, Dr. Ralph C.
    Ruoss, The Rev. G. Martin
    Stackel, Mr. William H.
    Steinhoff, Dr. L. H.
    Whittecar, The Rev. George R.
    Winters, Mrs. Roy L.
    Zeidler, The Rev. Clemens H.
  The United Presbyterian Church of North America
    Gibson, The Rev. Robert W.
    Moore, Dr. Ansley C.
    Rose, The Rev. J. Calvin

OTHER CHURCHES
  Lithuanian Reformed Church
    Pavilonis, Ing. Herman
  Estonian Evangelical Lutheran Church
    Viks, Propst Valter

ACCREDITED VISITORS NOMINATED BY THE U.S. CONFERENCE EXECUTIVE COMMITTEE

Applegarth, Miss Margaret T., *American Baptist Convention*
Curry, The Rev. A. Stauffer, *Church of the Brethren*
Freeland, The Rev. Paul, *Presbyterian Church in the U.S.*
Gotwald, Dr. Luther A., *United Lutheran Church in America*
Hategan, Father Vasile, *Roumanian Orthodox Church*
Jernagin, The Rev. W. H., *National Baptist Convention*
Knoff, Dr. Gerald E., *Methodist Church*
Letts, The Rev. Harold C., *United Lutheran Church in America*
Mather, The Rev. Thomas B., *Methodist Church*
Merle-Smith, Mrs. Van Santvoord, *Presbyterian Church in the U.S.A.*
Michaelsen, Dr. Robert, *Methodist Church*
Nace, Dr. I. George, *Evangelical and Reformed Church*
Nelson, Prof. John O., *Presbyterian Church in the U.S.A.*
Pepper, Dr. Almon R., *Protestant Episcopal Church*
Peters, Dr. John T., *Presbyterian Church in the U.S.A.*
Row, The Rev. W. Harold, *Church of the Brethren*
Vander Kolk, Prof. Justin, *Reformed Church in America*
Warfield, Dr. Gaither P., *Methodist Church*
Wilson, Dr. B. Norris, *Congregational Christian Churches of the U.S.A.*

ACCREDITED VISITORS INVITED FROM THE GENEVA OFFICE

Aasgaard, The Rev. Johan A., *Evangelical Lutheran Church*
Amstutz, Mrs. Celeste B., *Methodist Church*
Apostol, The Rev. Janos, *Christian Reformed Church of Brazil*
Bevilacqua, The Rev. Jose, *Association of Evangelical Churches of Puerto Rico*
Chou, Miss Ivy, *Methodist Church*
Davidson, Principal Lewis, *Presbyterian Church of Jamaica*
Farmer, The Rev. Garland S., *International Convention of Disciples of Christ*
Fierla, Bishop Wladyslaw, *Polish Evangelical Lutheran Church in Exile*
Gammon, Miss Billy, *Presbyterian Church of Brazil*
Hallman, The Rev. E. Emerson, *Canadian Council of Churches*
Illidge, Dr. Eugenio, *Presbyterian Church of Colombia*
Irwin, Señor Roberto, *Presbyterian Church in Venezuela*
Kuechlich, Dr. Reinhold, *Evangelical United Brethren*
Luxton, Rt. Rev. G. N., *Church of England in Canada*
Poulton, The Rev. Fred N., *Canadian Council of Churches*
Saulpaugh, Miss Ivane, *Protestant Episcopal Church*
Tan, Mr. Hoyfa, *Chinese Christian Churches in Indonesia*
Wissa, Mrs. Esther F., *Protestant Evangelical Church of Cairo*

VISITORS FROM MEXICO SPECIALLY INVITED

Baez-Camargo, Miss Rosenda
Diaz, Mrs. Fidentia Z. de
Diaz, Mr. Juan
Eliosa, Mr. Ernest
Garcia, Mr. Samuel
Groves, Mr. John
Lopez de Lara, Mr. Daniel
Macin, Mr. Paul
Matzigkeit, Mr. Wesley

Perez, Mr. Eufrasio
Santana, Miss Amelia
Tinoco, Mr. David A.
Velasco, Mrs. Evila G.
Velasco, Mr. Gustavo
Yanez, Mr. Moises
Zambrano, Mr. Saul

The List of Member Churches

AUSTRALASIA
Methodist Church of Australasia

AUSTRALIA
Church of England in Australia and Tasmania
Congregational Union of Australia
Federal Conference of Churches of Christ in Australia
Presbyterian Church of Australia

AUSTRIA
Evangelische Kirche A.u.H.B. in Oesterreich (Evangelical Church of the Augsburgian and Helvetic Confessions)

BELGIUM
Eglise chrétienne missionnaire belge (Belgian Christian Missionary Church)
Union des Eglises évangeliques protestantes de Belgique (Union of Protestant Evangelical Churches of Belgium)

BRAZIL
Federaçao sinodal (Federation of Lutheran Synods)
Igreja metodista do Brasil (Methodist Church of Brazil)

CANADA
Churches of Christ (Disciples)
Church of England in Canada
Presbyterian Church in Canada
United Church of Canada
Yearly Meeting of the Society of Friends

CEYLON
Methodist Church in Ceylon

CHINA
China Baptist Council
Chung Hua Chi-Tu Chiao-hui (Church of Christ in China)
Chung Hua Sheng Kung Hui (Church in China)
North China Kung Li Hui (North China Congregational Church)

CYPRUS
Church of Cyprus

CZECHOSLOVAKIA
Ceskobratska Cirkev Evangelicka (Evangelical Church of Czech Brethren)
Evangelicka Cirkev A. V. na Slovensku (Evangelical Church in Slovakia, Augsburgian Confession)
Ref. Cirkev na Slovensku (Reformed Christian Church in Slovakia)

DENMARK
Baptist Union of Denmark
Den Evangelislutherske Folkekirke i Danmark (Church of Denmark)

EGYPT
Coptic Orthodox Church
Patriarchate of Alexandria

ETHIOPIA
Ethiopian Church

FINLAND
Suomen Evankelis-luterilainen Kirkko (Evangelical Lutheran Church of Finland)

FORMOSA
Tai-oan Ki-tok Tiu-lo Kau-hoe (Presbyterian Church in Formosa)

FRANCE
Eglise de la confession d'Augsbourg, d'Alsace et de Lorraine (Evangelical Church of the Ausburgian Confession in Alsace and Lorraine)
Eglise évangélique luthérienne de France (Evangelical Lutheran Church of France)
Eglise réformée d'Alsace et de Lorraine (Reformed Church of Alsace and Lorraine)
Eglise réformée de France (Reformed Church of France)

GERMANY
Altkatholische Kirche in Deutschland (Old Catholic Church in Germany)
Evangelische Brueder-Unitaet (Moravian Church)
Evangelische Kirche in Deutschland (Evangelical Church in Germany)
  Evangelische Kirche von Berlin-Brandenburg
  Pommersche evangelische Kirche
  Evangelische Kirche von Schlesien
  Evangelische Kirche der Kirchenprovinz Sachsen
  Evangelische Kirche von Westfalen
  Evangelische Kirche im Rheinland
  Evangelisch-lutherische Landeskirche Sachsens[1]
  Evangelisch-lutherische Landeskirche Hannovers[1]
  Evangelisch-lutherische Kirche in Bayern[1]
  Evangelisch-lutherische Kirche in Thüringen[1]
  Evangelisch-lutherische Landeskirche Schleswig-Holsteins[1]
  Evangelisch-lutherische Landerskirche im Hamburgischen Staate[1]
  Evangelisch-lutherische Landeskirche Mecklenburgs[1]
  Braunschweigische evangelisch-lutherische Landeskirche[1]
  Evangelisch-lutherische Kirche in Lübeck[1]
  Evangelisch-lutherische Landeskirche in Schaumburg-Lippe[1]
  Evangelische Landeskirche in Württenberg
  Evangelisch-lutherische Kirche in Oldenburg

[1] This Church is directly a member of the World Council of Churches in accordance with the resolution of the General Synod of the United Evangelical Lutheran Church of Germany, dated 27th January 1949, which recommended that the member Churches of the United Evangelical Lutheran Church should make

GERMANY—*continued*
  Evangelische Kirche in Deutschland—*continued*
    Evangelisch-lutherische Landeskirche Eutin
    Evangelische Kirche in Hessen und Nassau
    Evangelische Landeskirche in Kurhessen-Waldeck
    Vereinigte evangelisch-protestantische Landeskirche Badens
    Vereinigte protestantische Kirche der Pfalz
    Evangelische Landeskirche Anhalts
    Bremische Evangelische Kirche
    Evangelisch-reformierte Kirche in Nordwestdeutschland
    Lippische Landeskirche
  Vereinigung der deutschen Mennonitengemeinden (Mennonite Church)

GOLD COAST
  Presbyterian Church of the Gold Coast

GREECE
  Ekklesia tes Ellados (Church of Greece)
  Greek Evangelical Church

HUNGARY
  A Magyarorszagi Evangelikus Egyhaz (Lutheran Church of Hungary)
  A Magyarorszagi Reformatus Egyhaz (Reformed Church of Hungary)

ICELAND
  Evangelical Lutheran Church of Iceland

INDIA
  Church of India, Pakistan, Burma, and Ceylon
  Church of South India
  Federation of Evangelical Lutheran Churches in India
  Mar Thoma Syrian Church of Malabar
  Orthodox Syrian Church of Malabar Catholicate
  United Church of Northern India and Pakistan

INDONESIA
  Geredja Kalimantan Evangelis (Church of Kalimantan)
  Gredja Keristen di Soelawesi Tengah (Toradja Church)
  Gredja Kristen Djawi Wetan (East Java Church)
  Geredja Masehi Indjili di Minahasa (Church of Minahassa)

---

the following declaration to the Council of the Evangelical Church in Germany concerning their relation to the World Council of Churches:

"The Evangelical Church in Germany had made it clear through its constitution that it is a federation (Bund) of confessionally determined Churches. Moreover, the conditions of membership of the World Council of Churches have been determined at the Assembly at Amsterdam. Therefore, this Evangelical Lutheran Church declares concerning its membership in the World Council of Churches:

(i) It is represented in the World Council as a Church of the Evangelical Lutheran confession.

(ii) Representatives which it sends to the World Council are to be identified as Evangelical Lutherans.

(iii) Within the limits of the competence of the Evangelical Church of Germany it is represented in the World Council through the intermediary of the Council of the Evangelical Church of Germany."

302   THE EVANSTON REPORT

INDONESIA—*continued*
    Gredja Masehi Indjili di Timoer (Protestant Church of Timor)
    Hoeria Kristen Batak Protestant (Batak Church Sumatra)
    Geredja Geredja Keristen Djawa di Djawa Tengah (Javanese Christian Churches in Central Java)
    Geredja Protestant Maluku (Church of the Moluccas)
    Protestantse Kerk in Indonesie (Protestant Church in Indonesia)

IRAN
    Synod of the Evangelical Churches of North Iran

ITALY
    Chiesa Evangelica Metodista d'Italia (Evangelical Methodist Church of Italy)
    Chiesa Evangelica Valdese (Waldensian Church)

JAPAN
    Nippon Kirisuto Kyodan (United Church of Christ)
    Nippon Sei Ko Kwai (Anglican Church in Japan)

JORDAN
    Greek Orthodox Patriarchate of Jerusalem

KOREA
    Korean Methodist Church
    Presbyterian Church of Korea

LEBANON (SEE ALSO SYRIA)
    Union of the Armenian Evangelical Churches in the Near East

MEXICO
    Iglesia Metodista de Mexico (Methodist Church of Mexico)

NETHERLANDS
    Algemene Doopsgezinde Societeit (General Mennonite Society)
    Bond van Vrije Evangelische Gemeenten in Nederland (Union of Free Evangelical Congregations)
    Evangelisch Lutherse Kerk (Evangelical Lutheran Church)
    Nederlands Hervormde Kerk (Dutch Reformed Church)
    Oud-Katholieke Kerk (Old Catholic Church)
    Remonstrantse Broederschap (Arminian Church)
    Unie van Baptisten Gemeenten in Nederland (Union of Baptist Congregations)

NEW ZEALAND
    Associated Churches of Christ in New Zealand
    Baptist Union of New Zealand
    Church of the Province of New Zealand (Church of England)
    Congregational Union of New Zealand
    Methodist Church of New Zealand
    Presbyterian Church of New Zealand

NORWAY
    Norske Kirke (Church of Norway)

PHILIPPINE ISLANDS
United Church of Christ in the Philippines

POLAND
Kosciol Ewangelicko-Augsburski w Polsce (Evangelical Church of the Augs-
burgian Confession in Poland).
Polski Narodoway Kosciol Katolicki (Catholic Church of Poland)

RUMANIA
Biserica Lutherana Ungara din Romania (Hungarian Lutheran Church in
Rumania)
Biserica Protestanta Evangelica din Romania dupa Confesiunea dela Augsburg
(Protestant Evangelical Church, Augsburgian Confession)
Biserica Reformata din Romania (Transylvanian Reformed Church)

SOUTH AFRICA
Bantu Presbyterian Church of South Africa
Church of the Province of South Africa
Congregational Union of South Africa
Methodist Church of South Africa
Ned. Gereformeerde Kerk van de Kaap Provinsie (Dutch Reformed Church of
South Africa of the Cape Province)
Ned. Hervormde of Gereformeerde Kerk van Zuid-Afrika in Transvaal
(Dutch Reformed Church of South Africa in Transvaal)
Nederduits Hervormde Kerk van Afrika (Dutch Reformed Church of Africa)
Presbyterian Church of South Africa

SPAIN
Iglesia Evangélica Española (Spanish Evangelical Church)

SWEDEN
Svenska Kyrkan (Church of Sweden)
Svenska Missionsförbundet (Mission Covenant Church of Sweden)

SWITZERLAND
Christkatholische Kirche der Schweiz (Old Catholic Church)
Schweizerischer Evangelischer Kirchenbund (Swiss Protestant Church Federa-
tion)

SYRIA (SEE ALSO LEBANON)
Evangelical Synod of Syria and Lebanon
Greek Orthodox Patriachate of Antioch

THAILAND
Church of Christ in Thailand

TURKEY
Oecumenical Patriarchate of Constantinople

UNITED KINGDOM AND EIRE
Baptist Union of Great Britain and Ireland
Baptist Union of Scotland
Churches of Christ in Great Britain and Ireland

UNITED KINGDOM AND EIRE—*continued*
  Church of England
  Church of Ireland
  Church of Scotland
  Church in Wales
  Congregational Union of England and Wales
  Congregational Union of Scotland
  Episcopal Church in Scotland
  Methodist Church
  Methodist Church in Ireland
  Moravian Church in Great Britain and Ireland
  Presbyterian Church of England
  Presbyterian Church in Ireland
  Presbyterian Church of Wales
  Salvation Army
  United Free Church of Scotland

U.S.A.
  African Methodist Episcopal Church
  African Methodist Episcopal Zion Church
  American Baptist Convention
  American Evangelical Lutheran Church
  American Lutheran Church
  Augustana Evangelical Lutheran Church
  Christian Methodist Episcopal Church
  Church of the Brethren
  Congregational Christian Churches of the United States of America
  Evangelical and Reformed Church
  Evangelical United Brethren Church
  Holy Apostolic Catholic Church of the East (Assyrians)
  International Convention of Disciples of Christ
  Methodist Church
  Moravian Church in America (Northern Province)
  Moravian Church in America (Southern Province)
  National Baptist Convention, U.S.A., Inc.
  Polish National Catholic Church of America
  Presbyterian Church in the United States
  Presbyterian Church in the United States of America
  Protestant Episcopal Church
  Reformed Church in America
  The Religious Society of Friends:
    Five Years Meeting of Friends
    General Conference of the Religious Society of Friends
    Religious Society of Friends of Philadelphia and Vicinity
  Romanian Orthodox Episcopate of America
  Russian Orthodox Greek Catholic Church of North America
  Seventh Day Baptist General Conference
  Syrian Antiochian Orthodox Church (Archdiocese of New York and all North America)
  United Evangelical Lutheran Church
  United Lutheran Church in America
  United Presbyterian Church of North America

WEST AFRICA
Church of the Province of West Africa

WEST INDIES
Anglican Church of the West Indies

YUGOSLAVIA
Reformed Christian Church of Yugoslavia

OTHER CHURCHES
Eesti Ev. Lut. Usu Kiriku (Esthonian Evangelical Lutheran Church)
Lietuvos Ev. Reformatu Baznycia (Lithuanian Reformed Church)

Appendices

1. DRAFT STATEMENT ON THE
PURPOSE AND FUNCTION OF THE BASIS[1]

The World Council of Churches is an instrument at the service of the churches which enables them to enter into fraternal conversation with each other, to co-operate in various fields, and to render witness together to the world. It is not a new church (even less a super-church) and does not perform ecclesiastical functions.

Since the Council desires to make clear to the churches and to the world what it is, what it does, and who are its members, it has adopted a *basis*. The first article of its Constitution formulates this Basis in the following words: "The World Council of Churches is a fellowship of churches which accept Jesus Christ as God and Saviour." This Basis performs three functions:

(1) It indicates the *nature* of the fellowship which the churches in the Council seek to establish among themselves. For that fellowship, as a fellowship of churches, has its own unique character. It has a specific source and a specific dynamic. The churches enter into relation with each other, because there is a unity given once for all in the person and work of their common Lord and because the Living Lord gathers His people together.

(2) It provides the *orientation point* for the work which the World Council itself undertakes. The ecumenical conversations which take place in the World Council must have a point of reference. Similarly the activities of the Council must be submitted to an ultimate norm and standard. The Basis provides that standard.

(3) It indicates the *range* of the fellowship which the churches in the Council seek to establish.

The acceptance of the Basis is the fundamental criterion which must be met by a church which desires to join the Council. The limits of each society are dependent upon its nature. By joining together the churches seek to respond to the call and action of their Divine Lord. The World Council must therefore consist of churches which acknowledge that Lord as the second person of the Trinity.

While the Basis is therefore less than a confession, it is much more than a mere formula of agreement. It is truly a basis in that the life and activity of the World Council are based upon it. And the World Council must constantly ask itself whether it is faithful to its Basis.

Each church which joins the World Council must therefore seriously con-

[1] As adopted by the Assembly on the recommendation of the Committee on General Policy (1)

sider whether it desires to participate in a fellowship with this particular Basis. On the other hand the World Council would overstep the limits it has set for itself if it should seek to pronounce judgment as to whether any particular church is in fact taking the Basis seriously. It remains the responsibility of each church to decide itself whether it can sincerely accept the Basis of the Council.

2. RECOMMENDATIONS CONCERNING THE DIVISION OF STUDIES

INTRODUCTORY

The Evanston Assembly will open up new and larger opportunities for the development of ecumenical and missionary thinking. A chief factor in this situation is the proposal to set up a Division of Studies, which will also serve the International Missionary Council and include four departments: Faith and Order, Evangelism, Church and Society and Missionary Studies. This last Department will be sponsored by the International Missionary Council.

This proposal marks a new departure in two ways. It takes account of the increasing convergence in thought and outlook of the ecumenical and missionary movements, thus facilitating closer co-operation between older and younger churches. It provides a framework which will make for greater flexibility in the shaping of study programmes and will enable the departments—if so desired—to join forces in a concerted approach to given problems.

The aim of the Division has been defined as follows: "to serve the churches by promoting ecumenical studies on the fundamental issues of their faith and life, so that they may increasingly think together, advance in unity, render common witness, and take common action in the social and international field."

The programme of the Division for the coming years must obviously be determined in the light of the deliberations of the Evanston Assembly and the meeting of the Executive Committee of the International Missionary Council. The Department on Faith and Order has already had its major projects fixed by the Faith and Order working committee in August, 1953. Broadly speaking, the programme will include two distinct though closely connected stages: (a) the follow-up of Evanston by promotion of study of the Assembly reports in the churches; (b) the development of new long-range projects. The latter task in particular will require a period of careful exploration and planning by the Division, working in close association with the Ecumenical Institute and the other departments in the Division of Ecumenical Action.

The Assembly Committee dealing with the Division of Studies may therefore wish to formulate its recommendations to the Assembly in broad terms, authorizing the Central Committee and the Committee on the

Division of Studies to shape a detailed programme which will take full account of the varied interests of the Council and its member churches.

The proposals listed below are thus merely to be regarded as a basis for discussion, illustrating possible priorities. They are the outcome of a considerable volume of consultation with advisers and correspondents in many countries. For the sake of brevity, the proposals are simply listed without developing the arguments favouring their selection. It will be profitable to consider them against the background of the ecumenical surveys prepared for the six sections at the Assembly, and their analysis of the tasks confronting the churches at the present time.

The following questions should be kept in mind in examining these proposals:

What should be the objectives of ecumenical study?

How should priorities be chosen?

What methods have proved most fruitful in the past? What new methods may be envisaged?

What can be done to make ecumenical study more truly an enterprise undertaken *by* the churches for the churches?

Should each department promote its own programme? Or should the Division as a whole centre its programme around one or more themes, exploring them from the different angles of the several departments?

How should the study projects of the departments within the Division of Ecumenical Action be integrated with the programme of the Division of Studies?

PROJECTS

1. *General Projects of the Division*

The executive staff of the Division will carry a broad range of responsibilities. These will include stimulation of ecumenical thought among the churches, planning and co-ordination of the Division's own activities, and maintenance of relationships with other divisions and departments. It is moreover essential that the Division should have sufficient staff resources to enable it to carry out important projects, which do not fall within the confines of its specialized departments. The following have been recommended:

I. *An ecumenical approach to the interpretation of the Bible*

A good deal of work has already been done on this subject, which is so fundamental for all ecumenical studies. So far the main focus has been the interpretation of the biblical teaching on social questions. These studies could be continued in a wider context and with particular reference to evangelism and the presentation of the gospel to modern man.

II. *The training of the ministry*

A long-range enquiry to be conducted in conjunction with the enquiry undertaken by the International Missionary Council in selected younger church areas. An important aspect of such a study would be the further-ance of ecumenical outlook in theological education. Initial step: an exploratory conference of theological educators to advise the Division on issues and methods for this enquiry.

III. *Editing of a series of ecumenical and missionary surveys*

2. Department on Faith and Order

The primary task of the Commission on Faith and Order is to carry on basic studies of questions pertaining to Christian unity. Following the Third World Conference on Faith and Order at Lund, 1952, plans for the study of the following questions during the coming years have already been formulated, and partially implemented, by the working committee of the Faith and Order Commission:

I. *The Church as understood in the light of the doctrines of Jesus Christ and the Holy Spirit*
II. *The ways and meaning of Christian worship*
III. *Christian tradition and the various church traditions*
IV. *"Proselytism" as a problem within the World Council of Churches*
V. *Social and cultural factors affecting church unity*

With these studies already under way, the Commission on Faith and Order seeks counsel, not on what shall be studied, but on how its work is to be related directly to the churches in their common concern to express their unity in Christ.

The following questions need to be discussed:
I. How can the reports prepared by study commissions of the Faith and Order Commission be given wider circulation among the churches, and how can churches make effective responses to such reports?
II. How can the numerous centres of experiment and study on matters of unity be connected by channels of communication which pass through the Faith and Order Commission and its secretariat?
III. What specific problems of inter-church relations may be illuminated by a study of "proselytism"?
IV. How may occasions be promoted, where permitted, for the common worship of Christians from various confessions and denominations? Is this a proper responsibility of the Faith and Order Commission? (see *Lund Report*, p. 35).
V. How may the social and cultural factors affecting church unity be brought to light, examined, and dealt with by the Faith and Order Commission as well as by divided churches?

3. Department on Evangelism

To what extent would it be desirable and feasible to shape joint projects with the Department on Missionary Studies?

It is suggested that the Department—in addition to its assistance to the churches in planning their evangelistic activities—should concentrate on two types of study: surveys of evangelism in different situations or areas, and a thorough enquiry on one or two problems of particular importance in the field. Here the question needs to be faced whether the conditions and problems confronting the churches in different parts of the world are not in fact so different that the Department should promote enquiries on a regional basis (e.g. the emphasis on industrial evangelism in certain countries, and on rural evangelism in others).

I. *Descriptive and evaluative surveys*

(*a*) Continuation of the present series of national or regional surveys. Projects under way or envisaged: South America, the United States, Scandinavia, Germany, Ceylon, Burma, a Muslim country.

(*b*) Problem surveys on:

(i) The use of the Bible in evangelism (in collaboration with the United Bible Societies).

(ii) The evangelistic emphasis and practice of the "sects" (in collaboration with the International Missionary Council and the United Bible Societies).

(iii) The needs and problems in rural evangelism.

II. *The mission of the Church to workers*

Combining study and pioneering experimentation, the project would include:

(*a*) A series of case studies on:

(i) Approaches actually used in evangelism among workers;

(ii) The religious assumptions and convictions of workers, and their attitude to Christianity;

(*b*) An information bulletin carrying regular reporting of experiments, projects and studies in this field, which would give a sense of fellowship in common endeavour.

III. *The Christian approach to the Jews*

It has further been suggested that the World Council—through the Department of Evangelism—should associate itself more closely with the projects of the International Committee on the Christian Approach to the Jews. If so, in what way?

4. *Department on Church and Society*

The primary task of the Department on Church and Society is to carry on basic studies of "the crucial problems of society about which the churches should declare their common mind and take action."

In the first place it is proposed that the Department sponsor a number of regional study conferences and consultations as soon as possible after Evanston. The purpose of these meetings would be to discuss the Assembly

report on social questions in relation to concrete situations, and to determine the particular projects for further study. It is suggested that there be:

(*a*) Three regional consultations, one in South America, one in Africa,
and one in East Asia. These three meetings would take as their general
theme: "The Christian Responsibility for the Social Problems in the
Regions Concerned," discussing this in the light of the Evanston report.
(The first two especially would be in the nature of consultations seeking
to concentrate on fact-finding and on crystallizing the issues which need
to be considered in the churches).

(*b*) Two study conferences dealing with the issues in the Evanston
report which specifically concern Western countries. One of these meetings would be held in Europe and the other in North America (unless it is
felt that more would be gained by a joint meeting of Europeans and
Americans).

Specific Issues

In the studies carried on since Amsterdam certain issues have emerged
which will undoubtedly receive major attention at the Assembly, and are
likely to become the subject of these post-Evanston meetings and the basis
of the programme of the Department. These are as follows:

I. *The Christian Responsibility for the Social Development of the Under-Developed
Countries,* including:

(*a*) Appraisal of the moral problems involved in changing economic
and political conditions in the under-developed countries.

(*b*) The problem of creating a social ethos conducive to responsible
social living.

(*c*) The encounter between Christian and non-Christian social ethics.

II. *The Christian Responsibility for the Political and Economic Problems of
Western Countries,* including:

(*a*) Christian thinking about political ethics in relation to the growth
of the social planning state. (Special problems in Europe due to the
development of supra-national economic and political integration).

(*b*) Relation between domestic social policies and international
economic and political responsibilities (e.g. the contribution of Western
"privileged" countries in supporting efforts to achieve a responsible
society in under-developed countries).

(*c*) The appeal of communism to workers, intellectuals and youth, in
some countries of the West.

III. *Church and Society in Communist Lands*

Survey of the moral and spiritual problems faced by people living in
communist societies.

Whether or not these or other issues are selected for emphasis, the
regional meetings proposed above will be the chief means for carrying
forward study in the year following Evanston. The preparation of reports

and studies on such topics is envisaged in preparation for, or as an outcome of, the various conferences and consultations. For the topic "The Christian Witness in Communist Countries," it is proposed that the Department continue to issue reports similar to those issued by the present Study Department on the subject.

Publications

The Department on Church and Society is also expected "to disseminate the results of these studies," "to keep the churches informed about important developments in society," and "to acquaint the churches with action taken by other churches in this field." For this purpose it is proposed to publish occasional study documents on the projects outlined above, and a quarterly information bulletin on *Church and Society*.

Additional Projects

The following projects have been proposed as important study topics, if the help of additional staff should be offered by interested churches :

I. *The Church as a Social Institution in a Changing Society*—a sociological study of the ways in which the life of the Church is shaped by the prevailing social, economic and political structures of the particular societies in which it lives, and the problems this raises for Christians in a period of great social change.

II. *Racial and Ethnic Tensions*—in pursuit of the issues raised by the Evanston section on this topic.

III. *Basis of an International Ethos*—jointly with the Commission of the Churches on International Affairs, the staff member in charge to be related to the C.C.I.A. and to the Division of Studies.

IV. *Human Relations in Industrial Life*—the Christian witness in relation to industrial tension and in particular to the labour movement.

V. *Sex and Family Life*—an exploratory survey of the thought and activities of the churches in this field, possibly leading to a more permanent enquiry. Undertaken jointly with the Department on Work for the Laity and the Department on Co-operation between Men and Women in Church and Society.

VI. *The Christian Understanding of Work* (jointly with the Department on Laity).

5. *Department of Missionary Studies*[1]

I. *Life and Growth of the Younger Churches*

A long-term enquiry focussed on the understanding of their task by younger churches, as missionary churches which represent the Universal Church in a local setting. (With field studies, promotion of discussion, and experimentation).

[1] These plans of the present Research Secretariat of the International Missionary Council were in the first place considered by the Executive Committee of the I.M.C. in July, 1954.

(*a*) New ways of worship (jointly with the Department on Faith and Order).

(*b*) Presenting the gospel to adherents of other faiths (continuing the discussions of the I.M.C. Conferences at Tambaram, 1938, and at Willingen in 1952; jointly with the Department of Evangelism).

(*c*) The inter-action of the Church, and its cultural and religious environment in non-Christian societies; the need for new patterns of church life (jointly with the Department on Church and Society).

(*d*) Re-shaping missionary strategies.

II. *Reform of the Training of the Ministry*
Continuation of the current fact-finding and interpretative surveys undertaken in selected younger church areas.

III. *Christian Missions in China—an attempt at an appraisal*
Preparation of a volume incorporating relevant material, and the circulation of papers.

IV. *A Projected Series of Missionary Research Pamphlets*
 —Towards a Theology of Missions
 —Missionary Vocation
 —African Marriage and Family Life
 —The Bible in the Life of the Younger Churches (by the United Bible
   Societies)
 —Healing in the Church's Mission—a discussion of principles and
   problems of modern medical missions
 —The Responsibility of Churches and Missions in the Field of Education,
   particularly with regard to Africa
 —Urban Evangelism in Africa

3. RECOMMENDATIONS TO THE COMMITTEE ON THE DIVISION OF STUDIES OF A SUB-COMMITTEE OF THE STUDY DEPARTMENT COMMITTEE

A meeting of the above sub-committee was held at 7 p.m. on August 17th in the First Methodist Church, Evanston. There were present: Dr. John Baillie (in the chair), Dr. Devanandan, Dr. Menn, Dr. Van Dusen, Dr. F. W. Tomkins, Dr. H. H. Harms, Dr. Ehrenström and Canon Alan Richardson (secretary).
The following resolutions were agreed:—

I. PROMOTION OF EVANSTON FOLLOW-UP BY THE DIFFERENT MEMBER CHURCHES
That the Steering Committee be asked to make provision for a half-hour period at one of the plenary sessions of the Assembly for the consideration

of the follow-up of Evanston. Member churches should then be urged to incorporate the findings of the Assembly in their life and thought, and specific ways in which this can be done should be suggested. (Good examples to which reference might be made would be the post-Amsterdam campaign of the Methodist Church in the U.S.A. during the first six months of 1949, and the post-Amsterdam follow-up of the Church of Scotland.) The Assembly should request the member churches "to report in due course the results of their study and action to the Central Committee."

It was agreed that the General Secretary of the W.C.C. should be asked to send a special letter to the churches, enclosing copies of the available Assembly publications, notifying them of the above request, and suggesting specific ways in which they might introduce the concerns, utterances, and actions of the Assembly in their regular programmes.

A similar half-hour should likewise be set aside for this purpose in the accredited visitors' programme.

II. PUBLICATIONS

A. Under W.C.C. Sponsorship

1. *A cheaply produced booklet* containing the Assembly's pronouncements upon the Main Theme, the Assembly Message, the Section Reports, and relevant resolutions : to be printed as quickly as possible.

2. *A series of six booklets* (with index of subjects), each containing the Survey (with possibly a supplement to it) and the Section Report, with an explanatory commentary describing the course of the discussion, bringing out the principal issues, and ending with questions for study. The various parts of this study guide should be edited in each case by the secretary or some other competent person in the Section. The series should be published in English in October. The form of publication of the French and German editions will require further discussion with the appropriate ecumenical agencies in those areas. It was noted that the Study Department Committee and the Sections' Co-ordinating Group have strongly urged such a reprinting of the Surveys with their corresponding Section Reports.

3. *The October number of The Ecumenical Review.* This will contain a series of general appraisals of the Assembly together with interpretative articles on the discussions of the Main Theme groups and of the six Sections.

B. Under National Sponsorship

1. Popular interpretations of the Assembly for use with the wider public. Since conditions vary so much from country to country, this very important task must be left to the different national ecumenical councils, etc.

2. *Booklets in various languages* (other than English, German, and French), containing the Main Theme document, the Section Reports, and the explanatory comments (as suggested above under A. 2). In order to expedite the production of such national editions, the Division of

Studies should send the Study Guide (i.e. the explanatory commentary on the reports plus the study-questions) in typescript to the national ecumenical agencies as a model to be adapted to the different national situations.

III. THE INITIATION OF A NEW PHASE OF ECUMENICAL STUDY

That the follow-up work thus described should not be regarded as an isolated enterprise, related to a past event, but rather as aiming at a more vigorous participation by the churches in the new W.C.C. programmes of ecumenical study and action.

IV. W.C.C. DEPARTMENTS AND STAFF

That all W.C.C. departments and commissions be instructed to emphasize the utterances and actions of the Assembly in all their work during the coming winter, and that the staff be instructed to give considerable time during the next few months to the stimulation of national follow-up programmes through personal visits and contacts. The Division of Studies should circularize national ecumenical study agencies, theological schools and inter-seminary movements, organizations of laymen's work, women's work and youth work, denominational and interdenominational bodies, etc.

V. REGIONAL CONFERENCES

That the staff of the Division of Studies be authorized to arrange a series of regional conferences in various parts of the world, similar in character to the pre-Evanston Asian conference at Lucknow; and that it be recommended to the Finance Committee that the provision of $20,000 in the budget for the year after Evanston, allocated for the Third Assembly, be allocated for the follow-up work of the Second Assembly.

4. STATEMENT ON FINANCE

The main concern of the Finance Committee will be the budgets of the World Council and the financial aspects of the programme. The Department of Finance and Administration is a service department and its activities result in the main from the programmes of the other divisions and departments. The Finance Committee will doubtless wish to review the results of the initial years and to include in its report to the Assembly some comment on those results; a report on the operations since the Amsterdam Assembly and on the activities of the Department of Finance and Administration is given in *The First Six Years*. The Finance Committee will certainly need to lay down general principles and plans for the financing of the work in the next period; a suggested annual general budget for the post-Evanston period is submitted at the end of this report, see pages 320 and 321.

The following is an annotated draft agenda for the main items to be considered by the Finance Committee:

I. GENERAL BUDGET

   (a) *Expenditure*

   (i) 1948–1953—consideration of report in *The First Six Years.*

   (ii) Post-Evanston—examination of the suggested budget, department by department, in the light of experience and of the proposed new structure and organization. There will also be need for constant liaison between the Finance Committee and the other Working Committees at the Assembly, since the other committees may wish to make recommendations which would have an effect on the budget.

   (b) *Revenue*

   (i) 1948–1953—consideration of report in *The First Six Years.*

   (ii) Post-Evanston—consideration of the contributions which should be requested from member churches in the period after the Second Assembly.

   (c) *Reserves*

   (i) General Reserve—consideration of present level, desirable level, and future allocations from annual budgets.

   (ii) Reserve for Second Assembly—consideration of provisional estimates of receipts and expenses for the Evanston Assembly.

   (iii) Reserve for Third Assembly—consideration of proposed annual provision.

   (iv) Ecumenical Institute—consideration of present level and desirable level.

   (v) Other Reserves.

   (d) *Investment Policy*

   (e) *Properties*

II. DEPARTMENT OF INTER-CHURCH AID AND SERVICE TO REFUGEES— SERVICE PROGRAMME

   (a) 1948–1953—consideration of report on financial aspects in *The First Six Years.*

   (b) Post-Evanston—consideration of financial problems and responsibilities involved. (Note: This budget will be controlled by the Executive Committee and by the Committee of the Division of Inter-Church Aid and Service to Refugees.)

   (c) Reserve position.

III. COMMISSION OF THE CHURCHES ON INTERNATIONAL AFFAIRS.

The C.C.I.A. is, of course, a separate entity created by the I.M.C. and the W.C.C. and financed by contributions from both organizations. Its accounts and budget should, however, be examined by the Committee.

   (a) 1948–1953—consideration of financial report which will be circulated at Evanston.

   (b) Post-Evanston—consideration of suggested budget, which will be circulated at Evanston, and of World Council financial contribution and responsibility.

IV. BUDGET OF U.S. CONFERENCE FOR THE W.C.C.

This body, which was originally called "World Council of Churches: Conference of U.S.A. Member Churches," was created after the Amsterdam Assembly to meet the special needs of the situation in the U.S.A. (See the section on the New York Office in *The First Six Years*.) It has its own budget but the Central Committee fixes a maximum upper limit to that budget; the limit was fixed at $50,000 for 1949 but was increased in subsequent years and the maximum fixed for 1954 is $70,000.

Suggested Annual General Budget after the Evanston Assembly

The tables (on pages 320 and 321) set out a suggested annual general budget for the World Council of Churches for a full year in the post-Evanston period in which the full programme proposed to the Assembly is in operation. The suggested budget is based upon past experience of actual expenses and upon proposals which are to be submitted separately by the Central Committee to the Assembly concerning the organization and structure of the World Council of Churches in the period following the Evanston Assembly.

The suggested budget is not a precise budget for operations in 1955 but a budget of revenue and expenditure in a year in which the proposed new structure and organization becomes fully operative. Furthermore, the provision made for certain expenses is based on average levels rather than on precise estimates calculated from the salaries of individuals at present occupying positions or the 1955 programmes of particular divisions or departments. Thus the same amount is provided for salaries in respect of each of the departments which have only one Executive Secretary, whereas in practice the cost of salaries for each department will vary according to such factors as whether the Executive Secretary is a married person with children or a single person. Similarly, provision for travel expenses and for the cost of meetings and conferences has been made at standard levels for each department whereas in particular years, individual departments may have expenses for these items greater or less than the average of all departments. Experience in the first five years, however, has shown that in considerable degree the variations compensate one another and the suggested budget submitted to the Assembly can be considered as representing a fair presentation of the expected expenditure under the proposed new structure and organization.

Under the Rules of the World Council of Churches, as adopted by the Amsterdam Assembly, it is provided that the Central Committee shall vote the annual budget of the Council. It will, therefore, be necessary for the Central Committee at its meeting immediately following the Assembly to give approval for a 1955 budget based upon the general financial decisions taken by the Assembly. A second reason for which it will be necessary to submit to the Central Committee at its meeting immediately after the Assembly a budget for 1955 which will differ from that which is set out in the tables on pages 320 and 321 is that it is unlikely that it will be possible to put into effect for the whole of 1955 the full programme recommended to the Assembly. The suggested budget should, therefore, rather be regarded as a forecast of the revenue and expenditure which would be required if and when the revised structure and organization suggested to the Assembly were put fully into effect.

The suggested budget totals $421,000 which represents an increase of $58,000 as compared with the budget for 1949 adopted by the Amsterdam Assembly and totalling $363,000, and an increase of $66,000 by comparison with the budgets approved by the Central Committee for the years 1953 and 1954.

The increase of $66,000 arises from changes of two different types:

(a) an increase of $18,000 arises from the inclusion in the General Budget of provision for the salary and travel expenses of the Associate General Secretary for the Division of Inter-Church Aid and Service to Refugees and also of the expense of the Secretary for Publicity for inter-church aid and refugee work, who under the new proposals will be a member of the staff of the new Department of Information. In addition to including the expenses within the General Budget, provision has been made on the revenue side of the budget for a corresponding transfer of income from the Service Programme budget of the Division of Inter-Church Aid and Service to Refugees. This increase of $18,000 thus neither represents an increase in total expenditure nor gives rise to any need for increased revenue from member church contributions to the General Budget.

(b) the remainder of the increase in the expenditure budget amounting to about $48,000 does necessitate increased revenue from member churches and is made up of an increase of about $18,000 in the grant to the C.C.I.A., an increase in expenditure amounting to about $15,000 arising from the creation of a Department of Information (the comparative figures in the budget tables indicate an increase of about $25,000 in expenses but about $10,000 is merely a transfer of expenses from the Service Programme budget as mentioned in the preceding paragraph) and provision in the General Budget for the expenses of the Department on Work for the Laity amounting to $9,700—expenses which for the last few years have been carried by the Service Programme budget of the Department of Inter-Church Aid and Service to Refugees. The slight further increase is primarily due to provision for completing the team of Associate General Secretaries.

On the revenue side, the budget calls for a contribution of $21,000 from the Service Programme budget of the Division of Inter-Church Aid and Service to Refugees, to cover the $18,000 mentioned above and a contribution of $3,000 for work done by the Youth Department for inter-church aid activities, and for revenue of $400,000 from contributions from churches associated in the Council and from private gifts for the General Budget.   This figure represents an increase of $80,000 or 25 per cent by comparison with the revenue budget of $320,000 for revenue from this source for the General Budget in 1954. This increased revenue is necessary to cover the increase of expenses mentioned in the previous paragraph and, secondly, to replace the amount of $35,000 withdrawn in 1954 from the General Reserve for the Ecumenical Institute to cover part of the expenses of the Institute in 1954. It will be recalled that at the Amsterdam Assembly,

it was decided that in 1949 $60,000 should be withdrawn from the reserve
for the Institute towards the annual expenses of that department and that in
each succesive year the amount withdrawn from the reserve for the Institute
should be reduced by $5,000. The budget for the Ecumenical Institute
adopted by the Amsterdam Assembly amounted to $65,000 so that an
amount of $5,000 was to be contributed in 1949 from general revenue for
the General Budget towards the annual expenses of the Institute and the
amount so contributed was to be increased by $5,000 in each year. In
practice, it was found that the Ecumenical Institute could be operated on a
budget of not $65,000 but $60,000, and the budget was accordingly
reduced. At the end of 1954, there will remain a balance of about $50,000
in the General Reserve for the Institute and it is recommended that that
reserve should not be drawn upon for the annual budgets in the period
between the second and third Assemblies, but that the full expense of the
Ecumenical Institute should be borne out of the annual revenue for the
General Budget.

The probable level of budgets in the period following the Evanston
Assembly was discussed by the Central Committee at its meeting at Lucknow in December 1952/January 1953, and by the Executive Committee at
its meeting in August 1953. It became clear in the course of those
discussions that increased revenue would be needed if the proposals
concerning the structure and functioning of the World Council in the
period following the Evanston Assembly were to be adopted. The Executive Committee, therefore, decided to call to the attention of member
churches that there might be need for an increase of approximately 25 per
cent in the total giving of member churches and to ask that consideration
should be given by the appropriate officers or committees of each church to
this provisional indication of needs.

Suggested Annual General Budget (Expenses) for Consideration by Evanston Assembly Compared with 1954 General Budget[1]

Swiss Francs

	1954 Budget	Suggested Budget	Suggested Staff
General Secretariat:			
Geneva	217,080	224,660	Gen. Sec., 1 Sec.
New York	196,880	196,880	Exec. Sec., 1 or 2 Secs.
Far East	12,840	12,840	1 Sec.
London	10,660	—	—
(sub-total)	*(437,460)*	*(434,380)*	
Division of Studies:			
Divisional Staff .	150,500	{ 88,000	A.G.S., 1 Sec.
Church and Society .		{ 41,500	1 Sec.
Faith and Order, Eur. Exp.	63,500	60,500	1 Sec.
Faith and Order, U.S.A. Exp.	27,820	—	—
Evangelism . . .	30,000	41,500	1 Sec.
(sub-total)	*(271,820)*	*(231,500)*	
Division of Ecumenical Action:			
Divisional Staff . .	—	54,500	A.G.S.
Ecumenical Institute .	256,800	256,800	{ Director, Asst. Dir. } 2 Prof.
Youth Geneva . .	90,660	81,500	2 Secs.
„ New York .	47,080	59,920	—
Laity	—	41,500	1 Sec.
Co-operation of Men and Women . . .	37,000	41,500	1 Sec.
(sub-total)	*(431,540)*	*(535,720)*	
Division of Inter-Church Aid:			
Divisional Staff . .	—	37,240	A.G.S.
Contribution to C.C.I.A. .	137,090	214,000	A.G.S.
Library	16,250	18,000	
Finance & Administration	—	—	Director, 3 Secs.
Department of Information	41,200	147,000	Director, 3 Secs.
Grant to E.P.S. . . .	12,840	12,840	
General Reserve . .	21,400	85,600	
Reserve for Third Assembly	149,800	85,600	
	1,519,400	1,801,880	

[1] The model budget approved by the Assembly for the post-Evanston period is the above budget, modified as indicated on p. 250 of this report to a total of frs.1,887,480.

SUGGESTED ANNUAL GENERAL BUDGET (EXPENSES)
FOR CONSIDERATION BY EVANSTON ASSEMBLY
COMPARED WITH 1954 GENERAL BUDGET[1]

Dollars

	1954 Budget	Suggested Budget	Suggested Staff
General Secretariat:			
Geneva	50,720	52,490	Gen. Sec., 1 Sec.
New York . . .	46,000	46,000	Exec. Sec., 1 or 2 Secs.
Far East	3,000	3,000	1 Sec.
London	2,490	—	—
(sub-total)	*(102,210)*	*(101,490)*	
Division of Studies			
Divisional Staff . .	35,160	20,560	A.G.S., 1 Sec.
Church and Society .		9,700	1 Sec.
Faith and Order, Eur. Exp.	14,830	14,130	1 Sec.
Faith and Order, U.S.A. Exp.	6,500	—	—
Evangelism . . .	7,010	9,700	1 Sec.
(sub-total)	*(63,500)*	*(54,090)*	
Division of Ecumenical Action:			
Divisional Staff . .	—	12,730	A.G.S.
Ecumenical Institute .	60,000	60,000	{ Director, Asst. Dir. 2 Prof. }
Youth Geneva . . .	21,180	19,040	2 Secs.
,, New York .	11,000	14,000	—
Laity	—	9,700	1 Sec.
Co-operation of Men and Women . . .	8,650	9,700	1 Sec.
(sub-total)	*(100,830)*	*(125,170)*	
Division of Inter-Church Aid:			
Divisional Staff . .	—	8,700	A.G.S.
Contribution to C.C.I.A. .	32,030	50,000	A.G.S.
Library	3,800	4,210	
Finance & Administration	—	—	Director, 3 Secs.
Department of Information	9,630	34,340	Director, 3 Secs.
Grant to E.P.S. . . .	3,000	3,000	
General Reserve . .	5,000	20,000	
Reserve for Third Assembly . . .	35,000	20,000	
	355,000	421,000	

[1] The model budget approved by the Assembly for the post-Evanston period is the above budget modified as indicated on p. 250 of this report to a total of $441,000.

5. THE REPORT OF THE JOINT COMMITTEE OF THE INTERNATIONAL MISSIONARY COUNCIL AND THE WORLD COUNCIL OF CHURCHES

The Joint Committee at its last meeting in July 1952 "saw more clearly than ever before that the inseparable oneness of Mission and Unity, as the deep meaning of the Church's existence, is basic to all the issues the Church has to face in the ecumenical movement." The Committee, therefore, put certain key questions on this subject to the conferences at Willingen and Lund. Thus, in this and other ways, the original impetus of the document on "The Calling of the Church to Mission and Unity," issued by the Central Committee of the W.C.C. at Rolle in 1951, is passing into the thinking of a wider constituency.

Meanwhile another impetus had come from the East Asian Study Consultation which met in December 1952 at Lucknow. That meeting called for still more serious consideration of the relationships between the W.C.C. and the I.M.C. The Central Committee of the W.C.C., meeting immediately afterwards at Lucknow, referred this request to the Joint Committee. This was the direct origin of the meeting at Königstein, Germany.

The work of the Spirit, we believe, is found in the total ecumenical movement of which the W.C.C. and the I.M.C. are two organized manifestations. In reflecting on this, and in the light of recent developments in the relationship of the two bodies, the Joint Committee believes that their association is also a witness to the work of the same Spirit. This association has already been worked out practically in a number of instances with signal success. It has been found possible to arrange for many common tasks to be performed through joint action. The Commission of the Churches on International Affairs was established by both bodies and is dependent upon them, while at the same time enjoying considerable freedom in carrying out its functions. The East Asia Secretaryship is a significant expression of our association and an effective instrument of joint action. The responsibility for co-ordinating emergency inter-church aid and relief outside Europe has been entrusted by both bodies to the Department of Inter-Church Aid and Service to Refugees of the W.C.C. It has now been proposed that the Division of Studies of the W.C.C. should also be the Division of Studies of the I.M.C., and that it should include a Department of Missionary Studies of which the Executive Secretary would be the Research Secretary of the I.M.C. Measures are being taken to ensure closer ties in public relations and information.

While welcoming these developments "in association," and the deepening conviction in many quarters that the two bodies belong together in one calling and purpose, the Joint Committee realizes that it has not yet become clear whether this association should necessarily lead to a single organization or whether it can best be furthered by the joint action of two "autonomous but inter-dependent councils." The Committee is aware that within the constituencies of both bodies there are divergent views on this question. These divergencies indicate the necessity for deeper thought on the whole matter and for a willingness to be led to conclusions which cannot yet be defined.

At the same time the Committee has become increasingly conscious that there are great issues and intractable problems which vitally concern the evangelistic outreach and world mission of the Church, and which are not being adequately faced by either the I.M.C. or the W.C.C. Political regionalization, the destruction of familiar patterns of life, the vitality of non-Christian faiths are problems which call for attention. The Committee is clear that such matters should not be delegated immediately to an existing department of either body or to a special committee. They require in the first instance careful study to find out how the combined resources in thinking and action of both bodies may be most effectively applied to them. Further, within the world-wide Christian fellowship itself there are new movements which must urgently occupy the attention of both bodies, for example manifestations of Christian missionary zeal outside the life of the older denominations, and the new awareness among the denominations themselves, partly due to the influence of the ecumenical movement, of their own world-wide confessional groupings. These are matters which call for joint consideration.

The Joint Committee has increasingly become an effective instrument for dealing with matters of common concern. Consequently it has decided to ask the parent bodies to strengthen its membership, and to provide it with a secretariat, so that it can itself undertake this new phase of joint consideration of common problems.

Proposed Constitution of the Joint Committee

(1) The I.M.C. and the W.C.C. shall each officially appoint six representatives to the Joint Committee. In order to secure the best possible coverage of confessions and areas, the officers of both bodies shall consult with each other before nominations are submitted to their respective governing committees.

(2) The officers of the I.M.C. and the W.C.C., in consultation, shall appoint the chairman of the Joint Committee, who shall be an additional member.

(3) The officers of the I.M.C. and the W.C.C., in consultation, shall make recommendations to their respective bodies concerning the appointment of the secretariat of the Joint Committee and the methods of financing the appointment.

(4) The General Secretaries of the I.M.C. and the W.C.C., and such other members of staff as may be required, shall sit with the Joint Committee.

Proposed Functions of the Joint Committee and its Secretariat

The Joint Committee shall be an advisory committee to the I.M.C. and the W.C.C. It shall have no authority to act independently in its own name. Its functions shall be:

(1) To help the two bodies to keep prominently before their member

churches and constituent councils their common responsibility for the evangelistic outreach and world mission of the Church.

(2) To study major aspects of the common tasks confronting the two bodies, and to make specific recommendations concerning the policies to be followed by the two bodies.

(3) To keep under review the ways by which the two bodies are co-operating, and to suggest new ways.

(4) And, in so far as may arise from the above, to continue to study the organizational implications of their developing relationships. Examples are: (a) the study of ways and means whereby the member councils of the I.M.C. may be constructively related to the work of the W.C.C. and the national councils of churches in countries of the older churches related to the missionary movement; (b) the study of the advantages, disadvantages, and implications of a full integration of the I.M.C. and the W.C.C.

Proposed Plan for the Division of Studies

Consideration was given to the best way of relating the study work of the W.C.C. and the I.M.C. A plan was submitted which had been carefully studied by the staff of both bodies and after discussion and modification was passed for submission to the Executive Committee of the W.C.C. and the *Ad Interim* Committee of the I.M.C., as follows:

(a) The Division of Studies of the W.C.C. as outlined in the Report of the Committee on Structure and Functioning shall also be the Division of Studies of the I.M.C.

(b) In addition to the present provisions for Faith and Order, Church and Society, and Evangelism, there shall be a Department of Missionary Studies of which the Research Secretary of the I.M.C. shall be the Executive Secretary.

(c) The Central Committee of the W.C.C., in appointing the members of the working committees for Faith and Order, Church and Society, and Evangelism, shall consult with the I.M.C. The administrative committee of the I.M.C., in appointing the members of the working committee of the Department of Missionary Studies, shall consult with the W.C.C. The Central Committee of the W.C.C., in appointing the additional members of the divisional committee, shall consult the I.M.C.

(d) The Associate General Secretary of the W.C.C. responsible for the Division, and the Executive Secretaries for Faith and Order, Church and Society, and Evangelism, shall be appointed, and their salaries and expenses paid, by the W.C.C. The Executive Secretary of the Department of Missionary Studies shall be appointed, and his salary and expenses paid, by the I.M.C. The expenses of the working committee of the Department of Missionary Studies shall also be met by the I.M.C.

(e) The members of staff of the Division shall work under the leadership of the responsible Associate General Secretary, but the location of the Department of Missionary Studies shall be left for the I.M.C. to decide.

REPORT ON EAST ASIA, AFRICA, AND LATIN AMERICA

EAST ASIA

(1) The decisions of the Bangkok Conference which led to the appointment of a Joint Secretary of the W.C.C. and the I.M.C. for East Asia have been justified by the experience of the past three years. The Secretary has rendered effective pastoral service to the churches and Christian councils of the region and has established his position as the accepted interpreter and symbol of the two bodies which he represents.

(2) The work of the East Asia Secretary in the next phase should continue the pastoral emphasis but include the task of relating the various activities of the W.C.C. and I.M.C. to the life and work of the churches and councils in the region.

(3) Less continuous travel will be required than during the past three years. Such travel as is undertaken should normally be related to specific tasks or occasions.

(4) It is, therefore, desirable that an office of the East Asia Secretary be established in a suitable centre. In the present circumstances this might, for the time being, be located in India.

(5) The parent bodies should consult and decide regarding any budget adjustments which may be necessary.

(6) The Committee recommends the nomination of Dr. R. B. Manikam for appointment as Joint East Asia Secretary for a further period of three years from 1st January 1955.

AFRICA

(1) In reviewing the total situation in Africa (south of the Sahara) the Committee noted the following facts:

(a) The growth of a new African self-consciousness.

(b) The acuteness of the racial problem in many parts of Africa and the need for the Christian Church to play a constructive role in relation to it.

(c) The rapid increase in industrialization and the consequent disintegration of African patterns of life.

(d) The need for education in responsible Christian citizenship.

(e) The intensity of the encounter between an advancing Islam and a growing Christian community.

(f) The necessity for a deeper understanding of what an indigenous church should be.

(2) These facts point to the urgent need for a regional approach to Africa and closer co-operation between churches and between Christian councils in Africa.

(3) The Joint Committee recommends that the I.M.C. be asked to take the initiative (on behalf of both W.C.C. and I.M.C.) in assisting councils,

churches, and missionary societies to discover what further co-operative action, especially on a regional basis, may be taken to meet these needs.

(4) In the judgment of this Committee it is advisable that a special Africa Committee (or Commissions) be set up, administratively related to the I.M.C., but with adequate W.C.C. representation, and that this committee should report from time to time to the Joint Committee.

LATIN AMERICA

(1) Looking at the Christian task in the world, the Joint Committee is aware of the need in Latin America for increased regional co-operation, and for relating such co-operation to the world Christian fellowship.

(2) The Committee recognizes that this must be worked out in Latin America—possibly by a conference convened and held within the region. It is therefore recommended that Dr. John Mackay and the Reverend Rudolfo Anders, as Chairman and Vice-Chairman of the I.M.C., be asked to consult with Christian leaders in Latin America as to the best means of achieving a comprehensive consultation in Latin America on these matters, or alternative means for achieving the ends in view.

The Commission of the Churches on International Affairs

The Joint Committee received from Dr. Nolde a report on the recent activities of the C.C.I.A. It recommended strongly to the two bodies that this Commission should be continued on its present basis, which had proved so satisfactory. It noted the need for increased income to the C.C.I.A. in order to deal more realistically with the present obligations as regards staff; the need to strengthen the international character of the officers and staff; the inevitable limitation of the range of the Commission, even in the matter of denials of religious liberty; and the new possibilities of co-operation with the Division of Studies and the Department of Information in securing a wider participation on the part of the membership of the churches in the issues dealt with by the Commission.

The Christian Approach to the Jews

The Joint Committee noted:

(a) that this subject would appear on the agenda of the Section on Evangelism of the Evanston Assembly;

(b) that the symposium to be published on this subject was to be made available to the members of that Section;

(c) that the World Council is now represented by three members on the Committee on the Christian Approach to the Jews;

(d) but that it had not proved possible to give such full and concentrated attention to this subject as it deserves in view of its inherent importance;

and decided:

> that this subject should be fully discussed at one of the first meetings of the Joint Committee after the summer of 1954 and that the Committee on the Christian Approach to the Jews be asked to prepare for the Joint Committee the documentation required for this discussion.

6. STATEMENT ON THE HOPE OF ISRAEL

In view of the decision of the Assembly on Friday to omit any reference to the hope of Israel in its Statement on the Main Theme, we feel it our duty to offer an explanation of our convictions in the hope that it will help toward closer understanding with those from whom we differed.

Our concern in this issue is wholly biblical and is not to be confused with any political attitude toward the State of Israel.

We believe that Jesus Christ is the Saviour of all mankind. In Him there is neither Jew nor Greek, but we also believe that God elected Israel for the carrying out of His saving purpose. Jesus Christ as Man was a Jew. The Church of Jesus Christ is built upon the foundation of the Apostles and Prophets, all of whom were Jews, so that to be a member of the Christian Church is to be involved with the Jews in our one indivisible hope in Jesus Christ. Jesus, the Messiah of Israel, was accepted by Gentiles but rejected by His own people. Nevertheless God is so gracious and mighty that He even makes the crucifixion of His Son to be the salvation of the Gentiles (Rom. 11: 11). Whether we are scandalized or not, that means that we are grafted into the old tree of Israel (Rom. 11: 24), so that the people of the New Covenant cannot be separated from the people of the Old Covenant.

The New Testament, however, speaks also of the "fulness" of Israel, when God will manifest His glory by bringing back His "eldest son" into the one fold of His grace (Rom. 11: 12–36; Matt. 23: 29). This belief is an indispensable element of our one united hope for Jew and Gentile in Jesus Christ. Our hope in Christ's coming victory includes our hope for Israel in Christ, in His victory over the blindness of His own people. To expect Jesus Christ means to hope for the conversion of the Jewish people, and to love Him means to love the people of God's promise.

In view of the grievous guilt of Christian people towards the Jews throughout the history of the Church, we are certain that:

> the Church cannot rest until the title of Christ to the Kingdom is recognized by His own people according to the flesh.[1]

We cannot be one in Christ nor can we truly believe and witness to the promise of God if we do not recognize that it is still valid for the people of the promise made to Abraham. Therefore we invite all men to join with us

[1] Findings of the Pre-Evanston Conference of the American Committee on the Christian Approach to the Jews, at Lake Geneva, August 8th–11th, 1954.

in praising and magnifying that God who "concluded them all in unbelief that He might have mercy upon all" (Rom. 11 : 32).

Signed

H. Berkhof, *Holland*
M. Boegner, *France*
A. Koechlin, *Switzerland*
P. Maury, *France*
T. F. Torrance, *Scotland*
H. Vogel, *Germany*
J. Sittler, *U.S.A.*
O. S. Tomkins, *England*
J. Smemo, *Norway*
E. Schlink, *Germany*
H. L. Yochum, *U.S.A.*
N. A. Winter, *U.S.A.*

H. d'Espine, *Switzerland*
R. S. Louden, *Scotland*
H. F. Schuh, *U.S.A.*
A. E. Haefner, *U.S.A.*
J. Hromadka, *Czechoslovakia*
D. G. May, *Austria*
J. P. Van Heest, *Holland*
M. Niemöller, *Germany*
A. H. Ewald, *U.S.A.*
L. Pap, *Hungary*
S. B. Coles, *Canada*
G. Stratenwerth, *Germany*

7. STATEMENT BY DELEGATES FROM THE DUTCH REFORMED CHURCHES IN SOUTH AFRICA

On behalf of all the delegates from the Dutch Reformed Churches in South Africa we wish to state that we would have felt happier if the report of the Committee on Intergroup Relations and the proposed resolutions attached thereto had been put to the Assembly to be received and referred to member churches for their consideration and report to the Central Committee. We appreciate the argument that no resolution of this Assembly has mandatory power over member churches and that certain recommendations, and especially Resolution No. 1, are intended to stimulate the independent thought and action of certain churches in specific situations. But we feel constrained to say that, at this stage of our ecumenical discussions on these matters, it may have the opposite effect by so prejudicing the issues at stake for some churches that fruitful action for them will be gravely jeopardized. We would deplore it deeply if the impression were created that this report and these resolutions are intended as the last word in a matter that vitally affects the mission of some churches and which, we feel bound to say, has not been considered in all its aspects during our talks at Evanston.

However, we are not offering an amendment, nor do we intend to record our votes against what is being proposed. At this stage we dare not commit our churches either way but wish to keep the door open for further conversation. We wish to place on record that we have experienced at Evanston much evidence of what we truly believe to be real Christian goodwill and an attempt to understand the peculiar difficulties we have to face. In response to that we now pledge ourselves personally to the task of urging our respective churches to apply themselves as urgently as possible to the study of the report and to communicate their findings to the Central Committee as soon as possible.

Signed

W. A. Landman, *Ned. Geref. Kerk van Suid-Afrika*
C. B. Brink, *Ned. Herv. of Geref. Kerk van Suid-Afrika*
A. J. G. Oosthuizen, *Ned. Herv. Kerk van Afrika*

8. A STATEMENT OF THE EASTERN ORTHODOX DELEGATES CONCERNING THE MAIN THEME OF THE ASSEMBLY

Being entrusted with the responsibility of representing the Orthodox member churches at this Assembly of the World Council of Churches, we are in duty bound to present the following comments on the Report of the Advisory Commission on the Main Theme: "Christ, the Hope of the World."

(1) We are happy to express our general agreement with the Report of the Advisory Committee. Ever since Pentecost, the Orthodox Church has been proclaiming to the world that Christ is the Hope and especially in our own time she is persistently re-affirming that all human hopes must be interpreted and judged, condemned, or amended, in the light of this hope. That at this decisive moment of its life the World Council of Churches unanimously felt that Christians should proclaim this hope to the world, and should alert themselves of their responsibilities in a world full of distress and suffering, makes us rejoice exceedingly.

(2) But this general agreement makes it even more necessary to state clearly, on the one hand, what we regard as not fully acceptable from the standpoint of the Orthodox Church, and, on the other, what we consider as requiring further development in the Report, and formally to draw attention to certain points which are not touched upon in the Report at all. Obviously, in these few remarks we cannot give a full confession of the Orthodox conception of the Christian Church. It must be affirmed, to begin with, in stronger terms, that the Christian Hope is grounded on Christian Faith. It is grounded on the belief that God takes a personal interest in human life and human history. God so loved the world as to give His only begotten Son. The Christian Hope is grounded in the belief that Jesus Christ, Incarnate Lord, came down from Heaven to save men. He accomplished the work of salvation on the Tree of the Cross and He manifested the new life for humanity in His glorious resurrection. He established upon earth His Holy Church which is His Body in which by the power of the Holy Spirit He abides with man for ever. The Church of Christ is one loving Body of Christ in which all generations of believers are united in the new life in Christ.

It is misleading to describe the Church simply as "the pilgrim people of God" and to forget that the Church Triumphant and Church Militant are but One Body. It is precisely in this unity that the Christian Hope is grounded. The Church is the great Communion of Saints. We upon earth live and strive in communion with the glorious "cloud of witnesses" revealed through the ages and are strengthened by the intercessions of the Theotokos and the Saints within whom we join in adoration of Christ our Redeemer.

(3) The Report justly stresses the importance of the belief in the second coming of Christ for the Christian Hope. However, we strongly believe that it is necessary to place an adequate emphasis on the actual presence of the Kingdom of God in the Church. The Kingdom has been founded by God through the Incarnation of His Son, the Redemption, the Resurrection, the Ascension of Christ in glory and the descent of the Holy Spirit. It has been existing on earth since Pentecost and is open to all men, bestowing to all who enter the power transforming and renewing human existence now on earth. Life eternal is not only an object of future realization; it is given to those who were called by the Word of God in the Sacrament of Baptism (Rom. 6) and is continuously renewed through participation in the Holy Eucharist. Nothing has been left undone by God for our salvation and for the immediate transformation of human existence. Thus our participation in the renewed life of the Kingdom of God is a present reality as well as a future fulfilment.

(4) The hope in Christ is itself a gift of the Holy Spirit and no one can confess Him as Lord and Saviour except by the Holy Spirit. It would be in vain to preach Christ as the Hope of the World without mentioning divine action and acknowledging the reality of grace which is the sole source of this hope. The tragedy of the fallen world consists precisely in its inability to hope in Christ without the help of grace. Moreover, this hope is meaningful and fruitful only inasmuch as it leads man into the real life in Christ which pre-supposes the continuous action of the Holy Spirit within us.

(5) The paragraphs of the Report dealing with the unity of the Church raise serious doubts. This subject will be treated in full in the Section on Faith and Order, but it should be noted that some of the ideas expressed in the Report lead to interpretations which cannot be accepted from the standpoint of the Orthodox Church.

The power of God is operating in the midst of human weakness. We never can fulfil all the demands which Christ makes upon us and in humility and repentance we must acknowledge our limitations and shortcomings, applying steadfastly for an increase of our faith and strength. And yet it is in the Church that we find this strength. The reality of the New Life is never compromised or annulled by our failures. Thus, the Church of Christ, as the realized Kingdom of God lies beyond Judgment, whereas her members being liable to sin and error are subject to Judgment.

(6) In proclaiming that Christ is the Hope of the world, we must not lose sight of the reality that Christ is not separated from His Father and the Holy Spirit. Hope in Christ cannot be separated from the hope in God, the

Father, and God, the Holy Spirit. Of all the promises of Christ, the most precious is when He asserts that the Holy Trinity will abide in us (John 14: 23; 15: 26; 16: 13–16; 17: 21–26). Life eternal is but fellowship with the Divine Trinity.

(7) Hope in Christ must be interpreted in its true content. We place our hope in the Incarnate Son of God, in Whom we also have become sons of God, the Father, and co-heirs with Christ. This sonship constitutes the foundation, the content, and the aim of our Christian Hope. Adoption by the Father renders man a "new creation." In Christ the Fatherhood of God has been revealed to us and communion with Him has been given. Through Jesus Christ, the Son of God, the Father bestows upon us the knowledge of truth, divine love, sanctification, eternal life, and ultimately participation in the divine nature (theosis).

(8) Hope in Christ means hope in the Blessed Trinity. The Orthodox Church gives clear expression to this truth in one of her prayers: "My Hope is the Father; my Refuge is the Son; my Shelter is the Holy Spirit; Holy Trinity, glory to Thee."

(9) Finally, we do not believe that the analysis of false hopes given in the Report is adequate and complete. False doctrines, which are mentioned in the Report, especially that of communism, threaten the whole of human existence, threaten human personality as such. All of these de-humanize life. It is this aspect of false hopes with which the Church is primarily concerned. The danger for man which these false doctrines present appears to be sorely underestimated in the Report. If we seek at the present time in our troubled and distorted world, a true basis for human hope, we must profess emphatically that it is only in the Church of God, Holy, Catholic, and Apostolic, that this basis can be found, since the Church is the "pillar and ground of Truth."

9. THE OFFICERS AND STAFF PERSONNEL OF THE ASSEMBLY

Presiding Officers

The Presidents of the World Council:
Bishop Eivind Berggrav
Dr. Marc Boegner
The Archbishop of Canterbury
Bishop G. Bromley Oxnam
The Archbishop of Thyateira

The Chairman of the Central Committee:
The Bishop of Chichester

The Vice-Chairman of the Central Committee:
Dr. Franklin Clark Fry

The Chairman of the Commission on Faith and Order:
Archbishop Yngve Brilioth

The Chairman of the Study Department Commission:
Dr. Henry P. Van Dusen
Bishop C. K. Jacob

The General Secretary

Dr. W. A. Visser 't Hooft

The Steering Committee

Chairmen:	The Bishop of Chichester
	Dr. Franklin Clark Fry
Secretary:	Dr. Robert S. Bilheimer
Members:	The Bishop of Armidale
	Bishop Eivind Berggrav
	Dr. Marc Boegner
	Archbishop Yngve Brilioth
	The Archbishop of Canterbury
	Dr. Leslie Cooke
	Professor George Florovsky
	Sir Kenneth G. Grubb
	Professor J. L. Hromadka
	Bishop C. K. Jacob
	Dr. Alphons Koechlin
	Bishop H. Lilje
	President John A. Mackay
	Metropolitan Mar Juhanon
	Bishop William C. Martin
	Dr. J. Earl Moreland
	Dr. Martin Niemöller
	Bishop Lesslie Newbigin
	Bishop G. Bromley Oxnam
	Metropolitan Panteleimon
	Mr. Charles Parlin
	Dr. E. A. Payne
	Mrs. Leslie Swain
	Mr. Charles Taft
	The Archbishop of Thyateira
	President Henry P. Van Dusen

Credentials Committee

Chairman:	Dr. M. E. Aubrey
Members:	Professor H. S. Alivisatos
	Bishop Ivan Lee Holt
	Dr. Douglas Horton
	The Bishop of Malmesbury
	Pastor D. W. Niesel

NOMINATIONS COMMITTEE

Chairman: Dr. J. Earl Moreland
Members: Professor Basil Ioannidis
Bishop H. Lilje
Pastor Pierre Maury
Mr. Rajaiah D. Paul
The Rev. David Say
Mrs. Leslie Swain

THE OFFICERS OF THE MAIN THEME GROUPS

Group 1 Chairman: Principal Russell Chandran
Secretary: Dr. H. L. Yochum
Group 2 Chairman: Dr. Charles Malik
Secretary: Canon Stanley L. Greenslade
Group 3 Chairman: Professor W. S. Tindal
Secretary: Dr. Ferdinand Sigg
Group 4 Chairman: Dr. Martin Niemöller
Secretary: Canon William W. Judd
Group 5 Chairman: Principal A. L. Haddon
Secretary: Dr. Joseph Sittler
Group 6 Chairman: Dr. Reuben Nelson
Secretary: Mr. Kenneth Yohan-Masih
Group 7 Chairman: Dr. Gerald Cragg
Secretary: Dr. Allan Watson
Group 8 Chairman: Dr. Stewart Herman
Secretary: The Bishop of Johannesburg
Group 9 Chairman: The Bishop of London
Secretary: Dr. John E. Skoglund
Group 10 Chairman: Bishop H. Lilje
Secretary: Principal Herbert Cunliffe-Jones
Group 11 Chairman: The Bishop of Bombay
Secretary: Dr. Herbert Gezork
Group 12 Chairman: Professor H. Alivisatos
Secretary: Dr. James David Salmond
Group 13 Chairman: Dr. Harold Roberts
Secretary: The Bishop of Gibraltar
Group 14 Chairman: Principal John Marsh
Secretary: The Rev. Robert Tobias.
Group 15 Chairman: Professor H. d'Espine
Secretary: Canon Hugh G. G. Herklots

The Main Theme Co-ordinating Group consisted of the Chairman and Secretaries of the Main Theme Groups. Its officers were:

Chairman: Bishop H. Lilje
Secretaries: Dr. Ralph Hyslop
Dr. Keith Bridston

MESSAGE DRAFTING GROUP

Bishop Lesslie Newbigin, Chairman
Dr. Charles W. Ranson, Secretary
Dr. Charles Malik
Dr. Nathan M. Pusey
Professor Pierre Burgelin
Dr. Kathleen Bliss
Bishop G. Noth
Dr. Robert L. Calhoun, Consultant
The Rev. M. M. Thomas, Consultant

THE OFFICERS OF THE SECTIONS

Section I. Faith and Order
Chairman: Archbishop Yngve Brilioth
Vice-Chairmen: Canon O. S. Tomkins
                   Metropolitan Juhanon
Secretary: Dr. J. Robert Nelson
Liaison Officer: Dr. Floyd Tomkins

Section II. Evangelism
Chairman: Bishop R. C. Raines
Vice-Chairmen: Canon T. O. Wedel
                   Bishop E. G. Gulin
Secretary: The Rev. D. T. Niles
Liaison Officer: Dr. R. W. Barstow

Section III. Social Questions
Chairman: Dr. C. L. Patijn
Vice-Chairmen: Dr. J. C. Bennett
                   Dr. E. C. Sobrepena
Secretary: The Rev. Paul Abrecht
Liaison Officer: The Rev. Charles West

Section IV. International Affairs
Chairman: Sir Kenneth Grubb
Vice-Chairmen: Dr. O. Frederick Nolde
                   Professor H. Alivisatos
Secretary: Dr. Richard Fagley
Liaison Officer: Dr. Walter W. Van Kirk

Section V. Intergroup Relations
Chairman: Dr. Roswell P. Barnes
Vice-Chairman: The Rev. P. K. Dagadu
Secretary: Dr. Norman Goodall
Liaison Officer: Dr. J. Oscar Lee

Section VI. The Laity
Chairman: Dr. Kathleen Bliss
Vice-Chairmen: Mr. R. D. Paul
                   Dr. Reinold von Thadden
Secretary: Dr. H. H. Walz
Liaison Officer: Dr. Cameron P. Hall

The Sections' Co-ordinating Group consisted of the Chairman, Secretary, and Liaison Officer of each Section. Its officers were:

Chairman: Dr. Henry P. Van Dusen
Secretary: Dr. Nils Ehrenström

THE OFFICERS OF THE COMMITTEES ON W.C.C. BUSINESS

Committee 1. General Policy
    Chairman: Bishop William C. Martin
    Vice-Chairman: Dr. A. Koechlin
    Secretaries: Dr. Samuel McCrea Cavert
                      The Rev. Kenrick Baker
    Liaison Officer: Dr. W. J. Gallagher

Committee 2. Division of Studies
    Chairman: Dr. H. Meyer
    Vice-Chairman: Dr. T. E. Jessop
    Secretaries: Dr. H. H. Harms
                      Dr. Rajah Manikam
                      Mr. John Turnbull
                      The Rev. D. T. Niles
                      Dr. J. Robert Nelson
                      The Rev. Paul Abrecht
                      The Rev. E. Nielsen
    Liaison Officer: Dr. W. Menn

Committee 3. Division of Ecumenical Action
    Chairman: Bishop Angus Dun
    Vice-Chairman: Professor Pierre Burgelin
    Secretaries: Dr. Hendrik Kraemer
                      Dr. H. H. Walz
                      Miss Madeleine Barot
    Liaison Officer: Miss Dorothy Asch

Committee 4. Division of Inter-Church Aid and Service to Refugees
    Chairman: Dr. E. Emmen
    Vice-Chairman: Dr. J. W. C. Dougall
    Secretaries: Dr. Edgar Chandler
                      Dr. Wayland Zwayer
    Liaison Officer: The Rev. Raymond Maxwell

Committee 5. Department of Information
    Chairman: Dr. Ernest A. Payne
    Secretary: The Rev. John Garrett
    Liaison Officer: The Rev. Russell Stevenson

Committee 6. Department of Finance and Administration
    Chairman: Dr. Eugene Carson Blake
    Secretary: Mr. Frank Northam
    Liaison Officer: Mr. Georges Lombard

Committee 7. Commission of the Churches on International Affairs
Chairman: Dr. Erling Wikborg
Secretary: Dr. Elfan Rees
Liaison Officer: The Rev. Philip Eastman

The Committees' Co-ordinating Group consisted of the Chairman, Secretary and Liaison Officer of each Committee. Its officers were:

Chairman   Mr. Charles P. Taft
Secretaries: Dr. Robert C. Mackie
                  Dr. R. H. Edwin Epsy

ACCREDITED VISITORS' PROGRAMME
Steering Committee

The Rev. George Appleton
Oberkirchenrat Dr. Beckmann
Dr. C. Bonnevie-Svendsen
Dr. J. Leslie Dunstan
The Rev. Dr. B. Hivale
The Rt. Rev. Stephen E. Keeler
Dr. Marjorie Reeves
The Rev. H. J. F. Wesseldijk
Bishop Michael Yashiro
Mr. Stephan Shostah
Secretaries: The Rev. Howard Schomer
             The Rev. Jacques Beaumont

10. SOME STATISTICS OF THE SECOND ASSEMBLY OF THE WORLD COUNCIL OF CHURCHES

				Clergy	Women	Laymen	Total
Delegates	..	..	..	383	44	75	502
Accredited Visitors	..	..	..	328	111	60	499
Consultants	..	..	..	93	15	37	145
Youth Consultants	..	..	..	36	31	29	96
Fraternal Delegates	..	..	..	23	3	5	31
Observers	..	..	..	24		1	25
				887	204	207	1298

The 1,298 official participants came from 179 churches in 54 countries. Of these the 502 delegates represented 132 member churches in 42 countries. The 376 staff included:

177 executive and secretarial staff, interpreters, translators.
70 stewards;
57 aides;
72 press and broadcasting staff;

646 press people were accredited at the Assembly of whom 322 represented the secular press, 195 the religious press, 76 the foreign press, and 53 radio. These figures for the press form no basis for comparison with the foregoing since a number of people came to Evanston in a double capacity.

In addition there was a large number of general visitors, wives of participants, etc., of whom no records were kept.

THE CONSTITUTION OF THE WORLD COUNCIL OF CHURCHES

As adopted by the Assembly at Amsterdam, 30th August 1948, *and amended at Evanston, 26th August* 1954

I. Basis

The World Council of Churches is a fellowship of churches which accept our Lord Jesus Christ as God and Saviour. It is constituted for the discharge of the functions set out below.

II. Membership

Those churches shall be eligible for membership in the World Council of Churches which express their agreement with the basis upon which the Council is founded and satisfy such criteria as the Assembly or the Central Committee may prescribe. Election to membership shall be by a two-thirds vote of the member churches represented at the Assembly, each member church having one vote. Any application for membership between meetings of the Assembly may be considered by the Central Committee; if the application is supported by a two-thirds majority of the members of the Committee present and voting, this action shall be communicated to the churches that are members of the World Council of Churches, and unless objection is received from more than one-third of the member churches within six months the applicant shall be declared elected.

III. Functions

The functions of the World Council shall be:

(i) To carry on the work of the two world movements for Faith and Order and for Life and Work.

(ii) To facilitate common action by the churches.

(iii) To promote co-operation in study.

(iv) To promote the growth of ecumenical consciousness in the members of all churches.

(v) To establish relations with denominational federations of world-wide scope and with other ecumenical movements.

(vi) To call world conferences on specific subjects as occasion may require, such conferences being empowered to publish their own findings.

(vii) To support the churches in their task of evangelism.

IV. Authority

The World Council shall offer counsel and provide opportunity of united action in matters of common interest.

It may take action on behalf of constituent churches in such matters as one or more of them may commit to it.

It shall have authority to call regional and world conferences on specific subjects as occasion may require.

The World Council shall not legislate for the churches; nor shall it act for them in any manner except as indicated above or as may hereafter be specified by the constituent churches.

V. Organization

The World Council shall discharge its functions through the following bodies:

(i) An Assembly which shall be the principal authority in the Council, and shall ordinarily meet every five years. The Assembly shall be composed of official representatives of the churches or groups of churches adhering to it and directly appointed by them. Their term of office shall begin in the year before the Assembly meets, and they shall serve until their successors are appointed. It shall consist of members whose number shall be determined by each Assembly for the subsequent Assembly, subject to the right of the Assembly to empower the Central Committee, if it thinks fit, to increase or to diminish the said number by not more than twenty per cent. The number shall be finally determined not less than two years before the meeting of the Assembly to which it refers and shall be apportioned as is provided hereafter.

Seats in the Assembly shall be allocated to the member churches by the Central Committee, due regard being given to such factors as numerical size, adequate confessional representation and adequate geographical distribution. Suggestions for readjustment in the allocation of seats may be made to the Central Committee by member churches or by groups of member churches, confessional, regional or national, and these readjustments shall become effective if approved by the Central Committee after consultation with the churches concerned.

The Assembly shall have power to appoint officers of the World Council and of the Assembly at its discretion.

The members of the Assembly shall be both clerical and lay persons—men and women. In order to secure that approximately one-third of the Assembly shall consist of lay persons, the Central Committee, in allocating to the member churches their places in the Assembly, shall strongly urge each church, if possible, to observe this provision.

(ii) A Central Committee which shall be a Committee of the Assembly and which shall consist of the President or Presidents of the World Council, together with not more than ninety members chosen by the Assembly from among persons whom the churches have appointed as members of the Assembly. They shall serve until the next Assembly, unless the Assembly otherwise determines. Membership in the Central Committee shall be distributed among the member churches by the Assembly, due regard being given to such factors as numerical size, adequate confessional representation and adequate geographical distribution. Any vacancy occurring in the membership of the Central Committee between meetings of the Assembly shall be filled by the Central Committee upon nomination of the church or churches concerned.

The Central Committee shall have the following powers:

> (*a*) It shall, between meetings of the Assembly, carry out the Assembly's instructions and exercise its functions, except that of amending the Constitution, or modifying the allocation of its own members; (*b*) It shall be the finance committee of the Assembly formulating its budget and securing its financial support; (*c*) It shall name and elect its own Officers from among its members and appoint its own secretarial staff; (*d*) The Central Committee shall meet normally once every calendar year, and shall have power to appoint its own Executive Committee. QUORUM: No business, except what is required for carrying forward the current activities of the Council, shall be transacted in either the Assembly or the Central Committee unless one-half of the total membership is present.

VI. APPOINTMENT OF COMMISSIONS

The World Council shall discharge part of its functions by the appointment of Commissions. These shall be established under the authority of the Assembly, whether they be actually nominated by the Assembly or by the Central Committee acting under its instructions. The Commissions shall, between meetings of the Assembly, report annually to the Central Committee which shall exercise general supervision over them. The Commissions may add to their membership clerical and lay persons approved for the purpose by the Central Committee.

In particular, the Assembly shall make provision by means of appropriate Commissions for carrying on the activities of Faith and Order and of Life and Work.

There shall be a Faith and Order Commission of which the following shall be the functions:

> (i) To proclaim the essential oneness of the Church of Christ and to keep prominently before the World Council and the churches the obligation to manifest that unity and its urgency for the work of evangelism;

(ii) to study questions of faith, order and worship with the relevant social, cultural, political, racial and other factors in their bearing on the unity of the churches;

(iii) to study the theological implications of the existence of the ecumenical movement;

(iv) to study matters in the present relationships of the churches to one another which cause difficulties and need theological clarification;

(v) to provide information concerning actual steps taken by the churches towards reunion.

The Commission shall discharge these functions in accordance with a constitution approved by the Central Committee.

In invitations to World Conferences on Faith and Order, it shall be specified that such conferences are to be composed of official delegates of churches which accept Jesus Christ as God and Saviour.

VII. Other Ecumenical Christian Organizations

(i) Such World Confessional Associations and such Ecumenical Organizations as may be designated by the Central Committee may be invited to send representatives to the sessions of the Assembly and of the Central Committee in a consultative capacity, in such numbers as the Central Committee shall determine.

(ii) Such constituent bodies of the International Missionary Council and such nation-wide councils of churches as may be designated by the Central Committee may be invited to send representatives to the sessions of the Assembly and of the Central Committee in a consultative capacity, in such numbers as the Central Committee shall determine.

VIII. Amendments

The Constitution may be amended by a two-thirds majority vote of the Assembly, provided that the proposed amendment shall have been reviewed by the Central Committee, and notice of it sent to the constituent churches not less than six months before the meeting of the Assembly. The Central Committee itself, as well as the individual churches, shall have the right to propose such amendment.

IX. Rules and Regulations

The Assembly or the Central Committee may make and amend Rules and Regulations concerning the conduct of the Council's business, of its Committees and Departments, and generally all matters within the discharge of its task.

The World Council of Churches has been incorporated under Swiss Law and has the attributes of a legal entity according to articles 60 and following of the Swiss Civil Code.

THE RULES OF THE WORLD COUNCIL OF CHURCHES[1]

The World Council of Churches shall be governed by the following Rules which are to be interpreted in the light of its Constitution:

I. Membership of the Council

Members of the Council are those churches which have agreed together to constitute the World Council of Churches and those churches which are admitted to membership in accordance with the following rules:

1. Churches which desire to become members of the World Council of Churches shall apply to the General Secretary in writing. Under the word churches are included such denominations as are composed of local autonomous churches.

2. The General Secretary shall submit such applications to the Central Committee (see Article II of the Constitution) together with such information as will be sufficient to enable the Assembly or the Central Committee to make a decision on the application.

3. The following criteria, among others, shall be applied, in addition to the primary requirement of the Constitution that churches eligible for consideration for membership shall be those "which express their agreement with the Basis upon which the Council is formed."

[1] As amended and adopted by the Second Assembly.

(a) *Autonomy*. A church which is to be admitted must give evidence of autonomy. An autonomous church is one which, while recognizing the essential interdependence of the churches, particularly those of the same confession, is responsible to no other church for the conduct of its own life, including the training, ordination and maintenance of its ministry, the enlisting, development and activity of the lay forces, the propagation of the Christian message, the determination of relationship with other churches and the use of funds at its disposal from whatever source.

(b) *Stability*. A church should not be admitted unless it has given sufficient evidence of stability in life and organization to become recognized as a church by its sister churches, and should have an established programme of Christian nurture and evangelism.

(c) *Size*. The question of size must also be taken into consideration.

(d) *Relationship with other churches*. Regard must also be given to the relationship of the church to other churches.

4. Before churches which are recognized as full members of one of the confessional or denominational world alliances with which the Council co-operates are admitted, the advice of these world alliances shall be sought.

5. A church which desires to resign its membership in the Council can do so at any time. A church which has once resigned, but desires again to join the Council, must again apply for membership.

II. THE ASSEMBLY

1. OFFICERS AND BUSINESS COMMITTEE

(a) At the first business session of the Assembly the Executive Committee shall present its proposals for the chairmanship of the Assembly and for the membership of the Business Committee of the Assembly.

(b) Additional names may also be proposed at the first or second business session by any group of six members of the Assembly. Such proposals must be made in writing.

(c) Election shall be by ballot unless the Assembly shall otherwise determine.

2. COMPOSITION OF THE ASSEMBLY

(*a*) *Members*. Full membership of the Assembly is confined to delegates appointed by the constituent churches to represent them.

(*b*) *Alternates*. The Central Committee shall make regulations for the appointment of alternates and for their duties and functions if and when appointed.

(*c*) *Consultants*. The Executive Committee is authorized to invite persons who have a special contribution to make to the deliberations of the Assembly or who have participated in the activities of the World Council. Such consultants will be appointed after consultation with the churches to which they belong. They shall be entitled to speak on the invitation of the Chairman but not to vote.

(*d*) *Observers*. The Executive Committee is authorized to invite a limited number of observers from churches which have not joined the World Council of Churches. Observers will not be entitled to speak or to vote.

(*e*) *Fraternal Delegates*. The Executive Committee is authorized to invite fraternal delegates from organizations with which the World Council of Churches entertains relationship. They shall be entitled to speak on invitation of the Chairman but not to vote.

(*f*) *Youth Delegates*. The Executive Committee is authorized to invite youth delegates who will be entitled to attend the full sessions. They shall be entitled to speak on invitation of the Chairman but not to vote.

3. AGENDA

The Agenda of the Assembly shall be determined by the Executive Committee and presented by it for approval to the first business session of the Assembly. Any member may move to have included in the Agenda such items of business as he may have previously notified to the Executive Committee.

III. PRESIDIUM

1. The maximum number of Presidents shall be six.
2. A President shall be ineligible for immediate re-election when his term of office ends.

3. The term of office of a President shall end at the adjournment of the next Assembly following his or her appointment.

4. The President or Presidents shall be entitled to attend the Assembly with full right of speech even if they are not appointed as delegates by their churches.

5. The President or Presidents shall be *ex officio* members of the Central Committee and of the Executive Committee.

IV. NOMINATIONS COMMITTEE OF THE ASSEMBLY

1. At an early session of the Assembly, the Assembly shall appoint a Nominations Committee, on which there shall be appropriate confessional and geographical representation of the membership of the Assembly.

2. The Nominations Committee in consultation with the officers of the World Council and the Executive Committee shall draft proposals concerning (*a*) the President or Presidents of the World Council of Churches, and (*b*) a list of persons proposed for membership of the Central Committee.

3. The Nominations Committee shall present its nominations to the vote of the Assembly for its acceptance or revision. In making nominations, the Nominations Committee shall have regard to the following principles:

(*a*) the personal qualifications of the individual for the task for which he is to be nominated;

(*b*) fair and adequate confessional representation;

(*c*) fair and adequate geographical representation;

and shall satisfy itself as to the general acceptability of the nominations to the churches to which the nominees belong.

4. It shall be open to any six members of the Assembly acting together to put forward in writing other nominations.

5. Election shall be by a ballot unless the Assembly shall otherwise determine.

V. CENTRAL COMMITTEE

1. MEMBERSHIP

(*a*) The Central Committee shall consist of the President or Presidents of the World Council together with not more than ninety members elected by the Assembly (see Constitution, paragraph V (ii)).

(*b*) Any member church, not already represented, which desires to be represented directly on the Central Committee, shall have the right to send one representative to the meetings of the Central Committee, provided it does so at its own expense. Such a representative shall be entitled to speak but not to vote.

(*c*) If a regularly elected member of the Central Committee is unable to come to the meeting, the church to which the absent member belongs shall have the right to send a substitute, provided that the substitute is ordinarily resident in the country where his church has its headquarters. Such a substitute shall be entitled to speak and to vote.

(*d*) Chairmen and vice-chairmen of divisional and departmental committees and commissions who are not members of the Central Committee have the right to attend Central Committee sessions as consultants without vote.

(*e*) Consultants for the Central Committee may be appointed by the Executive Committee after consultation with the churches of which they are members. They shall be entitled to speak but not to vote.

(*f*) Members of the staff of the World Council appointed by the Central Committee as specified under Rule IX, 1, shall have the right to attend the sessions of the Central Committee unless on any occasion the Central Committee shall otherwise determine. When they do so attend it shall be as consultants and without the right to vote.

(*g*) The newly appointed Central Committee shall be convened by the General Secretary during or immediately after the meeting of the Assembly.

2. OFFICERS

(*a*) The Central Committee shall elect its own Chairman and Vice-Chairman or Vice-Chairmen to serve for such periods as it shall determine. They shall be entitled to attend the Assembly as consultants, should they not be re-appointed as delegates by their churches.

(*b*) The Central Committee shall appoint a Nominations Committee which shall:

(i) nominate individuals to the Central Committee for the offices of Chairman and Vice-Chairman or Vice-Chairmen of the Central Committee;

(ii) nominate individuals for election as President, if between Assemblies need arises for such appointments, under the power conferred on the Central Committee by the Constitution and Rules;

(iii) nominate members of the Executive Committee of the Central Committee;

(iv) nominate members of the divisional committees and departmental working committees.

In making nominations, the Nominations Committee of the Central Committee shall have regard to the principles set out in Rule IV, 3, and in applying principles (*b*) and (*c*) to the nomination of members of the divisional committees and the departmental working committees, shall consider the representative character of the combined membership of all such committees. Any member of the Central Committee may make alternative proposals.

(*c*) Election shall be by ballot unless the Committee shall otherwise determine.

(*d*) The General Secretary of the World Council of Churches shall be *ex officio* secretary of the Central Committee and the chairman of the Finance Committee of the World Council of Churches shall be *ex officio* its treasurer.

3. MEETINGS

(*a*) The Central Committee shall meet ordinarily not less than once every year. An extraordinary session of the Central Committee shall be called, whenever one-third or more of the members requests a meeting to be called or when in the opinion of the Executive Committee that is desirable.

(*b*) A quorum of the Central Committee shall be forty voting members. The General Secretariat shall take all possible steps to ensure that there be adequate representation from each of the main confessions and from the main geographical areas of the membership of the World Council of Churches.

(*c*) The Central Committee shall have power to determine its own place of meeting and to fix the date and place for the meetings of the Assembly.

4. FUNCTIONS

The Central Committee shall have the following duties:

(*a*) It shall, between meetings of the Assembly, carry out the general policy laid down by the Assembly and take such actions as shall be necessary to carry out the decisions of the Assembly. It shall have authority to make decisions and take action in all matters where decision or action is required before the Assembly can meet again, provided that it shall not make any decision or take any action inconsistent with the policies laid down by the Assembly.

It shall have the following sub-committees:

(i) Finance Committee (a standing committee);

(ii) Nominations Committee (newly appointed at each meeting);

(iii) Reference Committee or Committees (appointed as needed at each meeting) to advise the Central Committee on any other questions arising which call for special consideration or action by the Central Committee.

(*b*) It shall vote the Annual Budget of the Council.

(*c*) It shall deal with matters referred to it by member churches.

(*d*) It shall consider applications for membership received between meetings of the Assembly.

(*e*) It shall have the responsibility of setting up such divisions and departments and regional offices or representations as may be necessary to carry out the policy laid down by the Assembly. It shall appoint divisional and departmental committees and their chairmen and vice-chairmen. It shall determine the general policy to be followed in the work of the divisions and departments of the World Council.

(*f*) It shall report to the Assembly on the actions it has taken during its period of office, and shall not be discharged until its report has been received.

VI. EXECUTIVE COMMITTEE

1. APPOINTMENT

(*a*) An Executive Committee shall be elected by the Central Committee at its first meeting after its appointment by the

Assembly, and shall hold office until the next meeting of the Central Committee. Its elected members shall be eligible for re-election.

(*b*) The Executive Committee shall consist of the President or Presidents of the World Council *ex officio* and the Chairman and Vice-Chairman of the Central Committee *ex officio* and of twelve other members of the Central Committee. Substitutes shall not be permitted to attend in place of elected members.

(*c*) The Chairman of the Central Committee shall also be the Chairman of the Executive Committee.

(*d*) The officers shall have the power to invite others to attend a meeting of the Executive Committee for consultation, always having in mind the need of preserving a due balance of the confessions and of the geographical areas.

(*e*) The General Secretary of the World Council of Churches shall be *ex officio* the secretary of the Executive Committee.

2. FUNCTIONS

The Executive Committee is a committee of the Central Committee appointed by it and responsible to it. The Executive Committee shall, between meetings of the Central Committee, carry out the decisions of the Central Committee and implement the policy laid down by it. The Executive Committee shall have no authority to make decisions on policy except that in circumstances of special urgency it can take provisional decisions. It may only issue public statements under the circumstances laid down in Rule X 4. It shall have power to appoint Associate General Secretaries and heads of departments provisionally but such appointments shall be subject to confirmation by the Central Committee. It shall supervise the operation of the budget and have power to impose limitations on expenditure if necessary.

VII. DIVISIONAL AND DEPARTMENTAL COMMITTEES

1. There shall be a small committee for each division whose responsibility shall be to carry out the aim of the division. It shall be responsible for the preparation and presentation to the Central Committee of the reports of the division's work.

It shall propose to the Central Committee the names of persons to fill the offices of secretary or secretaries to the division and, on the basis of proposals from the departmental working committees, of secretary or secretaries in the departments within the division.

2. Divisional committees shall be appointed by the Central Committee as follows:

(*a*) For the Division of Studies and the Division of Ecumenical Action, the committees shall consist of three persons who are not members of any departmental working committee within the division plus the chairman and one other member of each departmental working committee within the division. One of the two representatives of each departmental working committee must be a member of the Central Committee.

(*b*) For the Division of Inter-Church Aid, the committee shall consist of seven members, at least two of whom shall be members of the Central Committee.

Departmental secretaries shall normally be present at the meetings of divisional committees.

3. There shall be a working committee for each department appointed by the Central Committee and responsible for the preparation of the departmental programme for submission to the divisional committee and for the execution of the programme. It shall propose to the divisional committee the names of persons to fill the offices of secretary or secretaries in the department. The chairmen of departmental working committees shall be *ex officio* members of the appropriate divisional committees. Departmental working committees shall have power to call in *ad hoc* consultants as needed on particular problems. In the case of the Ecumenical Institute and the Graduate School of Ecumenical Studies, their boards shall be regarded as the working committees. Normally a working committee shall consist of fifteen members at least one of whom shall be a member of the Central Committee.

VIII. Financial Provisions

1. The draft annual budget of the World Council of Churches shall be prepared for presentation to the Finance Committee of the Central Committee by the General Secretariat, assisted by the Department of Finance and Administration, on the basis of proposals made by the divisional committees.

2. The Finance Committee of the Central Committee shall have the following duties:

(*a*) To present annually to the Central Committee an account of income and expenditure for the previous twelve months, and a balance sheet in respect of operations of all departments of the World Council of Churches.

(*b*) To present annually to the Central Committee in advance of the commencement of each year, a budget covering the operations of all the departments of the World Council of Churches.

(*c*) To consider and make recommendations to the Central Committee on all financial questions concerning the affairs of the World Council of Churches, such as:

Approval of budgets or increases in budgets;
Approval and granting of discharge for the accounts in respect of completed periods;
Accounting procedures;
Investment policy;
Principle governing scales of salaries and pensions and travel expenses and other such expenses;
Basis of calculation of contributions of member churches;
Methods of raising funds;
Appointment of auditors, who shall be appointed annually by the Central Committee and shall be eligible for re-election.

The committee shall have power to consider all matters concerning the World Council of Churches in so far as they bear upon its financial position.

3. The items of the budget of a division may be subsequently varied by the divisional committee at its discretion provided the authorized total be not exceeded, and the policy of the division be thereby advanced.

IX. STAFF OF THE WORLD COUNCIL OF CHURCHES

1. The General Secretary, the Associate General Secretaries, and the heads of departments shall be appointed by the Central Committee.

2. The normal terms of appointment for an Associate General Secretary shall be five years and for a head of department three years. Unless some other period is stated in the resolution making the appointment, the term of office of members of the staff of the World Council shall be from the date of the appointment until three months after the end of the next meeting of the Central Committee. All appointments made for a term exceeding one year shall be reviewed one year before expiring.

3. Retirement shall be at 65 for men and 60 for women or not later than the end of the year in which a staff member reaches the age of 68 for men and 63 for women.

4. If the position of General Secretary becomes vacant, the Executive Committee shall appoint an acting General Secretary.

5. The General Secretariat (i.e. General Secretary and Associate General Secretaries) is responsible for carrying out the decisions of the Assembly, the Central Committee, and the Executive Committee.

6. The General Secretariat shall be responsible for the conduct of the business of the Council, for relations with member churches and other ecumenical bodies, for the preparation and administration of the meetings of the Assembly, of the Central Committee and of the Executive Committee, for the general supervision and co-ordination of the activities and publications of the commissions and departments of the Council, for the interpretation of the work of the Council to the churches and the public, and for carrying on of activities not otherwise assigned.

7. The General Secretariat shall have the right to attend the meetings of departmental committees and other meetings called under the auspices of the Council.

X. Public Statements

1. In the performance of its functions, the Council through its Assembly or through its Central Committee may publish statements upon any situation or issue with which the Council or its constituent churches may be confronted.

2. While such statements may have great significance and influence as the expression of the judgment or concern of so widely representative a Christian body, yet their authority will consist only in the weight which they carry by their own truth

and wisdom and the publishing of such statements shall not be held to imply that the World Council as such has, or can have, any constitutional authority over the constituent churches or right to speak for them.

3. The Executive Committee or any commission of the Council may recommend statements to the Assembly or to the Central Committee for its consideration and action.

4. No committee or commission of the Council other than the Central Committee shall publish any statement until it has been approved by the Assembly, except that in circumstances of immediate urgency statements may be published by any commission of the Council on matters within its own field of concern and action, if approved by the Chairman of the Central Committee and the General Secretary, and in these cases the committee or commission shall make it clear that the World Council of Churches is not committed by any statement set forth in this manner.

5. In cases of exceptional emergency, statements may be issued by the Chairman of the Central Committee on his own authority after consultation with the Vice-Chairman of the Central Committee and the General Secretary provided that such statements are not contrary to the established policy of the Council.

6. Nothing in these regulations shall contravene the special provisions of the Constitution regarding the Commission on Faith and Order.

XI. CONSULTATIVE RELATIONSHIPS

1. INTERNATIONAL MISSIONARY COUNCIL

The officers and chief executive secretaries of the International Missionary Council shall be invited to sit with the Assembly and the Central Committee as consultants. (*Note:* See also Constitution No. VII.)

2. NATIONAL COUNCILS

(*a*) The World Council, recognizing that national councils of churches or national Christian councils have been established in a number of countries for purposes of fellowship and co-operation with one another and for the promotion and support of ecumenical activities and other common interests within their own area, shall invite selected national councils to enter into working relationships as associated councils.

(*b*) The purpose of such working relationships shall be to help national councils in their work and to encourage them to help the World Council of Churches in the promotion of ecumenical activities in the area concerned and in the furthering of the plans and policies which the Central Committee has laid down for the various divisions and departments of the Council.

(*c*) These councils shall be regularly designated to receive invitations to send a fraternal delegate to the Assembly and a consultant to the Central Committee (in accordance with Section VII (ii) of the Constitution).

(*d*) Opportunity shall be provided at the time of any meeting of the Assembly or Central Committee for the representatives of national councils to meet together for mutual consultation.

(*e*) While the World Council retains the right to deal with its member churches directly, no action shall be taken by it which would disturb any already existing fellowship or ecumenical organization within a nation or region.

(*f*) Any member church which prefers to have direct relationships with the World Council in any field of work can have such direct relationships.

(*g*) The following criteria, among others, shall be applied by the Central Committee in selecting national councils for these working relationships:

(i) that the national council accept the Basis of the World Council of Churches or express its willingness to co-operate on that Basis;

(ii) that there be prior consultation with the member churches of the World Council in the area concerned;

(iii) that there be prior consultation with the International Missionary Council in the case of national councils which are members of that body;

(iv) that the membership of the national council consist wholly or to a large extent of churches which hold membership in the World Council of Churches;

(v) that the national council have an interest in the work of the World Council of Churches and be willing to work for that Council;

(vi) that the national council give evidence of stability and have a staff with time to devote to World Council concerns.

(*b*) In the case of countries where national missionary councils exist, whether integrated in or associated with national councils of churches or independently, the Central Committee may invite such a national missionary council to send a fraternal delegate to the Assembly and a consultant to the Central Committee.

3. WORLD CONFESSIONAL ASSOCIATIONS

Such world confessional associations as may be designated by the Central Committee shall be invited to send fraternal delegates to the Assembly, and consultants to the Central Committee.

XII. LEGAL PROVISIONS

1. The duration of the Council is unlimited.

2. The legal headquarters of the Council shall be at Geneva. Regional offices may be organized in different parts of the world by decision of the Central Committee.

3. The World Council of Churches is legally represented by its Executive Committee or by such persons as may be empowered by the Executive Committee to represent it.

4. The World Council shall be legally bound by the joint signatures of two of the following persons: the President or Presidents, the Chairman and Vice-Chairman or Vice-Chairmen of the Central Committee, and the General Secretary. Any two of the above-named persons shall have power to authorize other persons, chosen by them, to act jointly or singly on behalf of the World Council of Churches in fields circumscribed in the power of attorney.

5. The Council shall obtain the means necessary for the pursuance of its work from the contributions of its member churches and from donations or bequests.

6. The Council shall not pursue commercial aims but it shall have the right to act as an agency of inter-church aid and to publish literature in connection with its aims. It is not entitled to distribute any surplus income by way of profit or bonus among its members.

7. Members of the governing bodies of the Council or of the Assembly shall have no personal liability with regard to the obligations or commitments of the Council. The commitments entered upon by the Council are guaranteed solely by its own assets.

XIII. Rules of Debate during Sessions of the Assembly and the Central Committee

1. The responsibilities of the Chairman shall be to announce the opening, suspension and adjournment of the meeting; he shall ensure the observance of the Rules of Debate; he shall grant the right to speak and declare the debates closed; he shall put questions to the vote and announce the result of the voting. His decision is final. If the Chairman's decision as to the result of voting is challenged, a vote shall immediately be taken on the motion: "that the Chairman's decision be reconsidered"; and reconsideration shall be permitted, if a majority of the members present and voting, vote in favour of this motion. On all matters of order, the Chairman's decision is final. He shall not make a motion himself.

2. If any member desires to propose a motion not on the agenda, he shall be permitted to have his motion read. A vote shall be immediately taken and his motion shall be admitted if a majority of the members present and voting, vote for its inclusion in the agenda.

3. All motions and amendments must be proposed and seconded. They must be handed to the Chairman in writing, and read before a vote is taken. A motion for receiving and adopting the report of a committee or for carrying out any recommendation mentioned in it need not be seconded. The Chairman has a casting vote only.

4. Any motion or amendment may be withdrawn by leave of the Assembly.

5. All speeches must be addressed to the chair.

6. No member shall speak more than once on the same motion or amendment, except that the mover shall have the right to reply.

7. When an amendment has been proposed it shall be put to the vote first and, if the amendment be adopted, the amended motion becomes a substantive motion.

8. During the discussions in full session speeches shall be limited to seven minutes. The bell shall be rung after five minutes as a warning to the speaker and again after a further two minutes when the speaker must sit down. Only that part which remains of ten minutes shall be allowed for translations.

9. Those who desire to speak during the free discussions in full session must hand to the Secretary as early as possible cards with their names, the capacity in which they are attending the Assembly, their church connection, and whether they desire to support or to oppose the motion.

10. Any member may at any time move the closure of the debate, whether any other delegate has signified his wish to speak or not. If application is made for permission to speak against the closure, it may be granted to not more than two speakers. If the motion of closure is adopted by a majority, the Chairman shall declare the debate closed.

11. Any member may submit a point of order or procedure to the Chairman, and may, if necessary, interrupt a speaker for the purpose.

12. Voting, unless otherwise decided by vote of the Assembly, shall be by show of hands. The Chairman shall first ask those in favour of the motion, and then those opposed to vote. A majority of those voting shall determine the decision. Those who abstain from voting may, if they wish, have the fact and the number of abstentions recorded. The Chairman may, if he thinks fit, appoint members to act as tellers, and he shall do so in any case of doubt as to the result of the vote.

13. The three official languages are English, French, and German. A speech made in any one of these languages shall, if desired, be summarized or translated into the other two. It shall be the duty of the Secretary to make arrangements for such translation. A member may speak in a language other than English, French, or German on condition that he arrange for the translation of his speech into one of the three official languages.

14. The rules of debate for the Central Committee are the same as those for the Assembly except that rules 8 and 9 shall not apply.

XIV. REVISION OF RULES

Amendments to these Rules may be moved at any meeting of the Assembly, or, at any meeting of the Central Committee by any member and may be adopted by a two-thirds majority of those present and voting, except that no alteration in Rules I, V, and XIV shall come into effect until it has been confirmed by the Assembly. Notice of a proposal to make any such amendment shall be given in writing at least twenty-four hours before the meeting of the Assembly or Central Committee at which it is to be moved.

Index[1]

---

[1] Figures in italics indicate official texts of reports or resolutions as adopted by the Assembly.